Political Economy and Settlement Systems of Medieval Northern Morocco

An archaeological-historical approach

Said Ennahid

BAR International Series 1059
2002

Published in 2016 by
BAR Publishing, Oxford

BAR International Series 1059

Political Economy and Settlement Systems of Medieval Northern Morocco

ISBN 978 1 84171 439 4

BAR Publishing is the trading name of British Archaeological Reports (Oxford) Ltd. British Archaeological Reports was first incorporated in 1974 to publish the BAR Series, International and British. In 1992 Hadrian Books Ltd became part of the BAR group. This volume was originally published by Archaeopress in conjunction with British Archaeological Reports (Oxford) Ltd / Hadrian Books Ltd, the Series principal publisher, in 2002. This present volume is published by BAR Publishing, 2016.

Printed in England

BAR
PUBLISHING

BAR titles are available from:

BAR Publishing
122 Banbury Rd, Oxford, OX2 7BP, UK
EMAIL info@barpublishing.com
PHONE +44 (0)1865 310431
FAX +44 (0)1865 316916
www.barpublishing.com

In memory of my father

ACKNOWLEDGEMENTS

This monograph was completed with the help of several individuals and institutions. I thank the members of my dissertation committee for their comments and suggestions. The guidance and support of Dr. Charles Redman, chair, was instrumental not only in the completion of this project but throughout my graduate career. I thank Dr. Nancy Benco for a decade of mentoring, assistance, and friendship. She provided valuable insight throughout the different stages of this project. I am grateful to Dr. Benco for allowing me to include al-Basra's compositional data into the instrumental neutron activation analysis presented in this study. The clarity of the final draft owes a great deal to Dr. Benco's editorial comments and suggestions. I thank Dr. Geoffrey Clark and Dr. Steve Falconer for their guidance, advice, and friendship over the years.

Mme Joudia Hassar-Benslimane, director of the Institut National des Sciences de l'Archéologie et du Patrimoine in Rabat, graciously facilitated the completion of this project. I am grateful to Dr. Arleyn Simon for her support, encouragement, and for making my "tenure" at the Archaeological Research Institute a memorable experience.

Travel and analytical costs for this research were generously supported by The National Science Foundation (Doctoral Dissertation Improvement Grant: SBR-9808443), The Wenner-Gren Foundation for Anthropological Research (Predoctoral Grant: 6388), the Arizona State University Chapter of Sigma Xi, the Department of Anthropology at Arizona State University, and the Barakat Foundation. Travel and fieldwork were also partly funded through a National Science Foundation grant awarded to Dr. Nancy Benco (SBR-9618369).

The instrumental neutron activation analysis (INAA) was conducted through the subsidy program at the Archaeometry Laboratory at the Missouri University Research Reactor (MURR). This program is administered by Dr. Hector Neff and Dr. Michael Glascock and supported by a National Science Foundation grant (SBR-9802366). I thank Dr. Hector Neff and Dr. Michael Glascock for their assistance in the completion of the INAA chapter.

Many colleagues and friends in Morocco and the United States deserve special thanks for their help at the various stages of this research. I thank Ahmed Ettahiri (La Conservation de Chella), Abdelfettah Ichkhakh (La Conservation de Volubilis), Hamza Ouassini and Mustapha Ramdani (Inspection des Monuments Historiques, Tangier), Hicham Hassini and Ibrahim Mlilou (Délégation régionale du Minstère des Affaires Culturelles, Larache), Nouzha Boudouhou, Nancy Mahoney, Andrew Duff, Alanna Ossa, Billy Graves, Steve Swanson, Chris Fisher, Donna Glowacki, Kim Savage, Kurt Fangmeier, and Heather Hoyt.

The completion of this monograph would not have been possible without the love, encouragement, and unwavering support of my family and my close friend Lama Jamjoum.

TABLE OF CONTENTS

LIST OF FIGURES

LIST OF TABLES

LIST OF TRANSLITERATIONS OF ARABIC CHARACTERS

Consonants[1]

ء	’ (Except when initial)
ب	b
ت	t
ث	th
ج	dj
ح	h
خ	kh
د	d
ذ	dh
ر	r
ز	z
س	s
ش	sh
ص	s
ض	d
ط	t
ظ	z
ع	‘
غ	gh
ف	f
ق	k
ك	k
ل	l
م	m
ن	n
ه	h
و	w
ي	y

Long Vowels

ا ى	â
و	û
ي	î

Short Vowels

َ	a
ُ	u
ِ	i

Diphthongs

َ و	aw
َي	ay

Articles

ال	al-
ال	-l- (if between two vowels)

ة	a; at (construct state)

[1] Adapted from the Encyclopedia of Islam.

Chapter 1

INTRODUCTION

The field of Islamic archaeology in Morocco has grown substantially during the last two decades. The establishment of the Institut National des Sciences de l'Archéologie et du Patrimoine (INSAP) in Rabat, and its collaboration with archaeological teams from different parts of the world infused the field with new ideas and energy. This monograph is a result of such collaboration.

This study builds on the results of recent archaeological investigations in northern Morocco. More specifically, it derives its theoretical framework from a model that was formulated in the course of these investigations by Boone, Myers, and Redman (1990). Archaeological research in northern Morocco was designed to test ideas about state formation and urban growth during the Islamic period (see Boone and Benco 1999). Based on the Boone et al. model, this study examines the material impact of changing political economies on settlement systems in northern Morocco from the ninth to the fifteenth centuries A.D.

Geographically, northern Morocco forms a triangle bounded by the cities of Tangier, Rabat/Salé, and Fez (Figure 1.1). Prior to the Islamic period, this area formed a Roman province known as *Mauretania Tingitania* (from Tingis, Roman for Tangier, which was the capital). By the late Islamic period, this area was composed of the three provinces of Fez, Habṯ, and Azg̱hâr (Leo Africanus 1956).

The chronological scope of this monograph - the ninth to the fifteenth centuries - encompasses the rise, the growth, and the eventual collapse of four major dynastic states: the Idrisids, the Almoravids, the Almohads, and the Marinids. Most importantly, it is within this time period that radical changes in the political economy and settlement systems of medieval Morocco occurred.

The beginning of the ninth century marked the establishment of the first dynastic state in Morocco under the leadership of Idrîs II (A.D. 803-829). The end of the fourteenth and the beginning of the fifteenth centuries witnessed radical changes in the political, economic, and socio-cultural structures of the country: (1) the intensification of Spanish and Portuguese military incursions against Moroccan coastal ports, (2) the rerouting of gold traffic towards the east - at the expense of Moroccan trade centers, and (3) the rise of Bedouin tribes (e.g., Ma'ḵil in the south). All these factors negatively affected the Marinid economy and disrupted settled life. Ultimately, it led to the collapse of the Marinid state. It was the end of a golden era and the beginning of a long period of political, economic, and cultural decline.

This chapter discusses the main objectives of the research and provides a theoretical overview of its central premises. It concludes with a brief outline of the subsequent chapters.

Objectives of the Research

This study has three main objectives. First, it uses documentary evidence to examine the political economy of medieval Moroccan dynastic empires based on the premise that there was a shift in state finance from reliance on agricultural surplus (Idrisid period) to reliance on long-distance gold trade (subsequent dynastic periods). Second, this research utilizes textual and numismatic data to document the material impact of changing political economies on the size, location, and distribution of settlements. It is argued that change in the economic structure of Moroccan dynastic empires triggered a shift in settlement patterns from a multitiered hierarchy of settlement size to a "primate" one.

Third, the study investigates local exchange and community interaction between the Idrisid provincial capital of al-Basra and its hinterland. This is a central, yet poorly understood aspect of the Idrisid political economy. Toward this end, it uses multiple lines of evidence: (1) archaeological field survey, (2) ceramic compositional data (instrumental neutron

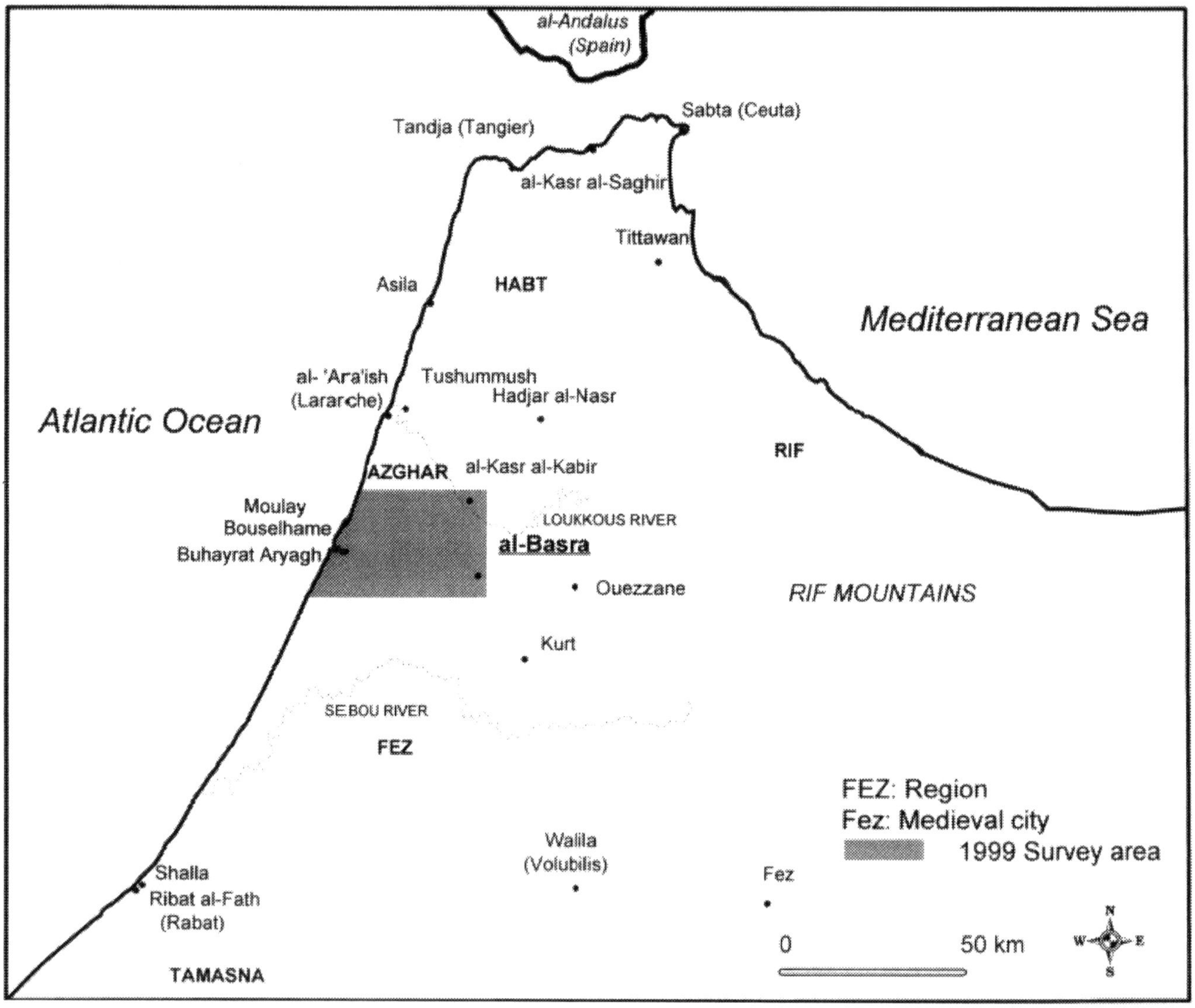

Figure 1.1 Map of Northern Morocco.

activation analysis, INAA), and (3) documentary and ethnoarchaeological evidence. Compositional data were used to ascertain that the ceramic material found in the al-Basra hinterland was produced in the city, and to identify a number of patterns of pottery distribution across the region. Documentary and ethnoarchaeological data were used to explain the nature and scale of al-Basra's local exchange system with an emphasis on pottery production and distribution.

Theoretical Background

This study of the political economy and settlement systems of medieval Moroccan dynastic empires draws most of its theoretical background from a conceptual model that was formulated a decade ago by Boone et al. (1990).[1] According to this model, the political economy of medieval Morocco was based on two economic sectors for generating the surplus needed to finance state institutions and their attached personnel: agriculture and long-distance gold trade. The model views agrarian-based surplus as essential to the early states of medieval Morocco and long-distance gold trade as the primary source of revenue for later dynastic empires. The dichotomy between these two mechanisms of surplus production may be approached from the standpoint of a shift from an agrarian-based finance system during the Idrisid period to a wealth finance system during subsequent dynastic periods. Most importantly, the model equates each finance system to a particular settlement system.

Figure 1.2 illustrates the main premises of the model. The political economy and settlement systems of medieval northern Morocco are divided into two major phases: (1) an early phase represented by the Idrisid state (ca. A.D. 789-974), and (2) a later phase represented by subsequent dynastic empires (the Almoravid empire ca. A.D. 1073-1147, the Almohad empire ca. A.D. 1130-1276, and the Marinid empire ca. A.D. 1258-1420).[2]

In the Idrisid state, the political economy was primarily agrarian-based and the settlement system was multitiered and hierarchical. Provincial capitals (e.g., al-Basra) were located

[1] The main ideas discussed in this model were first formulated by Boone and Redman (1982). See also Boone and Benco 1999:53-55.

[2] See Chapter 2 for details on dynastic chronologies.

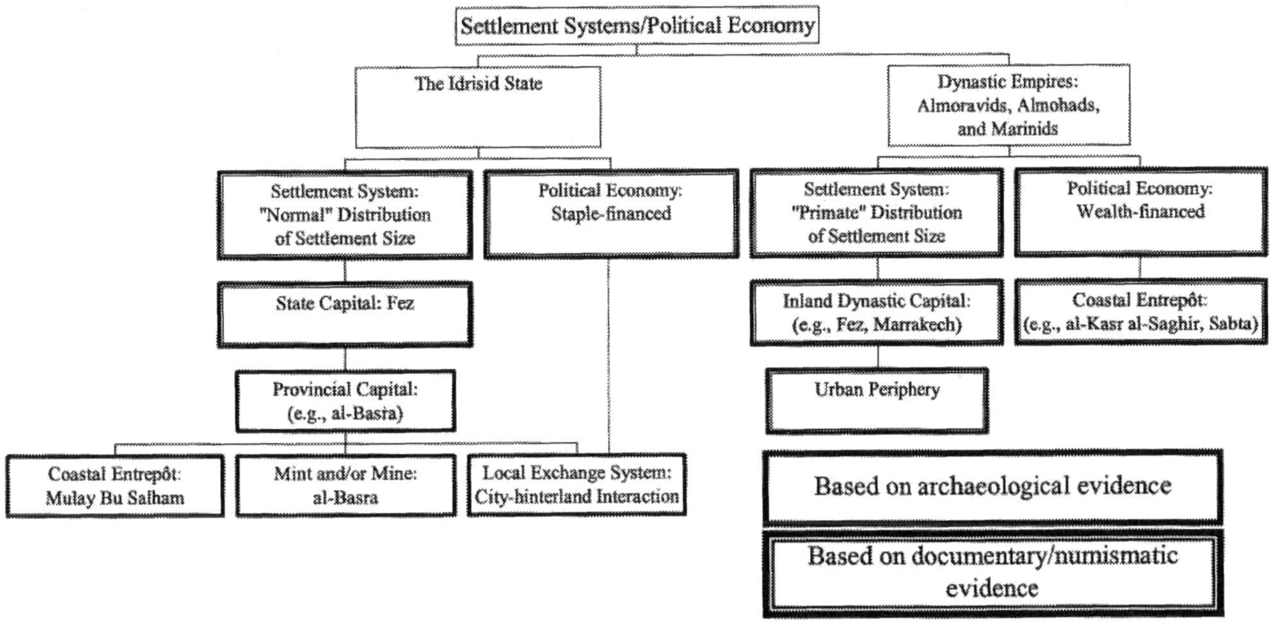

Figure 1.2 Conceptual Model of the Political Economy and Settlement Systems of Medieval Moroccan Dynastic Empires (9th-15th Centuries A.D.) (Based on Boone et al. 1990).

in rich agricultural lands and were surrounded by smaller sites in the hinterland. Fez, the capital of the Idrisid state, was the largest city within the system. Arranged hierarchically below Fez, were provincial capitals that housed self-sufficient and semi-independent politico-economic entities. Each provincial capital was in control of important agricultural and/or mining resources. Smaller towns and villages surrounded provincial capitals.

Exchange activities operated at two levels: (1) a local level involving the provincial capital and its hinterland, and (2) a regional level involving the provincial capital, nearby coastal entrepôts, and a number of provincial towns. The city of al-Basra represents a model Idrisid provincial capital with its own coastal entrepôt (Buhayrat Aryagh or Mulây Bû Salhâm) and its own mint (Eustache 1955, 1970-71). Other examples of Idrisid cities and their ports include, Kasr ‘Abd al-Karîm and Tushummush, Hadjar al-Nasr and Asîla, Nakûr and al-Mazamma, and Aghmât and Kûz (Cressier 1992; Cressier and Garcia-Arenal 1998; Cressier et al. 1992; Rosenberger 1967).

The Idrisid period came to a close as new economic horizons began to open for medieval Morocco. The rerouting of sub-Saharan gold traffic had a positive economic impact on Morocco. The Berber tribal groups living on the northern fringes of the Sahara quickly took advantage of the lucrative Saharan trade (Devisse 1972a, 1972b, 1988; Devisse and Hrbek 1988; Vanacker 1973). One of these groups - the Almoravids - eventually took control of the long-distance gold trade.

The emergence of the Almoravid empire in the eleventh century marks the beginning of the second phase. The Amoravid finance system relied almost exclusively on revenues from long-distance trade. The new economy gave rise to a “primate” settlement system in which the capitals of the interior (especially Fez and Marrakech) became substantially larger in size (up to three times larger) than other urban centers.

According to the model proposed by Boone et al. (1990:631-632), urban growth occurred along three principal “discontinuities” that separated distinct economic spheres. The first discontinuity operated in inland Morocco and triggered the growth of inland capitals, which functioned as hubs of long-distance trade between Bilâd al-Sûdân (sub-Saharan West Africa), Morocco, and the rest of the Mediterranean Basin. The second discontinuity was at the geographic periphery of dynastic empires: the Atlantic coast, the Mediterranean coast, and the northern fringes of the Sahara. The urban centers that developed along this periphery were mostly coastal entrepôts involved in transshipment activities. The third discontinuity separates two much smaller economic spheres: the urban and rural economies.

According to the model, the growth and long-term survival of a medieval Moroccan city depended on two factors: (1) the degree of economic integration that developed between a city and its hinterland and (2) the extent of the city’s political and economic involvement with the state (Boone et al. 1990: 641-642). Two types of urban centers were particularly prominent in this new setting: (1) inland dynastic capitals that, in addition to their role in long-distance trade, developed strong economic ties with their immediate hinterland, and (2) coastal entrepôts whose mercantile activities were sufficiently strong to be able to survive the withdrawal of state control and to flourish on their own.

Sequence of Presentation

Following the introduction, this monograph is organized into six chapters. Chapter 2 describes the methodology used in the study. It is composed of two sections. The first section describes the methods utilized to examine documentary evidence, and the second describes the archaeological survey methods. This chapter also includes a critical analysis of medieval Arabic documentary sources and an assessment of their potential for settlement studies.

Chapter 3 reviews the body of archaeological research on regional and micro-regional settlement patterns in northern Morocco in the last 25 years. This chapter addresses some of the difficulties of Islamic archaeology in Morocco, such as the lack of good ceramic and architectural sequences. It concludes with a discussion of a curious pattern observed by several archaeologists in Morocco: the ubiquitous association of archaeological sites and marabouts.[3]

Chapter 4 examines the political economy of medieval Moroccan dynastic empires using a vast corpus of medieval Arabic documentary sources. Based on the argument that the transition from the Idrisid period to subsequent dynastic periods was accompanied by a change in the sources of state finance, this chapter is divided into three sections. The first section defines the concepts of staple finance and wealth finance systems and demonstrates their relevance to explain the political economy of medieval Morocco. The second and third sections examine the political economies of the Idrisid state and subsequent dynastic states with an emphasis on the importance of agricultural surplus (staple finance) for the former and sub-Saharan gold trade for the latter.

Chapter 5 examines the material impact of changing political economies on medieval Moroccan settlement patterns. Using documentary and numismatic evidence, this chapter demonstrates that there was a shift in settlement patterns from a multitiered and hierarchical distribution of settlement size during the Idrisid period to a "primate" one during subsequent periods. It concludes with a critical analysis of the results derived from both lines of evidence.

Chapter 6 examines local exchange and community interaction between al-Basra and its hinterland. It describes the results of instrumental neutron activation analysis (INAA), the technique that was used to examine ceramic samples collected around al-Basra region, and, more specifically, to ascertain that these samples were produced at al-Basra. In addition to compositional data, documentary and ethnoarchaeological data were used to shed more light on the al-Basra's local exchange system, an important component of the Idrisid political economy.

Finally, Chapter 7 summarizes the findings of this study along three main axes: (1) theoretical contributions, (2) methodological contributions, and (3) substantive contributions. It concludes with a number of suggestions for future research.

The system of transliteration of Arabic words used in this study was adapted from the Encyclopedia of Islam (see List of Transliterations of Arabic Characters). Names and places familiar to English-speaking readers were not transliterated (e.g., Fez, Marrakech, Idrisids, Almoravids).

[3] The term *marabout* (from Arabic *murâbiṯ*) is defined as "(1) a Muslim monk or hermit, especially in Africa: Muslim ascetic: Muslim holy man or saint. (2) a tomb or shrine erected to a marabout." *Webster's Third New International Dictionary of the English Language Unabridged*, G&C. Merriam Company, Springfield, Massachusetts, 1964. The term *murâbiṯ* originates from *ribâṯ*, which refers to a fortified convent usually located at border zones between Muslim and non-Muslim territories (e.g., Ribâṯ al-Fatẖ). For more information on this important religious and military institution in medieval Islamic societies, see Brett and Fentress 1996:142-149; Chabbi and Rabbat 1995.

Chapter 2

METHODOLOGY OF THE RESEARCH

The main methodological aspect of this research is the combination of documentary evidence with archaeological survey data to investigate political economy and settlement systems of medieval Moroccan dynastic states. As Boone et al. (1990:630) argued, "available documentary sources for early North African state societies can be effectively combined with anthropological insight to formulate interpretive models to derive more meaning from the archaeological record." On the one hand, textual sources were examined for information on medieval economy and settlement patterns. Textually derived locational information was also effectively used to search for archaeological sites. On the other hand, archaeological survey data were used to investigate the local exchange system between the city of al-Basra and its hinterland communities (Figure 1.2). Ceramic samples found at a number of sites around al-Basra were analyzed using instrumental neutron activation analysis (Chapter 6).

This chapter is divided into two sections. In the first section, I present the sources I used in this study and follow that by a critical analysis of their potential for archaeological investigations. I also discuss how textual data were recorded and subsequently incorporated in this study. In the second section, I discuss how the archaeological field survey was conducted.

Methods for the Analysis of Documentary Evidence

Presentation of Textual Sources

This study is based on information derived from 23 textual sources. Appendix A contains a chronological listing of these sources. Depending on the nature of the source, its time period, and the origin and qualifications of its author, each source contributed differently to enhance our understanding of the political economy and settlement systems of medieval northern Morocco.

The documentary sources used in this study fall into two main categories: historical chronicles and geographical accounts. These two categories are different in terms of their subject matter and their methodology. Historical chronicles, as their name indicates, are essentially a narrative of historical (mostly political) events, such as battles, sieges, enthronement of kings, and the rise of new dynasties. Economic, social, and ethnographic information forms only a secondary layer in such narratives. Geographical accounts, on the other hand, are concerned with the topography and geography of the localities described, as well as with the social and economic aspects. Political events are referred to only in passing. I used historical chronicles primarily to shed light on the political events that accompanied the emergence, growth, and eventual collapse of medieval Moroccan dynastic states. For data on medieval economy and settlement systems, I relied almost exclusively on geographers' accounts.

Except for the book of al-Mu<u>k</u>addasî (1994), which was translated into English (*the Best Divisions for Knowledge of the Regions*, translated by Basil Anthony Collins), all the other archival sources I consulted are either in Arabic (original text) or in French (translations)[1]. Most of the medieval textual material cited in this study is quoted from French translations. I did not provide my own translations for two main reasons. First, I intended the material cited, especially the information found in the synoptic table (Appendix B), to be as close to the original text as possible so that it could be used by students and scholars with a minimal risk of misinterpretation; the French translations quoted in this study are authoritative and widely cited in the literature. Second, translating a large number of medieval Arabic texts into English would require an expertise that is highly specialized.[2]

---

1 The original manuscripts are preserved in a number of private and public libraries in Morocco (e.g., the library of the *<u>Dj</u>âmi' al-<u>K</u>arawiyyîn* in Fez) and Europe (e.g., *La Bibliothèque Nationale* in Paris and the *Escorial* in Spain). For an excellent study on Moroccan libraries and their archival collections, see Benjelloun-Laroui 1990.

2 For a detailed discussion of some of the difficulties of translating medieval Arabic texts into English, see Levtzion and Hopkins 1981:3-4.

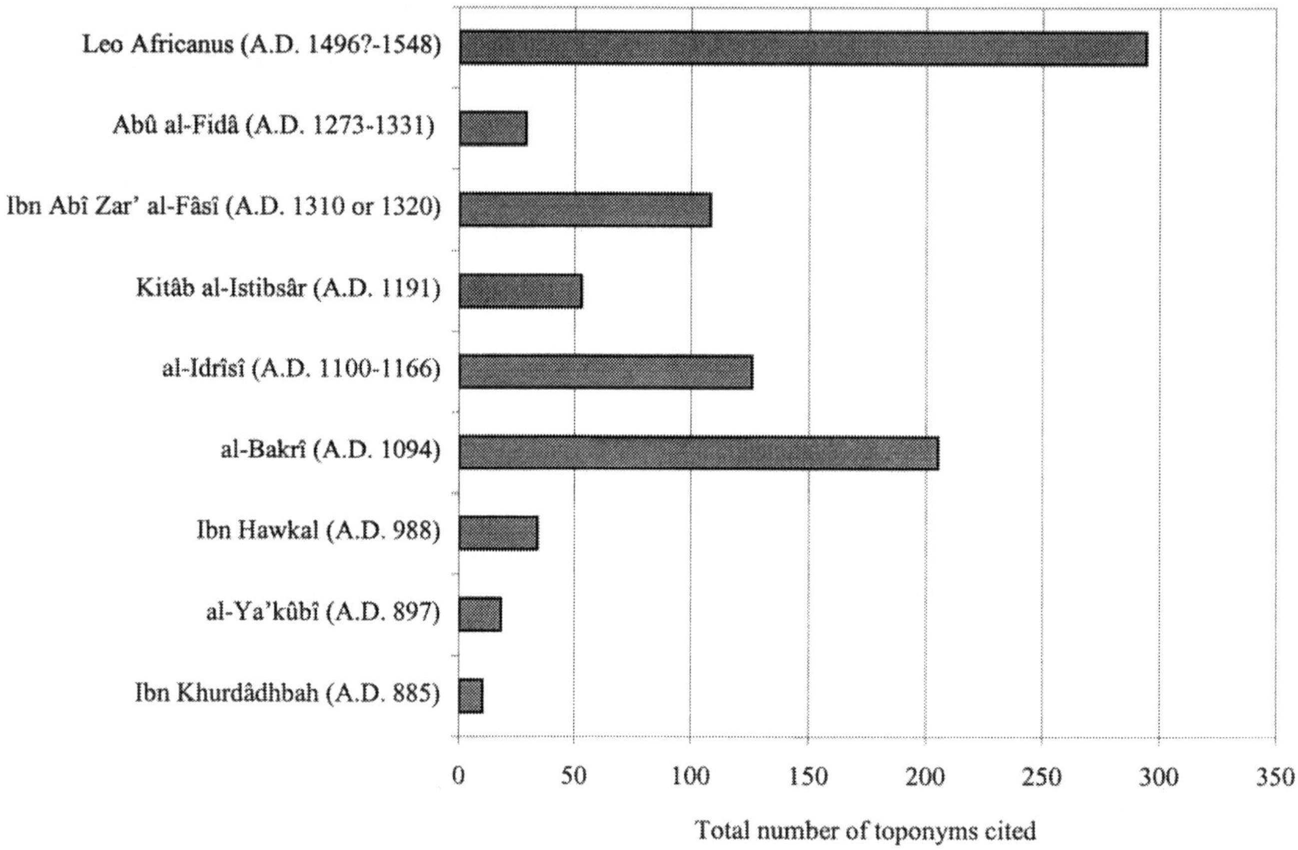

Figure 2.1 Distribution of Toponyms Cited in Textual Evidence. Data from Massignon (1906:46-47).

It is beyond the scope of this research to present an exhaustive overview of Arabic historico-geographical literature.[3] I will however briefly discuss one particular genre of Arabic geographical literature that is the most relevant to studies of settlement systems. The genre in question was named *al-Masâlik wa-l-mamâlik* (routes and kingdoms) by Blachère (1957:112) who chose this name because most of the books representative of this genre share the same title: *Kitâb al-Masâlik wa-l-mamâlik* (Blachère 1957:110-200; Maqbul 1965:579-582; Miquel 1967:267-330; Pellat 1991:639).

The *Masâlik wa-l-mamâlik* literature is relevant to settlement studies because it is particularly concerned with providing a purely descriptive inventory of settlements and the distances between them, layout of road networks, topographic features, and administrative boundaries. In fact, the earliest example of the *Masâlik wa-l-mamâlik* literature is the *masâlik* of Ibn Khurdâdhbah (A.D. 885). It was intended for the use of secretaries and military officials in the 'Abbasid bureaucracy, which explains the austerity and monotony of the prose. Ibn Khurdâdhbah held the very sensitive office of director of the Post and Intelligence Department (*Sahib al-barîd wa-l-khabar*). Later examples of the *masâlik* books were intended for a wider audience of merchants and travelers. As opposed to administrative manuals or practical guides, the information was delivered in more detail and in a more polished literary form.

The difference between the *Masâlik wa-l-mamâlik* and previous Arabic geographical genres is not only in style but also in methodology. Previous Arab geographers were mostly armchair scholars who relied on secondary sources in their writings. The information they provided is, therefore, uncertain if not unreliable. The geographers of the *Masâlik wa-l-mamâlik* school, on the other hand, relied first and foremost on direct observation (*'iyân*), and only secondarily on earlier written sources and oral information gathered from travelers and merchants. Their writings are, therefore, more reliable.

With a few exceptions, all the important sources used in this research, especially early ones, were written by geographers who belong to the *Masâlik wa-l-mamâlik* school: Ibn Khurdâdhbah (A.D. 885), al-Ya'kûbî (A.D. 889-890), Ibn al-Fakîh (A.D. 903), al-Istakhrî (A.D. 951), Ibn Hawkal (A.D. 988), al-Mukaddasî (A.D. 946-988), al-Bakrî (A.D. 1094), and al-Idrîsî (A.D. 1100-1166)[4]. In fact, the work of one them (*Ahsan al-takâsîm* of al-Mukaddasî) is considered to be the culmination of this genre (Blachère 1957:113; Miquel 1967:322-330). As shown in Figure 2.1, until the twelfth century, the *Masâlik wa-l-mamâlik* geographers contributed a large body of toponymic material for the early medieval period in Morocco. This material constituted the core of the settlement data discussed in this study. In the absence of a large-scale archaeological survey of northern Morocco, the contribution of these geographers is instrumental to settlement studies.[5]

3 For a detailed discussion, see Maqbul 1965, 1995; Miquel 1967.

4 There is no consensus as to which medieval geographer to include in the *Masâlik wa-l-mamâlik* school and which to exclude from it. The geographers included here are from classifications proposed by different scholars (see Pellat 1991).

5 For an overview of medieval textual sources on Morocco, see Massignon 1906:46-47; Siraj 1995b:31-62.

Of the 23 textual sources used in this research, five of them were most instrumental: (1) Ibn Hawkal, (2) al-Mukaddasî, (3) al-Bakrî, (4) al-Idrîsî, and (5) Leo Africanus (A.D. 1496?-1548). Notably, the first four geographers were all prominent members of the *Masâlik wa-l-mamâlik* school. In the remaining of this section, I will provide a brief overview on the life and work of each of these geographers.[6]

These textual sources cover a time period that extends from the tenth to the sixteenth centuries (see Appendix A). The works of al-Mukaddasî, Ibn Hawkal and al-Idrîsî feature a series of maps. While these maps are undoubtedly valuable sources of information for the study of medieval Arabic cartography, their utility for settlement studies is limited. They are too broad to allow accurate site identification. I used ancient maps primarily to get a sense of the general distribution of medieval settlements.

Ibn Hawkal (Abû-l-Kâsim Muhammad Ibn 'Alî al-Nasîbî) was born in Baghdad. He is famous for his book *Kitâb sûrat al-ard* (the Picture of the Earth) completed in A.D. 988. Ibn Hawkal wrote *Kitâb sûrat al-ard* after meeting with al-Istakhrî (A.D. 951) who encouraged him to do so and authorized him to correct and expand his *Kitâb al-masâlik wa-l-mamâlik* (the Book of Routes and Kingdoms). Ibn Hawkal visited North Africa, Spain, and the confines of sub-Saharan Africa between A.D. 947 and A.D. 951. This author was a geographer, a traveler and a merchant all at the same time. Hence, he developed keen eyes for assessing the economic situation of the countries he visited. It is possible that Ibn Hawkal was also a missionary (*dâ'iya*) at the service of the Fatimid government. His description of the Maghrib reveals his sympathy for the shi'îte movement.

The information found in Ibn Hawkal's book was instrumental to this research. It is original, accurate, and detailed, especially for the geographic area under investigation. "Ibn Hawkal's original contribution is most obvious in the chapters on the West, namely the Maghrib, Spain and Sicily." (Levtzion and Hopkins 1981:43). Although Ibn Hawkal incorporated a large section of the *masâlik* of al-Istakhrî in his book, his personal stamp overshadowed that of his mentor. It was derived, as he states himself, from first-hand experience and trustworthy sources (Ibn Hawkal 1967:66, 83). Ibn Hawkal was careful to indicate which data he personally collected through direct observation and which materials he borrowed from earlier sources. This scholarly practice gave even more scientific value to his work.

Ibn Hawkal's text is an important source for reconstructing the political economy of the Maghrib. Being a business-oriented author, Ibn Hawkal paid close attention to economic aspects; his text includes information on prices of basic staple goods, tax revenues, and market exchange. Ibn Hawkal's also provided original and detailed information on the gold trade between the city of Sidjilmâsa and sub-Saharan West Africa, and on nomadic populations living on the fringes of the Saharan desert (Levtzion and Hopkins 1981:43-44).

The value of Ibn Hawkal's text in term of toponymic information is limited compared with al-Bakrî's text, for example (Figure 2.1); his description of medieval Morocco is mainly concerned with major urban centers as he, himself, pointed out (Ibn Hawkal 1967:66). Ibn Hawkal, however, provided detailed cartographic information in the form of maps that accompany his text. As shown in Figures 2.2 and 2.3, Ibn Hawkal's map of the Maghrib is detailed and quite advanced for its time. It is in fact one of the most detailed medieval maps of the Maghrib, if compared, for example, with al-Mukaddasî's map (1994:199).

Al-Mukaddasî[7] (Shams al-Dîn Abû 'Abd Allâh Muhammad Ibn Ahmad Ibn Abî Bakr al-Bannâ' al-Shâmî) was born in Jerusalem around A.D. 945. He is considered to be the best representative of Arabic geographical literature of the second half of the tenth century. His book, *Ahsan al-takâsîm fî ma'rifat al-aklîm* (the Best Divisions for Knowledge of the Provinces) written in A.D. 985, is the first true geography of the Islamic world of his time. Al-Mukaddasî's rigorous methodology and his systematization of the subject matter are the most original traits of his work. Al-Mukaddasî (1994:215-216) states in one of the passages of his book that: "One of the excellences of our book is avoiding what others have mentioned; and the most objectionable feature of their books is that their methods are in every way opposite to ours... But read our book, and you find that it speaks for itself only, and, of its kind, somewhat like an orphan, is unique in its organization." *Ahsan al-takâsîm* is held in high regard by modern scholars; Wheatley (1976:361) considers this book "as one of the most ambitious studies of human organization ever to be attempted in the medieval world. Nor was it to be repeated."

Ahsan al-takâsîm is a valuable source for scholars investigating settlement systems in complex societies. It provides a wealth of geographic, economic, and administrative information covering a very wide region extending from the Atlantic Ocean to the Indus River, and from the Caspian Sea to the Sub-Saharan desert.

Ahsan al-takâsîm reveals a conscious effort to standardize medieval Arabic geographical literature, especially in terms of settlement typology. The majority of earlier descriptions consisted of dry and monotonous inventories of place-names with no attention to settlement hierarchy.

Al-Mukaddasî's relied on several lines of evidence, including direct observation (*'iyân*), notes he had gathered during twenty years of travel around the Islamic world, reliable oral sources, government archives, and earlier geographical accounts. His book is accompanied by a series of maps established according to his classification system. His description of the Maghrib, which he apparently did not visit, is valuable from a toponymic

6 Material on al-Bakrî, al-Idrîsî, al-Mukaddasî, Ibn Hawkal, and Leo Africanus was synthesized from Bosworth et al. (1986); Levtzion and Hopkins (1981); Lévi-Provençal (1960); Maqbul (1965); Miquel (1971, 1993); Oman (1971).

7 Material on al-Mukaddasî was synthesized from Miquel (1967, 1987, 1993); al-Mukaddasî (1963).

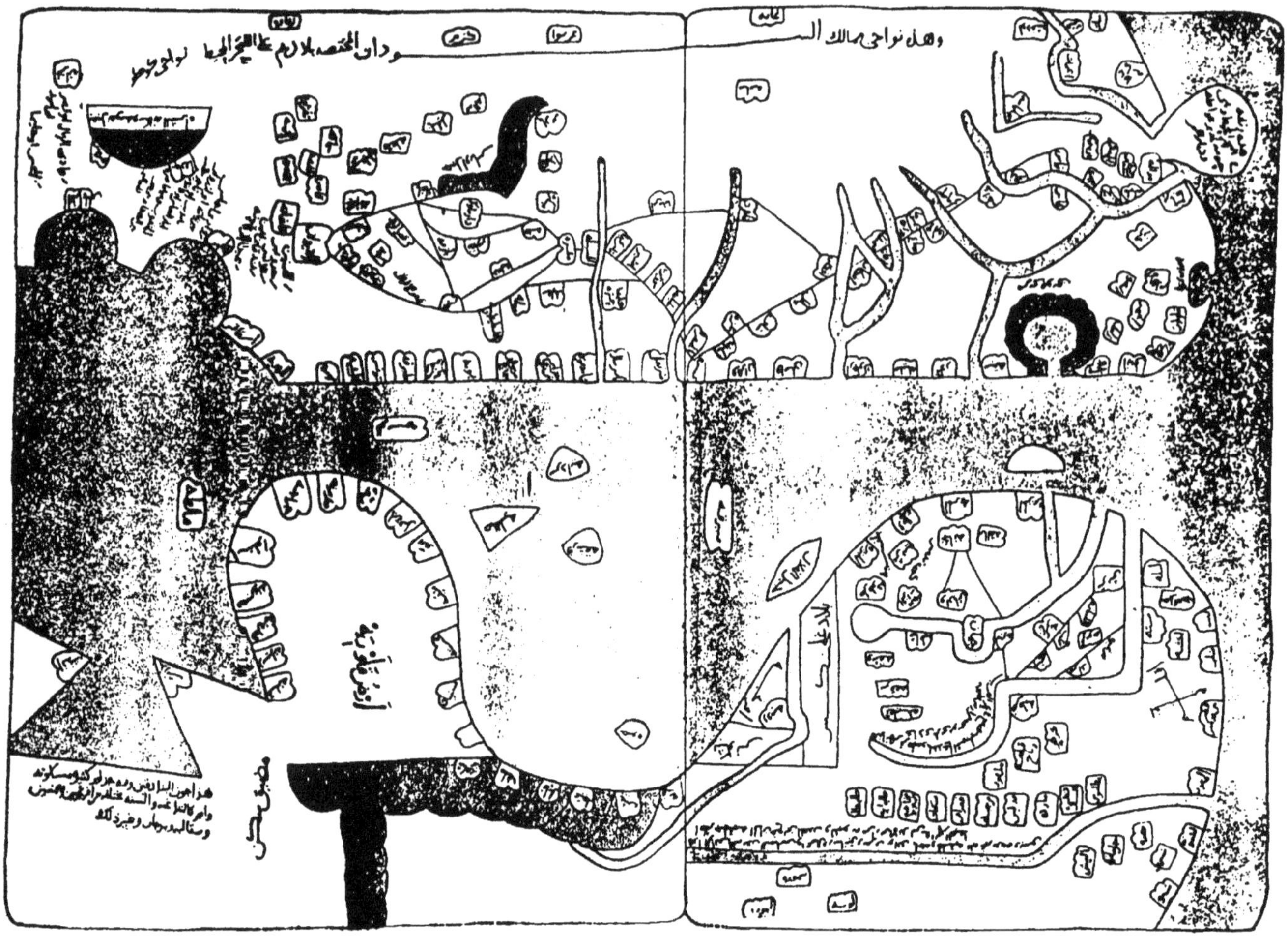

Figure 2.2 Map of the Mediterranean Basin by Ibn Hawkal (A.D. 988).

and organizational standpoint; al-Mukaddasî listed a total of 51 place-names just within the district of Fez and its adjacent territory.

Abû 'Ubayd al-Bakrî ('Abd Allâh Ibn 'Abd al-'Azîz Ibn Muhammad Ibn Ayyûb) was a native of al-Andalus (Muslim Spain). Although he never visited the Maghrib, the section of his *Kitâb al-masâlik wa-l-mamâlik* (the Book of Routes and Kingdoms), which describes medieval Morocco, is one of the richest, most accurate, and most reliable accounts available for the early medieval period of Morocco (Lévi-Provençal 1960:156). Al-Bakrî's *Kitâb al-masâlik wa-l-mamâlik* was completed in A.D. 1068. The author died in A.D. 1094.

The sources of al-Bakrî are threefold: verbal information derived from travelers who actually visited Morocco, Cordovan official archives, and more importantly, the work of an earlier geographer named al-Warrâk.[8] As it was pointed out by Levtzion and Hopkins (1981:62-63), it is important for scholars using al-Bakrî's text to pay attention as to which material is taken from al-Warrâk and which is an original contribution of the author; al-Warrâk's description predates al-Bakrî's by almost a century. To complicate this matter, al-Bakrî occasionally omits citing his sources. In some instances, however, he updated his sources by providing information dating to the time when he was writing (A.D. 1068).

Al-Bakrî's book was the most important source used in this research. His description of the Maghrib is both original and detailed. It includes, in addition to administrative and geographical information, valuable insights on the ethnography and social and political history of the Maghrib (Levtzion and Hopkins 1981:62). Al-Bakrî's book constitutes one of the richest toponymic inventories of medieval place-names at our disposal (Figure 2.1).

Al-Idrîsî (Abû 'Abd Allâh Muhammad Ibn Muhammad Ibn 'Abd Allâh Ibn Idrîs al-'Âlî bi-Amr Allâh) also known as al-Sharîf al-Idrîsî, was a native of Sabta (Ceuta) in Morocco. His book, *Kitâb nuzhat al-mushtâk fî khtirâk al-âfâk* (The Pleasures of Him who longs to cross the Horizons)[9], is one of the most influential works of descriptive geography for the Maghrib and al-Andalus. It was completed in A.D. 1154. Al-Idrîsî died in A.D. 1166.

8 Muhammad Ibn Yûsûf al-Warrâk lived in Ifrîkiya (Tunisia) between A.D. 904 and A.D. 973. Al-Bakrî cited al-Warrâk repeatedly. Al-Warrâk wrote a roadbook, now lost, entitled *al-Masâlik wa-l-mamâlik*. He also wrote several monographs on a number of North African cities including al-Basra, Nakûr, Sidjilmâsa, Sabta, Tâhart, Wahrân (Oran), and Tunis.

9 Also called *Kitâb Rudjâr* (the Book of Roger) because Roger II, the Norman king of Sicily, commissioned it. The book was intended to accompany a large silver planisphere now lost.

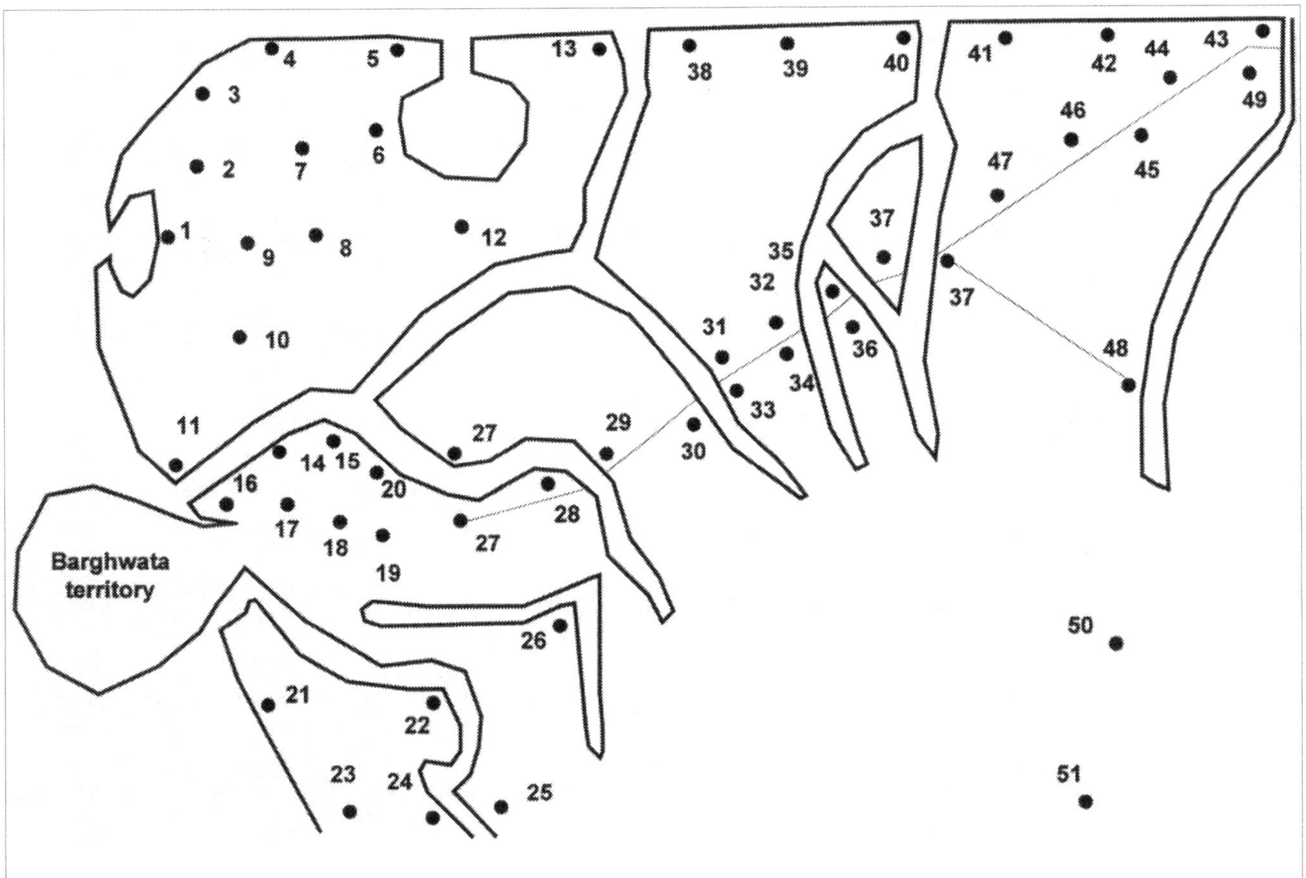

Figure 2.3 Map of Morocco by Ibn Hawkal (A.D. 988).

Al-Idrîsî's knowledge of Morocco was based on first-hand experience; thus his information is detailed and accurate (Figure 2.1). He did, however, copy several passages that described a number of medieval Moroccan cities from *Kitâb ṣûrat al-arḍ* of Ibn Hawkal. Al-Idrîsî was also indebted to al-Bakrî whose book he supplemented, confirmed, and elaborated on. He adapted the information found in al-Bakrî to fit his conceptual framework (i.e., astronomical division of the world into seven climes or *akâlîm*), and updated some of al-Bakrî data to account for current historical changes. Al-Idrîsî had at his disposal a number of independent sources of evidence, which allowed him access to original data, especially on trade patterns (Levtzion and Hopkins 1981:105).

Al-Idrîsî's *Nuzhat al-mushtâk* is accompanied by a series of maps, "which are on the whole the most accurate and complete of those in the Islamic tradition" (Levtzion and Hopkins 1981:104). Al-Idrîsî's map of the Maghrib, however, was of a limited importance to this study because it lacks the necessary resolution to allow site identification.

Leo Africanus[10], originally known as al-Hasan Ibn Muhammad al-Wazzân al-Zayyâtî, was born in Granada some time between A.D. 1489 and A.D. 1495. He traveled extensively across Morocco on several diplomatic and business trips in which he represented the Wattasid sultan of Fez. In A.D. 1517, al-Hasan al-Wazzân was captured by Sicilian corsairs while he was returning by sea from his pilgrimage to Mecca. The corsairs took him to Rome and offered him as a present to Pope Leo X. In A.D. 1520, he was baptized by the Pope who gave him his own name, Johannis Leo de Medicis. The editor of al-Hasan al-Wazzân's *Descrittione dell' Africa* (Description of Africa) referred to him as Giovanni Leone Africano, thus the name Leo Africanus. A few years before his death in A.D. 1548, Leo Africanus converted back to Islam.

Leo Africanus completed his *Descrittione dell' Africa* in A.D. 1526. This book was written in Italian based on notes that the author had gathered during his travels. The original text (in Italian) contains a large number of distorted place-names. Lhote, the editor of the French translation entitled *Description de l'Afrique* (Leo Africanus 1956), made several corrections and annexed a number of useful site identifications. Of all the textual sources consulted, Leo Africanus' book contained the largest number of place-names (Figure 2.1).

The *Descrittione dell' Africa* is the latest source used in this research. It provides a rich and colorful account of the economic, social and political life of Morocco at the beginning of the sixteenth century. The minute and almost photographic description of the city of Fez in the late middle ages is the best example in this regard. The *Descrittione dell' Africa* is a major source for the study of medieval Morocco.

Critical Analysis of Textual Sources

The documentary sources used in this study vary a great deal in terms of the resolution and the relevance of the information they provide. Prior to the time of Ibn Hawkal and al-Mukaddasî, the information found in the majority of Arabic sources was too poor and too broad to allow a sufficiently detailed reconstruction of medieval Moroccan settlement patterns.[11] These sources are, however, the only record at our disposal for the very early Islamic period in Morocco. This is particularly the case for a number of early eastern geographers, such as Ibn Khurdâdhbah (A.D. 885), Ibn al-Fakîh (A.D. 903), and al-Istakhrî (A.D. 951).

It is not surprising that the most detailed and reliable accounts at our disposal are those composed by geographers and chroniclers who lived in Morocco or al-Andalus, since they were more acquainted with the political, economic, and geographic conditions of the country than their distant contemporaries. As shown in Figure 2.1, the contribution of eastern geographers (Ibn Khurdâdhbah, al-Ya'kûbî, Ibn Hawkal, and Abû al-Fidâ) in terms of toponymic information is modest compared to geographers who lived in Morocco or al-Andalus. There was a tendency among medieval geographers to focus on northern Morocco - possibly because of the presence of a relatively well-established political authority - at the expense of the Middle Atlas, the High Atlas, and most areas south of Um al-Rabî' River, except for the Sûs region and the oases (Terrasse 1947a:38).

The use of textual records in archaeological investigations presents a number of challenges. Textual records are rarely, if ever, free from errors, discrepancies, exaggerations, fallacies, and bias-induced statements. The sources of inaccuracies in textual records are varied. While some are relatively easy to detect (e.g., copyist's mistakes), others are more elusive. The two most common sources of inaccuracies in Arabic medieval historical records are exaggeration and plagiarism.

Medieval authors are known for their propensity toward overstatement, either to please a particular audience (e.g., court historians depicting their masters and their deeds in a more favorable light) or to conform to a particular literary style and appeal to its readers (e.g., travel literature). In his *Mukaddima*, Ibn Khaldûn (1967), one of the most influential historians of the fourteenth century, wrote an eloquent passage on exaggeration as a major flaw of the medieval historical discourse:

> "[They] give free rein to their imagination, follow the whisperings of exaggeration, and transgress the limitations of customary experience, when speaking of the armies of contemporary states, or of states which existed in the recent past; or when discussing the troops of Muslim or Christian nations; or when enumerating the revenues of kings, or the taxes or dues levied by them; or when estimating the expenditure of the wealthy, or the fortunes of the rich. Should we, however, check up these figures by asking the responsible officials for the number of their troops, or the rich for a statement of their wealth, profits, and expenditures, the result is apt to come to less than a tenth of the popular estimate." (Issawi 1987:29).

Other common form of distortion, which is somewhat related to exaggeration, is political bias. Several medieval authors were known for their inclination to a particular dynasty or a religious movement, which was reflected in their work. Ibn Khurdâdhbah (and possibly al-Ya'kûbî) served as director of the Post and Intelligence Department (*Sahib al-barîd wa-l-khabar*) for the 'Abbasids of Baghdad, and wrote his *masâlik* for the 'Abbasid administration. Al-Ya'kûbî, Ibn Hawkal, and al-Mukaddasî were all sympathizers of the shi'îte movement, a fact which helps to explain their tendency to promote shi'îte ideology (e.g., Ibn Hawkal's positive statements in favor of the Fatimids).

Plagiarism was one of the most serious problems I encountered in analyzing textual sources. It is so widespread in medieval Arabic literature that each record had to be dissected to separate original material from a plagiarized one. By identifying the different layers of information found

---

[10] Material on Leo Africanus was synthesized from Bosworth et al. (1986).

[11] A notable exception is a passage written by the ninth century al-Ya'kûbî in which he described a medieval itinerary in northern Morocco (al-Ya'kûbî 1937).

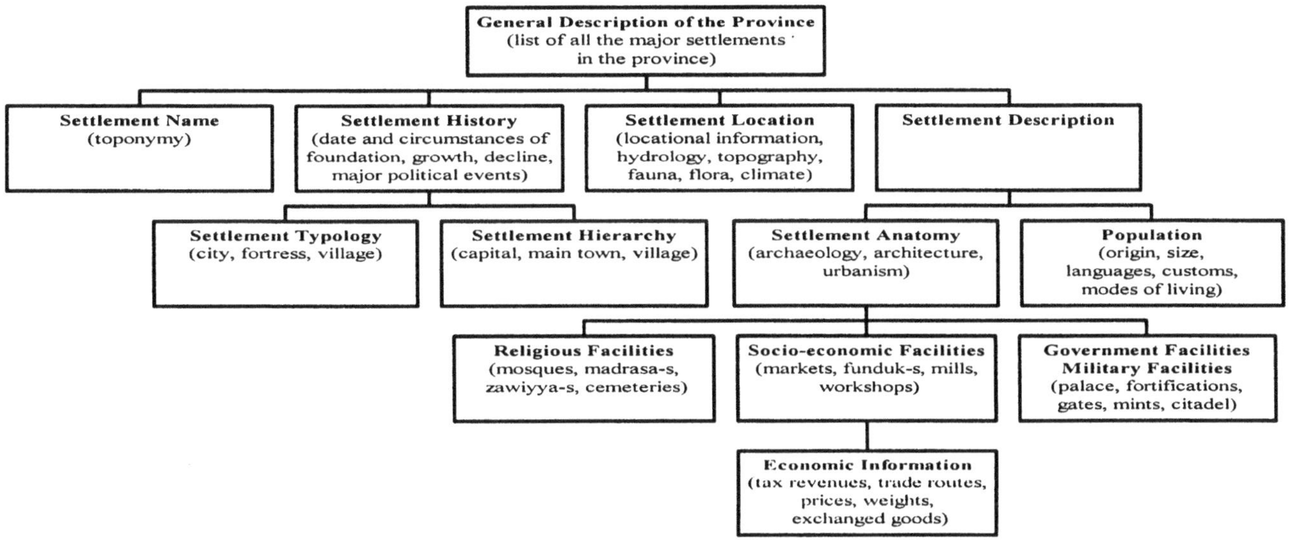

Figure 2.4 Schematic Classification of Settlement Data Found in Textual Evidence.

in textual sources, one could minimize the risk of basing interpretations on anachronistic and/or outdated information. The failure to recognize plagiarized material could lead to serious misinterpretations, especially when the plagiarized information was several centuries old. This could have important implications for textually based settlement studies. If the evidence used contains outdated material plagiarized from earlier sources, one could "recreate" the settlement system under investigation (i.e., assigning settlements to a time period during which they were in fact abandoned).

The textual sources used in this study, especially those written by Ibn Hawkal and his successors, contain several categories of settlement information. The number and order of these categories vary from one source to another. As the schematic drawing in Figure 2.4 shows, the main categories found in a typical description of a medieval settlement can be arranged hierarchically. The account begins with a general description of the province or district in which the settlement is located. It may include a map and a list of the major cities within the district (e.g., al-Mukaddasî 's description of the district of Fez). A more specific description follows, with details on settlement toponymy, location, chronology, size, and typology. These information categories are the most relevant to regional studies of settlement systems. In order to take full advantage of textual data, researchers need to be familiar with the nuances and subtleties of medieval Arabic settlement terminology. Appendix C lists the most common terms and expressions used in reference to settlement chronology, size, and typology.

Chronological data, such as foundation dates are usually indicated in broad terms which allow only a gross distinction to be made between pre-Islamic and Islamic settlements (e.g., "*madîna awwaliyya*" or ancient city). Information on site size is also given in similar broad terms (e.g., "*madîna âhila*" or populous city). Of course, this information acquires greater value when it is linked to other textual data, such as population size and/or tax payments. The terminology used to describe settlement typology is both the most specific and the most diverse. Al-Mukaddasî was the first geographer to establish a well-defined settlement terminology, which standardized medieval Arabic geographical literature.

As Figure 2.4 shows, textual records can also provide important information on the anatomy of a site and its political, economic and socio-cultural history. While information on site anatomy (e.g., description of public monuments, houses, outline of the city, etc) is primarily used in site-specific studies, information on population size, tax payments, and public facilities - in terms of number and size - is also used by archaeologists to establish settlement hierarchies, an important variable in studies of regional settlement systems.

Textual records are, however, inconsistent in terms of the amount of detail they provide for each category of settlement information. Major urban sites are described in more length than small settlements. Small hinterland communities are often described in very broad terms. For example, al-'Umarî (14th century A.D.), while describing al-Basra, states that: "its territory contains villages and agricultural fields... [translation by author]." (Fagnan 1924:79-80). Also, medieval geographers tend to focus in their descriptions of market exchange on luxury items at the expense of utilitarian goods. They paid more attention to regional and sub-regional exchange systems than to local ones. This is a serious drawback for studies of local exchange systems involving urban centers and their countryside. Archaeological evidence is essential in this regard (see Chapter 6).

Archaeological identification of historically documented sites increases when the texts provide detailed and specific information. Figure 2.5 shows the distribution of settlements according to whether or not they are archaeologically identified. There are still numerous sites that are historically documented, but yet to be identified by archaeologists. Notably, more than half of the Idrisid sites (25 out of a total of 43 sites) are virtually unknown archeologically (see Chapter 5).

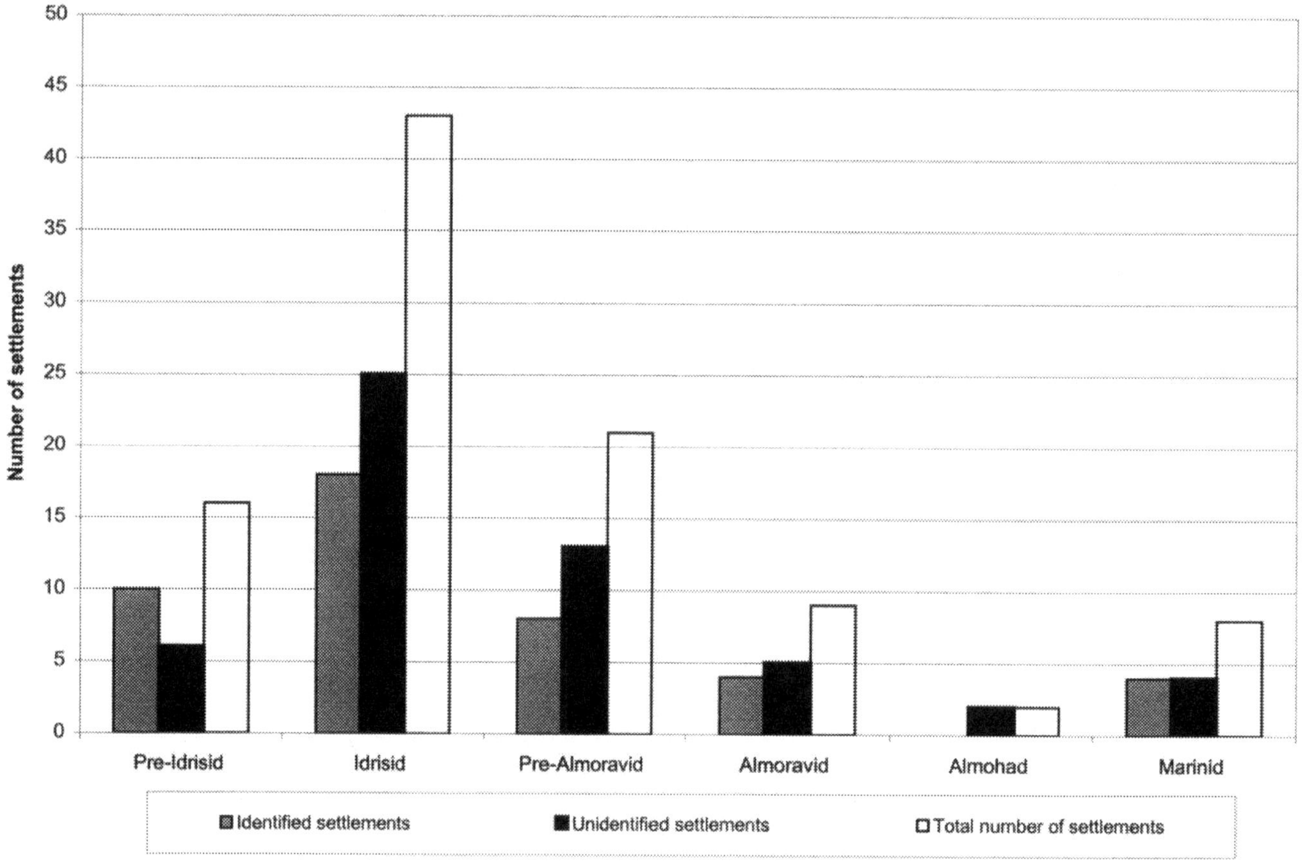

Figure 2.5 Number of Archaeologically Identified and Unidentified Settlements Known to Exist Historically in Northern Morocco by Time Period.

One of the problems of using textual sources to locate archaeological sites is the fact that these sources provide distances between settlements in a multitude of units. In medieval Arabic metrology, the *mar<u>h</u>ala*, the *mîl*, and the *barîd* are the most commonly used units for measuring distances between locations.

The *mar<u>h</u>ala* is the distance traveled in one day. According to al-Mu<u>k</u>addasî, it is the equivalent of six to seven *farsa<u>kh</u>s* or parasangs (one *farsa<u>kh</u>* equals 6 km). Elsewhere, his *mar<u>h</u>ala* equals 8.6 *farsa<u>kh</u>s* or the equivalent of 50 km.[12] The *mîl* is the equivalent of 2 km (al-Mu<u>k</u>addasî 1950:76 note 12). The *barîd*, which is the distance between two staging posts, is the equivalent of 11.5 km (al-Mu<u>k</u>addasî 1963:144 note 20). According to Ibn Rustah (1967:22), the *barîd* equals 12 *mîl* or 24 km.[13]

Several variables have to be taken into consideration while using these units of distance: (1) the modes of transport used at the time (e.g., horses, camels, mules, or on foot), (2) the nature of the physical landscape crossed (e.g., mountainous terrain vs. open desert), and (3) the season of travel (e.g., summer vs. winter).

In addition to these relatively fixed units of distance, site location is also expressed in a variety of broader statements, such as references to nearby natural landmarks (e.g., mountains, springs, woodland, or rivers) or cultural ones (e.g., sites or monuments). This type of locational information also presents some difficulties since the natural and built environments change constantly.

Recording of Textual Information

In this study of the works of 23 medieval Arab geographers and chroniclers (Appendix A), I analyzed each descriptive account in terms of toponymic information, site location, site chronology, site type, site size, and political/socio-economic information. In order to exploit textual data in a systematic manner, I designed a database using Microsoft Access. Each category of settlement information for each individual site was entered in a separate field.

The storage of textual information in a database form proved to be very useful in a number of ways. Using a system of keywords, I was able to search the database by site name, name of textual source, or any other variable of interest. Also, the assignment of textual data to separate fields allowed more consistency while recording textual information. The database created for the present research can be easily expanded to include more sites (e.g., sites beyond the boundaries of northern Morocco), more textual sources, and more categories of settlement information.

The data shown in Appendix B represent a synoptic table of settlement information derived from the database in question. Settlement names are listed alphabetically to facilitate

[12] Encyclopedia of Islam 1991, vol. VI, pp. 558-559.

[13] For details on medieval Arabic units of distance, see Elisseeff 1988; Hinz 1965; Ibn Rustah 1967:22.

reference. I ordered the textual information for each site in a chronological manner starting from the earliest source to the latest. Numismatic evidence, when available, is always listed at the end of each site description. For example, the earliest textual source on Fez is Ibn Khurdâdhbah (A.D. 885) and the latest is Leo Africanus (A.D. 1548). The main advantage of this classification system is that it allows the urban and economic growth (or decline) of each settlement to be monitored through a long period of time.

I used the database primarily to search for the following settlement variables: (1) settlement length of occupation, (2) phase of foundation, (3) state of occupation (occupied vs. abandoned), (4) archaeological status (identified vs. non identified), and (5) settlement size.

Settlement length of occupation refers to the number of centuries a particular settlement was occupied after it was first mentioned in textual sources. This is an important variable in assessing the survival rate of settlements through time. The phase of foundation refers to the dynastic period during which a settlement was founded. There are four major foundation phases:

Phase I: A.D. 789-974 (the Idrisid period)[14]

Phase II: A.D. 1073-1147 (the Almoravid period)

Phase III: A.D. 1130-1276 (the Almohad period)

Phase IV: A.D. 1258-1420 (the Marinid period)

State of occupation refers to whether a site was occupied or abandoned at a particular phase. This is important in assessing urban growth during each dynastic phase. The last variable examined was the archaeological status of settlements. This simply means whether or not a particular settlement was archaeologically identified. This variable proved useful in evaluating the potential of textual sources for identifying archaeological sites.

Settlement size was the most important variable in this study. It is by monitoring change in settlement size that one could document the shift in settlement systems from a multitiered and hierarchical pattern to a "primate" one or vice-versa. Table 2.1 shows the criteria I used for assigning each settlement to its corresponding settlement size class. In order to monitor change in settlement size from one phase to another, I adopted the settlement size classes[15] proposed by Vitorino Magalhaes Godinho, an economic historian of the Annales school (1947:134:135) (Table 2.1).

Settlement size data used in this study were derived from textual evidence either directly, as population estimates expressed in numbers of cooking hearths (*mawâkid*), or indirectly by examining the typology and anatomy of the settlement in question. A cooking hearth is the equivalent of a household. Godinho (1947:134) estimated the average size of the medieval family to be five persons (see also Massignon 1906:148 note 1); in order to convert the number of cooking hearths into actual numbers of inhabitants, Godinho multiplied the number of hearths by five. For example, based on the fourteenth-century chronicler Ibn Abî Zar' (1843:25-26, 1860:57), the city of Fez contained 89,236 households (or cooking hearths); if we use Godinho's formula, this figure would translate to a population size of close to 450,000 inhabitants. Fez would belong then to a settlement size class I (more than 100,000 inhabitants). In Table 2.1, the numbers of cooking hearths are distributed into six categories using Godinho's formula.

In the absence of direct textual evidence on settlement size in the form of numerical values, I devised a number of criteria to infer settlement size. The first criterion is based on settlement terminology. As listed in Appendix C, medieval authors used a number of terms and/or expressions to convey a relatively precise meaning about the type and size of the locality being described. For example, there is clear hierarchical distinction between a locality described as a *kasaba* (a provincial capital) and another described as a mere *karya* (a village). Similarly, a locality described as a "*madîna kabîra*" (a large city) was obviously larger in size than a "*madîna mutawassita*" (a mid-sized city). The second criterion is based on the anatomy of the settlement under investigation. A settlement that contained a large numbers of public facilities, such as mosques, public baths (*hammâm*), markets, workshops, and cemeteries was undoubtedly larger than one which lacked such facilities. Additional criteria for inferring settlement size were the presence of mints and the amount of tax payments paid to the central authority.

In Table 2.1 (last column), I show how these criteria were implemented in ascending order. I assigned to settlement size class VI (less than 2,000 inhabitants) all settlements described in textual evidence as "small urban settlements" or "rural settlements." This settlement class also includes sites with no numismatic evidence.[16] Settlement size class V (2,000 to 10,000 inhabitants) includes urban centers with public facilities and/or sites with numismatic evidence. A typical site within this settlement category is enclosed by a city wall of less than five gates and contains a relatively small congregational mosque of less than five aisles.[17] The sites assigned to settlement size class IV (10,000 to 25,000

[14] The chronology of the Idrisid period is derived from Eustache (1970a:1036). The chronology of subsequent dynastic periods is derived from Laroui (1995:362-366). The Almoravid and Almohad chronologies are based on the dates when tribal/religious leaders were officially proclaimed as rulers. The Marinid chronology is based on the date when tribal/religious leaders acquired the title of *Amîr al-Muslimîn* (the prince of the Muslims). The pre-Idrisid period refers to the phase that extends from the Arab conquest of medieval Morocco (*al-Futûh*) (A.D. 703-711) to the Idrisid period (A.D. 789). This is not to be confused with the pre-Islamic period, which extends from the end of the Roman period in A.D. 285 to the Arab conquest. The pre-Almoravid period refers to the phase between the collapse of the Idrisid dynasty (A.D. 974) and the rise of the Almoravids (A.D. 1073). During this period, medieval Morocco was conquered by the Fatimids, the Umayyads (Terrasse 1950:137:164) and the Zenata tribes (Terrasse 1950:165:181).

[15] I adopted Godinho's settlement size classes because they were used by Boone et al. (1990). Using the same settlement size classes allowed the comparison between the Boone et al. (1990) data and my own.

[16] This is based on the assumption that the presence of a mint implies the presence of a sizable urban center (see Chapter 5).

[17] This is based on the two assumptions: (1) the number of city gates reflects the perimeter of the area enclosed by city walls and the number of aisles in a congregational mosque reflects its size, (2) the area enclosed by city walls and the size and number of congregational mosques reflect population size.

Table 2.1 Criteria for Assigning Settlement Size Values

Frequency Distribution of Settlement Size Classes[a]		Direct Textual Evidence: Number of Hearths/Households[b] (in thousands)	Indirect Textual Evidence: Settlement Typology[c]/Anatomy
Class	*Number of Inhabitants (in thousands)*		
I	>100	>20	Metropolises of Fez and Marrakech at their height (150,000 dinars in tax payment).
II	50-100	10-20	Dynastic capitals of Fez, Marrakech, and Rabat at their height.
III	25-50	5-10	State Capital; Large Provincial Capital: more than one congregational mosque and/or 50,000 dinars or more in tax payment.
IV	10-25	2-5	Provincial Capital; Large Urban Center: presence of public facilities, city-wall (>5 gates), and/or congregational mosque (>5 aisles).
V	2-10	.4-2	Urban Center: presence of public facilities, city-wall (<5 gates), congregational mosque (<5 aisles), and/or presence of numismatic evidence (a mint).
VI	<2	<.4	Small Urban Settlement; Rural Settlement; Fortress; Coastal entrepôt; Caravansary; no numismatic evidence.

[a] After Godinho (1947:135)

[b] A cooking hearth (*mawk̲id*) is the equivalent of a household. One cooking hearth equals five persons (Godinho 1947:134).

[c] See Appendix C for a detailed list.

inhabitants) are mostly large urban centers or provincial capitals. A typical site within this settlement category is enclosed by a city-wall of more than five gates and contains a large congregational mosque of more than five aisles. Settlement size class III (25,000 to 50,000 inhabitants) is represented by state capitals and large provincial capitals. The most representative settlement within this class contains more than one congregational mosque and contributed an average of 50,000 dinars or more in annual tax payment to the state treasury. Only the cities of Fez, Marrakech, and Rabat were assigned to settlement size class II (50,000 to 100,000 inhabitants). These cities represent dynastic capitals at their peak. The two cities of Fez and Marrakech grew even more to become real metropolises each with a population of much more than 100,000 inhabitants. Both cities contributed more than 150,000 in annual tax payments (al-'Umarî 1927:171).

In Appendix D, I list all the settlements analyzed in this study according to their settlement size class and phase of occupation. Each phase represents a dynastic period (e.g., Phase I represents the Idrisid period). The first column shows the names of the settlements listed in alphabetical order, followed by the time period when they were founded or mentioned in textual records for the first time. Roman numerals indicate the values for settlement size classes (I, II, III, etc.). Settlements that were abandoned, destroyed, or not yet founded at a particular time period are represented by a zero. By using this table, one can easily follow temporal change in settlement size for each of the sites listed. For example, the city of al-Basra was an important provincial capital (settlement size class IV) during phase I (Idrisid period), then it decreased in size and became a regular urban center (settlement size class V) during phase II (Almoravid period). Finally, by phase III (Almohad period), the city has already collapsed (settlement size class represented by a zero).

Appendices B and D, and Table 2.1 are included in this study in order for other researchers to reproduce or verify my results in terms of using textual evidence to monitor change in medieval Moroccan settlement systems. Appendix B shows the "raw data" derived from textual sources and used in this study, Table 2.1 shows my criteria for inferring settlement size classes, and finally, Appendix D shows a list of all the settlements examined in this study and their size class values by dynastic period.

Archaeological Survey Methods

Base Map Preparation

As part of the archaeological-Historical approach, this study also involved a relatively large-scale archaeological survey in northern Morocco.[18] Prior to conducting field survey, I established a base map in which I marked the zones of potential importance (i.e., areas selected for thorough investigation). I based my judgement as to the importance of a particular zone on the following lines of evidence (in descending order of importance):

[18] The topographic coverage of the 1999 survey area includes the maps of Arbaoua (1/50,000 Feuille NI-30-XIII-3c), Lalla Mimouna (1/50,000 Feuille NI-29-XVIII-4d), and Moulay Bou salham (1/50,000 Feuille NI-29-XVIII-4c).

1. Documentary evidence (which also includes ancient maps)
2. Cartographic evidence (information derived from modern topographic maps)
3. Toponymic evidence (modern place-names associated with archaeological sites)
4. Oral tradition (information derived from local informants)

At this stage, I examined the documentary evidence looking specifically for information on site location. Once I established a list of all the sites for which locational information was provided, I sorted them by geographic area. Each geographic area corresponds to the area covered by a 1:50,000 topographic map. On the topographic map of the zones under investigation, I marked the zone boundaries based on textual evidence. Each zone was later surveyed with more intensity in search for textually documented sites.

Cartographic evidence consists of information found in modern topographic maps of the survey area. The topographic maps used in this project consist mainly of the 1:50,000 series, since the 1:25,000 series are not available for the survey area. I also consulted a number of regional maps of the 1:100,000 and 1:250,000 series.[19] In addition to topographic maps, the administrative map of Morocco (useful for administrative contacts), and a commercial road map (Michelin, Carte Routière et Touristique) proved very useful.

The cartographic information I examined in this project pertains to two types of features: (1) architectural features of archaeological significance and (2) purely geographical features. On Moroccan topographic maps, the following captions point to features/localities that are often associated with archaeological sites: "Ruins", "Roman ruins", "Dome" (*K̲ubba*), "Marabout" (*Sîyyid*), "Cemetery", "Walls", or "Walls in ruin". Upon inspection, several of these features revealed archaeological material. In fact, most of the sites located during this survey project were found near marabouts and old cemeteries. I will discuss in more detail the curious association between archaeological sites and marabouts in Chapter 3.

The geographical features that are the most determinant of Islamic site location, and all human site location for that matter, are water, food resources, and protection against the elements and other competitors. According to the fourteenth century Ibn Abî Zar‘ (1843:16, 1860:36), the ideal [Islamic] city is the one that embodies the following five constituents: (1) water resources, (2) arable land, (3) wood resources, (4) solid fortifications, and (5) a government (*al-Sulṯân*).

On topographic maps, I marked the areas that were particularly rich in water resources (e.g., areas located near important springs and/or watercourses) and/or those for which there were natural defensive features (e.g., areas enclosed by outcroppings or located on tophills overlooking the surrounding landscape). These areas were inspected during the field survey. Most woodland areas shown on topographic maps of northern Morocco date to recent historical times. Therefore, it was not possible to effectively use this attribute (i.e., proximity to wood resources) in search for archaeological sites. The vast and dense woodlands often described by medieval authors had long disappeared after centuries of overexploitation. Since I did not have soil maps at my disposal, I was not able to investigate the potential of soil fertility for encouraging human settlement.

[19] Topographic maps for Morocco are available through *La Division de la Cartographie* in Rabat.

Toponymic evidence refers to a number of modern place-names that are often associated with archaeological sites. The following toponyms are the most common ones: Sîdî al-Mak̲h̲fî (the hidden lord), s̲wayyar (small wall), k̲sar (fort), h̲ad̲j̲ra or h̲ad̲j̲ar (rock), karkûr (rock pile), h̲aws̲h̲ (enclosure) and briyyad̲j̲ (little tower). The toponym of Sîdî al-Mak̲h̲fî drew the attention of a team of archaeologists to a locality near the city of al-Basra. After close inspection around a small burial ground, a horde of 120 Almohad dirhams was found (Limane and Rebuffat 1995:300, note 9). Along the same lines, the Roman site of *Ad Novas* was found near a locality with the toponym of "Souiyar" and the Islamic site of H̲ad̲j̲ar al-Nasr was found near a village with the toponym of "al-H̲ad̲j̲ar".

Oral tradition constitutes an important source of information for archaeologists working in Morocco. Before surveying a particular zone, I usually spent some time talking to local residents to explain the purpose of my visit and the nature of my "job" (which was not always an easy task!). Such informal interactions are very important in building mutual trust and rectifying misconceptions. Once this first contact was established, I hired a local assistant. This proved extremely useful in coordinating contacts with local inhabitants and in finding a number of place-names not marked on topographic maps.

Almost invariably, I encountered the following terms used to describe archaeological sites: "*K̲dîm*" (ancient), "*Fransîs*" (colonial), "*Rûmân*" (Roman), or "*Bartk̲îz*" (Portuguese). It is somewhat curious that, in Moroccan oral tradition, the majority of ancient structures (or those believed to be old by the locals) are often attributed to the Portuguese and not the Roman period. One possible explanation is that the Portuguese presence in Morocco was relatively recent and remains within popular memory.

Field Survey

Using the base maps (i.e., topographic maps showing the zones of potential archaeological significance) established during the first phase, I then proceeded to the actual field survey. The survey crew consisted of archaeologists from the Institut National des Sciences de l'Archéologie et du Patrimoine (INSAP) in Rabat,[20] and a number of assistants (mostly local

[20] The Moroccan archaeologists who participated in this project are Hicham Hassini and Ibrahim Mlilou (Délégation régionale du Minstère des Affaires Culturelles, Larache), Hamza Ouassini and Mustapha Ramdani (Inspection des Monuments Historiques, Tangier), Ahmed Ettahiri (La Conservation de Chella), and Abdelfettah Ichkhakh (La Conservation de Volubilis).

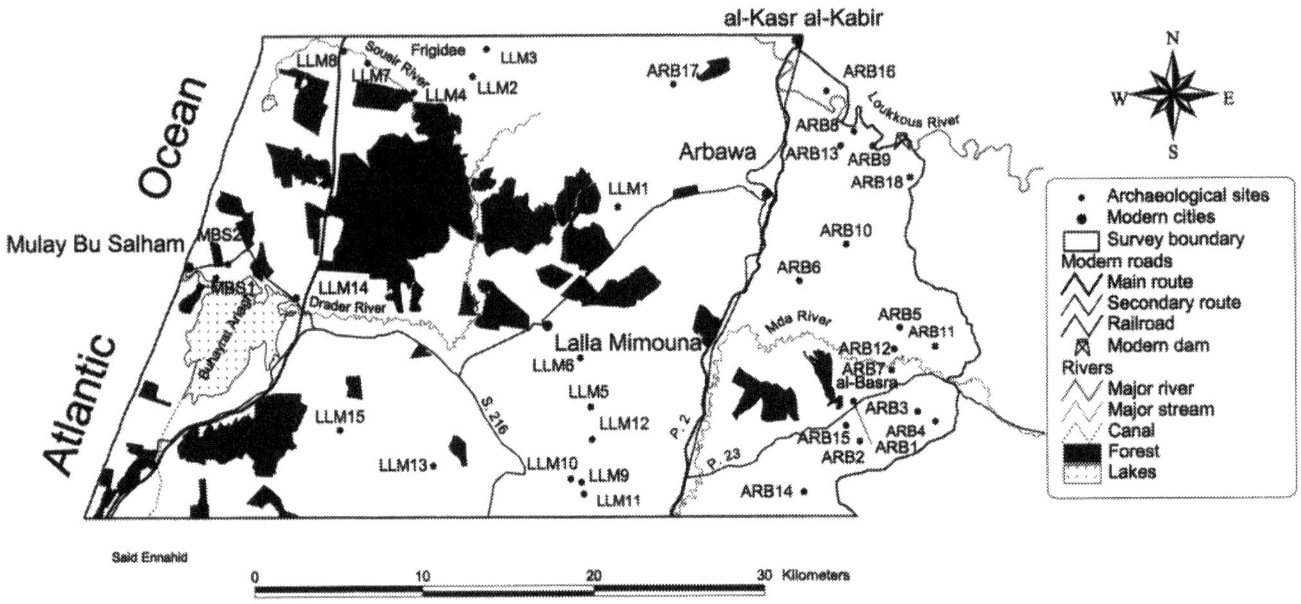

Figure 2.6 Map Showing the Survey Area Around Al-Basra and the Location of Its Hinterland Sites.

farmers) hired for short periods of time. Unfortunately, I was not able to have a field crew of more than three members at any one time.

Considering the size of the survey area (close to 1,200 km^2; Figure 2.6)[21] and the time constraints, systematic full-coverage was not possible. I proceeded instead by subdividing the survey area into several zones classified according to their archaeological potential. High priority zones (based on the lines of evidence discussed above) were thoroughly investigated.

The actual survey work consisted of driving to the edge of the zone of interest, and then systematically surveying it using transects spaced approximately 20 meters apart. The zone boundaries were either cultural (e.g., boundaries of agricultural fields, power lines, etc.) or natural (e.g., watercourses, woodlands, etc.) features, or a combination of the two. All the villages and especially all the cemeteries and marabouts encountered in each zone were inspected for surface scatters and archaeological features.

Low priority zones (i.e., areas for which there was no settlement information, be it textual, cartographic, toponymic, or verbal) were surveyed in a less systematic manner and with lower intensity. In most cases, only the large villages within the zone in question were visited and, occasionally, one or two of their residents were informally interviewed. Most of the zones of low priority were heavily affected by development projects and/or urban growth, which made it difficult to survey them. Among these projects were a highway along the Atlantic coast connecting Rabat to Tangier and a dam (Oued al-Makhazin Dam) southeast of Ksar Kebir. In addition, a large portion of the survey area has recently been converted into eucalyptus tree farms, which made it inaccessible to archaeological survey (Figure 2.6).

As shown in Appendix H, the information recovery system[22] used in the survey was designed to record as much survey data as possible (e.g., site provenience, site condition, site description, environmental setting, etc.). A form was filled out for each site. In order to record a site's coordinates, I employed a Magellan Trailblazer XL GPS unit (Global Positioning System), which was useful for surveying open areas with few or no landmarks recognizable on the topographic maps. In addition, I supplemented the GPS information with site coordinates (x, y, and z) recorded from topographic maps. This proved to be a good backup because in several instances, my GPS unit did not function properly due to weak satellite signals.

Sites numbers were assigned using a notational system composed of the first three letters of the topographic map in which the site was located, followed by a sequential number. For example "ARB 1" (al-Basra) represents the first site found in the area covered by the topographic map of Arbaoua. Each site was also assigned a name, which corresponded in most cases to the name of a nearby village. I included administrative (jurisdictional boundaries) and land-ownership information, which would be required to obtain an excavation permit.

To map the sites, I used a Brunton pocket transit and tape. Since most of the sites were only a few hundred meters in diameter (Appendix E), site area was easily determined based on the extent of ceramic surface scatter. If the site contains visible archaeological features that are too small to be included in the overall map, additional maps showing these features were included. This information was also supplemented with a detailed photographic record.

[21] This is the survey area covered during the 1999 field season. A previous field season conducted in 1998 did not provide the expected results (see Chapter 3).

[22] Modified after K. Kintigh (Ojo Bonito Archaeological Project, Arizona State University).

Three ceramic collection strategies were used: quantitative, diagnostic, and complete. A quantitative collection was made within 5 m by 5 m or 10 m by 10 m loci depending on the density of the surface scatter. All ceramic material found within a particular locus was collected. This strategy, which was used at a limited number of sites, generated quantitatively controlled samples from different loci of the site. In a diagnostic collection, all sherds with meaningful typological attributes (diagnostic) were collected (e.g., decorated sherds, glazed sherds, rims, handles, etc.). This strategy also involved the collection of a sample of all ceramic types present on the site. This strategy, which was used most frequently, provided a representative sample of ceramic types present at the site in a relatively short period of time. A complete collection, in which all surface material in a particular locus was collected, was made only at sites with light surface densities.

All collected pottery was classified and counted by diagnostic parts, decorative techniques, and glaze type. Major forms from each site were drawn and photographed. It was not possible to draw any precise conclusions on site chronology based on these surface collections. Islamic commonware pottery, which constitutes the bulk of my surface collections, is poorly studied. With a few exceptions, there are no good ceramic sequences for Islamic commonware pottery found in Morocco. The early Islamic city of al-Basra is the only archaeological site, within the survey area, for which a well-established ceramic typology is available (Benco 1987, 1989a, 1989c, 1995a; Benco and Blackman 1998; Ennahid 1992). Because of al-Basra ceramic chronology, however, it was possible to study local exchange and community interaction between the city and its hinterland through chemical analysis (see Chapter 6).

Because of the lack of good ceramic sequences for the Islamic period in most parts of Morocco, it was not warranted to invest a lot of time and effort in implementing the sophisticated survey methodologies and/or surface collection strategies discussed in the literature (e.g., Ammerman 1981; Fish and Kowalewski 1990; Lewarch and O'Brien 1981; Nance 1983; Plog et al. 1978; Redman 1973, 1987; Redman and Watson 1970; Schiffer et al. 1978). The lack of good ceramic sequences for Islamic sites is a serious impediment to the development of Islamic archaeology in Morocco (see Chapter 3).

Chapter 3

ARCHAEOLOGICAL SURVEY IN NORTHERN MOROCCO

The body of archaeological research - including studies of regional settlement patterns - on the Islamic period in Morocco is still at an early stage of the development.[1] Until a relatively recent date, most archaeological research in Morocco focused on Roman and pre-Islamic period sites at the expense of Islamic ones. This tendency was first introduced during the colonial period (A.D. 1912-1956), when a number of French classical archaeologists and historians - most of them members of the colonial bureaucracy - were searching for evidence to support colonial agendas (see Laroui 1995).

There is no doubt, however, that Moroccan Islamic archaeology owes a great deal to several colonial-period scholars, such as Terrasse, Marçais, Lévi-Provençal, and Le Toureau, to name a few. These scholars contributed to a better understanding of many aspects of Moroccan society (e.g., archaeology, history, ethnography, art and architecture). Colonial-period scholars wrote the earliest studies on Islamic urbanism in Morocco (e.g., the monographs on Fez, Rabat, and Marrakech), as well as the earliest descriptions of many Islamic archaeological sites.

Islamic archaeology in Morocco witnessed significant progress in the last few decades. The establishment of the Institut National des Sciences de l'Archéologie et du Patrimoine (INSAP) gave a much needed impetus to the discipline as a whole. In addition to training a new generation of archeologists, this institution is actively engaged in several international projects (U.S., France, and Spain) to excavate, salvage, document, and preserve archaeological sites and monuments.

This chapter reviews some of the recent studies of medieval regional and mircro-regional settlement patterns in northern Morocco. Regional settlement data were drawn primarily from previous research conducted in northern Morocco by a number of archaeologists. Micro-regional settlement data were collected during a survey project I conducted around al-Basra, an important Idrisid provincial capital. The last section examines a curious pattern I observed while conducting archaeological survey in the Moroccan countryside, namely, the ubiquitous association of archaeological sites and Marabouts. This chapter also addresses some of difficulties encountered by archaeologists conducting archaeological survey in Morocco.

Regional Settlement Patterns

The Rif Region

The Rif region, an arc-shaped area located between the Mediterranean Sea and the Rif Mountains (Figure 3.1), has been the object of several archaeological surveys for the last 25 years (Bazzana et al. 1983-84; Cressier 1981, 1983, 1992; Cressier et al. 1992 Touri 1988). Cressier has made a major contribution to our understanding of regional settlement patterns in the region.[2] Cressier combined archaeological survey and test excavation with the use of historical evidence, topographic maps, and aerial photography. His main focus was to study the nature of interaction between urban centers and their hinterland and that between Rifian urban centers and other urban centers in inland Morocco and al-Andalus.

Cressier identified three main phases of development of medieval Islamic settlements in the region from the ninth to

[1] For an overview of the literature on medieval regional settlement patterns and urban architectural and spatial organization in the Maghrib and the Iberian Peninsula, see Boone and Benco 1999. For a map showing the different sites and areas in Morocco that were investigated archaeologically and/or ethnographically during the last 100 years, see Cressier 1995:Figure 2.

[2] Some of the material discussed in this section was synthesized from Boone and Benco (1999:55-56).

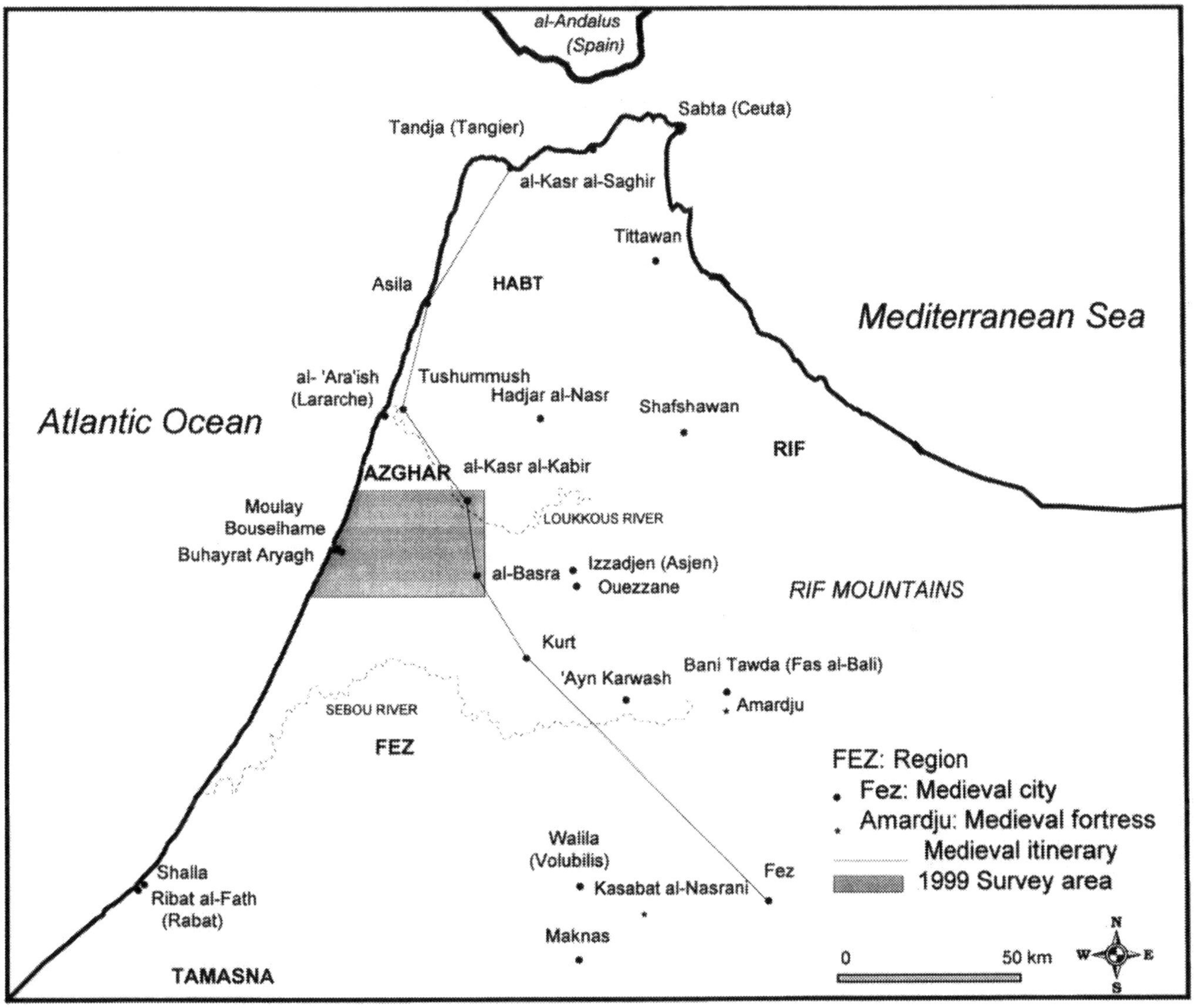

Figure 3.1 Map Showing the Major Archaeological Sites Investigated During the 1998 Field-Season.

the sixteenth centuries (Cressier 1992:175-176). During the first phase (from the ninth to the eleventh centuries A.D.), the few urban centers in the region, founded by Berber groups, were concentrated inland. The two main political powers in the region were the Idrisids in the west and the kingdom of Nakûr in the east. The second phase (from the mid eleventh to the fifteenth centuries A.D.) saw the growth of coastal settlements, which developed into important urban centers (e.g., Malîla, al-Mazamma, and Badîs). The development of the Rifian coast is to be equated with a change in medieval Moroccan political economy in which coastal entrepôts began to play an important role in long-distance trade networks between sub-Saharan West Africa, Morocco, and al-Andalus (Chapter 4). During this phase inland settlements decreased in size or were abandoned. The last phase (from the fifteenth to the sixteenth centuries A.D.) is marked by urban decline due to the Christian *Reconquista* and Spanish and Portuguese attacks on the Moroccan coasts. Several major coastal cities were captured (e.g., Sabta and Malîla). This period also saw an influx of refugees expelled from Spain. These refugees, used to urban life, brought a revival in urban activities in the Rifian interior zone. The city of S͟haf͟shawan, an important urban center in the region, was built by Muslim refugees.

Northwestern Morocco

Understanding urban growth and state formation in the Islamic period was at the core of a long-term archaeological project conducted in northwestern Morocco - the equivalent of the Roman province of "*Mauretania Tingitania*"[3] (see Boone and Benco 1999:53-55). During this project, several seasons of archaeological fieldwork were conducted at the Islamic-Portuguese coastal entrepôt of Qsar es-Seghir (al-K̲as̲r al-S̲agh̲îr) (Redman 1986b). In a second phase, a series of test excavations were conducted at five different sites: al-Basra, Mûlây Bû Salhâm, Nakûr, Badîs, and D̲jbîla (Redman 1983, 1983-84, 1986a). The most important contribution of this project to medieval settlement studies in Morocco is the formulation of an important conceptual model (Boone and Redman 1982; Boone et al. 1990) (see details in Chapter 1). The Boone et al. model opened new interpretive opportunities to studies of regional settlements in Morocco.

Using the Boone et al. model as a theoretical framework, I originally intended to examine how change in political

[3] For an inventory of some of the archaeological sites in northern Morocco, see Touri 1997.

economy affected settlement patterns and long-distance trade networks in northern Morocco. In 1998, I conducted an archaeological survey along the important medieval trade route that connected Fez to Tangier (Figure 3.1). I used documentary evidence as well as modern toponymic evidence to identify potential archaeological sites and then proceeded with archaeological survey. This methodology - as outlined in greater detail in the previous chapter - was followed during the next field season (1999) in the area around al-Basra.

While conducting this survey, several difficulties were encountered. Because of the size of the survey area - a 200-km transect - I was unable to implement the survey techniques minimally required to collect the data I needed. A far more serious problem is the lack of good ceramic sequences for Islamic sites in Morocco (Boone and Benco 1999:53, 57).

Compared with studies of Roman period ceramics, Islamic ceramic studies in Morocco have emerged only recently. There are, however, a few exceptions, such as a number of studies published during the colonial period (e.g., Delpy 1955; Deverdun and Rouche 1949; Marçais 1939; Ricard and Delpy 1931; Terrasse 1937; Terrasse and Meunié 1957). These studies contributed to the identification and dating of a number of ceramic types considered as index fossils (*fossil directeurs*) for various dynastic periods in Morocco and al-Andalus (medieval Spain) (see Grenier De Cardenal 1980). For example, *cuerda seca* ceramics first appeared during the Caliphate Period in al-Andalus (A.D. 942-1035), *sgraffito* ceramics appeared in the eleventh century, and "*les céramiques estampées*" (ceramics with floral and/or epigraphic motifs impressed into soft clay) date between the twelfth and fifteenth centuries.

In the last couple of decades, studies of Islamic ceramics have focused on plain utilitarian ware, which constitute the bulk of the ceramic material found at Islamic archaeological sites (e.g., al-Basra) (see Bazzana and Montmessin 1995; Benco 1987; De Cardinal-Breton 1985-1986; Ennahid 1992; Grenier De Cardenal 1980; Myers 1984; Redman 1986a; Taouchikht 1995). Ceramic typologies for a number of Islamic sites have been established (e.g., al-Basra, Qsar es-Seghir, and to a lesser extent, Walîla, Balyûnash, and Nakûr).

Despite this progress, it is still difficult to date Islamic archaeological sites based on surface collections when no index fossils are found. This was the case for most of the archaeological sites discovered during the first field season (1998). The ceramic material collected at these sites was mostly utilitarian ware with no distinctive features to allow any inferences about site chronology. The lack of visible archaeological features at most of these sites - except for the big urban centers - reduced even further the chances of dating them. Consequently, it was difficult to use survey data to monitor temporal change in settlement patterns.[4]

Furthermore, except for the major nodes along the Fez-Tangier route (e.g., al-Basra, al-Kasr al-Kabîr, and Tushummush), which have been archaeologically known for a long time, it was difficult to identify the other staging posts - mentioned in the historical texts - along this route. The majority of the archaeological sites found during this survey are not historically documented.

Because of the current limitations of using survey data to investigate regional settlement patterns, the next field season (1999) focused on a micro-regional settlement system centered around the Idrisid provincial capital of al-Basra. From a methodological point of view, the shift in geographical scope from a large area (northern Morocco) to a relatively small one (al-Basra region) allowed the recovery of archaeological data of better quality than those collected during the previous field season.

This study takes advantage of multiple lines of evidence. As discussed in the methodology chapter (Chapter 2), and outlined in Figure 1.2, historical and numismatic data were used mainly to address questions on political economy (Chapter 4) and regional settlements systems (Chapter 5), whereas archaeological data were used primarily to document settlement distribution around al-Basra and its local exchange system (Chapter 6).

Micro-Regional Settlement Patterns

Al-Basra Region

In order to investigate local exchange and community interaction between al-Basra and its hinterland, I conducted an archaeological survey in al-Basra region (Figure 2.6). This survey covered an area of close to 1,200 km². The survey area included three important nodes of the medieval route from Fez to Tangier: al-Basra, al-Kasr al-Kabîr, and Tushummush. I chose to investigate the area around al-Basra for three main reasons: (1) al-Basra is known historically as the most important urban center in the area, (2) al-Basra offers a typical example of an agrarian-based economy (Figure 1.2), and finally, (3) al-Basra is one of the few early Islamic sites in Morocco with a well-established ceramic and architectural sequences (Benco 1987, in press; Ennahid 1992). A preliminary survey in the al-Basra area (Ennahid 1995) showed encouraging results; al-Basra ceramic material was found at several sites in the hinterland of the city.

During the 1999 survey, more sites with pottery similar to that from al-Basra were found. Fifteen archaeological sites were especially important in this regard (Figure 3.2). A selected number of ceramic samples from these sites was subjected to chemical analysis (INAA) to ascertain the interaction between al-Basra and its hinterland communities. A detailed discussion of al-Basra's local exchange system and its settlement patterns - in light of INAA results - is included in Chapter 6.

Archaeological Sites and Marabouts

While conducting field survey in the Moroccan countryside, I was struck by the ubiquitous association of archaeological

[4] Only the survey data collected at the al-Basra's hinterland sites were analyzed in this study (Chapter 6).

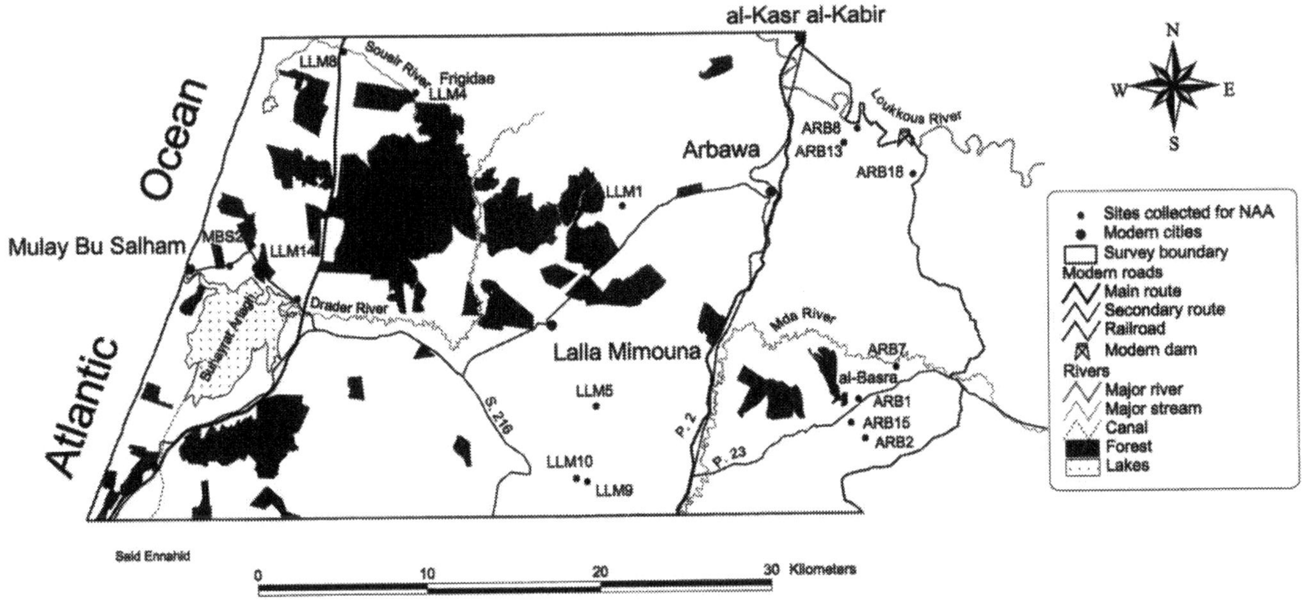

Figure 3.2 Map Showing the Survey Area Around Al-Basra and the Location of Archaeological Sites Collected for Instrumental Neutron Activation Analysis (INAA).

sites and marabouts. Although several studies have been written on maraboutism as a form of Moroccan popular culture (Alberich 1954; Calasso 1992; Dermenghem 1954; Doutté 1984; Lévi-Provençal 1953; Westermarck 1926, 1935), the relationship between maraboutism and archaeological site location is poorly understood. Moroccan archaeological literature has just recently began to investigate this curious phenomenon (Siraj 1995b:439-447). Since most archaeological surveys are conducted in the countryside, the following discussion will focus on rural marabouts.

A marabout is known in Moroccan oral tradition as *siyyid* (pl. *sâdât*). All saint names are preceded by the honorific title *Sîdî* or *Mûlây* for male saints, and *Lâlla* for female saints. Contrary to urban marabouts, for which there are exhaustive hagiographies[5] (biographies of saints or *manâkib*, in Arabic), rural marabouts are far less likely to be documented. We know very little about the saints buried in most rural marabouts.

Hagiographic evidence has proved instrumental in the study of the Islamic site of Hadjar al-Nasr in northern Morocco (Cressier et al. 1998). This site was discovered near the rural marabout of Sîdî Mazwar. Based on hagiographic evidence, Cressier et al. (1998:316) argued that Sîdî Mazwar was an Idrisid prince who came to Hadjar al-Nasr to devote his life to worship. Most importantly, Cressier et al. (1998:316) argued that the retreat of Sîdî Mazwar to Hadjar al-Nasr prior to A.D. 864 (date of the saint's death) implies that the city was not founded *ex nihilo*, in the beginning of the tenth century, as indicated by historical evidence, but rather a century earlier.

Marabouts, especially domed ones, constitute one of the main characteristics on the Moroccan rural landscape. From a practical point of view, they are ideal reference points for archaeologists conducting field survey, because (1) they are easily recognizable on the ground, and (2) their location is usually plotted on topographic maps. An additional advantage of using domed marabouts as reference points, is the fact that a large number of them are located on hilltops, possibly because they were originally meant to be seen from afar and from all directions.

There are three types of marabouts in northern Morocco[6]: (1) domed marabouts, (2) open-air saint burial sites, and (3) shrines (see Mikesell 1961:Figure 25). Domed marabouts, known locally as *Kubba* (Arabic for dome), form a whitewashed cubic structure barely big enough to host the saint sarcophagus. The choice of the building materials depends on the available local resources, both financial and natural. The central feature of these structures is a dome or *Kubba* - giving its name to the whole structure - placed right above the saint tomb[7]. In rural Morocco, marabouts are the focal point of a host of social, religious, and economic activities. Rural populations bury their dead around saint tombs and hold their annual fairs (*moussem* or *mawsim*) in honor of local patron saints. Marabouts are the meeting place of choice for rural women. Although it is against orthodox belief, rural women appeal to them - through votive offerings - for intercession in times of adversity (see Brett and Fentress 1996:225-227).

The second type of marabout is not associated with any type of architectural features. It is usually made of an open-air tomb surrounded by a modest stone and shrub enclosure known in Arabic as *hawsh*.[8] It is possible that the saints buried

5 For example, Mûlây Idrîs Zarhûn (Idris I, founder of the Idrisid dynasty), considered to be the patron of all saints in Morocco.

6 See also Eickelman 1976 and Geertz 1968.

7 Some marabouts are covered with a pyramidal roof. The architecture of marabouts - and rural architecture in general - is changing rapidly. Marabouts are now being built, or restored, using modern techniques and building materials; roofs made of tin plates are now replacing the old domes.

8 For a detailed discussion of the type of vegetation usually found near marabouts, see Mikesell 1961:107-110.

in this type of tombs were either less influential or that, the surrounding populations did not have the financial means to invest in a more elaborate memorial.

The last category of marabouts is represented by shrines or sacred sites. These are locations centered around an object or a feature, such as a tree or stone enclosure, that are considered as sacred ground by local populations. This practice may trace its origins to pre-Islamic pagan practices. Although categorically prohibited in orthodox Islam, these practices are widespread in rural Morocco. Rural shrines are often given saint names despite the absence of a sarcophagus.

In some cases, the sanctified object is an archaeological feature, such as a building block, that is either found *in situ*, or that was moved from a nearby location. This is the case of two shrines found near the Roman site of Zilil (Siraj 1995b:441-442). One type of rural shrine, known as *Sîdî al-Makhfî* (literally, "the hidden lord"), is of a particular interest to archaeologists. Compared to other sacred sites in rural Morocco, *Sîdî al-Makhfî* locations are the most often associated with archaeological sites (see Siraj 1995b:456-459). In a *Sîdî al-Makhfî* location near al-Basra, archaeologists found a horde of 120 Almohad dirhams (Limane and Rebuffat 1995:300, note 9).

The search for gold caches at sacred sites has been a special activity conducted by a group of people known as *Swâsa* (people from the Sûs region in southern Morocco). These are *fkîh* (reciters of the Koran) who engage in witchcraft, geomancy, and exorcism.[9] Using some sort of geomantic or talismanic writings, they roam the countryside in search for hidden treasures.

This practice has been known for several centuries as attested in the following passage by Leo Africanus (1956:225-226): "il existe aussi à Fez des hommes que l'on nomme Elcanesin [*al-kannâzîn*, from *kanz*, Arabic for treasure] qui s'occupent de chercher les trésors qui ont été enfouis dans les fondations des ruines antiques... ils sont absolument persuadés que, lorsque l'empire d'Afrique fut enlevé aux Romains (...) ils enterrerent dans les environs de Fez un grands nombre d'objects précieux et de valeur qu'ils ne pouvaient emporter avec eux... C'est dans cette vaine croyance que les Canesin [*al-kannâzîn*] fouillent la terre et détériorent souvent les édifices et les sépultures..."

Such activities cause a lot of damage to archaeological sites and to the Moroccan national heritage in general. Ancient coins and jewelry are often melted, once sold in the black market. Due to such illegal practices, valuable archaeological and numismatic data are lost.

The ubiquitous association of archaeological sites and marabouts[10] is not yet fully understood. From a chronological point of view, most archaeological sites predate the marabouts located within them. This is obviously the case of all Roman archaeological sites. One important question is why a marabout is built at or near an archaeological site. One possible answer is that an archaeological site may have been used first as a hermitage or retreat (*khalwa*, in Arabic) by a local saint. At a later date, when the saint died, the hermitage may have been transformed into a marabout. This process often led not only to the sanctification of the saint burial ground but the sanctification of the archaeological site as well. In the Dchar Jdid region in northern Morocco, several marabouts are located within Roman archaeological sites (see Siraj 1995b:444).

This interpretation is only partly applicable to Islamic sites, since some of the marabouts around Islamic sites are several centuries old, and may have been built prior, or shortly after the foundation of the Islamic sites in their vicinity. The marabout of Mûlây Bû Salhâm, near medieval Buhayrat Ariagh, was built in honor of a non-local saint who died around A.D. 951 (Ricard 1925:241). The town, now known as Mûlây Idrîs Zarhûn, was built around the sanctuary of Mûlây Idrîs al-Akbar (Idrîs I, the founder of the Idrisid dynasty who died in A.D. 793). The inhabitants of Mûlây Idrîs Zarhûn originally lived in Walîla (Roman Volubilis) before they moved to their new location during the second half of the eleventh century (Eustache 1970-71:163). The Idrisid site of Hadjar al-Nasr was possibly used as a hermitage by Sîdî Mazwar - an Idrisid prince who later became a saint - before it evolved into a city after he died in A.D. 864 (see Cressier et al. 1998).

Maraboutism and archaeology is an important subject of investigation that requires a multidisciplinary approach involving archaeologists, social anthropologists, and historians. It has the interpretive potential of contributing to the literature on the archaeology of religion and ethnicity.

9 See Leo Africanus 1956:216-220, for an account about such practices in medieval times.

10 Several archaeological sites found during the 1998 and 1999 field seasons were located near marabouts (see Appendix E).

Chapter 4

POLITICAL ECONOMY OF MEDIEVAL MOROCCO

Political economy is defined as the mechanism by which surplus is extracted in the form of tribute, taxes, or *corvée* labor to support state institutions administered by non-food-producing personnel (see Earle 1994:444; Hirth 1996:204-206). Most archaeological studies of political economy tend to focus on one of three economic activities: production, service, or distribution (see Hirth 1996). The data I will discuss in this chapter are related more to strategies of production and distribution than to service. According to Hirth (1996:209): "Production strategies are concerned with the control of surpluses generated in both food production and craft activity... Distribution strategies focus on direct and indirect control of resources moving through both mobilization and exchange networks." In this chapter, I will discuss the Idrisid political economy as an essentially agrarian-based economy (i.e., based on control of surplus generated through food production), and the political economy of post-Idrisid dynastic states as one based on the expropriation of proceeds from long-distance gold trade (i.e., control of exchange networks). These two types of finance systems will be referred to here as *staple finance* and *wealth finance*, respectively, terms that come from the works of D'Altroy and Earle (1985) and Earle (1994) on the Inka political economy.

According to the Boone et al. model, there was a shift in medieval Moroccan political economy from a reliance on agricultural surplus (staple finance) during the Idrisid period to a reliance on proceeds from long-distance gold trade (wealth finance) during subsequent dynastic periods. In the first section of this chapter, I will define the two central concepts of staple finance and wealth finance and discuss their relevance to the Moroccan context. In subsequent sections, I will demonstrate that there was, in fact, a major difference between the Idrisid period and later dynastic periods in terms of the nature of the surplus generated and the mechanisms implemented to generate it. Evidence for each time period will be discussed separately.

Staple Finance and Wealth Finance

The Boone et al. model postulates that there was a shift in medieval Moroccan political economy from an emphasis on the production and control of staple goods (Idrisid finance system) to an emphasis on control of gold trade networks and the expropriation of their proceeds (post-Idrisid finance system). In the anthropological literature, these two types of finance systems have been referred to as *staple finance* and *wealth finance*, respectively.

These two concepts were first used to describe the political economy of the Inka empire (D'Altroy and Earle 1985; Earle 1994). The Inka staple finance system involved payment of taxes in kind, such as grains, livestock, and clothing.[1] Commoner households, in return for using farming plots owned by the state, provided the state with *corvée* labor and staple goods. Staple revenue was then centrally managed by the state - in massive storage facilities - and later distributed as payment to state personnel and *corvée* laborers. This system of political finance is simple and direct since staple goods offered as payment are ready for household consumption (as opposed to payments in currency, which need to be converted into consumable goods through market exchange). A staple finance system, however, requires considerable investment in storage facilities and transportation systems. Because staple goods are characteristically bulky, heavy, and highly perishable, it must have been a "logistical nightmare" (Earle 1994:444-445) to transport these goods from the fields to state storage facilities and, to reduce to the minimum the amount of time they had to await in storage bins before they were distributed. Considering these limitations in managing staple goods, a staple finance system is most suitable for small agrarian states and for empires with highly dispersed activities

[1] Material on staple finance and wealth finance in the Inka political economy was synthesized from D'Altroy and Earle (1985); Earle (1994).

that can be financed by regional mobilizations (D'Altroy and Earle 1985:188).

The Inka wealth finance system involved "the use of valuables, primitive money, or currency as means of payment of taxes or tribute to a central authority, which then uses these goods and others manufactured by attached specialists to fund governmental activities, particularly political services" (D'Altroy and Earle 1985:193). Contrary to staple goods, wealth items are more manageable in terms of their transportability over long distances with minimum costs and their storability in smaller warehouses. Wealth finance is more appropriate for territorially extensive empires since it allows more central control over revenue and reduces dependence on regional administrators (wealth items being brought directly to the capital). Wealth items, however, have a limited intrinsic value and need to be converted into subsistence goods. In other words, in order for state officials and personnel to meet their subsistence needs, they will have to exchange these items for staple goods through a market system.

Staple finance and wealth finance systems are not mutually exclusive. They were isolated in the literature mainly for analytical or heuristic reasons. The political finance of archaic states typically involves a combination of the two systems (D'Altroy and Earle 1985:188). In the case of the Inka empire, these two systems played complementary roles. Staple finance was used to support local or provincial administrative activities, and wealth finance was used to support interregional functions (mostly integrative) managed by the central authority (D'Altroy and Earle 1985:188).

The concepts of staple finance and wealth finance may be applied to the context of the medieval Moroccan political economy. However, it should be emphasized that the Moroccan data do not offer the same fine-grained resolution as the Inka example. Moreover, the Maghribian context offers some major differences from its Andean counterpart.

Staple finance seems to have been the dominant form of political finance during the Idrisid period. Control of agricultural land was essential to the Idrisid economy. Staple finance must have been the most viable form of political finance for the Idrisid state considering its fragmentary nature; each Idrisid prince was in control of an agricultural region. As opposed to the Inka empire, the Idrisid state also had a currency and a market system. There is no archaeological or textual evidence, however, that the Idrisids maintained any type of storage facilities.

During the Almoravid period, wealth finance became the dominant form of political finance. Control of long-distance gold trade networks and the expropriation of a portion of the gold being exchanged, in the form of taxes, was the backbone of the Almoravid economy and that of subsequent dynastic empires (see Lacoste 1974). Moroccan dynastic empires, however, did not control the sources of gold. In other words, they did not control the production of wealth. Instead, they insured the protection of gold trade networks and the continuous flow of gold from its production locale (sub-Saharan West Africa) to its terminus (western Mediterranean Basin) along the trade routes.

Idrisid Finance System

Fiscal Resources

There is little documentary evidence on the Idrisids' finance system and virtually none on their fiscal system.[2] The few textual references available show that Idrîs II relied, in his rudimentary administrative apparatus, on Arab immigrants who came from al-Andalus and Ifrîḵiya. According to Ibn Abî Zar' (1860:28, 1964:57), Idrîs II appointed a vizier, a judge, and a secretary. Apparently, there was no special government official in charge of financial affairs. It is possible that the vizier was responsible for collecting and managing tax revenues of what was then a small state. Ibn Ḫawḵal, while describing the region around the city of Kurt, states that: "Tous les lieux de cette région [Kurt], ainsi que Tanger, appartiennent aux Edrisites, qui en recuiellent les taxes et les impôts [*dj̲ibâya* and *ḵharâdj̲*], ils possédent aussi la ville de Masa." (Ibn Ḫawḵal 1842:193). He does not, however, provide any further details on how the Idrisid fiscal resouces, especially the *ḵharâdj̲* (tax on farmland), were paid. Was the *ḵharâdj̲* paid in kind or in cash?[3] How was it collected? Who collected it? And where was it stored?[4] There is no doubt though that the proceeds from farmed land were a major component of the Idrisid finance system; upon the death of Idrîs II in A.D. 829, the territories of the Idrisid state were divided among his eldest sons (Eustache 1970a). Each principality corresponded to a major agricultural region of northern Morocco (i.e., importance of agricultural surplus to the Idrisid princes). However, unlike the case of the Inka empire, there is no evidence that the Idrisid state owned the land and that surplus was generated through *corvée* labor.

It is probable that the Idrisids levied additional taxes on the production of mines as was the case for the rulers of Sidj̲ilmâsa. Al-Bakrî reported that al-Yasa' (A.D. 814-815), ruler of Sidj̲ilmâsa, appropriated a fifth of the proceeds from the mines of Dar'a: "Il [al-Yasa'] préleva le quint (*ḵhumus*) sur le produit des mines du Dar'a [Tudg̲ha?]." (al-Bakrî 1965:286). In addition to taxes on farmland and mines, the Idrisids may also have collected other custom duties

[2] For an important study on the finance systems of Maghribian dynastic states (up to the thirteenth century) using historical data, see Hopkins 1958. Massignon (1906:178-184) also provides valuable textual information on dynastic states fiscal reforms.

[3] We know from a passage by al-Bakrî that flax (linen textiles?) was used as currency in market transactions: "Elle [al-Basra] s'appelle aussi Basrat al-Kattân 'Basra du lin' parce que, à l'époque où elle commença à se peupler, on y employait du lin en guise de monnaie dans toutes les opérations commerciales." (al-Bakrî 1965:216). It is possible that, in addition to payment in currency, a part of al-Basra's taxes were paid using flax (linen textiles?) as a form of rudimentary money.

[4] For archaeological examples of storage facilities associated with staple finance systems, see D'Altroy and Earle 1985; Webb and Frankel 1994. In Morocco, only ethnographic evidence for collective storage facilities (granaries) is available (see Jacques-Meunié 1951; Montagne 1929).

(*mûdjîbat, kabâlât,* and *mukûs*) on farmer's products brought to urban markets[5] or to coastal entrepôts for exportation overseas (e.g., Spain and Ifrîkiya).

Idrisid Agrarian-Based Economy

During the early Islamic period, medieval Morocco was a rich agricultural country. Several early medieval historical sources describe the fertility of the land of *al-Maghrib al-Aksâ* (medieval Morocco). Interestingly, the image of lush woodlands (e.g., the Ghumâra and Zarhûn regions) depicted in documentary evidence has changed since the Middle Ages. The causes of such change are primarily human induced. Centuries of overgrazing, deforestation[6], and a host of other natural and cultural processes have caused the deterioration of the ancient environment.

Tribal agriculturalists played an important role in the economy of early medieval Morocco, even after the development of the gold trade and the emergence of a merchant elite. Through a system of market exchange, farmers living in the hinterlands of urban centers brought their products to the cities to be exchanged for finished goods and services. The bulk of their products consisted of subsistence goods and raw materials (e.g., hides, cotton, flax, wool, wood, etc.).

Textual evidence indicates that medieval Moroccan cities were well supplied by their hinterland. The number of food processing facilities within a city may be used as an indirect index to gauge the city's needs in subsistence goods.[7] For example, the presence of a large number of mills suggests that large quantities of cereals were brought to the city from farming communities in the hinterland. According to al-Ya'kubî (1892:357-358), the city of Fez had 3,000 working mills (472 mills according to Ibn Abî Zar' 1843:25-26, 1860:57). Most of the agricultural production of medieval Morocco seems to have been exchanged through small-radius local exchange systems composed of a network of rural markets (*aswâk*, sing., *sûk*).

Since before the Islamic period, weekly tribal markets were the platform of local exchange between rural communities and neighboring urban centers (see Vanacker, 1973:673-674).[8] Weekly tribal markets were often located at the boundaries of ecological zones or socio-ethnically different groups so that products from communities of different subsistence modes could be exchanged (e.g., farmers vs. pastoralists). These markets were also strategically located at major crossroads so that a maximum number of villages would have equal access to the services and goods offered. Other factors determining the location of a market included the site's historic, religious, or symbolic significance (e.g., *baraka* or benediction).

Following a rotation system, rural markets were held at different locations every day of the week. This is reflected in market names, such as *Sûk al-Tnîn* (Monday market) or *Sûk al-Sabt* (Saturday market) (see Vossen 1984:368-369). This system had the additional advantages of serving the largest region possible and offering a secure and continual source of sustenance to a non-food producing class of artisans (e.g., potters, weavers, and blacksmiths), merchants, caterers, and entertainers. The textual evidence contains abundant information on weekly tribal markets, the type of commodities exchanged, the prices of goods, etc. Al-Bakrî (1965:212) states that there was a market "held every Friday" at the village of Nasr Ibn Djarw. He also mentioned a "busy" and "well-supplied" market called Sûk Fankûr located along the route between Aghmât and Fez (al-Bakrî 1965:294). In late medieval times, Leo Africanus (1956:175-176) refers to a market that was held "outside the city [of Maknâs] every Monday".

The textual evidence also shows that a number of settlements were named after nearby markets. The most important example in this regard is the city of al-Kasr al-Kabîr, which was known in medieval times as Sûk Kutâma (al-Bakrî 1965:215). An important tribal market was held at the location of what later became al-Kasr al-Kabîr. Historically, the Kutâma tribes inhabited the area around al-Kasr al-Kabîr. The agricultural prosperity of the Gharb (for which al-Kasr al-Kabîr was the chief-seat) is well documented, and this region is still one of the richest agricultural areas in Morocco.

Al-Bakrî's chronicle reveals an interesting pattern of urban development, that is the evolution of a tribal market (Sûk Kutâma) into a permanent location that later becomes a full-fledged urban settlement (the city of al-Kasr al-Kabîr). A similar process occurred at Asîla and Sidjilmâsa. At Asîla, the Kutâma built a mosque (*djami'*) that quickly became the focus of an important seasonal fair. At a later date, this fair site evolved into a city (al-Bakrî 1965:220). The site of Sidjilmâsa served as the location of seasonal market for water vessels and metal wares before it developed into a city (al-Bakrî 1965:285).

In areas with no specialized agricultural production, irrigation systems, or significant soil fertility, economic interaction was limited to small-scale local exchange systems between cities and their hinterlands or among hinterland communities. The most fertile areas of the country were involved in much broader exchange networks - in addition to local exchange systems. Several medieval cities were known for the production of a particular agricultural commodity.

In Sidjilmâsa, irrigated farms produced large quantities of cereals that were exported to Awdaghust (al-Bakrî 1965:283, 300). In al-Basra's region, cotton was one of the main products

[5] Some North African rulers went to great lengths to collect custom duties; Hopkins (1958:41), citing al-Bakrî, relates the case of Mu'iz Ibn Bâdîs who joined the city of al-Kayrawân to nearby suburbs by parallel walls so that to prevent merchants from entering the city without paying custom duties.

[6] The analysis of ethnobotanical remains recovered at al-Basra shows that large quantities of cork oak (Quercus suber) was used for charcoal in the metal production area (Benco, in press; Mahoney 1994).

[7] For a detailed account on the agricultural products and the main farming regions of medieval Morocco, see Siraj 1995a; Vanacker 1973.

[8] For ethnographic examples, see Fogg 1939, 1941; Troin 1975; Vossen 1984:367-369.

(Ibn Hawkal 1842:192, 1967:80, 1938-39:76).[9] It was exported to Ifrîkiya and other locations via the Lûkkûs River. According to Ibn Hawkal (1842:192): "les habitants de Basra s'embarquent avec des marchandises sur la branche [of Lûkkûs River] qui passe chez eux; ils decendent alors jusqu'á l'Océan, et se dirigent ensuite où ils veulent se rendre." The prosperity of al-Basra was largely due to the fertility of its soil and the abundance of its specialized agricultural production. Ibn Hawkal (1967:83) states that the city was involved in trade relations with the Barghwâta and al-Andalus via the coastal port of Mûlay Bû Salhâm (medieval Buhayrat Aryagh). In another passage, he states that "Buhayrat Aryagh communique avec l'océan où mouillent les vaisseaux espagnols qui viennent charger les produits agricoles de la région [of al-Basra and Biyâtha, near the city of Kurt]..." (Ibn Hawkal 1938-39:81).[10]

The development of specialized agriculture was instrumental to the development of both the industrial sector and gold-trade networks. There was an interdependence between specialized agriculturalists, artisans, and merchants. Products, such as cotton, wool, flax, and hides were used to manufacture highly valued finished goods destined for exportation to sub-Saharan markets. Al-Bakrî mentions that "Les moutons de Yerara sont d'une belle race... Leur laine, qui est d'une qualité superieure, s'emploie à Sidjilmâsa pour fabriquer des étoffes dont chaque pièce se vend à un prix qui dépasse 20 mithkâls" (al-Bakrî 1965:281).

Textual data on the early Islamic period in Morocco clearly show that agriculture was the backbone of the medieval Moroccan economy. The main sources of the Idrisid state finance system were linked to agricultural production (namely, taxes on farmland, custom duties levied on agricultural products brought to cities and tribal markets, and taxes on agricultural products brought to coastal entrepôts for exportation). Agriculture was also important to other sectors of the Idrisid economy, such as the industrial sector (i.e., supply of raw materials needed for the manufacture of finished goods) and exchange networks (local, regional, and macroregional exchange).

In addition to agricultural surplus as the main source of revenue for the Idrisid state, mining and long-distance trade provided secondary sources of revenue (see Garcia-Arenal and Manzano Moreno 1995:31, 1998:279, 282). Since the early Idrisid period, Idrisid rulers showed great interest in controlling the mining resources of the country. Rosenberger (1970b:89) argues that the military expedition to Tâza led by Idrîs I in A.D. 790 was possibly conducted in search for gold mines. Idrîs II conquered the rich mining region of Fazâz and took over the silver mine of Djabal 'Awwâm. Control of Fazâz insured a secure and continuous supply of silver for dynastic mints. The division of the Idrisid state after the death of Idrîs II clearly shows that control of important mining resources supplemented control of good arable land (see Rosenberger 1970c:103). The Idrisid prince 'Abd Allah acquired the mining cities of Tamdûlt (rich in silver) and Iglî (rich in copper); another Idrisid prince - Yahya - acquired the city of Dây (rich in copper)[11] (Colin 1936:197; Rosenberger 1970b:89).

As opposed to other examples of preindustrial states elsewhere (see Sinopoli 1994), there is little archaeological evidence to document the finance system of the Idrisid state. Characteristically, food items are perishable and, therefore, invisible in the archaeological record. Archaeological investigation can only be based on indirect evidence. Cressier (1984), for example, studied ancient irrigation systems and land tenure in the area around the archaeological site of Mastâsa based on the interpretation of aerial photographs. The analysis of faunal remains from al-Basra shows the dominance of domestic sheep (Ovis aries), domestic goat (Capra hircus), and domestic cattle (Bos taurus) (Benco, in press; Loyet 2000). Studies of al-Basra's ethnobotanical remains point to the dominance of domesticated wheat (primarily Triticum aestivum or Tricum durum) and barley (Hordeum) (Benco, in press; Mahoney 1994). With the exception of cotton, which was not documented archaeologically, these results seem to support documentary evidence, which indicate that al-Basra produced large amounts of dairy products and cereals.

Post-Idrisid Finance System

Finance Institutions and Fiscal Resources

Compared with the early Islamic period in Morocco, textual evidence on the finance institutions of post-Idrisid dynastic states is relatively specific and detailed. There is, however, an imbalance in textual sources in terms of the information they provide on how these institutions operated. We know relatively more on how state revenue was collected and far less on how it was disbursed (Hopkins 1958:49).

It was not until the Marinid period (from the thirteenth to the fifteenth centuries A.D.), that textual sources began to shed more light on the mechanisms by which the state financed its institutions. *Rawd al-kirtâs* of Ibn Abî Zar' (14th century A.D.) and the *Masâlik al-absâr* of al-'Umarî (14th century A.D.) are two notable examples in this regard (Ibn Abî Zar' 1860; al-'Umarî 1927). Textual evidence shows that post-Idrisid dynastic state revenue was stored in special facilities; cash revenue was placed in what was called "*buyût al-amwâl*" (literally, houses of money or treasuries) and revenue in kind was stored in what was called "*khazâ'in*" (warehouses). Hopkins (1958:52) cites a passage by Ibn 'Idhârî (13th century A.D.) in which this latter refers to a "*Khâzin 'ala-l-mâl al-*

9 See also Cressier et al. 1998:312; Siraj 1995a:196; Vanacker 1973:677. There is, however, no archaeological evidence for cotton production at al-Basra (Mahoney 1994).

10 A large quantity of Moroccan cereal production was exported to Spain. For details on trade in agricultural products between medieval Morocco and Spain in the twelfth century, see Picard 1995. Picard's study is based primarily on al-Zuhrî (1968), al-Idrîsî (1983) and Kitâb al-Istibsâr (1985). For later periods, see Dufourcq 1966.

11 According to al-Idrîsî (1983:46), the copper produced at the city of Dây was of an excellent quality. Some of the production of the city was retained for local use - in the manufacture of utensils and clothing accessories - the rest was exported to [distant] markets. For more details, see Rosenberger 1970c:125.

dhahabî" (guardian of cash revenue) and a "*Khâzin 'ala al-ta'âm*" (guardian of grain revenue). Unfortunately, there are no further indications on how revenue in kind (e.g., grains and other staples) was handled. It is possible that surplus in staple goods was used to feed dynastic troops.

Nevertheless, this passage clearly indicates that there were two distinct government officials, one in charge of guarding cash revenues and the other in charge of guarding revenues in kind. More importantly, it shows, albeit indirectly, the coexistence of two forms of finance systems: staple finance and wealth finance. There is, however, no archaeological evidence for storage facilities to support Ibn 'Idhârî's information.

The Almoravids (A.D. 1073-1147) were the first to introduce a true form of central government or "*makhzan*" (state apparatus, literally, a storehouse), operated by a full-time bureaucracy. The core of the Almoravid *makhzan* - as was the case with most North African dynastic states - was composed of the most prominent members of the ruler's tribe.[12] Under the reign of Yûsûf Ibn Tâshfîn (A.D. 1061-1107), the Amoravid tax revenues were substantial. They were derived from the two taxes instituted by the Koran (*zakât* and *'ushûr*), the *djizya* collected from the Jews and the Christians living in the cities, and from booties of holy war (Jihad) (Massignon 1906:178). Ibn Abî Zar' (1860:191, 238-9) states that Yûsûf Ibn Tâshfîn was one of the richest kings of the Maghrib, even without levying taxes. While it implies state prosperity, this statement should not be taken at face value. The Almoravids needed large amounts of money to support the costs of their widespread military campaigns, and they had to institute new taxes which were not prescribed by Islam, such as the "*kabâlât*" (taxes on trade), to pay for them.

The Almoravid rulers were strongly criticized by their successors (the Almohads) for reverting to such illegal fiscal measures. In a letter written by 'Abd al-Mû'min, the founder of the Almohad dynasty, to the population of Constantine, he wrote: "Leur pays dans le passé a eu à subir des vexations illégales, gabelles [*kabâlat*], taxes [*mukûs*] amendes [*maghârim*] de la part des misérables qui y régnaient et leurs gouverneurs: il ne souciait pas de leur appliquer exclusivement la législation des impôts obligatoires [*zakât* and *'ushûr*]. Mais grâce à la réforme réalisée par le mahdi [the Almohad spiritual leader], cet état de choses impie a été aboli, et les Almohades n'exigent de leurs sujets que les redevances fixées par la Sunna, et non plus les taxes abusives que les anciens maîtres du pays [the Almoravids] avaient instituées." (Lévi-Provençal 1941:27).

Although the letter clearly shows the opposition of the founder of the Almohad dynasty to raising unlawful taxes, later Almohad rulers instituted other new taxes, such as *al-fitra* (charity paid in Ramadân) and *al-mûdjibât* (octroi duties). The Almohad finance affairs were supervised by a special government official called *Sâhib al-Ashghâl* (minister of finance) located in Marrakech, the state capital (Hopkins 1958:51; Laroui 1995:170). This implies that the Almohad finance system was managed centrally and not delegated to provincial officials. However, there is a passage by Ibn Khaldûn in which he refers to a *Sâhib al-Ashghâl* appointed for the provincial city of Salâ by the Almohad Yûsûf (A.D. 1162). It is doubtful, however, that a *Sâhib al-Ashghâl* could be a local official (Hopkins 1958:51). Provincial towns were run by local administrators (*mushrif*) who were in charge of levying taxes on commercial transactions and exchanged commodities. Some of the fiscal proceeds levied by provincial towns may have been spent locally as payments to the sultan's garrisons, salaries for local officials and *shaykh* (tribal chiefs), or to finance public works and other services, with the rest sent to the central treasury.

The Marinid finance system is largely documented by the fourteenth-century geographer al-'Umarî. In his *Masâlik al-absâr*, al-'Umarî (1927:171) provides a list of tax revenues levied by the Marinid sultan Abû Sa'îd 'Uthmân II (A.D. 1310-1331) from 22 cities (Table 4.1). Similar to that of the Almohads, the Marinid finance system was centrally organized with provincial officials in charge of collecting fiscal proceeds and sending them to the central treasury. Some of the proceeds were spent locally to pay provincial state officials and maintain public works. Al-'Umarî (1927:171) pointed out that some taxes collected in the towns of Tazûta, Tittawân, Asîla, al-Kasr al-Saghîr (Qsar es-Seghir), and Tawrîrt were disbursed locally rather than sent to the state treasury. This form of local appropriation of state revenue is a variant of "regional mobilization," which results when the central authority allows provincial elite to draw labor and/or tribute from local communities in order to support themselves (Brumfiel and Earle 1987:4).

Sub-Saharan Gold Trade: Basis of Post-Idrisid Dynastic Political Economy

Before the eighth century, no "regular" long-distance exchange activities existed between medieval Morocco and sub-Saharan Africa.[13] Long-distance trade routes followed a diagonal course across the Sahara, running northeast-southwest to serve Egypt, southern Ifrîkiya, and Bilâd al-Sûdân.[14] It was not until the tenth century that a regular north-south route was established between Morocco and the sources of African gold (Devisse 1972a:49). The northeasterly route from Ghâna to Egypt through Ifrîkiya was substituted by a

[12] Lacoste (1974:13) states that: "the tribe - a political form of organization - constituted the embryo of a state. In North Africa the State was, in a sense, a confederation of tribes allied with the tribe of the ruler."

[13] According to Arab chroniclers, the conquest of the Sûs region (southern Morocco) in A.D. 734 brought back an immense booty in gold and slaves. Rosenberger (1970b:86 note 22), argues that if this military expedition did in fact reach sub-Saharan Africa, then it must have followed a route that was already known. If, however, it did not venture beyond the Sûs region, then a regular trade must have already been taking place, at this period, between the Sûs and Bilâd al-Sûdân. For more details on this issue, see Vanacker 1973:667.

[14] Information on long-distance gold trade networks was synthesized from Devisse (1972a, 1972b). For more details, see the following studies: Bovill 1968; Cahen 1981; Devisse 1988, 1996; Jacques-Meunié 1982; Lacoste 1966; Levtzion 1978; Messier 1974, 1980; Miller 1997; Vanacker 1973. The following studies provide detailed discussions on historical sources that describe medieval sub-Saharan West Africa: Cuoq 1975; Levtzion and Hopkins 1981; Mauny 1961.

Table 4.1 Tax Payments of Marinid Cities According to the 14th century al-'Umarî

Settlement Name	Tax Payment in Thousands of Mithkâl[a]
Tidjissâs	5
Tît	5
Safrawi	6
Al-'Arâ'ish	10
Bâdis	10
Azammur	20
Kasr 'Abd al-Karîm	20
Aghmât	25
Asafî	25
Tâzâ	30
Tangier	30
Ghasâsâ; al-Mazamma; Malîla	30
Anfâ	40
Salâ	40
Sabta	50
Maknâsa	60
Fez	150
Marrakech	150
Sidjilmâsa; Dar'a	150

Note: Data from al-'Umarî (1927:171).

[a]One mithkâl, also known as dinar, equals 4.25 grams of gold (Devisse 1972a:58 note 69; Miles 1965:297).

northerly one leading directly to Fez via Sidjilmâsa. Ibn Hawkal states that "The route from Egypt to Ghana went over them ('enormous deserts and sands') but the winds blew continually upon the caravans, heavy and light, and more than one heavy caravan was annihilated and light one exterminated; also the enemy attacked them and annihilated them on more than one occasion. So they abandoned this road and left it for [that of] Sijilmasa" (Levtzion and Hopkins 1981:45; see also Ibn Hawkal 1967:61).

The city of Sidjilmâsa, founded in A.D. 757 by Sufrîte Berbers, was the most important desert entrepôt for the long-distance gold trade in the Maghrib.[15] The Maghrâwa issued the first gold currency minted at the city in the tenth century. Ibn Hawkal (1967:61) relates that while visiting Awdaghust (modern Tegdaoust in Mauritania), he saw a promissory note (*sak*) in the amount of 42,000 dinars made to a merchant from Sidjilmâsa.[16] Since Sidjilmâsa was the gate to Bilâd al-Sûdân, its control ensured a monopoly over the long-distance gold trade. As a result, it was controlled by a succession of dynastic states, including the Idrisids, the Umayyads, the Fatimids, the Almoravids, the Almohads, and the Marinids.[17]

It appears that the Idrisids failed to conquer the southern fringes of Morocco and control sub-Saharan gold traffic (Brignon et al. 1967:67). They did not issue a gold currency, possibly because they did not have access to sub-Saharan gold. The Idrisids may have compensated for the shortage in gold by amassing agricultural surplus from hinterland farmers to fuel their political economy.

The Fatimids, on the other hand, amassed considerable revenues by imposing duties on gold-transporting caravans coming in and out of the city of Sidjilmâsa. In one passage, Ibn Hawkal states that "Mu'taz, during the period of his emirate there [in Sidjilmâsa] continuously received revenue from taxes on caravans setting out for the land of the Sûdân, as well as tithes, land tax, and old-established dues from what was bought and sold there, such as camels, sheep, cattle and other merchandise going out and coming in from Ifrîqiya, Fez, Spain, the Sûs, and Aghmât, along with other sums due from the Mint- to a total of about 400,000 dinars and this from Sijilmâsa and its district alone" (Levtzion and Hopkins 1981:47). After the fourteenth century, Sidjilmâsa was bypassed by the gold-transporting caravans that headed directly east to Ifrîkiya and Egypt (Lacoste 1984:80-81).

Before the Almoravid period, gold trade was facilitated by the Saharan nomads who guarded and guided caravans through the desert. According to Ibn Hawkal (1967:101-102), these nomads had no knowledge of agriculture and subsisted on the meat and dairy products of their herds. They derived the bulk of their resources from toll and protection fees they levied on caravans crossing their territories. The Almoravid empire originated from a coalition of the most powerful of these nomadic tribes - the Sanhâdja tribes of Mauritania - in the northern fringes of the Saharan desert (Terrasse 1950:213).[18] In A.D. 1054-1055, the Almoravids managed to establish control over the two end points of the western route of gold traffic: Awdaghust and Sidjilmâsa. Although the Almoravids controlled the gold traffic, they did not have direct access to sub-Saharan gold mines (Figure 4.1).

During the Almohad period, when the entire Maghrib was unified under one central government, the two main axes of long-distance gold trade (the western and eastern routes) were managed by one authority. The Almohads played a central role as intermediary agents between the sub-Saharan kingdoms and Europe. Several Maghribian coastal entrepôts

[15] A Moroccan-American team of archaeologists, directed by Ronald Messier, conducted several field-seasons at the site of Sidjilmâsa (Messier 1995, 1997). For more information on the city and its economic history, see Devisse 1985; Lessard 1970; Lightfoot and Miller 1996; Smith 1993; Terrasse 1936.

[16] "I have seen a warrant written concerning a debt owed by Muhammad b. Abî Sa'dûn in Awdaghust, and witnessed by assessors, for 42,000 dinars." (Levtzion and Hopkins 1981:45).

[17] Jacques-Meunié (1982) has a different view in this regard. She argues that the southern regions of Morocco (Sidjilmâsa, Eastern Dar'a, Wâdî Nûn, and the Sûs valley) were independent from dynastic control between the eleventh and sixteenth centuries. This region only occasionally recognized the nominal authority of the Sultan of Fez or Marrakech (Jacques-Meunié 1982:64). However, textual records do not support this view; according to al-'Umarî (1927:171), Sidjilmâsa and Dar'a paid 150,000 mithkâl (dinar) to the Marinid treasury.

[18] For more details on the Almoravid empire, see Conrad and Fisher 1982, 1983; Devisse and Hrbek 1988; Levtzion 1978; Messier 1974; Monaes Farias 1967; Monteil 1968; Norris 1971.

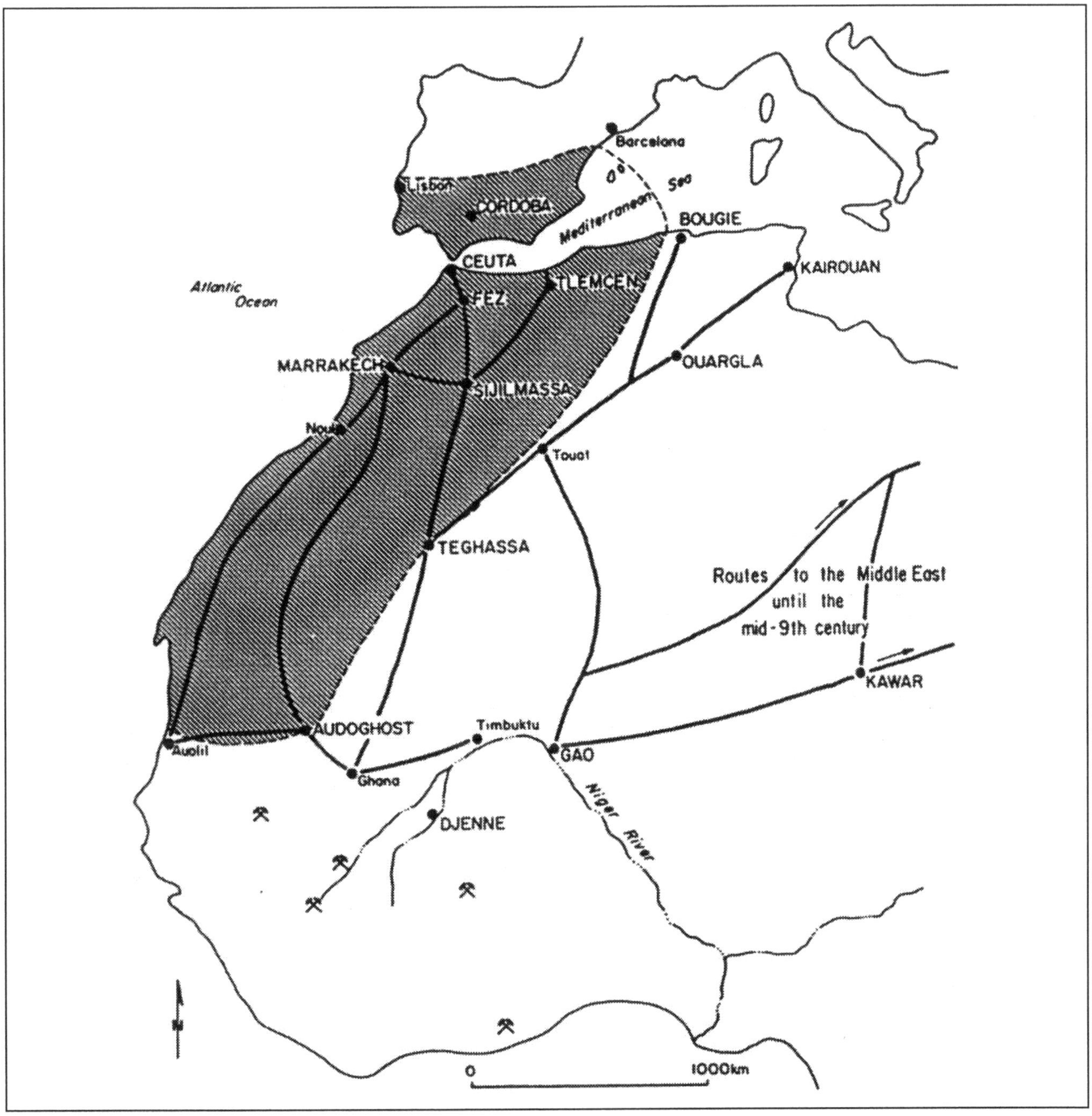

Figure 4.1 Map of Northwest Africa During the Almoravid Period (Dark Lines Indicate Gold Trade Networks. Mining symbols indicate West African Gold Sources). (Source: Boone et al. 1990:Figure 2).

(e.g., Tunis and Sabta) were visited by increasing numbers of merchants from Italy, France, and Spain.

In A.D. 1274, the Marinids conquered the city of Sidjilmâsa, thus becoming the new masters of the sub-Saharan gold trade. As with the two previous dynastic empires (i.e., the Almoravids and the Almohads), this trade constituted the foundation of the Marinid political economy. Several passages from the *Masâlik al-absâr* of al-'Umarî (1927:203, 206-207, 215) show that large amounts of gold were distributed to finance state institutions and support state officials. In addition, the salaries of local tribal chiefs and army officers were paid in minted gold.

By the fourteenth century, new developments occurred in the trade networks. The traffic along the eastern route, via Warghla, once again became active, leading to the decline of the economy of Sidjilmâsa (Brignon 1967:169). The Bedouin tribes of Ma'kil took advantage of the collapsing Marinid dynasty by establishing control of southern Morocco, including Sidjilmâsa (Brignon et al. 1967:169-170; Laroui 1995:199-202). They raided the few caravans that crossed their territory. The Ma'kil presence in southern Morocco had disastrous consequences on the economy and the political and social structures of the sedentary Berbers of the oases (Jacques-Meunié 1982:66-67), and the moribund Marinid economy worsened significantly when the Spanish and the Portuguese fleets occupied several Moroccan coastal entrepôts.[19]

[19] The Portuguese occupied Sabta (Ceuta) in A.D. 1415. Shortly afterwards (A.D. 1420), the Marinid dynasty collapsed.

Medieval Moroccan coastal entrepôts played an important role in the economy of post-Idrisid dynastic states.[20] They functioned as a platform for complex exchange networks between tribal agriculturalists, gold traders, and foreign merchants (mostly Portuguese, Spanish, and Italians). Inland tribal agriculturalists used coastal ports to channel their products to distant markets (in Spain and Ifrîkiya) where they received higher prices.[21] Gold traders visited coastal ports in search of European manufactured goods (especially fabrics), which were highly valued in sub-Saharan markets. And, finally, European traders came to Moroccan ports in search of sub-Saharan gold, slaves, raw materials, and cereals. By the middle of the fifteenth century, the Portuguese, who already occupied a number of Moroccan coastal ports, had begun to venture further south to ports closer to Bilâd al-Sûdân. Their goal was to bypass Maghribian traders and gain direct access to Sudanese gold and other commodities.[22] However, the Portuguese ultimately failed to establish new gold trade networks (Devisse 1972b:387).

In terms of items exchanged between medieval Morocco and Bilâd al-Sûdân, it seems that, at least until the tenth century, Morocco exported mainly agricultural and animal products (e.g., cotton, cereals, flax, and hides) and metals (e.g., copper and silver) to the south (Laroui, 1995:118). After the development of an important craft industry, Morocco also began to export finished goods (e.g., glazed ware, fabrics, glass items, leather items, jewelry, and metal wares). North African glazed ware has been found at several sub-Saharan sites (e.g., Azelik-Takadda in Niger and Tegdaoust, medieval Awdaghust in Mauritania). Using a variety of chemical and mineralogical methods of ceramic analysis, researchers are trying to trace the origin of the glazed ware found in sub-Saharan archaeological sites and to reconstruct medieval long-distance exchange networks between the north and south (Cressier and Picon 1995; Devisse and Picon 1995; Echalier 1976; El Hraiki et al. 1986, 1995; Louhichi and Picon 1983). These analyses indicate that more than half (55%) of the glazed ware found in Tegdaoust was produced in Sidjilmâsa (Cressier and Picon 1995:392; Devisse and Picon 1995:236). The locale of production of the glazed ware found at Azelik-Takadda has not yet been identified. The Azelik-Takadda glazed ware is, however, similar to that produced in Egyptian workshops (Cressier and Picon 1995:392).

Glazed ware was not, however, an important item of long-distance trade. The glazed items found in sub-Saharan Africa may have been destined for use by Maghribian merchants rather than for sub-Saharan markets (Cressier and Picon 1995:391). Most of the glazed sherds found at the site of Tegdaoust were associated with areas that appeared to be occupied by non-local groups (i.e., North African merchants) (Devisse 1972a:52; Devisse and Picon 1995:235-236). Furthermore, glazed ware and other ceramic items are difficult to transport over long distances because of their weight and risk of breakage.

Although gold and slaves were the main "commodities" exchanged between the Maghrib and sub-Saharan Africa, a number of unfinished commodities and raw materials, such as ivory, spices, indigo, ebony, and gum Arabic were also imported into North Africa. The value of the items exchanged between the Maghrib and sub-Saharan Africa depended primarily on: (1) the distance between the production and distribution centers, (2) the caravan's expenses incurred before and along the journey across the Sahara (e.g., buying well-fed camels; paying for the services of servants, guides, and guards; paying passage and protection fees to Saharan nomads), and (3) the amount of taxes and custom duties paid at ports of entry.[23]

As this historical overview on long-distance gold trade between the Maghrib and sub-Saharan Africa shows, sub-Saharan gold was important in the post-Idrisid dynastic political economy. According to Lacoste (1974:2): "The gold trade appears to have been a veritable 'conductor' of North African medieval history and as the motor of the development of the Maghreb during the Middle Ages."

West African gold was one of the most important wealth items for Maghribian states. It was a rare commodity, and, for a long period of time, its provenience was shrouded in mystery. As opposed to silver, which was found in several regions of medieval Morocco, the number of gold mines was small. Furthermore, medieval Moroccan gold production was insufficient to sustain the increasing need for this precious metal (Colin 1936; Eustache 1970b, 1970-71; Gsell 1928; Rosenberger 1964, 1970a, 1970b).[24]

The intermediate location of Morocco between gold producing regions of West Africa and the western Mediterranean was an important factor in insuring a regular flow of gold through the country. The proceeds from the gold traffic benefited both the ruling elite and the merchant class. The ruling elite collected a number of trade-related taxes in exchange for its role in facilitating and protecting gold trade networks.[25] The merchant class, which included prominent government officials as well as members of the ruling class,

[20] For more details on maritime trade and historical and/or archaeological discussions on a number of medieval ports, see Cherif 1991; Cressier 1992; Cressier et al. 1992; Eustache 1955; Picard 1996; Redman 1986b; Ricard 1938; Rosenberger 1967; Siraj 1995a.

[21] The rare shipwrecks, found in Europe, dating to the Islamic period show that amphorae were the main type of vessels used to store agricultural products and foodstuffs shipped overseas (Siraj 1995a:207). The Institut National des Science de l'Archéologie et du Patrimoine in Morocco is currently training Moroccan archaeologists to conduct underwater archaeology at a number of medieval ports.

[22] For more details on the Portuguese presence in Morocco, see Godinho 1947, 1969; Ricard 1936, 1955.

[23] The twelfth-century al-Idrîsî (1983) and the fourteenth-century Ibn Battûta (1859) provide detailed information on the logistics of Saharan trade. See also Godinho 1956.

[24] For a discussion of mining activities during the pre-Islamic period in Morocco, see Siraj 1995a:192-196.

[25] Al-Bakrî (1965:296) mentions that in A.D. 745, 'Abd al-Rahmân Ibn Habîb (governor of Ifrîkiya) dug a series of wells along the long-distance trade route linking the oasis of Bânî to the city of Awdaghust. Even private enterprises seem to have been involved in the maintenance of wells along trade routes; Devisse (1972b:371) cites the case of the thirteenth century al-Makkarî brothers' corporation. The state also built and maintained a series of "*manâzil*" or halting places for caravans (Elisseeff 1988).

invested part of its capital in caravans heading for Bilâd al-Sûdân (Lacoste 1974:12).

Gold trade with sub-Saharan Africa was not, however, financed by North African states. It was a private entrepreneurial activity conducted by wealthy merchants from trading cities, such as Fez, Sidjilmâsa, and Aghmât. As al-Idrîsî (1864-1866:76-77) notes "les habitants d'Aghmât sont riches et commerçants; il se rendent dans les pays des Noirs avec un grand nombre de chameaux... Durant la domination almoravide il n'était pas de gens plus riches que les habitants d'Aghmât."

In summary, as the Boone et al. model (1990) postulated, there was a shift in the political economy of medieval Morocco. The staple finance system that operated during the Idrisid period was to a large extent replaced by a wealth finance system during the post-Idrisid dynastic period. The wealth item *par excellence* in the post-Idrisid period was sub-Saharan gold. In most territorially extensive medieval empires, wealth finance was the most appropriate mechanism for supporting state institutions and its personnel. It was easier to transport over long distances and to store in state treasuries. It is possible that gold dust (*tibr*) brought from West Africa was first processed at the port of entry of Sidjilmâsa before it was transported to inland dynastic capitals.[26] According to al-Mas'ûdî (A.D. 956), "all the gold obtained (from the Western Sûdân) is struck into coins in the city of Sidjilmâsa." (Kamal 1926-1951:628, cited in Messier 1974:38).

While proceeds from the long-distance gold trade constituted the main source of revenue for post-Idrisid dynastic states, agriculture and craft production were also important components of post-Idrisid dynastic economy. The importance of agricultural surplus to state finance is reflected in a statement by the thirteenth-century chronicler Ibn 'Idhârî (cited in Hopkins 1958:52), in which he referred to a special state official (*Khâzin 'ala al-ta'âm*) in charge of guarding staple goods, presumably stored in state-owned warehouses.

During the post-Idrisid dynastic period, agricultural products were needed to supply the inland capitals and coastal entrepôts. Raw materials, such as flax and hides, were needed for the manufacture of finished goods to be exchanged with sub-Saharan West Africa. Furthermore, important fiscal proceeds were derived from taxes on agricultural products brought to state-controlled markets and coastal ports. Control of market exchange was an important component of the Almoravid economy since market transactions depended on the state monetary system (see Picard 1995:186).

Role of Makhzan Tribes in Post-Idrisid Dynastic Political Economy

In order to control an extensive territory, post-Idrisid dynastic states delegated some of their authority to local administrators, especially in regard to tax collection. In medieval Morocco, the central authority or *makhzan* often engaged a number of nomadic tribes - known as *makhzan tribes* or *gîsh* - to maintain order and, more importantly, to collect taxes from sedentary farmers (*ra'iyya tribes*) (Brignon et al. 1967:93; Terrasse 1950:285-288).[27]

Makhzan tribes are usually discussed in North African historical literature within the context of the "Arab invasion".[28] The "Arab invasion" refers to the encroachment upon the territories of sedentary populations - living along the coast and in the Atlantic plains - by the nomadic Arab tribes of Banî Hilâl from Upper Egypt. Rather than an act of trespass by undisciplined hordes of nomads, the Hilâlian infiltration was a deliberate political action initiated by the Almohad central authority.

In A.D. 1152, the Almohad ruler 'Abd al-Mu'min defeated the Banî Hilâl tribes in Sétif (the central Maghreb) and deported them to Morocco (Lacoste 1984:71; Laroui 1995:170). These tribes were needed to reinforce the Almohad army in the Jihad movement against Spain. From the Almohad period onwards, the enlistment of Arab nomads in the dynastic army became a common practice. They officially became *makhzan* tribes or *gîsh* as opposed to *ra'iyya* tribes.

In addition to their role in the dynastic armies, makhzan tribes were in charge of collecting taxes from subordinate sedentary farmers (*ra'iyya tribes*). In exchange for their military and tax collection services, the central authority exempted the tribes from paying *kharâdj* (tax on farmland), and offered them considerable fiscal concessions in the form of "*iktâ'*." The *iktâ'* is a system in which the central authority delegates its fiscal prerogative over a territory to a proxy (in this case the makhzan tribes), who collected the fiscal proceeds as payment for a particular service (Lacoste 1974:5).

By delegating such power to a proxy, the central authority was running the risk of strengthening the makhzan tribes who, eventually, might betray it. Makhzan tribes occasionally abused the authority invested in them by forcing subordinate tribes to pay excessive taxes (Lacoste 1984:79-81). The tribal chiefs also became actively engaged in the political scene by building alliances with prominent members of the ruling elite against their contenders. During periods of political instability and weakness of the central authority (e.g., the end of the Marinid period), they collected taxes for their own benefit.

The fiscal and military abuse of makhzan tribes caused considerable damage to settled life in medieval Morocco at the end of the Marinid period. Large agricultural areas were left barren after sedentary populations had abandoned their villages. Sedentary life was reduced to a small number of fortified villages and urban centers (Terrasse 1947a:52-53). In his description of Marrakech, Leo Africanus (1956:102) states that "Les terrains vacants sont plantés de palmiers, de vignes et d'arbres fruitiers parce que les habitants ne peuvent

[26] For more technical information on Sudanese gold (e.g., quantities of Sudanese gold transported, its quality, its minting into currency), see Devisse 1996.

[27] In addition to makhzan tribes, tax collection was also the prerogative of an elite troop made of Christian militiamen. For their influence on medieval Moroccan military architecture, see Terrasse 1953:400.

[28] See the following studies for more details: Idris 1968; Lacoste 1966:87-105; Laroui 1995:139-146; Marcais 1913; Poncet 1967.

pas avoir une palme de terrain cultivable hors des murs tant ils sont molestés par les Arabes [i.e., the Banî Ma'kil tribes]."

The increased role of the makhzan tribes in the post-Idrisid dynastic political economy also changed the political map of medieval Morocco. By the Marinid period, the country became divided into two distinct territories: (1) *Blâd al-makhzan*, or tax paying territories, and (2) *Blâd al-sîba*, or rebel territories (Terrasse 1947b:149). The former shrank as more and more populations refused to pay taxes and escaped to the mountains (the Rif and the Atlas Mountains). Only sedentary farmers living in open areas (e.g., the Atlantic plains) - thus within the reach of makhzan tribes - remained under the central authority (Terrasse 1947b:150).

Chapter 5

SETTLEMENT SYSTEMS OF MEDIEVAL NORTHERN MOROCCO

This chapter examines the material impact of changing political economies on medieval Moroccan settlement patterns. Based on documentary and numismatic evidence, it demonstrates that there was a shift in settlement patterns from a multitiered and hierarchical distribution of settlement size during the Idrisid period to a "primate" one during subsequent periods. The term "primate" is used in this study to describe a settlement system that is dominated by two anomalously large cities (the dynastic capitals of Fez and Marrakech); the next largest settlements are much smaller in size, therefore, creating a gap - in settlement size - between Fez and Marrakech and the rest of medieval Moroccan urban centers. Furthermore, in contrast to large dynastic capitals, which are highly integrated (vertical integration), the settlements at the lower levels of the settlement hierarchy are characterized by a weak horizontal integration.

This research utilizes an archaeological-historical approach that combines archaeological data with textual and numismatic evidence. In Chapter 2, I explained how each type of data was collected, classified, and analyzed in order to monitor change in settlement systems of northern Morocco from the ninth to the fifteenth centuries

The discussion is arranged along three main axes: (1) an analysis of textual evidence, (2) an analysis of numismatic evidence, and (3) a critical analysis of the results form both lines of evidence.

Hierarchy of Islamic Settlements in "A<u>h</u>san al-Ta<u>k</u>âsîm" of al-Mu<u>k</u>addasî

As discussed in Chapter 2, the *A<u>h</u>san al-ta<u>k</u>âsîm* of the tenth-century Arab geographer al-Mu<u>k</u>addasî[1] offers important insights into the hierarchy of Islamic settlements in the tenth century. Figure 5.1 shows al-Mu<u>k</u>addasî's hierarchy of Arab Islamic settlements. The domain of Islam (*mamlakat al-Islâm*) is composed of two subdivisions (the domain of Arabs or *mamlakat al-'Arab* and the domain of non-Arabs or *mamlakat al-'A<u>dj</u>am*) and fourteen provinces.[2] Al-Mu<u>k</u>addasî used two types of hierarchical systems; one for ordering regional/administrative units and the second for ordering settlement units (Ismail 1972:Figure 2). Since al-Mu<u>k</u>addasî did not clearly separate these two systems, they tend to appear as part of a single system. Regional/administrative units refer to large territorial divisions of homogenous features, such as climate, physical geography, and population. Settlement units are small entities, within regional/administrative units, which are economically and politically interdependent.

The difference between these two types of hierarchical systems is also a matter of abstraction as opposed to physical reality. Regional/administrative units are conceptual constructs with no physical bounds (e.g., the notion of *mamlaka*), whereas settlement units are concrete entities bounded in physical space (e.g., *madîna*).

Al-Mu<u>k</u>addasî's hierarchical model of settlements operates within two spheres of interaction: the *mamlakat al-Islâm* (domain of Islam) and the *i<u>k</u>lîm* (province). The former is the stage for broad regional networks of long-distance exchange, population movement, and various administrative and political interactions between different provinces within the domain of Islam as a whole. The latter domain (province) is better defined spatially and much smaller geographically. It consists of sub-regional and local exchange systems involving a metropolis and its districts and various cities and their hinterlands, all within the boundaries of a single province.

[1] *A<u>h</u>san al-ta<u>k</u>âsîm fî ma'rifat al-a<u>k</u>âlîm* (the best divisions for knowledge of the provinces) was written by al-Mu<u>k</u>addasî in A.D. 985.

[2] There were six Arab provinces (the Maghrib, Egypt, Arabia, <u>Sh</u>âm, Irâ<u>k</u>, and A<u>k</u>ûr) and eight non-Arab provinces (Miquel 1993:493).

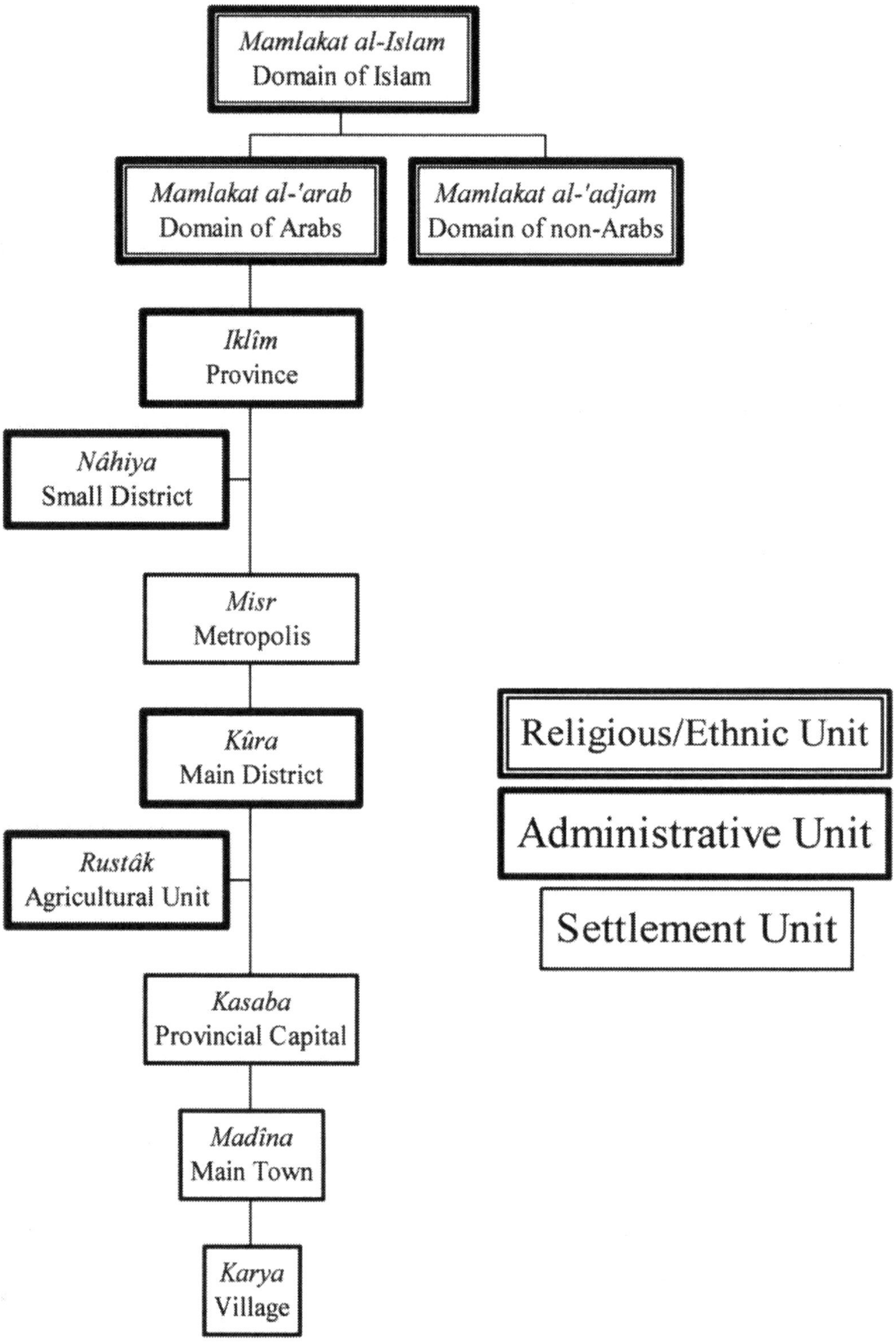

Figure 5.1 Hierarchy of Arab-Islamic Settlements in Ahsan Al-Takâsîm of Al-Mukaddasî (A.D. 985).

An important contribution of al-Mukaddasî to medieval Arabic geographical literature is his development of a specific terminology for settlement types.[3] He consistently used specific terms to convey specific meanings. The rigor of his vocabulary is illustrated in his use of the terms *Maghrib* (occident) and *Gharb* (west) - graphically similar in Arabic; he used the former to refer to the province composed of Morocco, Algeria, Tunisia, Libya, and al-Andalus (Muslim Spain), and the latter only when he wanted to add Egypt and al-Shâm (Syria) to the same province (al-Mukaddasî 1994:7).

According to al-Mukaddasî, medieval Arab settlements are composed of four territorial divisions (administrative units) and four settlement divisions (settlement units) (Figure 5.1).

[3] Basil's translation (al-Mukaddasî 1994) failed to account for such an important aspect of al-Mukaddasî's contribution; Basil gave several translations for the same term. For example "*madîna*" was translated as "town" (1994:200), as "chief-town" (1994:205) as "capital" (1994:200), and as "inner city" (1994:7). Similarly, the term "*nahiya*" was translated as "division" (1994:198), and as "region" (1994:206).

Territorial divisions consist of the following components listed in decreasing order of magnitude: *iklîm* (province), *kûra* (main district), *nâhiya* (territory), and *rustâk* (agricultural territory). The *iklîm* constitutes a homogeneous entity characterized by a uniform physical landscape and shared political and socioeconomic values among its dependencies. The *kûra* represents an administrative subdivision within the *iklîm*. The *kûra* is politically and economically subordinate to the *iklîm*. The *nâhiya* is another smaller subdivision within the *iklîm*. In his description of the province of al-Maghrib (North Africa), al-Mukaddasî used the term *nâhiya* to refer to an even smaller subdivision within the *kûra* (the two territories within the district of Fez).

The smallest territorial division in al-Mukaddasî's hierarchy is the *rustâk*. It represents a rural territory composed of a number of small towns and villages under the control of a main city. In his description of medieval Morocco, al-Mukaddasî used this term in reference to two medieval localities: Dar'a and Balad Gumâr. He wrote that the *rustâk* of Balad Gumâr "takes three days to traverse its length or its width; its entire area encompasses many prosperous villages" (al-Mukaddasî 1994:206). The economic importance of the *rustâk* is far greater than its modest hierarchical status within the province. Al-Mukaddasî states in this regard that "[one] should know that an area does not become illustrious by the number of its settlements, but rather by the importance of its rural districts [*rasâtîk* sing. of *rustâk*]" (al-Mukaddasî 1994:205).

The most relevant aspect of al-Mukaddasî's conceptual model to settlement studies is his hierarchical classification of settlement units. According to al-Mukaddasî, there are four hierarchical settlement divisions or settlement units: the *misr* (metropolis), the *kasaba* (provincial/district capital), the *madîna* (city), and the *karya* (village). The *misr* is the highest hierarchical unit of settlement within the province. Al-Mukaddasî defines it as "any town which is the seat of the highest authority, where the governmental bureaux [offices] are assembled, to which is assigned the functions of administration [and finance], and which, for the towns of the entire region constitutes a central place." (al-Mukaddasî 1994:50). The *misr* rules the surrounding districts (*kûra*) through a number of provincial capitals or *Kasabât*. The *kasaba* is the chief-seat of the provincial government. For example, the Idrisid capital of Fez was the *kasaba* of the district of *al-Sûs al-Adna* (Northern Morocco). The provincial capital controls the cities located within its administrative/political jurisdiction. It is the largest in size and the most prominent economically and politically.

The *madîna*[4] (city) is the unit of settlement of most interest to regional settlement studies. Al-Mukaddasî inventoried a large number of city-names for each district. Based solely on his book, it is possible to reconstruct the macro-regional settlement patterns of the entire Islamic world in the tenth century. Of course, such a reconstruction will reflect al-Mukaddasî's own perception of the Islamic world of his time. In other words, his inventories of city-names reflect his judgment on what he thought was worthy of mention (al-Mukaddasî 1994:205). His description also reflects the "general usage", and what was commonly understood and accepted by tenth century Islamic society. He stated in this regard that "we happen to mention some towns that are smaller than many villages in other regions, but which are widely known as towns. My scholarship is, of course, based on general usage" (al-Mukaddasî 1994:205). The smallest unit in al-Mukaddasî's settlement hierarchy is the *karya* or village. It refers to hinterland settlements around urban centers.

Al-Mukaddasî's hierarchical model is based on the assumption that every province must have districts, every district must have a capital, and every capital must have a number of cities. Metaphorically, he equates metropolises to kings, provincial capitals to chamberlains, cities to armies, and villages to foot soldiers (al-Mukaddasî 1994:50-51). In the tenth century, the Islamic world - as depicted by al-Mukaddasî - was composed of 17 metropolises, 67 provincial capitals, 50 chief-seats, and a large number of urban centers (*madâ'in*) and villages.

Idrisid Settlement System

Hierarchy of Idrisid Settlements in "Ahsan al-Takâsîm" of al-Mukaddasî

In addition to the marcoregional hierarchy of Islamic settlements, al-Mukaddasî's book offers one of the most detailed and systematically organized accounts of the Idrisid settlement system. According to this medieval Arab geographer, the province of al-Maghrib was composed of North Africa (except Egypt), al-Andalus (Muslim Spain) and Sicily. It contained two metropoles (*misr*) and six districts (*kuwra*). The metropoles were al-Kayrawân (Kairouan) and Kurtuba (Cordoba). The districts were Sidjilmâsa, Fez (also known as al-Sûs al-Adnâ), al-Sûs al-Aksâ, Barka, Ifrîkiya, and Tâhart. Only the district of Fez (i.e., northern Morocco)[5] will be discussed here since the other districts are beyond the geographic scope of this research.

The city of Fez was the capital (*kasaba*) of the district of Fez. This district was composed of two territories (*nâhiya*)–Tandja[6] and al-Zâb[7]–and 41 main cities (Figure 5.2). The 41 main cities - as listed by al-Mukaddasî - are: Al-Basra, Zalûl, al-Djâhid, Sûk al-Kutâmî, Wargha, Sabû, Sanhâdjâ, Huwwâra, Tîzâ [Tâzâ], Matmâta,Kazannâya, Salâ, Madînat Banî Karbâs,

4 In *Ahsan al-takasîm*, the term "*madîna*" is used either in a general context or in a specific one. In a general context, the term "*madîna*" means "urban center" (pl. *madâ'in*). In a more specific context, it means "chief-seat" (pl. *mudun*) (al-Mukaddasî 1963:13 note 15; Wheatley 1976:360).

5 In the description of al-Mukaddasî, the district of Fez also includes parts of southern Tunisia, and all of southern Algeria (al-Mukaddasî 1950:76 note 9).

6 The territory of Tandja is, geographically, the equivalent of Roman "Mauretania Tingitania". This territory was composed of 10 cities: Walîla [Volubilis], Madraka, Matrûka, Zakkûr, Ghuzza, Ghumîra, al-Hâdjir, Tâdjarâdjarâ, al-Baydâ', and al-Khadrâ' (al-Mukaddasî 1950:9). Tandja was also mentioned as a city: "Tandja that town so remote" (al-Mukaddasî 1994:198).

7 Al-Zâb territory is composed of Msîla, which is the capital of the territory, Makkara, Tubna, Biskra, Badîs [Badès], Tahûdha, Tawlâkâ, Djamîla, Bantiyûs, Adna, and Ashîr (al-Mukaddasî 1950:9).

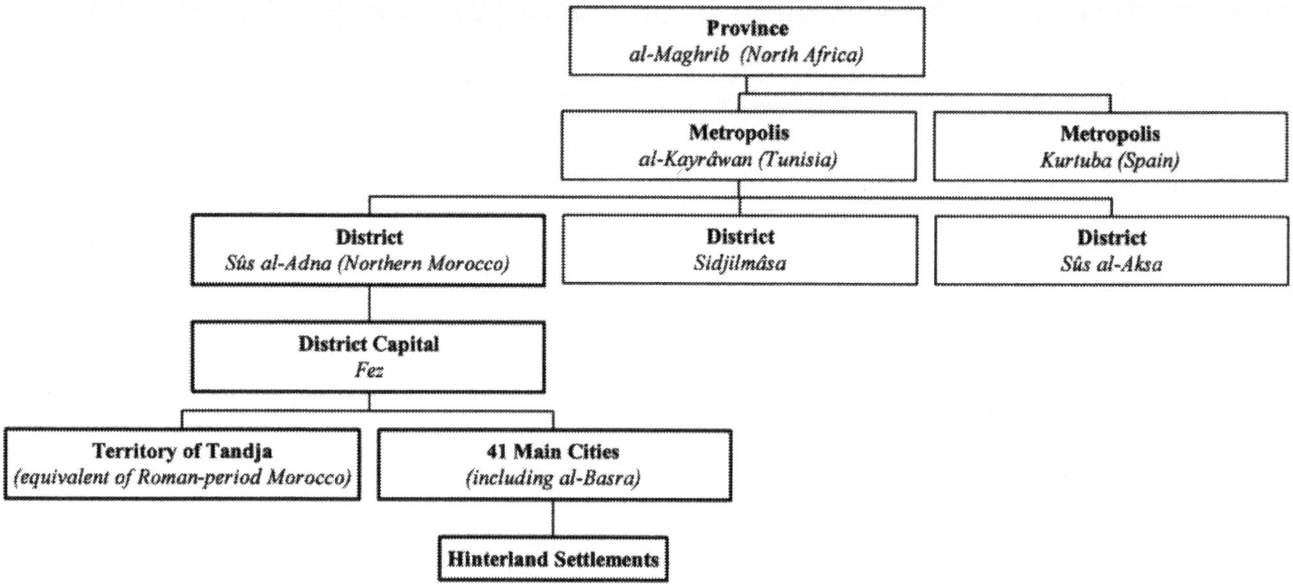

Figure 5.2 Hierarchy of Idrisid Settlements in Ahsan Al-Takâsîm of Al-Mukaddasî (A.D. 985).

Mazhâhiyya, Azîlâ, Sabtâ [Ceuta], Balad Ghumâr[8], Kal'at an-Nusûr, Nakûr, Balash, Marnîsa, Tâbarîdâ, Sâ', Miknâsa [Meknès], Kal'at Shamît, Madâ'in, Burdj n-Ûzikî, Tayûnû, Maksîn, Amlîl [Melilla], Amlâh Abî l-Hasan, Kastîna, Nafzâwa, Nikâwûs, Biskara, Kabîsha, Mâdînat Banî Zahhîk, Luwâta 'Abd Allâh, Luwâta Barkiyya, Akdhâr Ibn Shirâk, and Madînat Djabal Zâlâgh (al-Mukaddasî 1950:7-9).

Al-Mukaddasî's Idrisid settlement system was clearly multitiered and hierarchical (Figures 1.2 and 5.2). At the top was the city of Fez, the capital of both the state and the district; it figured prominently within the Idrisid settlement system. Below Fez, were the provincial capitals. This second level consisted of mid-sized cities located in rich agricultural areas. Based on al-Mukaddasî's description of northern Morocco, the Idrisid urban network was composed 51 cities - 41 within the district of Fez and 10 within the territory of Tandja. Although al-Mukaddasî provided us with a rich inventory of city names, his account does not include - for most of the cities he listed - any locational information, which limits his work in reconstructing Idrisid urban networks archaeologically.

Issues in Idrisid Urbanism

Except for al-Basra, and to a lesser extent Walîla and Hadjar al-Nasr, no Idrisid settlements have been the objects of archaeological investigations (Akerraz 1998; Benco 1987, 1990, 1994, 1995b, in press; Cressier et al. 1998). Most of what we know about Idrisid urbanism is based on textual and numismatic evidence. The most recent studies on Idrisid urbanism are several articles in a book edited by Cressier and Garcia-Arenal (1998).[9] These articles present the latest archaeological, textual, and numismatic evidence on a number of Idrisid cities. Among the issues addressed are: (1) the transition from the Roman to the Idrisid period and the emergence of the first Islamic cities in Morocco, (2) a typology of the Idrisid city and its functions, and, (3) an examination of the political and economic structure of the Idrisid state (Akerraz 1998; Cressier et al. 1998; Garcia-Arenal and Manzano Moreno 1998; Rosenberger 1998; Siraj 1998).

In this section, I focus on two issues in Idrisid urbanism that are insufficiently examined in the literature: (1) the definition of the Idrisid *madîna* (Idrisid city) in textual sources, and (2) a discussion of a specific component of Idrisid urbanism: the pairing of provincial capitals with their coastal entrepôts.

Although a large number of settlements are categorized as cities (*mudun*) by medieval geographers and chroniclers, there is no clear-cut definition of what a city is. Medieval authors did not explicitly discuss the minimum requirements - in terms of settlement size and/or the number and size of public facilities - for a settlement to qualify for urban status. Scholars are still debating on what constitutes an Islamic city. Is it the presence of city walls? Is it the presence of a congregational mosque[10] (*djami'*)? Or is it the presence of other features?

The fourteenth-century chronicler Ibn Abî Zar' (1843:16, 1860:36) lists five conditions necessary for an exemplary city: (1) water resources, (2) arable land, (3) wood resources, (4) solid fortifications, and (5) a government (*al-Sultân*). These conditions cover the most vital needs of the medieval city in terms of sustenance, protection[11], and administration. Unfortunately, only a handful of cities met all these conditions.

8 Balad Ghumâr (Ghumâra) was a territory of a tribal group rather than an urban center in the strict sense of the word.

9 This book is the result of two roundtables organized by the Casa de Velazquez (Madrid) in 1994 and 1995. The first one was on "Naissance de la Ville Islamique", and the second was on "La Ville Islamique du Haut Moyen-Age (al-Andalus-Maghreb)".

10 A congregational mosque or *masdjid djami'* is one in which Friday prayer is held.

11 City walls functioned primarily as defensive features against intruders, such as tribal nomads, and armies of political rivals. For a detailed discussion of the relationship between urban communities and their hinterlands, see Stambouli and Zghal 1976. For a recent study on medieval Moroccan fortifications, see Cressier 1995.

Several medieval geographers considered the presence of city walls as a determining factor for a given settlement to be categorized as a city. Al-Idrîsî (1864-1866:71-72, 1957:38) did not consider Dar'a (Tudgha?) as a "real" city but rather as a conglomeration of attached villages (*kura*) and buildings (*'imârât*). He emphasized that Dar'a (Tudgha?) was not enclosed by a rampart (*sûr*) or a ditch (*hafîr*). Similarly, Ibn Hawkal (1938-39:81) considers Hadjar al-Nasr as a *madîna* based, among other things, on the fact that the city was fortified. Interestingly, he does not mention the presence of a congregational mosque (*djâmi'*) in the city.

Leo Africanus' account on the foundation of the city al-Kasr al-Kabîr, despite its anecdotal and fictitious character, also points to the importance of city walls as a defining element of urban status: "[King al-Mansûr] fit construire d'importants et beaux palais et plusieurs maisons. A son départ, il les donna en récompense au pêcheur qui le pria de vouloir bien faire enclore ces palais et ces maisons d'une muraille... Cela fut fait et le pêcheur demeura le seigneur de la nouvelle petite ville" (Leo Africanus 1956:252-253).

There was no consensus among medieval geographers as to the importance of city walls in defining the "urbanness" of a settlement. Aghmât and Nfîs were considered to be major urban settlements, although it was clearly stated that they were not fortified.

The presence of a congregational mosque (*djâmi'*) - although not the most determining element - was highly regarded by medieval geographers. The number of congregational mosques within a city was often used as an indication of its prominence. For example, the city of Fez, the metropolis of the Maghrib, contained 785 mosques (Ibn Abî Zar' 1843:25-26, 1860:57). Al-Mukaddasî used the term *minbar* (congregational mosque, literally preacher's chair) instead of *madîna* to describe the district of Sidjilmâsa: "Dar'a commande un vaste canton; elle a plusieurs (mosquées-) cathédrales [*manâbir*] ... 'Arîsh désigne un canton où il y a plusieurs (mosquées-) cathédrales [*manâbir*]" (al-Mukaddasî 1950:29).

Although scientifically rigorous otherwise, al-Mukaddasî did not define what constitutes a city. In his hierarchy of Arab-Islamic settlements, the city (*madîna*) occupies an intermediate level between the provincial capital (*kasaba*) and the village (*karya*) (Figure 5.1). Furthermore, he states that "we happen to mention some towns that are smaller than many villages in other regions, but which are widely known as towns. My scholarship is, of course, based on general usage" (al-Mukaddasî 1994:205).

This passage introduces two new variables to the definition of the Islamic city: size and "general usage" or common appellation. Many medieval geographers based their distinction between cities and villages on size differences; obviously, a city is much larger than a village. For example, al-Idrîsî (1983:169) states that the city of Masîna was a big village that resembles a small city:[12] "grand village qui ressemble plutôt à une petite ville..." In a similar passage, al-Bakrî (1965:224) mentions that the Wargha river cuts through a conglomeration of villages that resemble cities:[13] "cette rivière [Wargha] coule dans un pays magnifique, au milieu d'une foule de villages qui ressemblent à des villes." While settlement size was an important element in assigning urban status to a given settlement, al-Mukaddasî's notion of "general usage" is much harder to account for through textual analysis, and much more so through archaeological investigation.

The second issue concerns a specific component of Idrisid urbanism: the pairing of provincial capitals with their coastal entrepôts. As shown in Figure 1.2, each Idrisid provincial capital had one or more coastal entrepôts to channel the agricultural production of the region under its control. Textual evidence confirms that this was a prevalent pattern during the Idrisid period. Several coastal entrepôts along the Atlantic and Mediterranean coasts served as active maritime outlets to a number of inland Idrisid provincial capitals: Mûlây Bû Salhâm (medieval Buhayrat Ariagh), and later on Tushummush, served as ports for al-Basra; Tigissâs and Tafardjannît were the ports of Djarâwa; Kûz was the port of Aghmât. The kingdom of Nakûr controlled several coastal entrepôts on the Mediterranean coast among which are the ports of Badîs and al-Mazamma.[14]

However, the use of a network of coastal outlets to channel the agricultural production of inland areas was an economic strategy that was implemented long before the Idrisid period. The Romans had established several ports and anchorage sites on Moroccan coasts and had used them to ship agricultural products, especially cereals. The most important Roman ports are: Sala Colonia (Shâlla), Thémiatyria (al-Ma'mûra?), Mulelucha (Buhayrat Ariagh), Lixus (Tushummush), Tingi (Tangier), Septem Fratres (Sabta), Parientina (Bâdis?), Ad Sex Insulas (Mazamma), and Rusaddir (Malîla) (Siraj 1995a:203).

The survival of Idrisid ports depended on the political and economic strength of the provincial capitals they serviced. After the death of Idrîs II and the division of the state into several principalities, each Idrisid prince attempted to encroach upon his rival's domain. The wars between provincial capitals weakened the Idrisid state and made it vulnerable to exterior threats (i.e., the Fatimids of Ifrîkiya and the Umayyads of Spain). As exchange networks between provincial capitals and their coastal entrepôts were disrupted, the Idrisid economy declined and eventually collapsed. Although a number of coastal entrepôts were abandoned, several others (e.g., Asîla, Tangier, Sabta, and Salâ) remained prosperous despite the political turmoil.

12 "karya kabîra kal madîna al-saghîra." (al-Idrîsî 1957:109).

13 "karârât kathîra shabîha bi al-mudun." (al-Bakrî 1965:224).

14 Notice that most of these coastal entrepôts were located at the mouth of major rivers (e.g., Tushummush on Lukkûs River, and Kûz on Tansift River). Other examples include al-Ma'mûra on Subû River, Salâ on Bû Ragrâg River, Azammûr on Um al-Rabî' River, Mâsa on Mâsa River, and Nûl on Nûl River. The location of medieval Moroccan ports in proximity of major rivers was due to the lack of naturally protected anchorage sites along the coasts.

Post-Idrisid Settlement System

Rise of Inland Dynastic Capitals

Boone et al. (1990) based their model on textually derived data drawn from the work of Godinho (1947). While the textual evidence discussed in the model showed that there was a shift in settlement systems, it was inconclusive for two main reasons.

First, the bulk of Godinho's textual data is derived from two medieval Arab geographers - al-'Umarî and Leo Africanus - whose works date to the fourteenth and sixteenth centuries, respectively. The settlement information provided by these two geographers is more detailed and more reliable for the Marinid period, which is at the end of the model's second phase, rather than the earlier periods. Second, and more importantly, Godinho's evidence lacks settlement size figures for the Idrisid and pre-Almoravid periods; his earliest figures begin with the Almoravid period and continue to the end of the Almohad period (Godinho 1947:135). This limitation is particularly serious because the phase during which the settlement shift occurred is not documented textually. Although Boone et al. (1990:641) acknowledge this shortcoming: "[the textual data they present] may only represent the tail end of a more radical shift in settlement size distribution," their documentary evidence represents only the aftermath of the phenomenon under investigation.

In order to obtain a better understanding of the circumstances that accompanied the settlement shift in question, textual data from a wider variety of sources, especially earlier ones, was needed. As a result I examined 23 medieval textual sources dating from the ninth to the sixteenth centuries (Appendix A). I recorded and systematically analyzed settlement information from 99 documented sites in northern Morocco (Table 5.1; Appendix D). Appendix B represents a synopsis of the textual data I examined in my investigation of medieval Moroccan settlement systems.

Using the same frequency distribution of settlement size classes as Godinho's (1947:134-135), I classified the 99 sites into six major groups (see details in Chapter 2). The distribution of settlement size classes by dynastic period shows, for the first time, that medieval Morocco witnessed a turning point in its settlement history under the Almoravids.

Table 5.1 Distribution of Settlements by Founding Period

Founding Period	Number of Settlements
Pre-Idrisid	16
Idrisid	43
Pre-Almoravid	21
Almoravid	9
Almohad	2
Marinid	8
Total	99

As the model predicted, there was a dramatic shift in the number of mid-sized settlements (Class V) between the Idrisid and Almoravid periods (Figure 5.3). The number of settlements dropped by nearly 70% (from 54 to 17 settlements) and continued to fall more gradually during later periods. Historical evidence attributes this decrease to the large-scale destruction that usually accompanied the emergence of a new dynastic empire and the collapse of an old one (e.g., Almoravids, Almohads). Independent and militarily self-sufficient mid-sized urban centers may have posed a threat to the ruling elite, and therefore, were destroyed (Boone et al. 1990:636; Boone and Benco 1999:54). Several mid-sized and small cities were destroyed because they did not have sufficient military manpower and/or defensive features to counterattack dynastic troops (Boone et al. 1990:Figure 3). Al-Basra is a typical example in this regard. Others were simply abandoned because their fragile economy was negatively affected by the prevailing political instability. Figure 5.3 also shows a more gradual decrease in the number of Class VI cities (less than 2,000 inhabitants), mostly during the Almohad and Marinid periods. The number of large settlements (Classes I, II, III, and IV) remained low throughout the Middle Ages.

During the Idrisid period when it served as the state capital, Fez was not significantly larger than the other Idrisid cities (Boone et al. 1990:641). During the Almoravid period, when it achieved primacy over all settlements, its population exceeded 100,000 inhabitants. By the Almohad period, it had become a true metropolis.[15] In the fourteenth century, under the reigns of al-Manṣûr and his son al-Nâṣir, Fez featured 785 mosques, 122 public fountains, 93 ḫammâms, 472 mills, and, most importantly, 89,236 households (Ibn Abî Zar' 1843:25-26, 1860:57-58). This number of households is the equivalent of nearly 450,000 inhabitants.[16] Although these figures may overestimate the population of a medieval city, it is clear that Fez was by far the largest city in northern Morocco at this time. The two prominent cities of the Maghrib, Fez and Marrakech, were at least three times larger than the largest city in the next settlement size class (25,000-50,000 inhabitants) (Boone et al. 1990:640).

Godinho's data show that mid-sized settlements continued to decrease over time (Table 5.2). The number of settlements in Class III (25,000-50,000 inhabitants) decreased by half from A.D. 1060-1217 to A.D. 1400-1415. Godinho's data show only a slight decrease in the number of settlements in Class V (2,000-10,000 inhabitants). This pattern is somewhat misleading since it was within this settlement size class (which includes al-Basra) that the radical shift occurred. The pattern differences shown in Figure 5.3 and Table 5.2 are due to differences in scope between Godinho's work and my own.

[15] "*madînat Fâs kutb wa madâr li muduni al-Maghrib al-Aksâ* [Fez is the pole and the center around which revolves the cities of *al-Maghrib al-Aksâ*]" (al-Idrîsî 1957:53).

[16] In medieval texts, population size is indicated by the number of cooking hearths or *mawâkid* (sing. *mawkid*). A hearth is the equivalent of a household. Godinho (1947:134) estimated the average size of the medieval family to be five persons; in order to convert the number of cooking hearths into actual numbers of inhabitants, Godinho multiplied the number of hearths by five. This is what I have done here.

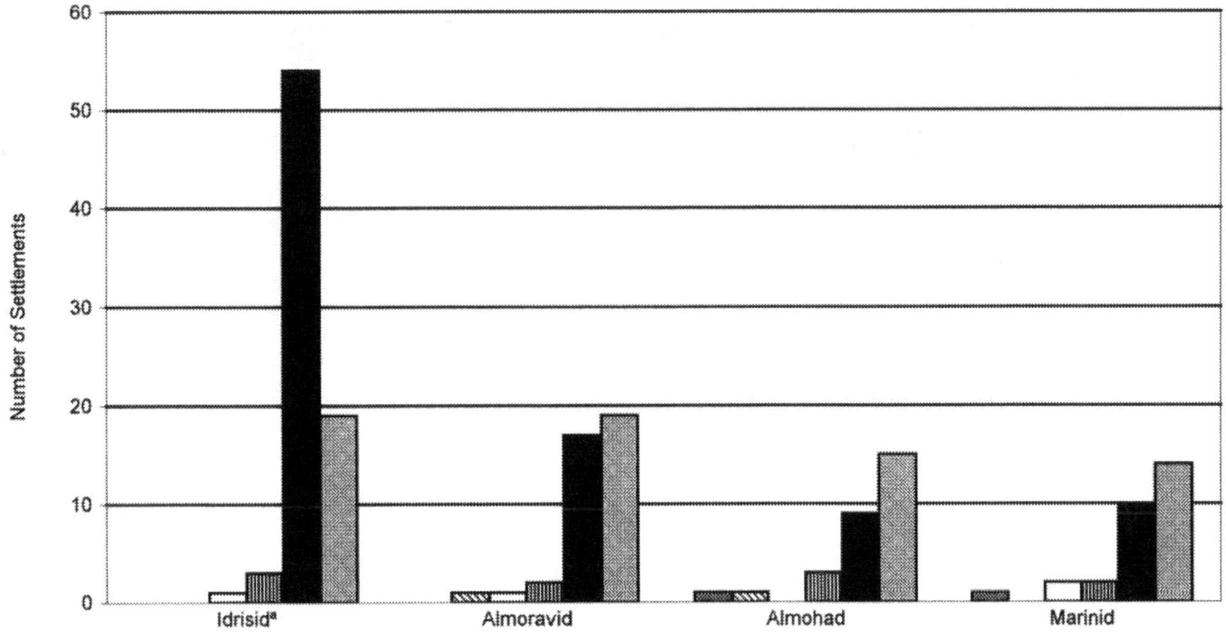

	Idrisid[a]	Almoravid	Almohad	Marinid
Class I: >100*	0	0	1	1
Class II: 50-100*	0	1	1	0
Class III: 25-50*	1	1	0	2
Class IV: 10-25*	3	2	3	2
Class V: 2-10*	54	17	9	10
Class VI: <2*	19	19	15	14

*Population Size (in thousands of inhabitants)

Note: The data presented in this figure are based on the information found in Appendix D.
[a]pre-Idrisid, Idrisid, and pre-Almoravid periods combined.

Figure 5.3 Distribution of Settlement Size Classes by Dynastic Period.

Table 5.2 Frequency Distributions of Settlement Size Classes of Medieval Moroccan Cities by Time Period.

Number of inhabitants	Number of Cities				
	A.D. 1060-1217	A.D. 1270-1350	A.D. 1400-1415	A.D. 1470-1510	A.D. 1525
More than 100,000	2	2	2	2	2
50,000-100,000	0	0	0	0	0
25,000-50,000	8	–[a]	4	3	3
10,000-25,000	15	46[a]	15	14	13
2,000-10,000	28	–[a]	25	26	24
Total	53	48	46	45	42

Note : Data from Boone et al. (1990:Table 1); Godinho (1947:135).
[a]Separate class data not available.

Godinho's work was broad in geographical scope and was mainly concerned with important urban centers. In addition, it was drawn almost exclusively from two textual sources dating to the later medieval period (al-'Umarî and Leo Africanus). By comparison, the geographical scope of my research was limited to northern Morocco. The textual data I used, however, was drawn from a wider variety of documentary sources that covered a longer period of time (from the ninth to the fifteenth centuries A.D.).

Based on the supposition that larger cities paid more taxes than smaller ones, one would expect to find, in the context of a "primate" settlement system (1) a significant gap between the tax payment of the largest cities and that of the next-largest ones, and (2) a strong correlation between tax payments and settlement size.

To test the first component of this hypothesis, I used data derived from al-'Umarî's *Masâlik al-abs̱âr fî mamâlik al-ams̱âr* (Pathways of Vision in the Realms of the Metropolises) (1927:171). The data consist of the tax payments of 22 medieval cities to the Marinid treasury under the reign of Abû Sa'îd 'Uṯhmân II (A.D.1310-1331). As shown in Table 4.1, the amount of taxes paid by Fez and Marrakech are substantially larger than any other city in medieval Morocco. It equals the tax payment of Siḏjilmâsa and Dar'a combined, and is 2.5 higher than Maknâsa, the city with the next largest tax contribution. Al-'Umarî's tax information clearly shows that a "primate" settlement distribution prevailed until the Marinid period (A.D. 1258-1420).

To test the second component of my hypothesis, I correlated al-'Umarî's tax information with settlement size data derived from Godinho's work (1947:134-135)[17] (Table 5.3). Figure 5.4 shows that there is a meaningful correlation between settlement size and the amount of tax payment (Spearman rank-order correlation: -0.843). This graph also shows that the two inland capitals of Fez and Marrakech are substantially larger (Class I) than other cities within the Marinid settlement system. In a "primate" settlement pattern, one would expect the absence of second-ranking urban centers (Class II). Although one value is shown in Class II, it represents the population estimate for an entire region (Sidjilmâsa-Dar'a) and not for an individual city. Godinho's settlement data - used to establish this graph - do not show any Class II (50,000-100,000 inhabitants) urban centers (Tables 5.2 and 5.3).

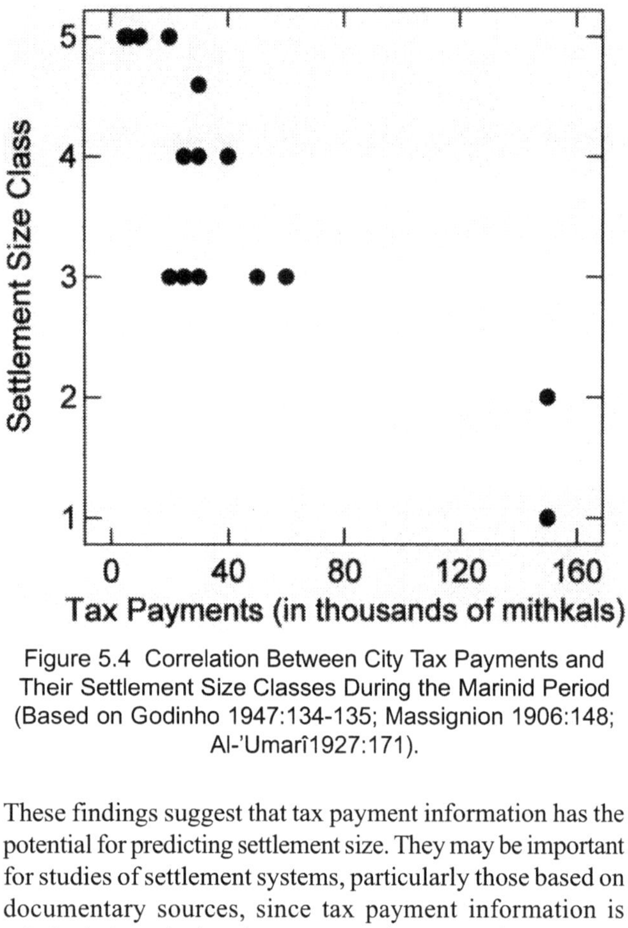

Figure 5.4 Correlation Between City Tax Payments and Their Settlement Size Classes During the Marinid Period (Based on Godinho 1947:134-135; Massignion 1906:148; Al-'Umarî1927:171).

These findings suggest that tax payment information has the potential for predicting settlement size. They may be important for studies of settlement systems, particularly those based on documentary sources, since tax payment information is relatively less elusive than concrete data on settlement size.

Post-Idrisid Urban Development

The analysis of textual sources in terms of urban development of post-Idrisid sites point to a number of interesting patterns. More than half of the textually documented sites (59 out of a total of 99 sites) were occupied for two to three centuries (Figure 5.5). Most settlements with such a relatively short occupation span date to the Idrisid and pre-Almoravid periods (Figure 5.6). These mid-sized inland settlements were abandoned and/or destroyed during the Almoravid conquest of northern Morocco. The territory that suffered the most from the Almoravid impact is that of the Barghwâta. The Almoravids totally devastated the territory of this rebel Berber state, destroying a large number of cities and villages.

Even a century later, the plains of Tâmasnâ (where the Barghwâta were settled) remained only sparsely populated (Terrasse 1947a:50). According to Leo Africanus (1956:158-159), the province of Tâmasnâ once contained close to 40 cities and 300 castles before it was totally destroyed by the Almoravid troops. In a reference to one of the descendents of Sâlih ibn Tarîf (founder of the Barghwâta state), al-Bakrî (1965:262) wrote that: "Il [Yûnus ibn Ilyâs ibn Sâlih ibn Tarîf] dépeupla trois cent quatre-vingt-sept villes, ayant passé au fil de l'épée tous les habitants, parce qu'ils lui avaient résisté." Although this statement is likely an exaggeration, it suggests that the Barghwâta territory (i.e., the province of Tâmasnâ) was densely occupied.

The transition from one dynastic period to the other was usually marked by intense warfare between competing political entities. On the one hand, dynastic warfare caused massive destruction of cities and resulted in the corrosion of settled life. On the other hand, it promoted the development of military architecture, for example, the fortification of cities and the construction of fortresses. The twelfth-century chronicler al-Baydak (Lévi-Provençal 1928:218-221) reported that the Almoravids had built a series of strategically located fortresses to stop the advance of the Almohad army, and listed the names of 24 of them.[18] During periods of relative political stability, medieval fortresses played new roles. They were used to control long-distance trade routes and to monitor the movement of rebel tribal groups, especially those living in the mountains (the Rîf and the Atlas) or near major crossroads. The fortress of Amardjû, near the city of Banî Tâwdâ, functioned as an Almoravid military outpost to repel the raids of mountainous Ghumâra tribes (al-Idrîsî 1983:101; Anonymous 1958:141-142).

Few urban settlements survived the repetitive cycles of political turmoil that accompanied dynastic wars. Only 10 settlements in northern Morocco were occupied for eight centuries or longer[19] (Figure 5.5). Significantly, half of these settlements functioned as coastal entrepôts. Of 14 coastal entrepôts in northern Morocco, 11 (80%) were occupied for

[17] Population estimates for the cities of Sidjilmâsa and Dar'a were derived from Massignon (1906:148) based on information found in Leo Africanus and Marmol.

[18] These fortresses are: Al-Fallâg [al-Fallâdj], al-Kal'a, al-Wulga [al-Wuldja], Âmargû [Amardjû], Ânsâ-n-Îmâdîdan, Âsakkâ-n-Kamât, Âsbûr [Ashbûr], Âsrû of Banû 'Abd Allâh, Âssikâbû, Dây, Haylâna, Karnâtâ, Luggâga [Ludjdjâgha], Nafîs, Tâdlâ (also Hisn Tâkazûrart), Tâfarkaggûnt, Tâgrârt, Târûlûlat-(a)n-Îgadmîwan, Tâsanûlt, Tâsgamârt [Tâsghamârt], Tasgaymût, [Tasghaymût], Tâzagdarâ [Tâzaghdarâ], Tûnaktâyân, and Wîrkân. Only three Almoravid fortresses have been investigated: Tasghaymût, Tûnaktâyân, and Amardjû. In fact, most of the fortresses listed by al-Baydak are not yet adequately identified. For more details on medieval Moroccan fortifications, see Cressier 1995.

[19] The settlements in question are the following Pre-Idrisid and Idrisid sites: al-Djazîra (Gezira), Fez, Idjâdjîn, al-Kasr al-Kabîr, al-Kasr al-Saghîr, Khamîs Matghâra (Camis Metgara), Maghîla, Sabta, Salâ, and Tangier.

Table 5.3 Settlement Size Estimates for Selected Medieval Moroccan Cities Based on Documentary Evidence.

Number of Inhabitants	Settlement Name
More than 100,000	Fez and Marrakech.
50,000-100,000	No cities.
25,000-50,000	Tâza, Sabta (before A.D. 1415), Maknâs [a], Azammur (height), Tît (height), and Aghmât-Urîka.
10,000-25,000	Malîla, Tangier, al-Kasr al-Kabîr [Kasr 'Abd al-Karîm] (height), Salâ-Rabat, Safim [Asfî], Tît (decline), al-'Arâ'ish (?) (15th-16th A.D.), and Anfâ.
2,000-10,000	Bâdis, Tagaca [Tidjissâs], al-Kasr al-Kabîr [Kasr 'Abd al-Karîm] (decline), al-'Arâ'ish (12th-13th A.D.), Azammur (decline beginning of 16th A.D.), Tît (16th A.D.), Safru (?) [Safrawi], Cacaca (?) [Ghasâsâ], al-Mazamma (?), and Aghmât-Aylân (?).

Note : Data from Godinho (1947:134-135).

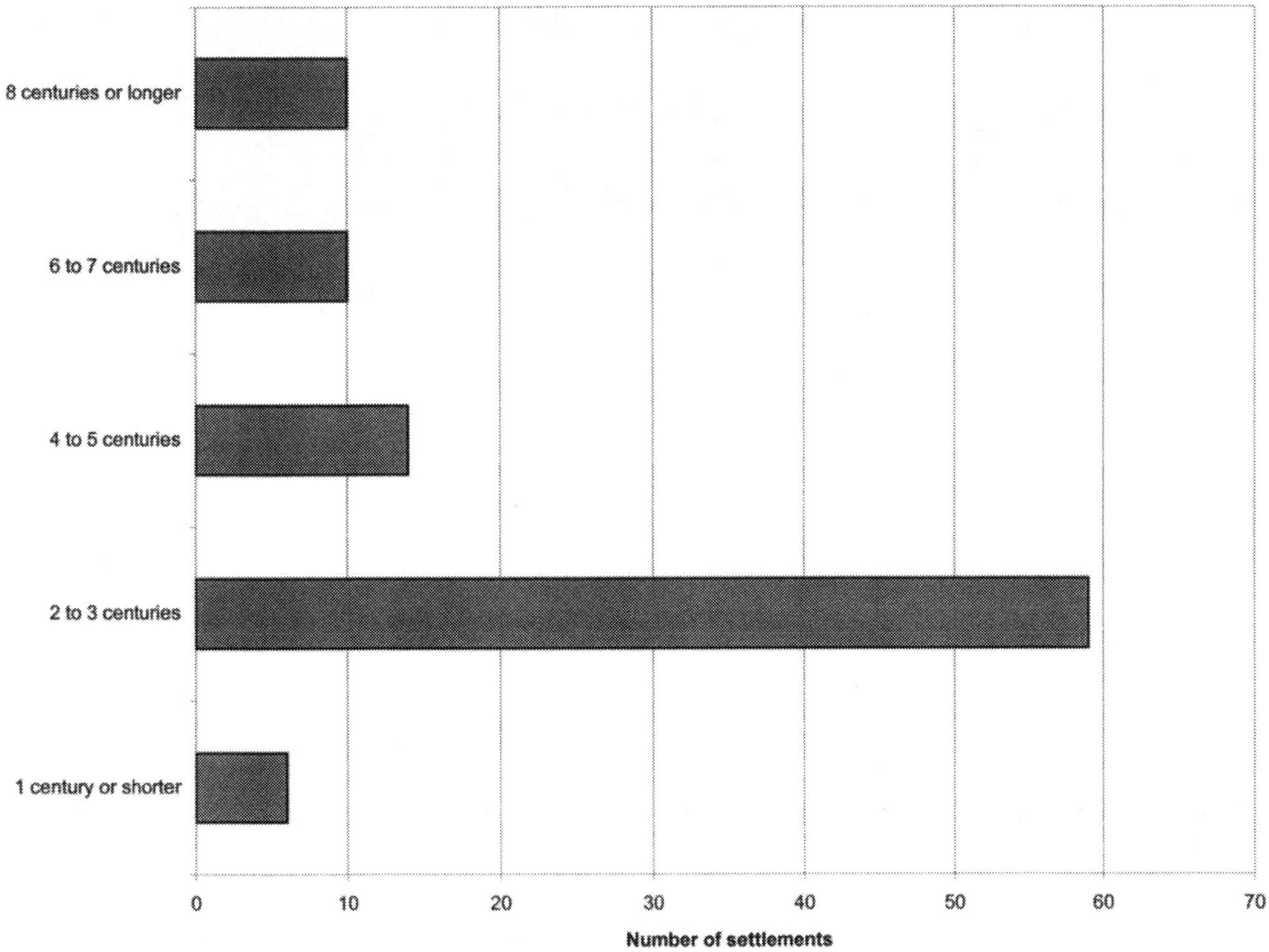

Figure 5.5 Distribution of Settlements by Length of Occupation (All Periods Combined).

more than seven centuries (Figure 5.7). All the coastal entrepôts in northern Morocco were founded prior to the Almoravid period. The shift in political economy that occurred during this period apparently triggered a change in the role of coastal entrepôts. Under the Idrisids, coastal entrepôts were economically and politically tied to provincial capitals (e.g., Buhayrat Aryagh functioned as the port of al-Basra). After the eleventh century coastal entrepôts assumed a greater importance. Dynastic control of long-distance trade offered them new economic opportunities. They became involved in a variety of mercantile activities, first under the watchful eye of state officials, but later as independent entities for their own benefit. Their economic autonomy from state control was key to their longevity.

My analysis of textual sources shows that medieval Moroccan urban networks declined continuously and irreversibly after the Idrisid period (Figure 5.8). The only

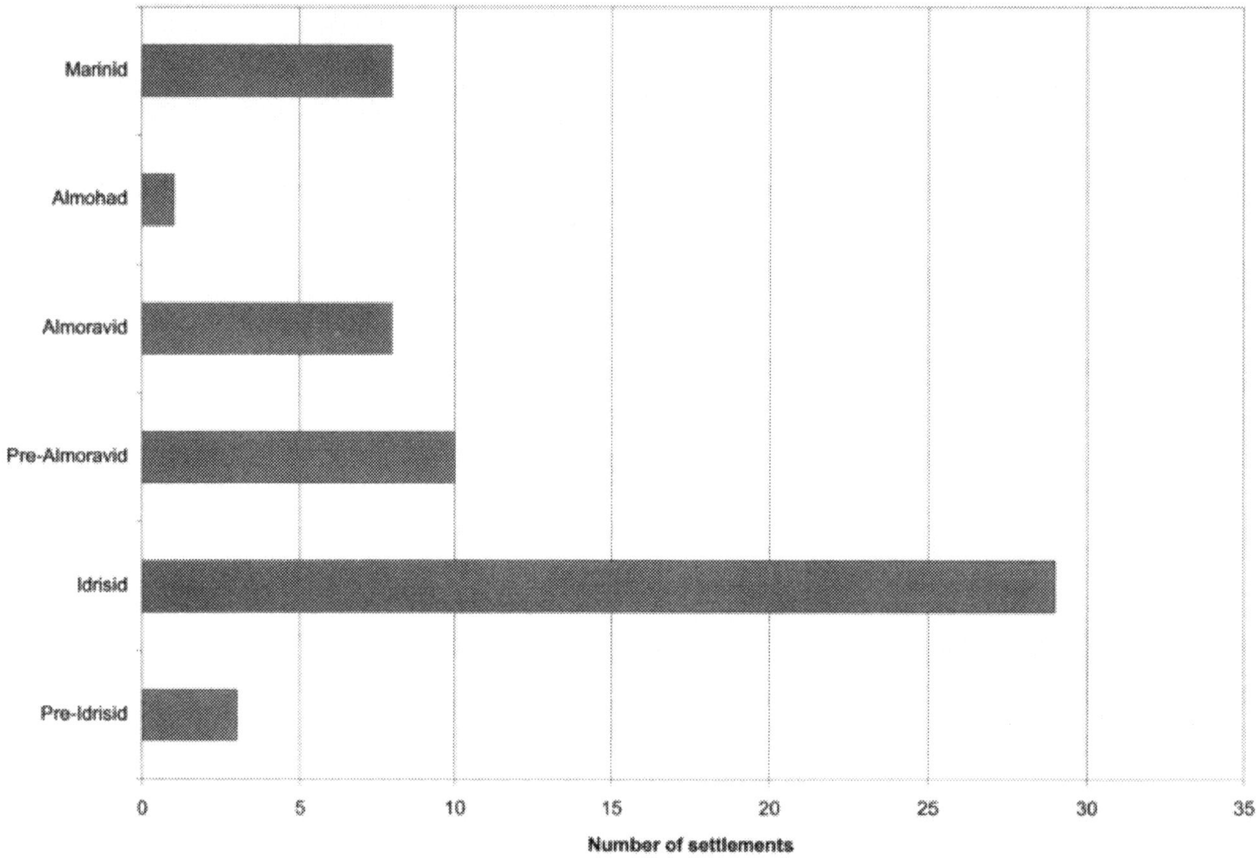

Figure 5.6 Distribution of Settlements Occupied Between Two to Three Centuries by Dynastic Period.

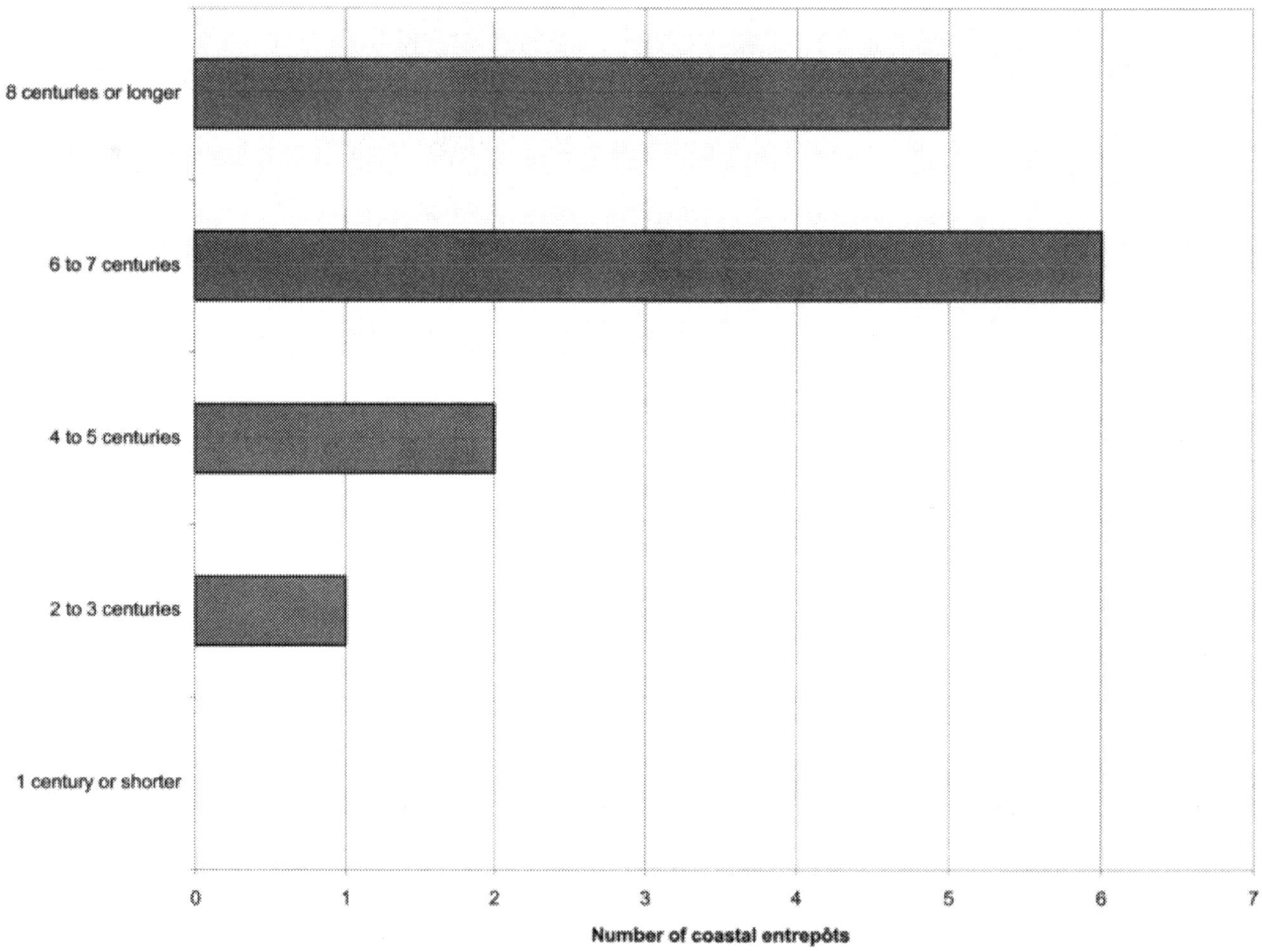

Figure 5.7 Distribution of Coastal Entrepôts by Length of Occupation (All Periods Combined).

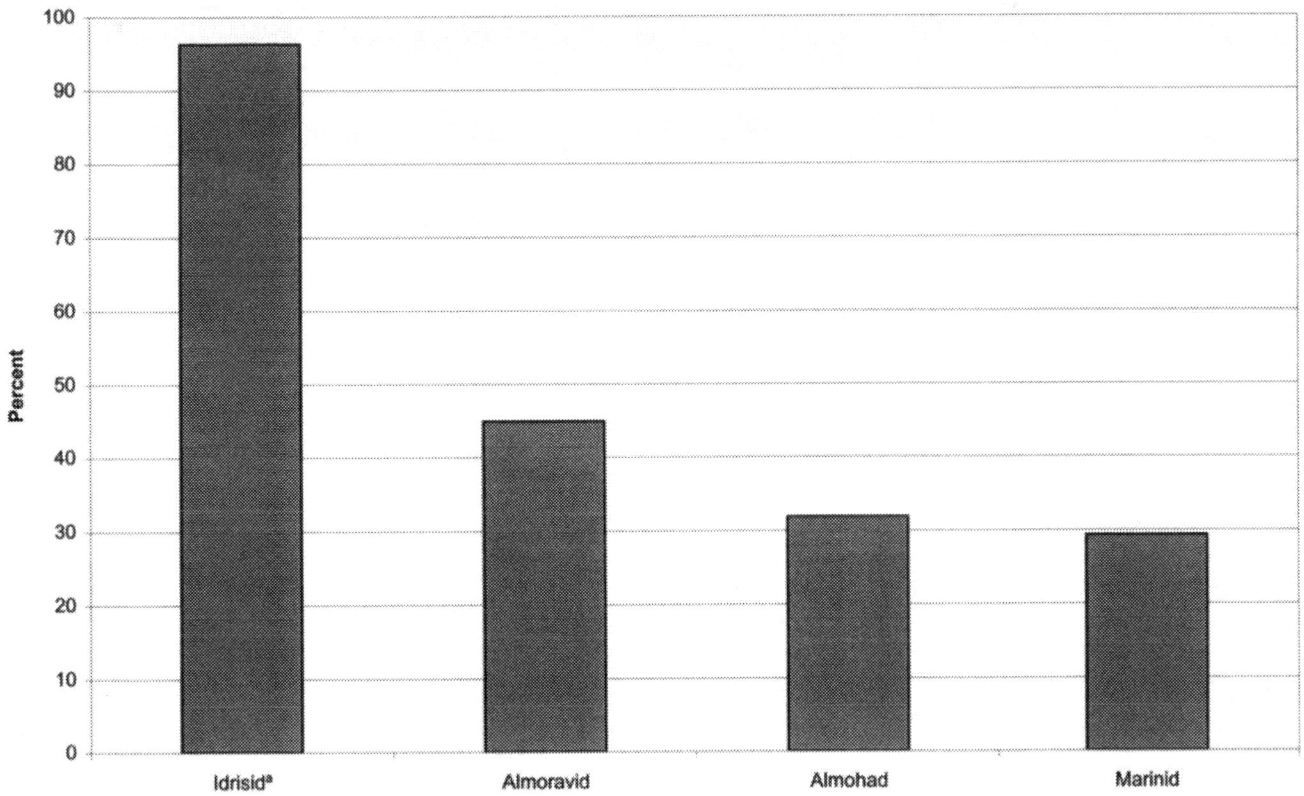

[a]pre-Idrisid, Idrisid, and pre-Almoravid periods combined.

Figure 5.8 Percent of Occupied Settlements by Dynastic Period.

exceptions were the dynastic capitals, such as Fez, Marrakech, and Ribâṯ al-Fatẖ (Rabat) which continued to grow through time. The Almoravid period marked the threshold when the number of abandoned or destroyed settlement outnumbered those that were still occupied. In the fifteenth century (Marinid period), only about 30% of all the original settlements in northern Morocco were still inhabited[20] (Figure 5.8).

In the fourteenth century, al-'Umarî (1927:162-166) listed only 26 cities as being the main urban settlements for the entire country.[21] In the sixteenth century, Leo Africanus pointed to a large-scale decline in settled life in several passages of his description of medieval Morocco: "Sur toute les collines de ce pays [the territory of Fez] on trouve de nombreux et très grands villages. Il est vrai qu'en raison des guerres passées les plaines sont peu habitées." (Leo Africanus 1956:169). In another passage, he wrote that: "Cette province [Azgẖâr] est une plaine dont le sol est excellent. Aussi a-t-elle été habitée par une population considerable et y exista-t-il des villes et des chateaux. Mais ces localités ont toutes été détruites à la suite d'une guerre dans les temps anciens et le sont restées. On n'en voit plus de traces aujourd'hui, à l'exception de quelques rares petites villes qui sont encore debout et habitées" (Leo Africanus 1956:250).

Although the texts cite warfare as the major cause of settlement abandonment, other factors, such as famine and epidemics, may have been equally devastating. Ibn Abî Zar' (1843: 21, 1860:48) mentioned the "great famine" of A.D. 1222-1240 which, in his terms, caused "the abandonment of the country." A plague in A.D. 1348-1350 may have caused significant reductions in populations and settled life. In Europe, the plague decimated between 1/8 and 2/3 of the population; similar estimates may be applied to medieval Morocco (Brignon et al. 1967:153). Episodes of famines and epidemics are often accompanied by riots and dissidence, which could have caused further settlement disruption.

The analysis of textual evidence also indicates that urban networks in medieval northern Morocco reached their fullest extent at a surprisingly early stage. The Idrisid period witnessed the highest number of newly founded settlements. A total of 43 settlements were founded, or at least mentioned for the first time in textual records, during this period (Figure 2.5). Although a large number of Idrisid sites were destroyed by the Almoravids, the few that remained were reoccupied and formed the backbone of medieval Moroccan urban networks.

Several settlements in northern Morocco were founded long before the Islamic period (e.g., Sala Colonia [Sẖâlla], Lixus [Tusẖummusẖ], Septem Fratres [Sabta], and Tingi [Ṯandjia]). Nevertheless, the majority of urban centers in northern Morocco were built by Islamic dynastic states. According to Leo Africanus (1956), the majority of cities in the northern provinces of Morocco (i.e., Fez, Azgẖâr, Tâmasnâ, and Habṯ) were founded during the Islamic period (Figure 5.9).

20 I assumed that a given settlement was abandoned if it is not mentioned in later sources.

21 These cities are: Agẖmât, al-'Arâ'isẖ, al-Kaṣr al-Sagẖîr, al-Mazamma, Anfâ, Asafî, Azammûr, Aṣîla, Bâdis, Fez, Gẖaṣâṣâ (al-Kudya al-Baydâ'), Kaṣr 'Abd al-Karîm, Maknâsa, Malîla, Marrakech, Ṣa, Sabta, Ṣafrawi, Salâ, Sidjilmâsa, Tangier, Tâzâ, Tâzûṯa, Tidjîsâs, Ṯîṯ, and Tiṯawîn.

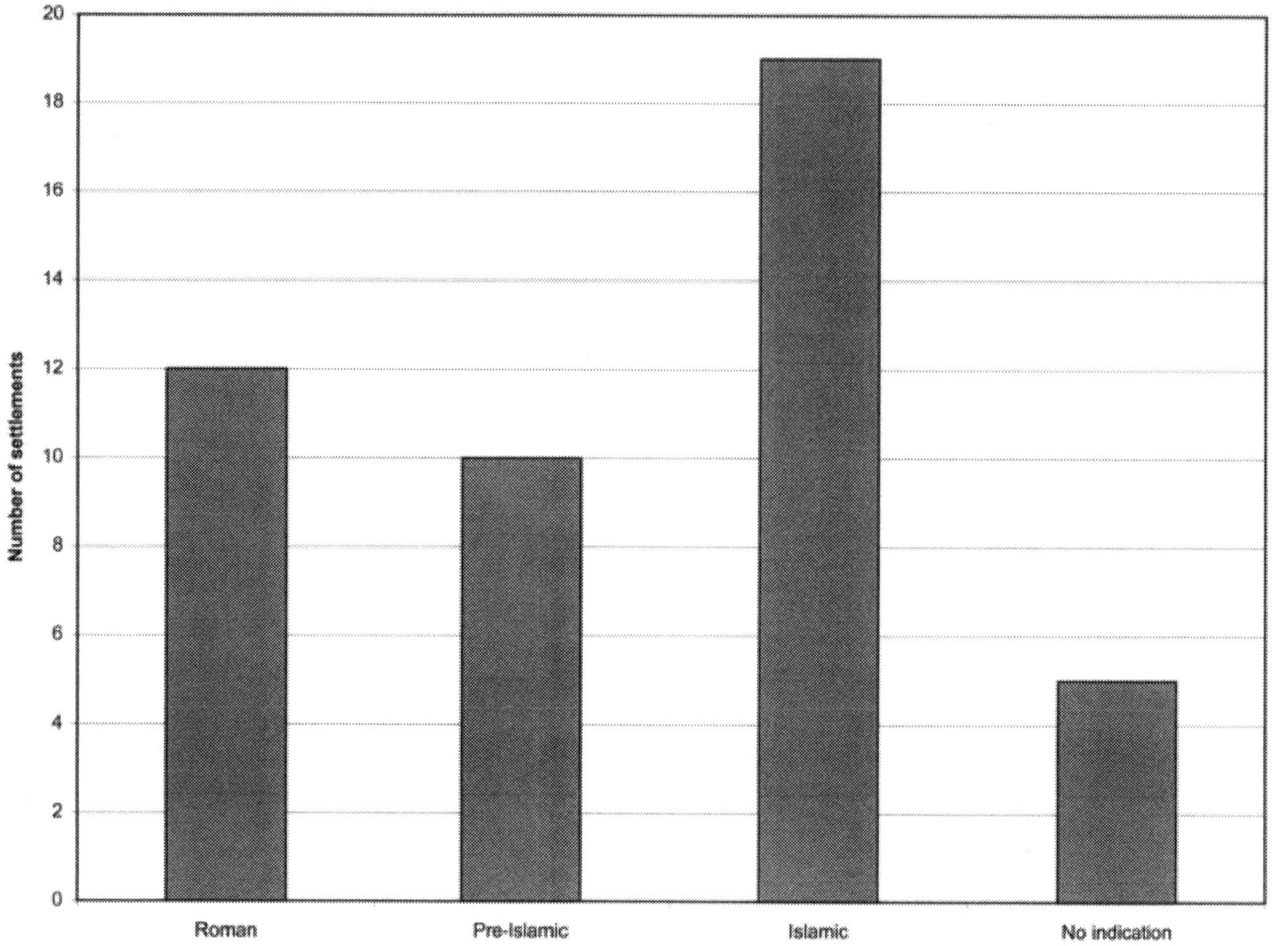

Figure 5.9 Distribution of Settlements in Northern Morocco by Founding Period (Based on Leo Africanus 1956).

Numismatic Evidence: Production and Spatial Distribution of Medieval Moroccan Mints

Numismatic evidence constitutes an important supplement to archaeological data and textual sources. In fact, for several medieval settlements (especially during the Idrisid period), it is the only source available. The two main references I used to document the production and spatial distribution of medieval Moroccan mints are Eustache (1970b, 1970-71) and Hazard (1952).

Eustache (1970b:96-101) lists 52 medieval Moroccan mints[22] dating from the Idrisid to the ʻAlawite periods and their locations (46 different locations). Each entry contains the mint's name, location (proposed or actual), and dynastic affiliation (i.e., the first dynasty that issued currency at the mint). Hazard (1952:328-344), on the other hand, provides an "index of mints" dating from the Almoravid to the Marinid periods. In this index, the coins (mostly dinars and dirhams) issued by individual mints are listed by year of emission and by dynastic affiliation. Each study (Eustache 1970b and Hazard 1952) contains a map of the mints discussed in the text. The graphs shown in this section were based on counts derived from the information found in Eustache's list of mints and Hazard's index of mints.

[22] This list includes the Idrisid mint of Tilimsân (modern Tlemcen in Algeria).

Idrisid Mints

According to numismatic evidence, the Idrisids struck their currency at more than 20 mints (Brethes 1939; Colin 1936; Eustache 1970b, 1970-71). In his influential study of Idrisid currency (*Corpus des Dirhams Idrissites et Contemporains: Etudes sur la numismatique et l'histoire Monétaire du Maroc*), Eustache (1970-71:105) listed 23 Idrisid-period mints, including Tilimsân in Algeria and two other mints for which no transliteration was proposed.[23]

As Table 5.4 shows, 16 mints were founded by the Idrisid dynasty: al-ʻÂliya, A<u>gh</u>mât, Amaʻdan, A<u>s</u>îla, Baht, al-Ba<u>s</u>ra, Ikam, Mrîra, Subû, Tâ<u>dj</u>râ<u>dj</u>ra (Tâgrâgra), Tahlît, War<u>gh</u>a, Warzî<u>gh</u>a, Wa<u>t</u>î<u>t</u>, Wâwmahnâ, and Waza<u>kk</u>ûr. Another six mints were not Idrisid foundations, but issued Idrisid currency: I<u>dj</u>arhân, <u>T</u>an<u>dj</u>a, Tilimsân, Tud<u>gh</u>a, Walîla, and Zîz (Eustache 1970b:101). The mint at Tud<u>gh</u>a issued both Idrisid and non-Idrisid dirhams (bearing the name of local princes). The Idrisids may have been allowed to mint their currency at Tud<u>gh</u>a after reaching an agreement with the local prince who controlled the mint (Eustache 1970-71:132-133).

It is not the concern of this research to delve into the corpus of numismatic evidence for each Idrisid mint. Instead, I will

[23] Eustache's list does not include *A<u>gh</u>mât*, which also issued Idrisid dirhams (Laallaoui 1993).

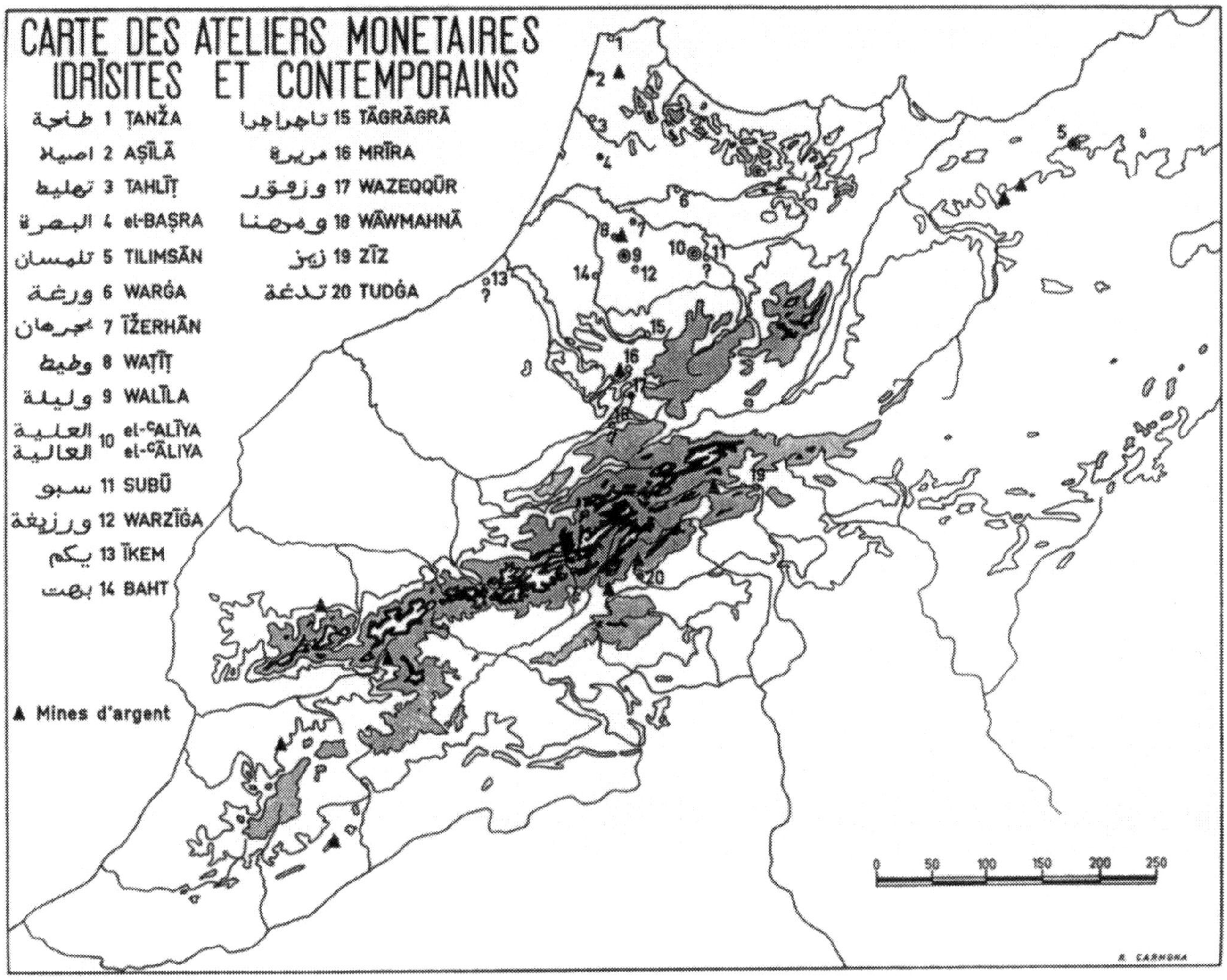

Figure 5.10 Map of Idrisid Minting Sites. (Source: Eustache 1970-71).

adopt a more global approach with an emphasis on the distribution of Idrisid mints and its implication for settlement patterns. The use of numismatic evidence to address settlement pattern issues is based on the assumption that the presence of a mint implies the presence of an urban center. There is no doubt that a mint was an important government facility; it was the location where wealth was converted into currency. A mint was also a center for propagating state ideology; the currency bears the name and the credo or emblem of the ruling authority.[24] Considering its economic and political importance, a mint had to be protected by a military garrison and some type of monumental defense features (Eustache 1970-71:110), and was likely situated within the perimeter of an urban center. The linkage of a mint with an urban center is supported by toponymic data. Nearly half of the Idrisid minting sites are named after watercourses[25] (e.g., Ikam, Subû, Wargha, Zîz), which, while not absolutely required for the functioning of a minting facility, are critical for an urban center. I would suggest that the names of the Idrisid mints were, in fact, the names of urban settlements located near rivers to insure a permanent water supply for the city.

From a purely numismatic point of view, the inscription of the terms *madîna* (city) and *ma'din* (mine/mint) on a number of Idrisid dirhams offers additional support to my argument. On an Idrisid dirham minted at Waṯîṯ in 200 A.H. (A.D. 815-816), the mint name was inscribed as *ma'din Waṯîṯ*. On a number of dirhams minted the same year by Idrîs II at al-'Aliya, Mrîra, and Wazakkûr, the mint names were preceded by the words *madînat Idrîs* (the city of Idrîs II). As Eustache (1970-71:160) argued, this is evidence that the term *ma'din* (mine/mint) was used in parallel to the term *madîna* (city) to refer to a foundation by Idrîs II. The mint names inscribed on Idrisid dirhams were, in fact, the names of actual urban settlements and not those of geographically isolated minting facilities.

It is unclear, however, why a number of Idrisid mints/cities are not mentioned in textual sources. As Table 5.4 shows, there are no references in the textual record to Ama'dan, Idjarhân, Ikam, Mrîra, Waṯîṯ, and Wâwmahnâ. It is possible that these mints were located in small urban centers that were intentionally ignored by medieval authors, but it is curious that the presence of a mint would not have warranted

24 See for example, Ben Romdhane 1978 for a study of the ideological aspects of the Almohad currency.

25 See Eustache's list for details (Eustache 1970b:96-100). Tahlît, although not a name of a watercourse, is the name of a city that al-Baydak mentioned near the Lûkkûs River (Lévi-Provençal 1928:149).

Table 5.4 Idrisid Minting Sites

Name of Mint	Idrisid Founding	Textual Evidence	Identification Status
Aghmat[a]	Yes?	Yes	Yes
al-'Âliya (Fez)	Yes	Yes	Yes
al-Basra	Yes	Yes	Yes
Ama'dan	Yes	No	No
Asila	Yes	Yes	Yes
Baht	Yes	Yes	No
Idjarhan	No	No	No
Ikam	Yes	No	No
Mrîra	Yes	No	No
Subu	Yes	Yes	No
Tadjrâdjrâ	Yes	Yes	No
Tahlît	Yes	Yes	No
Tandja	No	Yes	Yes
Tilimsân	No	Yes	Yes
Tudgha	No	Yes	No
Walîla	No	Yes	Yes
Wargha	Yes	Yes	No
Warzîgha	Yes	Yes	No
Watît	Yes	No	No
Wâwmahna	Yes	No	No
Wazakkur	Yes	Yes	No
Zîz	No	Yes	No

Note: Data from Eustache (1970, 1970-71).
[a] Laallaoui (1993).

the mention of the urban center where it was housed. It is equally possible that these particular mint names referred to government minting facilities within urban centers. Mrîra, although not mentioned in any textual record, was definitely an urban center since an Idrisid dirham contains the following inscription: *Mrîra madînat Idrîs* (Mrîra the city of Idrîs II). Oddly, Fez and al-'Âliya are two names for the same city, but there is no single Idrisid dirham with the name of Fez on it, and no single textual reference to the name of al-'Âliya.[26]

Except for al-Basra and Walîla, there is little archaeological evidence on Idrisid minting sites. In fact, the majority of Idrisid mints are yet to be adequately identified and investigated. Figure 5.10 shows a map of Idrisid mints based on Eustache's work. Eustache based his identifications primarily on toponymic data, such as the names of watercourses and topographic landmarks (Eustache 1970b:96-100). Despite its tentative nature, the map of Idrisid mints points to a number of patterns.

Most Idrisid mints are concentrated in northwestern Morocco. This was the location of most Idrisid strongholds. Walîla was the Idrisid's first base of operations, and Fez was the capital of the state. The population of this region showed an allegiance to the Idrisid dynasty from its inception (e.g., the Awraba tribes of Walîla). Northwestern Morocco was also a rich agricultural region. Considering the importance of agricultural surplus to the Idrisid finance system, it is natural that the Idrisids maintained strong control over this region.

Figure 5.10 shows two areas with no Idrisid minting sites: the Rîf (Northeastern Morocco) and the Tâmasnâ (the Atlantic plains between the Bû Ragrâg River and the Um al-Rabî' River).[27] These two areas were outside Idrisid control. The Rîf and Tâmasnâ were controlled by two independent political entities, respectively, the kingdom of Nakûr and the kingdom of Barghwâta. The former was founded by Salîh Ibn Mansûr in A.D. 809 and lasted until A.D. 917. The second was founded by Salîh Ibn Tarîf in A.D. 744. The kingdom of Barghwâta remained independent from dynastic control until it was eradicated by the Almoravids.

The map of Idrisid mints also shows that the southern region of the Idrisid state (al-Sûs al-Aksâ) was rich in mining resources, especially silver mines. There is no numismatic evidence for any minting activities in this area, although this is not conclusive proof that Idrisid minting sites did not exist in the region; there could be a number of Idrisid dirhams that are yet to be discovered. Overall, the available evidence points to the rarity of Idrisid currency in southern Morocco. In a passage by al-Bakrî describing al-Sûs al-Aksâ (southern Morocco), he notes that broken pieces of jewelry were used as silver currency because minted dirhams were rare[28] (al-Bakrî 1965:308).

Post-Idrisid Dynastic Mints

Numismatic evidence for post-Idrisid dynastic states offers additional information for understanding medieval Moroccan political economy and settlement systems. Dynastic states struck their currency at 16 known mints[29] (Figure 5.11). Except for Fez (al-'Aliya), Tudgha, and Tandja, all of these mints were founded after the tenth century (the end of the Idrisid period). Many Idrisid mints may have been abandoned as the result of the emergence of a new political economy (wealth finance).

In contrast to Idrisid mints, which depended primarily on silver, post-Idrisid dynastic mints were based on gold. It appears that proximity to gold trade networks was more important than proximity to silver resources.[30] The flow of

[26] The proof that al-'Âliya and Fez refer to the same location is found in an Idrisid dirham inscribed with the expression: "*al-'Âliya madînat Idrîs*" (Eustache 1970-71:146).

[27] The mints of Taghasâ and Nakûr in the Rîf region did not mint any Idrisid dirhams. They did, however, issue 'Abbasid and Umayyad currencies, respectively.

[28] In the same passage, al-Bakrî (1965:308) added an intriguing piece of information in which he referred to a mithkâl (gold currency) named after a mint administrator!

[29] Only mints found in Morocco are discussed in this section. For a complete list of dynastic mints in the Maghrib and al-Andalus, see Hazard 1952:328-344.

[30] However, post-Idrisid dynastic states did not totally abandon the exploitation of mining resources, especially silver and copper (Rosenberger 1970a, 1970b).

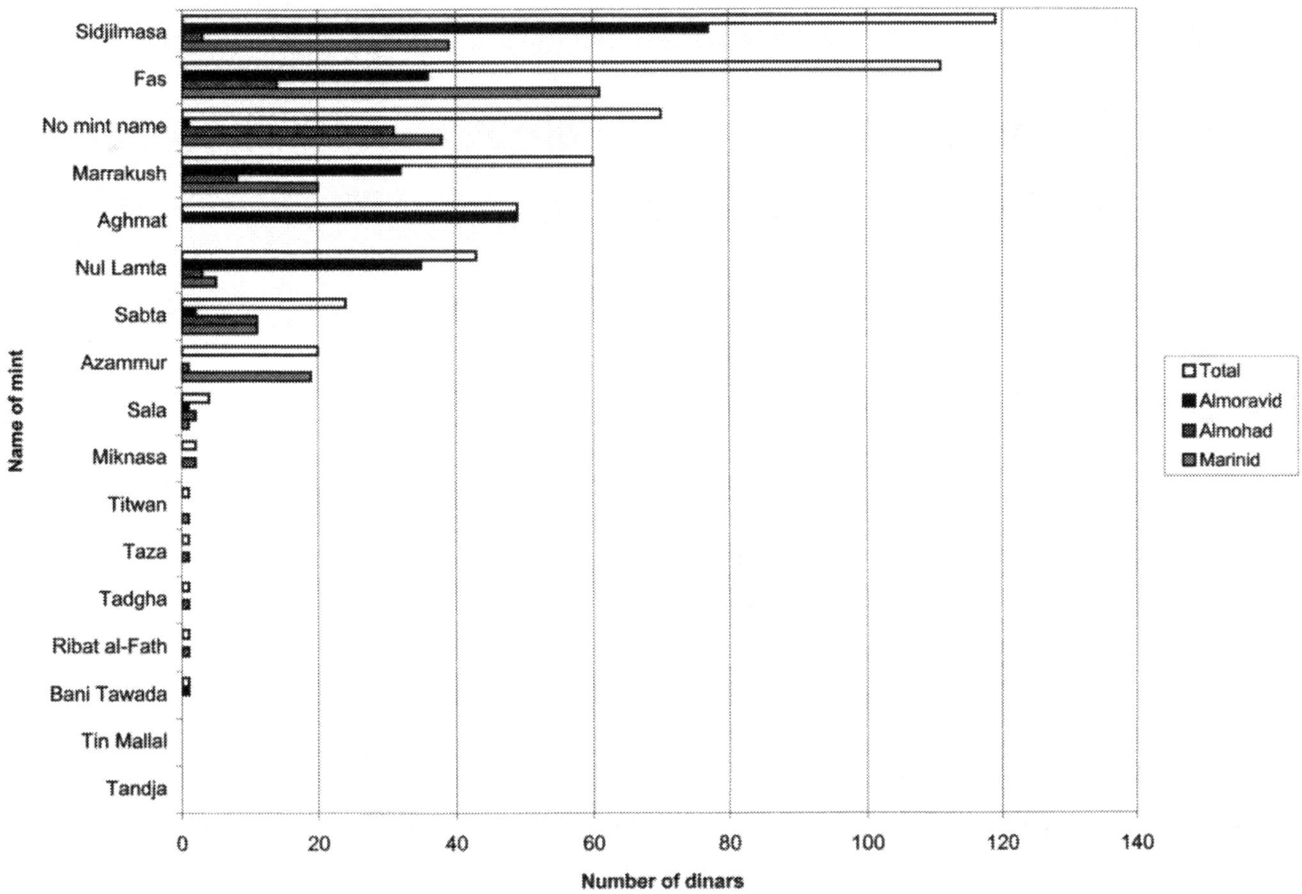

Figure 5.11 Medieval Moroccan Dynastic Mints and Their Gold Currency Production.

gold allowed Moroccan mints to issue large amounts of dinars (gold currency), which replaced the dirham as the unit of state currency.[31] In fact, the dinar became the unit of currency for all international transactions. Several medieval authors praised the high quality of gold currency issued by Moroccan dynastic states, especially the Almoravids and the Almohads.

As Figure 5.11 shows, the mints that produced most dinars were located in major inland dynastic capitals. The minting sites of Sidjilmâsa, Fez, Marrakech, and Aghmât contributed nearly 70% of the total number of dinars issued in Morocco. Sidjilmâsa was the gate to sub-Saharan gold[32] and Fez, Marrakech, and Aghmât were the most prominent hubs of long-distance trade in the Mediterranean basin. The four mints with the next highest minting activity are prominent coastal entrepôts (Nûl Lamta,[33] Sabta, Azammûr, and Salâ); these contributed nearly 20% of the total number of dinars issued in Morocco.

The overall picture that emerges from the numismatic information is that the two prominent urban forms of post-Idrisid dynastic states (inland dynastic capitals and coastal entrepôts) played a leading role in the new political economy by converting sub-Saharan gold into wealth (in the form of gold currency). It is somewhat surprising that little numismatic evidence is associated with the mints of Ribât al-Fath (Rabat) and Tandja (Tangier) which were, respectively, a prominent dynastic capital and a leading coastal entrepôt at this time.

The large quantity of dinars issued by the Almoravid dynasty is yet another indication of its prominent role in the long-distance gold trade. The Almoravid dinars constitute nearly 50% of the total corpus of dinars known to date[34] (Figure 5.12). The Marinids also minted considerable quantities of dinars. The relatively low amount of known Almohad dinars does not necessarily reflect a decrease in gold trade activities; instead, it may be due to the small number of Almohad coins discovered so far. The Almohads maintained the largest number of dynastic mints (13 mints)[35] after the Idrisids (Figure 5.12), indicating that they actually processed considerable quantities of sub-Saharan gold.

The large quantities of gold coins struck at dynastic mints suggest that the revenues to support local governorships were collected locally from passing caravans, rather than being distributed centrally through the state capital (Marrakech and, subsequently, Fez) (Boone et al. 1990:635).

31 The dinar is minted in gold, the dirham in silver, and the *fals* (smallest denomination) in copper (Miles 1965a, 1965b; Udovitch 1965).

32 There is an important passage by al-Mas'ûdî (A.D. 956) in which he states that "All the gold obtained (from the Western Sûdân) is struck into coins in the city of Sidjilmâsa" (Kamal 1926-1951:628, cited in Messier 1974:38).

33 For a discussion of the role of medieval Nûl Lamta in maritime trade, see Picard 1996:50-51.

34 For a detailed discussion of the Almoravid gold currency, see Messier 1974, 1980.

35 Based on data from Hazard (1952:328-344).

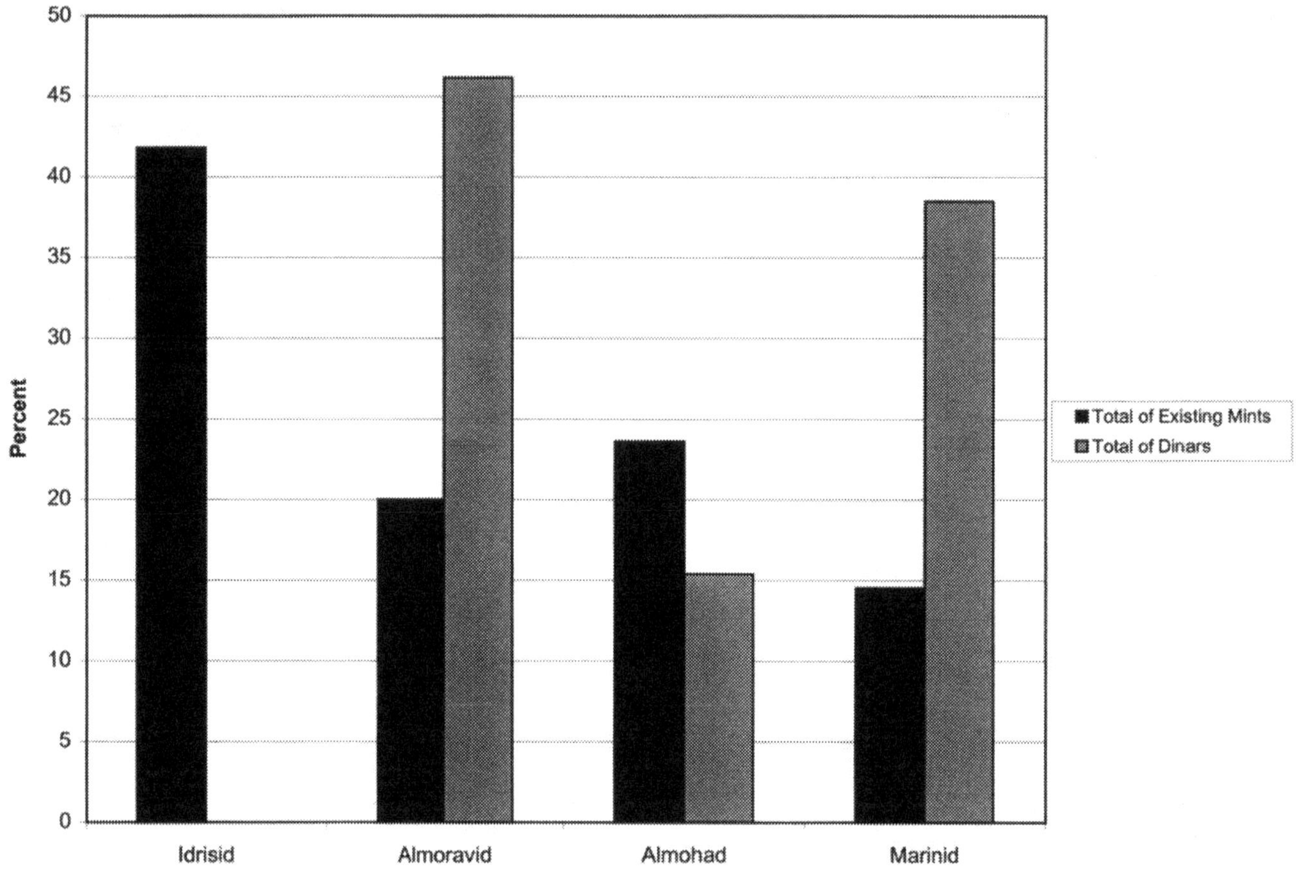

Figure 5.12 Distribution of Minting Sites and Dinars by Dynastic Period.

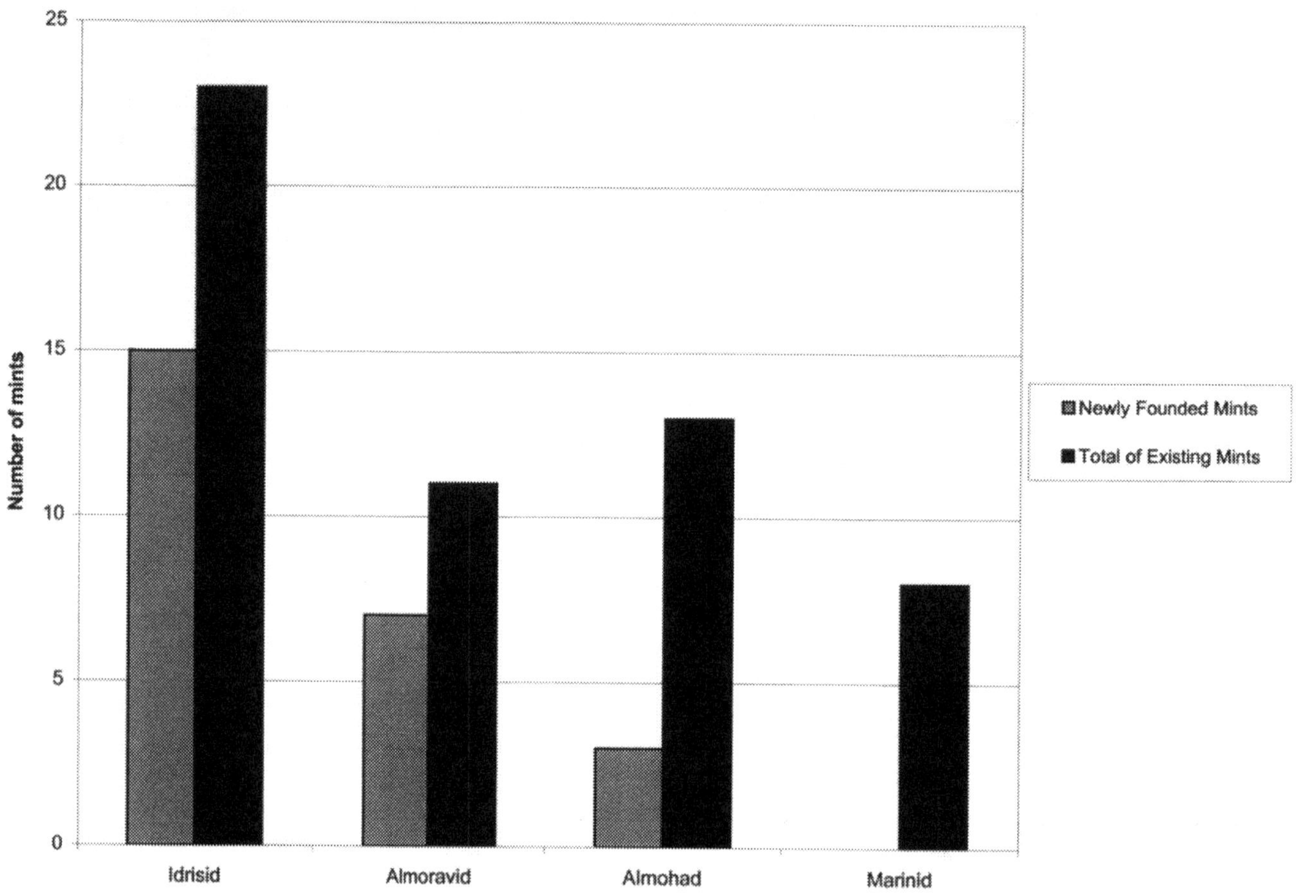

Figure 5.13 Distribution of Minting Sites by Dynastic Period.

Textual sources are not clear as to how state revenues were distributed at the central level. The only explicit textual reference to this is that the Almohads appointed a *Sâhib al-ashghâl*, or the equivalent of the minister of finance, who was based in Marrakech, the state capital (i.e., an officer of the central government) (Hopkins 1958:50-51; Laroui 1995:170). At the provincial level, a *mushrif* (local administrator) was in charge of the apparatus of local customs and, possibly, the mint (*sikka*).

This examination of minting sites by dynastic period indicates that the number of newly founded dynastic mints decreased after the Idrisid period (Figure 5.13). The Idrisids established the largest number of new mints known to date[36] (15 mints), but only a few were reused in later periods. The Marinids did not found any minting sites of their own, but instead reused existing ones. It is the Almoravid dynasty that laid the foundation of the minting network for the post-Idrisid period (seven newly founded mints).

It is possible that the Idrisids built anew (and reused) the largest number of mints because their state was politically and economically fragmented into several semi-independent principalities. Subsequent states, on the other hand, maintained fewer mints because their system of government and their political economy was more elaborate and more centralized. It is also possible that post-Idrisid dynastic states intentionally reduced the number of their minting sites so that they could effectively monitor the process of converting gold into currency.

Discussion

In this discussion, I focus on one main issue: were the results/patterns presented in this chapter affected by the inherent limitations and biases of the textual and numismatic sources? Textual and numismatic sources strongly point to an intense process of urbanization during the early Islamic period in Morocco. Based on these sources, there were 80 settlements in medieval northern Morocco between the pre-Idrisid and pre-Almoravid periods (Table 5.1). More than half of them (43 settlements) were occupied during the Idrisid period (or at least was mentioned by sources dating to this period). From the Almoravid period onward, only 19 new settlements were added to the list of medieval settlements in northern Morocco (Table 5.1).

It is possible that the high number of settlements associated with the early Islamic period in Morocco (i.e., prior to the Almoravid period) is due to the nature of the textual sources examined. All the texts documenting this time period were written by geographers of the *Masâlik wa-l-mamâlik* school: Ibn Khurdâdhbah (A.D. 885), al-Ya'kûbî (A.D. 889-890), Ibn al-Fakîh (A.D. 903), al-Istakhrî (A.D. 951), Ibn Hawkal (A.D. 988), al-Mukaddasî (A.D. 946-988), and al-Bakrî (A.D. 1094). The main subject matter of this school was the inventory of cities and the distances between stage-posts and was compiled initially for postal services and later for merchants and travelers (see Chapter 2 for more details). For example, al-Mukaddasî (1950:7-9) listed 41 cities within the district of Fez alone. Later geographers were less concerned with site inventory than with providing in-depth descriptions of major cities.

Numismatic evidence also supported the existence of a large number of early Islamic sites in northern Morocco. The list of known Idrisid settlements (43 settlements) was increased by including 13 minting sites, some of them known exclusively from numismatic evidence.

It is legitimate to ask whether the settlement counts associated with pre-Almoravid periods were somewhat "inflated" compared with those of later periods. In other words, was the transition from the Idrisid to the Almoravid period accompanied by a less radical decrease in mid-sized settlements (Class V) than shown in Figure 5.3? If all the cities mentioned exclusively in the *Masâlik wa-l-mamâlik* lists of the ninth and tenth centuries (17 settlements)[37] and all the sites known exclusively from numismatic evidence (8 Idrisid mints)[38] are excluded, the graph in Figure 5.3 displays a less marked decline. The total number of Class V settlements of the early Islamic period (i.e., pre-Idrisid, Idrisid, and pre-Almoravid periods) is reduced from 54 to 29.

Even with the exclusion of these 25 "questionable" sites (17 sites of the *Masâlik wa-l-mamâlik* lists and 8 Idrisid mints), there is still a strong case for a significant decrease in urban development from the early to the later Islamic periods. The total number of Idrisid sites (i.e., founded during the Idrisid period or mentioned by authors of the ninth and tenth centuries) is still twice as high as that of the Almoravid period (18 sites vs. 9 sites). Likewise, the total number of early Islamic sites (i.e., pre-Idrisid, Idrisid, and pre-Almoravid sites) in northern Morocco is still significantly larger than that of later Islamic sites (55 sites vs. 19 sites).

These results indicate the presence of a very active phase of urban development during the early Islamic period in northern Morocco compared with later periods. They are further supported by a statement made by Terrasse more than 50 years ago: "Jusqu'aux Idrissides le Maroc du Nord semble avoir conservé ses cités romaines. Des Idrissides aux Almoravides les créations se multiplièrent: Idrissides, Miknasa et Zénètes furent tous des fondateurs de villes: en deux siécles le Maroc du Nord renouvela presque complètement son équipements urbain" (Terrasse 1947a:45). More recent literature on medieval Moroccan urbanism also indicates intense urbanization during the Idrisid period compared with later periods (Cressier et al. 1998:313; Garcia-Arenal and Manzano Moreno 1998:259, 264, 276; Rosenberger 1998:229, 236).

36 Excluding Tilimsân, Aghmât, and two other Idrisid mints for which no transliteration was proposed by Eustache (1970b:101, 1970-71:175-176).

37 These cities are: Balash, Djarmâna, Fankûr, Ghuzza, al-Hadjîr, al-Djâhid, Kal'at Shamît, al-Khadra, Madînat Djabal Zâlâgh, Madrâka, Malhas, Matrûka, Mudrîka, Tadjrâdjra, Tâwarat, Wargha, and Zallûl.

38 These mints are: Baht, Idjarhân, Subû, Tadjrâdjra, Tahlît, Wargha, Warzîgha, and Watît.

One last point needs to be made: that is, the disparity between the picture depicted by textual and numismatic evidence and that depicted by archaeological research. In contrast to textual and numismatic evidence, which points to a settlement pattern dominated by early Islamic sites, archaeological investigations indicate that only the al-Basra's hinterland sites can be confidently identified as early Islamic sites (see Chapter 6). The difficulty to identify early Islamic sites in the archaeological record can be explained in several ways. Most important of all is that early Islamic sites are hard to recognize archaeologically because the sequence of Islamic ceramics is poorly understood (see Chapter 3). Even a site as important as al-Basra would be hard to date with surface data alone because of the type of ceramics found on the surface, which consist mostly of commonware pottery and no "index fossils." This situation is less likely to occur in the case of a late medieval site; the ceramics will be relatively easier to date, and there is a higher probability that more architectural remains will be found and tentatively dated.

As shown in Figure 2.5, during the early Islamic period (especially the Idrisid period) the number of settlements that are known to exist historically but have not yet been identified by archaeologists exceeds that of settlements known from both archaeology and documentary evidence. The difference between these two categories of settlements (identified vs. unidentified) is less marked for the post-Idrisid periods.

Early Islamic sites may be harder to locate archaeologically because many of them are smaller in size; when they were abandoned and/or destroyed, they disappeared from the archaeological record faster than would larger sites. Several medieval sites in Morocco were literally dismantled by centuries of quarrying. The most vivid example of this process is the site of al-Basra. Of a 2.05 km of fortifications enclosing an area of 30 ha, only a heavily damaged portion of about 220 m still stands. Al-Basra's city walls would have disappeared completely if archaeologists had not intervened recently. Although al-Basra was a large medieval city (it had ten gates and a congregational mosque), it would have been relatively hard to identify archaeologically, even with the assistance of textual and numismatic evidence, if the city walls had disappeared completely and its toponym had been forgotten. It is likely that a large number of early medieval sites disappeared from the archaeological record because they were dismantled, their location deserted or reoccupied by rural populations, and their toponyms forgotten.

In the absence of a regional and long-term archaeological survey of northern Morocco, textual and numismatic evidence offers important insights on medieval Moroccan urbanism. There is no doubt that the picture as it emerged from these sources of evidence will be modified as more archaeological data come to light. The examination of more textual sources, more numismatic data, and more archaeological evidence - as it becomes available - will hopefully lend more credence to the arguments presented here.

Chapter 6

THE PROVINCIAL CAPITAL OF AL-BASRA AND ITS HINTERLAND: A STUDY OF LOCAL EXCHANGE AND COMMUNITY INTERACTION

In this chapter, I investigate an important aspect of the Idrisid political economy, namely local exchange and community interaction. The Idrisid agrarian-based political economy produced a multitiered and hierarchical settlement system; Fez, the dynastic state capital, functioned as the core of the system and was surrounded by a number of provincial capitals that controlled important agricultural land. Smaller towns and hinterland villages surrounded each of these provincial capitals. Along with relatively large-scale regional exchange systems between the provincial capitals, small local exchange systems, involving each provincial capital and its surrounding communities, also were in operation.

In order to investigate local exchange networks between al-Basra and its hinterland, I used chemical characterization of ceramics by instrumental neutron activation analysis (INAA). The chemical signature of archaeological specimens from al-Basra was used as a reference for identifying chemical groupings within the regional data. The study consisted of 145 samples collected from 15 hinterland sites in al-Basra's region (Table 6.1; Figure 3.2), 114 samples from al-Basra itself, and 62 samples collected by Benco from traditional potters working in northern Morocco today.

This research is based on the premise that al-Basra and its hinterland were involved in a local exchange system, in which pottery was a widely exchanged commodity. The concept of local exchange is used here to refer to the movement of goods or services or both within the context of a single settlement system (Johnson 1975:285-286). Although there is ample textual evidence that commodities other than pottery were exchanged between the city of al-Basra and its hinterland, I focus exclusively on pottery for two reasons: (1) pottery is relatively easy to trace to a single source or source zone, and (2) pottery survives, unlike other commodities (e.g., cotton, flax, cereals, and dairy products) that are perishable and, therefore, harder to recover and/or trace archaeologically. Both documentary and ethnoarchaeological evidence indicate that pottery was sold in markets along with other commodities. In other words, there is no reason to believe that the mechanisms of pottery distribution were entirely different from those of other commodities. Based on this observation, I assume that the mechanisms of pottery exchange (derived from archaeological and ethnoarchaeological evidence) reflect those of other commodities (described in textual records).

Al-Basra was an important pottery production center as attested to by the presence of two pottery kilns and large quantities of excavated ceramic material, including a number of wasters. More than 100,000 potsherds were recovered from the site during the first two seasons alone[1] (Benco 1987:62; Benco, in press). Production surplus was exchanged with neighboring villages. There is no evidence (e.g., presence of kilns or wasters) that hinterland communities manufactured their own wheelmade pottery using the same clay sources as al-Basra potters. Considering the small size of the hinterland villages (Appendix E), it may have been more cost effective for them to procure their pottery from al-Basra that producing their own wheelmade utilitarian ware.

The aim of the INAA study was to determine if the pottery collected at hinterland sites might have been produced at al-Basra. If the chemical composition of hinterland ceramics was similar to that of al-Basra's pottery, one could argue that

[1] Regardless of possible breakage rates differences, this is a very large quantity if compared, for example, to the "22,000 ceramic pieces (intact and shards)" recovered at the important archaeological site of Siḏjilmâsa in three field seasons (Lightfoot and Miller 1996:88; see also Messier 1997).

Table 6.1 Hinterland Sites Included in INAA Study

Site Number	Site Name	No. of Specimens	Basra Core[a]	
			No. of Specimens	*Percent*[b]
ARB2	al-Ghzalat	10	9	90
ARB7	Bhalla	10	5	50
ARB8	Jahjouka	10	9	90
ARB13	Sidi Bou Douma	10	4	40
ARB15	Kudyat Srafah	10	9	90
ARB18	Ketama	10	10	100
LLM1	Shkayfa	10	10	100
LLM4	Frigidae	5	4	80
LLM5	Sidi an-Niyya	10	9	90
LLM8	Sidi Ahmed Bourziguine	10	8	80
LLM9	el-Arab	10	10	100
LLM10	Kudyat Sma	10	10	100
LLM14	Sidi Yssef	15	12	80
MBK1[c]	al-'Asimi	5	3	60
MBS2	Douar Riah	10	6	60
Total		145	118	_

[a] Basra Core refers to the main chemical group identified in this study.

[b] Percent of the total number of specimens submitted.

[c] This site is not shown on Figure 3.2. It is located at about 21 km southeast of al-Basra.

al-Basra served as a major pottery production center, as well as an important distribution center.

Al-Basra offers an ideal setting for using INAA to investigate local exchange and community interaction. The site is relatively well documented historically. It was the object of numerous textual descriptions by various medieval geographers and chroniclers (Appendix B). Moreover, during the last 20 years, several seasons of archaeological investigations at al-Basra have substantially enhanced our understanding of the site and the Idrisid period in general (Benco 1987, 1990, 1994, 1995b, in press; Redman 1983, 1983-84). Finally, and most importantly, al-Basra is one of the few Islamic sites for which compositional data are available (Benco and Blackman in preparation, 1998). Thanks to the generosity of Nancy Benco, I was able to incorporate the al-Basra data, along with the ethnographic database, into my analyses.

This chapter is composed of three main components: (1) a historical-archaeological overview on al-Basra, (2) a presentation of INAA methodology and al-Basra INAA results, and (3) a discussion of the Idrisid local exchange system as reflected by al-Basra INAA results on the one hand, and historical and ethnoarchaeological evidence on the other.

Al-Basra: A Brief Overview

The city of al-Basra is located in northern Morocco at about 40 km from the Atlantic coast (Figure 1.1). Al-Basra was founded by the Idrisid dynasty around A.D. 800. After the death of Idrîs II, the Idrisid state was partitioned into a number of semi-independent principalities, each governed by one of his sons (Eustache 1970a). Al-Basra served as the provincial capital of an important agricultural region. The political history of al-Basra was a turbulent one, due to competition over power between the various descendents of the Idrisids on the one hand, and between regional powers, namely, the Fatimids and the Umayyads, on the other (Benco 1987:16-28; Eustache 1955:228-234, 1970-71:118-122; Yver 1960). Archaeological evidence suggests that the city was probably abandoned sometime in the late eleventh or the twelfth century (Benco 1987:16).

There is a relatively large corpus of textual sources on medieval al-Basra (Appendix B). Documentary evidence points to al-Basra as a prominent provincial capital in northern Morocco. Al-Bakrî (1965:216-217) states that the city "surpasse toutes les localités voisines par l'étendue de ses pâturages et le nombre de ses troupeaux." Ibn Abî Zar' (1860:130) referred to al-Basra as an Idrisid capital: "Leur [speaking of the Idrisids] domination s'étendit depuis le Sous el-Aksa jusqu'à la ville d'Oran, et ils eurent pour [dynastic] capitale Fès, et plus tard El-Basra." Along the same lines, Abû al-Fidâ (1848:184-185) states that: "Le chef-lieu de la province était autrefois Basra... Après la destruction de la ville, le chateau de 'Abd al-Karîm (al-Kasr al-Kabîr) prit le rang de capitale."

Textual evidence also documents trade between al-Basra and nearby cities and distant regions (e.g., Ifrîkiya) (Ibn Hawkal 1938-39:76, 1967:83). Some of al-Basra's production was transported via the Lukkûs River to Tushummush (Ibn Hawkal 1842:192). This was al-Basra's second coastal entrepôt; Mûlây Bû Salhâm (medieval Buhayrat Ariagh) served as an earlier coastal entrepôt for the city (Eustache 1955). The city

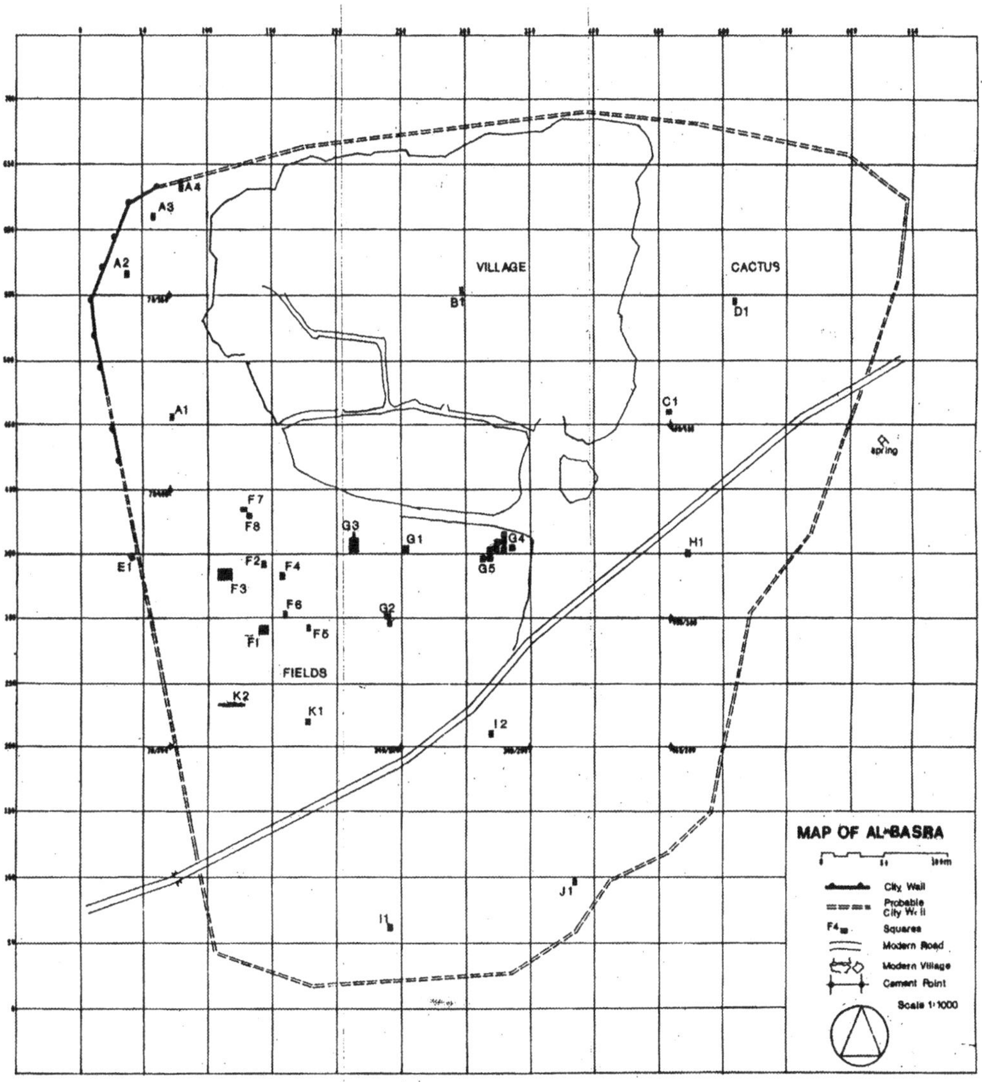

Figure 6.1 Map of Al-Basra Showing the Visible Traces of the Fortification Wall and the Location of Excavation Units At the Site. (Source: Benco 1994).

minted its own currency, as attested to by the discovery of dirhams bearing its name (Eustache 1970-71:118-122).

Archaeological Investigations at al-Basra

Al-Basra is one of the few medieval Islamic cities in Morocco that has been excavated systematically. The site has been the object of several seasons of archaeological investigations over the last twenty years (Benco 1987, 1990, 1994, 1995b, in press; Redman 1983, 1983-84). Al-Basra covers an area of about 30 ha. The only visible feature at the site is the northwest portion of the city wall (about 220 m in length) (Figure 6.1). Archaeological excavations at the site revealed substantial architectural remains including a cistern, a number of well preserved house complexes, and a water canalization system, to mention a few.

The chronology of the site consists of three main phases of occupation: early (Phase I), middle (Phase II), and late (Phase III). Phase I was characterized by substantial stone architecture, flagstone pavements, and water drains. Phase II was characterized by well-built limestone walls and pebbled and plastered floors. Phase III was characterized by poorly built stones walls, often adjacent to Phase II structures. Phase III marks the final collapse of al-Basra as an urban center (Benco 1990). Based on radiocarbon analyses of wood charcoal, the early phase (Phase I) was dated to ca. A.D. 550-890, the pre-Idrisid period; the middle phase (Phase II) to ca. A.D. 780-953, which corresponds to the Idrisid period, and a late phase (Phase III), which covers the post-Idrisid period (Benco 2000).

For the purpose of this study, the most important findings were two updraft kilns located about 50 m from each other. Both kilns are roughly the same size, about 4 m by 4 m. These two kilns appear to have operated at different time periods, one (F3) during the earliest occupation (Phase I) and the second (F1) during the middle occupation (Phase II). They were built using the same construction technique and building materials; a series of transverse fired brick arches supporting the flue-lined floors of the firing chambers (Benco 1989a:102) (Figures 6.2a and 6.2b). The finding of these two kilns, in addition to the presence of many wasters scattered across the site, constitute strong evidence that al-Basra was an important pottery production center for most of its 300-year history.

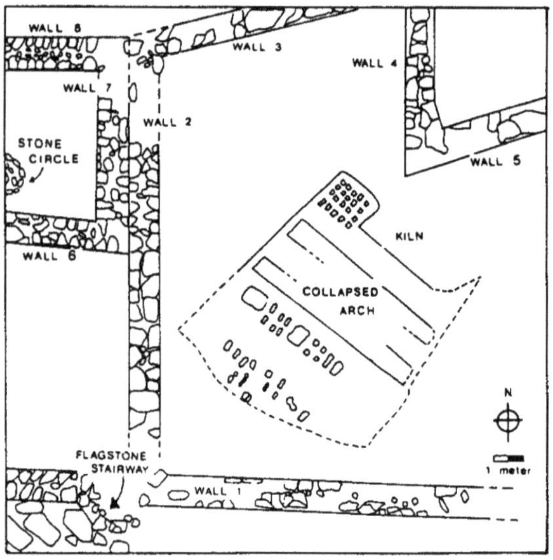

Figure 6.2a Plan of F3 West Excavation Unit Showing the Kiln Floor and Collapsed Arch and Walls of Later Structures. (Source: Benco 1990).

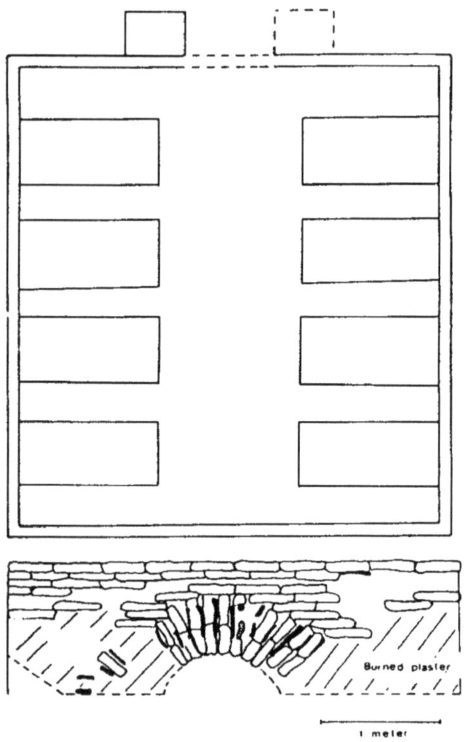

Figure 6.2.b Updraft Kiln in F3 West Excavation Unit. Upper: Plan of Kiln Showing Eight Arches, Central Corridor, and Projected Entrance. Lower: Front View of Arch, Showing Brick, Tile, and Stone Construction. (Source: Benco 1990).

In contrast with most Islamic sites in Morocco, a ceramic typology for the site of al-Basra has long been established (Benco 1987, 1989c; Ennahid 1992). Most of al-Basra's collection consists of undecorated wheelmade storage and serving jars, pitchers, bowls, and oil lamps. Handmade cooking vessels and imported glazed ware constitute only a small portion of the total assemblage.

Al-Basra pottery is composed of three main ware categories. The dominant one is buff ware, which represent more than 80% of the total collection. Depending on the amounts of quartz contained in buff ware, Benco (1987:66-67) identified three subgroups within this ware category: sandy, fine, and very fine. A far less dominant ware category is cream ware. It is characterized by a highly calcareous cream-colored paste. This ware category constitutes 15% of the total assemblage. Cream ware is often found in the form a spoutless pitcher that is sometimes decorated with painted motifs. The last ware category is represented by glazed ware. It constitutes only 2% of al-Basra pottery. Glazed ware is believed to be a non-local production, possibly originating from other production centers in the Maghrib or al-Andalus. The chemical compositional analysis of the al-Basra pottery has clearly discriminated between these three ware categories[2] (Figure 6.3) (Benco and Blackman 1998).

Compositional Analysis: Methodological Issues

Sample Description

In order to investigate the local exchange system that involved al-Basra and its hinterland, 145 potsherds from 15 archaeological sites around the city were analyzed by INAA at the University of Missouri Research Reactor Center (MURR) (Table 6.1). This pottery was selected because of its similarity to ceramic material from al-Basra. The similarity was apparent in both vessel forms and ware categories. In fact, the observed similarity was the trigger for conducting INAA to determine whether the ceramics in question were also compositionally similar to al-Basra material.

These 15 sites were discovered during the 1999 archaeological survey, which I conducted in al-Basra region (Figure 3.2). All of the 145 potsherds submitted for compositional analysis originated from surface collections since no excavations were conducted at any of the newly found sites. In general, 10 ceramic specimens from each site were selected for INAA. The pottery consisted entirely of wheelmade plain wares. Most are buff wares of various textures, although cream, orange, and gray wares are also represented (Appendix F).[3] The majority of the samples consist of vessel forms similar to those used by Benco in her compositional analysis of al-Basra ceramics (Forms 40, 41, 42, 43, 44, 48, and 80) (see Benco 1987:70-81; Appendix E).

The INAA study of al-Basra ceramics conducted by Benco and Blackman (Benco and Blackman in preparation, 1998) at the Conservation Analytical Laboratory at the Smithsonian Institution, utilizing the research reactor at the National Institute of Standards and Technology (NIST) consisted of 92 ceramic samples from three phases of occupation at al-Basra. Their sample also included a number of kiln wasters, two fragments of kiln bricks, and 20 clay samples collected from clay deposits within a 3-km radius of the site. The analysis identified three distinct compositional groups, which correspond to the three main ware categories found at the site: buff, cream, and glazed wares (Figure 6.3) (Benco and Blackman 1998).

2 For a detailed discussion of the al-Basra INAA results, see Benco et al. (in preparation).

3 Because of its length, this table is placed in Appendix F.

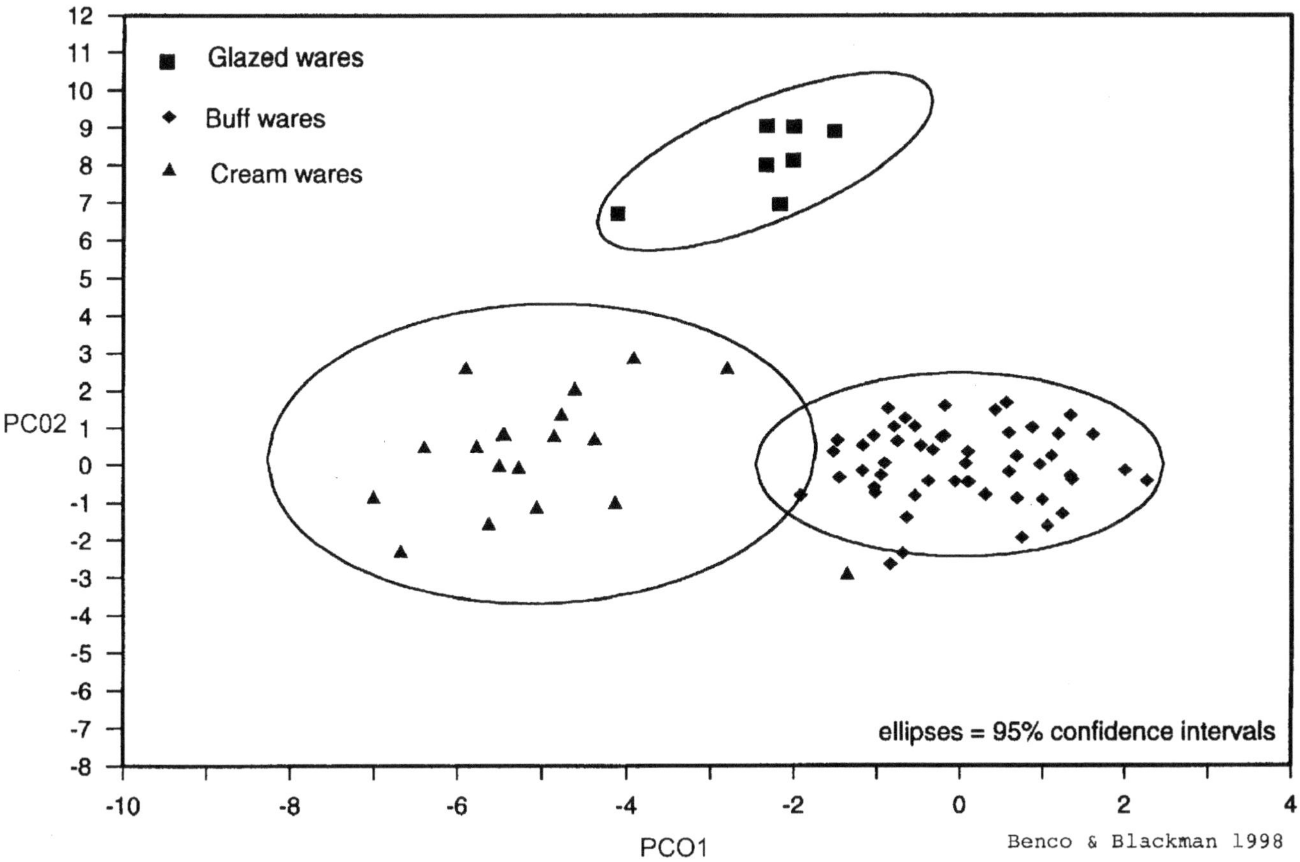

Figure 6.3 Al-Basra's Three Main Compositional Groups. (Source: Benco and Blackman 1998).

In addition to archaeological samples from al-Basra and its hinterland, this project also incorporated INAA compositional data for ceramics and raw materials collected by Benco from four ethnographic contexts in northern Morocco (26 pottery samples and 36 raw clay samples). These data were collected to document the changes that occur in chemical composition of ceramic materials as they are culturally modified by potters from raw clays into finished products (Benco 1992). These data were analyzed at MURR (Neff and Glascock 1993). The ethnographic data consist of clays, tempers, and pottery vessels from four pottery producing communities in northern Morocco: Tetouan, Ksar el-Kebir, Beni Kissane (on the Mediterranean coast), and Ain Koub (in the Rif mountains). The first two represent major pottery production centers and the last ones are small rural communities of part-time potters (Benco 1989b; El-Hraiki 1989; Vossen and Ebert 1986). The ethnographic ceramics and raw materials from these four communities can be easily discriminated chemically. The ethnographic data provided compositional information for raw materials collected in the survey area. One of the ethnographic contexts, Ksar el-Kebir, lies within 20 km of al-Basra and less than 10 km from three hinterland sites (ARB 8, ARB 13, and ARB 18).

Sample Preparation and Analysis

INAA is used to characterize archaeological materials (e.g., ceramics, obsidian) and relate them to specific sources based on their chemical signatures. INAA provides precise and simultaneous determination of up to 32 or 33 major, minor, and trace elements reported in concentrations of parts-per-million (ppm) per gram of material. This method was first applied to archaeological materials in the late 1950s (Rice 1987:396-398).[4]

The following discussion of how the samples were prepared and how the method is implemented is drawn from Neff and Glascock (2000). Glascock (1992) also provides a detailed discussion of the various aspects of this highly complex and technical method. A small fragment of each ceramic sample was cleaned using a silicon carbide burr to eliminate painted, slipped, and contaminated surfaces. The scraped specimens were washed with deionized water and allowed to dry in air for several hours. Fragments of the sample were then crushed in an agate mortar to yield a fine powder. MURR retains a part of each specimen, unpowdered, for its archives. The powder samples were oven-dried at 100 degrees C for 24 hours. Approximately 150 mg of powdered sample were placed in polyethylene vials used for short irradiations. At the same time, 200 mg of powdered sample were weighed into high-purity quartz vials used for long irradiations. Reference standards were submitted along with the unknown samples. The reference standards used by MURR are SRM-1633a (coal fly ash) and SRM-688 (basal rock). Samples of SRM-278 (obsidian rock) and Ohio Red Clay, which are treated as unknowns, were submitted along with the unknown samples for quality control purposes.

At MURR, neutron activation analysis of ceramics consists of two irradiations and a total of three gamma counts. A short

[4] For a historical overview of the archaeological application of INAA, see Neff 1992.

irradiation is carried out through the pneumatic tube irradiation system. As described by Glascock (1992) and Neff and Glascock (2000), samples in the polyethylene vials are sequentially irradiated, two at a time, for five seconds at a neutron flux of 8 x 10^{13} n/cm^2/s. The 720-second count yields gamma spectra containing peaks for the following nine short-lived elements: aluminum (Al), barium (Ba), calcium (Ca), dysprosium (Dy), potassium (K), manganese (Mn), sodium (Na), titanium (Ti), and vanadium (V). The samples in quartz vials are exposed to a thermal neutron flux of 5 x 10^{13} n/cm^2/s for 24 hours. This long irradiation is analogous to the single irradiation implemented at most other laboratories. After the long irradiation, samples are allowed to decay for seven days, then washed to eliminate contamination, and counted for 2,000 seconds (the "middle count") on a high-resolution germanium detector coupled to an automatic sample changer. This middle count determines the following seven medium half-life elements: arsenic (As), lanthanum (La), lutetium (Lu), neodymium (Nd), samarium (Sm), uranium (U), and ytterbium (Yb). An additional three-to four-week period of decay follows and the samples are counted again for 10,000 seconds. This final count determines the 17 long half-life elements: cerium (Ce), cobalt (Co), chromium (Cr), cesium (Cs), europium (Eu), iron (Fe), hafnium (Hf), nickel (Ni), rubidium (Rb), antimony (Sb), scandium (Sc), strontium (Sr), tantalum (Ta), terbium (Tb), thorium (Th), zinc (Zn), and Zirconium (Zr).

Statistical Considerations

The analyses performed at MURR produced elemental concentration values for 32 or 33 elements in most of the submitted samples. In some cases, the elemental concentration of Nickel (Ni) was too low to be detected, resulting in missing data. The Smithsonian-NIST data set includes only 26 of the 33 elements determined by MURR. This is due to the fact that NIST uses a single irradiation whereas MURR uses two. In order to combine the Smithsonian-NIST and the MURR databases, only the 26 elements commonly detected by the two laboratories were considered. NIST data were calibrated for compatibility with MURR data using conversion factors obtained by calculating ratios of the means of replicated Ohio Red Clay check standard analyses undertaken by the two laboratories.

The following discussion is synthesized from Glascock (1992) and Neff and Glascock (2000). Prior to the statistical analysis of the data, raw elemental concentration values were converted to base-10 logarithms. The use of log-transformed concentrations instead of raw counts compensates for difference in magnitude between major elements, such as iron, aluminum, and potassium on the one hand, and trace elements, such as the rare earth or lanthanide elements, on the other hand. The transformation to base-10 logarithms also provides a more nearly normal distribution for many trace elements, hence facilitating the application of clustering and other multivariate procedures (Baxter 1994).

Considering the large amounts of data generated by INAA studies, the use of advanced statistical methods is usually required. The main objective of statistical analyses of compositional data is to identify groups of similar chemical signatures within the analytical database. According to the "provenance postulate" (Weigand et al. 1977 cited in Neff and Glascock 2000), these groups are assumed to represent geographically restricted sources or source zones. The identification of sources or source zones is achieved by comparing the measured elemental concentrations of the unknown groups to those of the known ones, and noting the presence of kiln wasters in the groups.

Most pottery characterization studies use bivariate plots (two-dimensional scattergrams) to visually inspect multidimensional data and to identify possible patterning. Highly correlated elements tend to form well-defined clusters. Confidence levels are often calculated and shown on the bivariate plots as ellipses surrounding correlated subgroups. Bivariate plots can be used to display either the original concentration data or linear combinations of the original data (i.e., principal components or discriminant functions) (Glascock 1992:17). Although bivariate plots are limited to two-dimensional display of the data, calculation of Mahalanobis distance allows the assessment of how well-separated the different groups are on multiple dimensions.[5]

Prior to calculating Mahalanobis distances (probability of membership), archaeologists use cross-validation (or "jackknifing"); the specimen being evaluated is removed from its presumed group of membership so that it does not influence the group centroid in the direction of the specimen. This problem is called "stretchability" (Harbottle 1976) and is especially encountered in dealing with small groups. All the probabilities discussed in this chapter are cross-validated.

Results of Instrumental Neutron Activation Analysis (INAA)

The INAA study identified one major core group (the Basra core group), seven smaller groups (Basra-1, Basra-2, Basra-3, Basra-4, EM-1, Hinterland-1, and Hinterland-2), and a number of unassigned specimens. Table 6.2 shows the number of samples in each compositional group. Appendix F lists the al-Basra's hinterland samples characterized by INAA at MURR according to their subgroup affiliation. The al-Basra samples analyzed at NIST are not included in this appendix. This information will be published in a joint article by Benco, Ennahid, Blackman, and Neff (Benco et al. in preparation). The first column shows the sample's subgroup affiliation. The second one provides the sample's identification number. At MURR, each sample is assigned a unique analytical identification number with a three-letter prefix (usually the researchers' initials) and a three-number suffix (the sequential number of specimens submitted). Al-Basra's hinterland samples are numbered BSR001 through BSR145 (N=145). Columns 3, 4, 5, 6, and 7 refer, respectively, to site name, site number, type of ware category, typological attributes, and site chronology. The last column shows the probability of membership of each specimen in the Basra Core Group based

5 For details, see Sayre 1975 (cited in Glascock 1992, Neff and Glascock 2000) and Bishop and Neff (1989).

Table 6.2 Distribution of INAA Samples by Chemical Compositional Groups

Chemical group	No. of Samples (MURR only)[a]	No. of Samples (NIST and MURR combined)[b]
Basra Core	118	133
Basra-1	0	23
Basra-2	0	21
Basra-3	0	13
Basra-4	0	7
EM	0	9
Hinterland-1	5	7
Hinterland-2	8	8
Unassigned Specimens	14	38
Total	145	259

[a]Samples from al-Basra hinterland sites analyzed at MURR.
[b]Samples from al-Basra and its hinterland sites analyzed at NIST and MURR, respectively.

on cross-validated (jackknifed) Mahalanobis distances from this group centroid. For a specimen to be assigned to the Basra Core Group, it must show above 1% probability of membership in it. This may seem a very low cutoff threshold, but based on Mahalanobis Distance calculations, all specimens assigned to the Basra Core Group still have a very low percent probability of belonging to other groups (typically below 0.0005%). In other words, if specimen A shows 99% probability of membership to the Basra Core Group and specimen B only 1% probability of membership to the same group, that does not mean that specimen A is "more representative" or a better group member than specimen B. The Basra Core Group is characterized by a range of variation and all its members are equally representative of that range. The probabilities for other groups are not shown in Appendix F because these groups are too small to test (i.e., too small to calculate a non-singular variance-covariance matrix) (Hector Neff, personal communication 2001).

Appendix G assembles the elemental concentrations of the archaeological specimens submitted to MURR (N=145). These data are the result of two irradiations and three counts (a total of 33 elements determined). The inclusion of the raw data generated for this project will make it possible for other researchers to recreate the groupings, evaluate my arguments about them, and compare and/or complement their own compositional data with mine. The following description of the various chemical groups identified in the MURR and NIST data sets is synthesized from the MURR report written by Neff and Glascock (2000).

The Basra Core Group

Most of the archaeological pottery from the hinterland sites, together with a substantial portion of the pottery from al-Basra itself, falls into a single chemical group, referred to as the Basra core group. Of the 145 ceramic samples from the hinterland sites, 118 samples (82%) can be confidently assigned to the Basra core group (Tables 6.1 and 6.2). All the 133 samples included in this group (118 hinterland samples analyzed at MURR and 15 samples from al-Basra analyzed at NIST) show above 1% probability of membership based on cross-validated Mahalanobis distances from the group centroid. All specimens excluded from this group show less than 1% probability of membership, in most cases far less.

The fact that most of the pottery from al-Basra region (i.e., the site and its hinterland) belongs to a single chemical group suggests that the bulk of the archaeological (or more tentatively, Idrisid) pottery produced in the region came from a single source or source zone (i.e., the same area of clay deposits). While none of the al-Basra clay samples fall into the Basra core group, one kiln waster from al-Basra does. This provides additional support for local production at al-Basra.

Further support is provided by Benco's ethnographic database, which is derived from four pottery production centers in northern Morocco. The inclusion of this database allows the range of geographic variation in ceramic compositions in northern Morocco to be evaluated. As shown in Figure 6.4, chromium and cesium clearly discriminate ceramics and raw materials from (1) Tetouan and Beni Kissane (two communities to the north of al-Basra), (2) the Basra core group ceramics, and (3) ethnographic materials from Ksar el-Kebir and Ain Koub. Although the Basra core group overlaps with ethnographic materials from Ksar el-Kebir and Ain Koub on chromium and cesium, a rubidium-cobalt plot (Figure 6.5) clearly discriminates it from Ksar el-Kebir, and a cobalt-zinc plot (Figure 6.6) clearly discriminates it from Ain Koub.

These plots clearly indicate that the Basra core group constitutes a chemically homogenous group. It has its own chemical signature that neatly discriminates it from compositional groups elsewhere in northern Morocco. More importantly, the majority of samples from hinterland sites ARB 8, ARB 13, and ARB 18, which are located in the vicinity of Ksar el-Kebir (less than 10 km from Ksar el-Kebir; see Figure 3.2) fall into the Basra core group (Table 6.1; Appendix F). This suggests that the samples from these sites were not produced using clay materials from the vicinity of Ksar el-Kebir and that the al-Basra's clay sources are distinct from nearby sources.

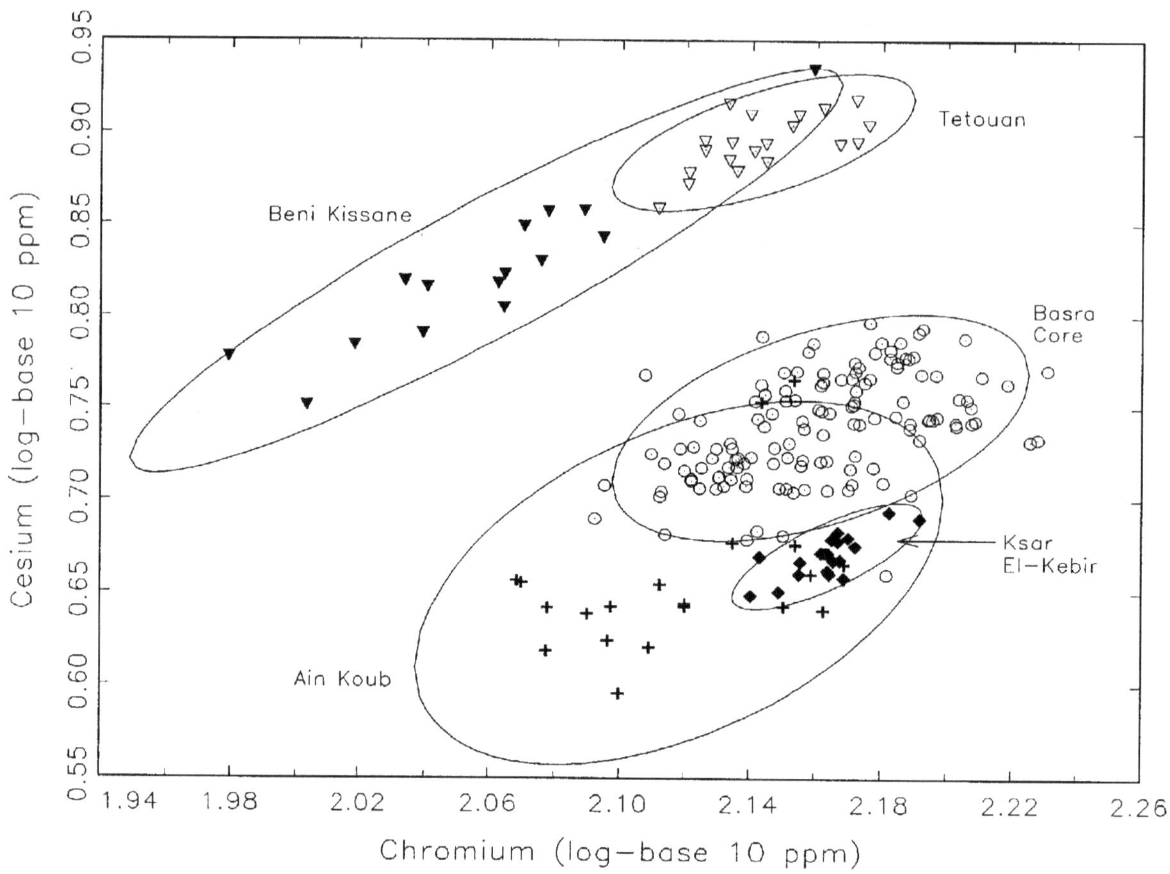

Figure 6.4 Bivariate Plot of Chromium and Cesium Concentrations in Northern Morocco Ethnographic Data and in the Basra Core Group Defined in This Study. Ellipses Represent 90% Confidence Level for Membership in the Groups.

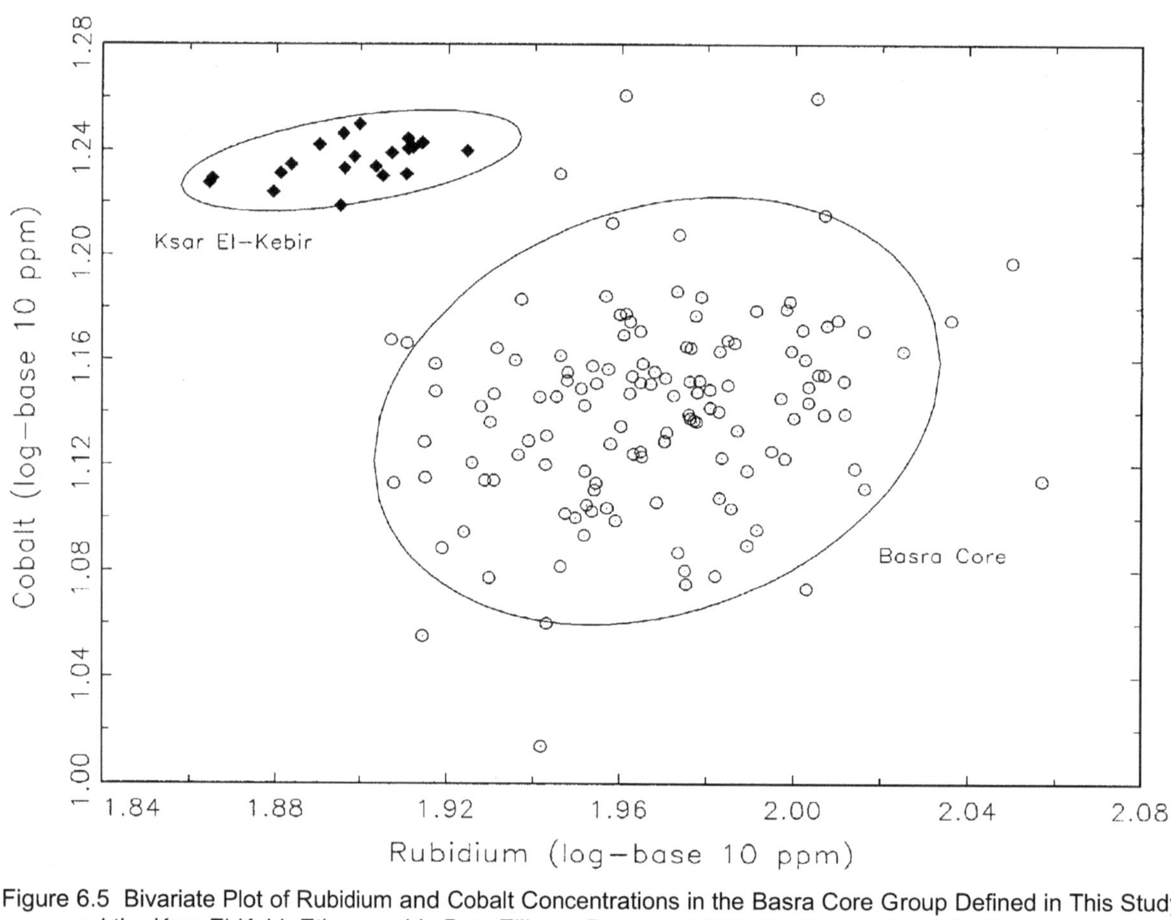

Figure 6.5 Bivariate Plot of Rubidium and Cobalt Concentrations in the Basra Core Group Defined in This Study and the Ksar El-Kebir Ethnographic Data.Ellipses Represent 90% Confidence Level for Membership in the Groups.

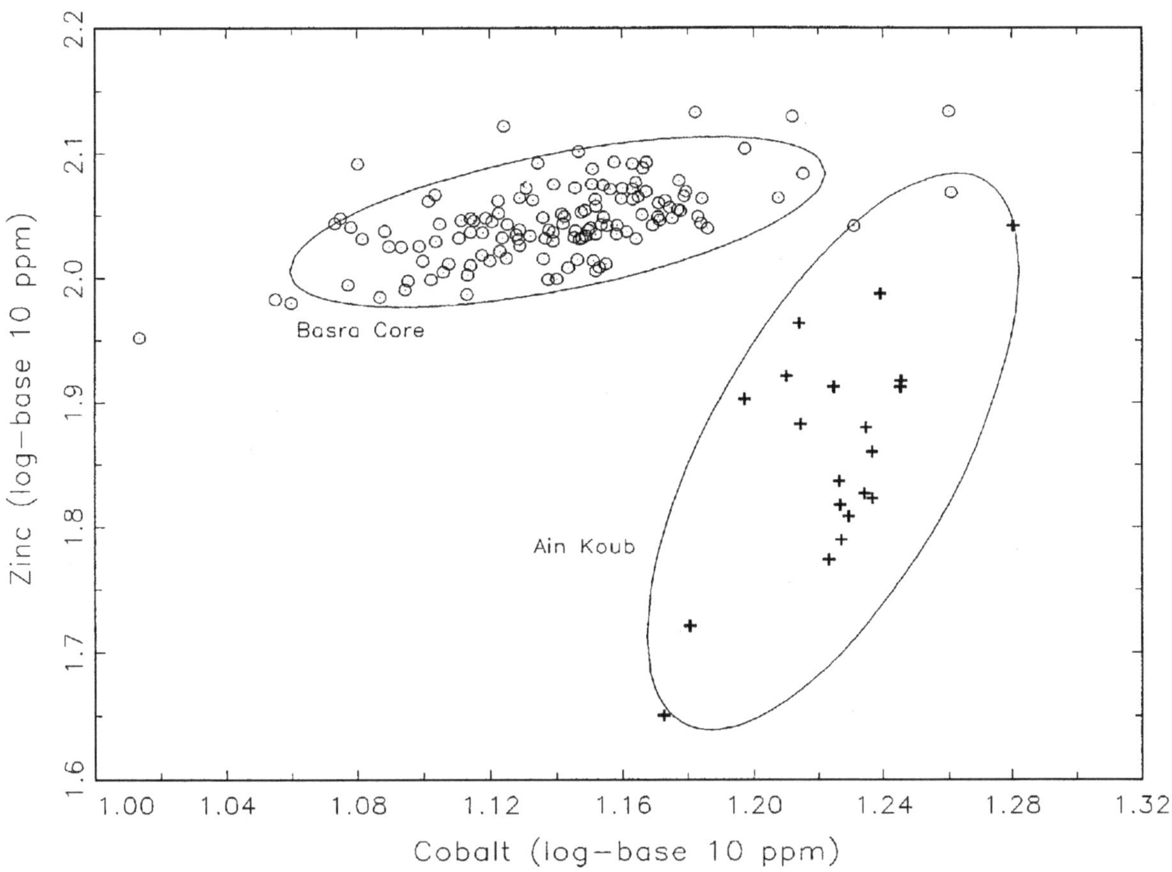

Figure 6.6 Bivariate Plot of Cobalt and Zinc Concentrations in the Basra Core Group Defined in This Study and the Ain Koub Ethnographic Data. Ellipses Represent 90% Confidence Level for Membership in the Groups.

The Basra-1 Group

In addition to the main chemical group, the Basra core group, several smaller groups were identified in the NIST-MURR databases. A well defined one is designated as Basra-1 group. This group consists of cream ware specimens from al-Basra and corresponds to the cream ware compositional group defined by Benco and Blackman (1998) (Figure 6.3). The Basra-1 group is characterized by very high concentrations of calcium (Figure 6.7). This group includes three clay samples from al-Basra, which indicates that cream wares were produced locally. None of the cream ware samples from al-Basra hinterland sites approaches the levels of calcium concentrations observed in the Basra-1 group. Al-Basra cream ware pottery was possibly not intended for exportation to hinterland sites.

The Basra-2, 3, and 4 Groups

The Basra-2, 3, and 4 groups constitute small groups of samples from al-Basra that were analyzed at NIST. Although none of the samples belonging to these groups shows more than a 1% probability of membership in the Basra core group, many bivariate projections of the data show these groups as overlapping with the Basra core group. Figure 6.7 shows that while these three groups overlap with the Basra core group, they generally have higher calcium concentrations than the latter. The Basra-1 group has the highest levels of calcium concentrations.

One way to interpret the compositional groups shown in Figure 6.7, is to view the ceramic raw materials of al-Basra region as falling along a continuum from calcareous to non-calcareous. The Basra-1 cream wares represent the calcareous end of the compositional continuum, whereas the Basra core group (mostly buff wares) represents the non-calcareous end of the continuum. The Basra-2, 3, and 4, then, represent intermediate compositions along this continuum.

The Basra-2 and 4 groups may be viewed as minor compositional variants of ceramic raw materials present in al-Basra region. The fact that clay samples from al-Basra are included in both groups agrees with the hypothesis that these compositions are local. The Basra-2 and 4 groups represent compositional variants that are relatively low in heavy rare earth elements, especially lutetium, compared with the Basra core group (Figure 6.7). Lower lutetium may arise from slight variations in non-plastic constituents, such as lower proportions of amphiboles. A chromium-scandium plot clearly discriminates the Basra-2 and 4 groups (Figure 6.8). The Basra-4 group has lower concentrations of many elements, especially transition metals. This is also possibly due to a difference in the texture of wares in each group: the Basra-2 group contains more refined pastes that are less diluted by quartz grains. Three clay samples included in the Basra-2 group are sieved, which is consistent with this interpretation.

The Basra-3 group is discriminated best from the Basra core group by enriched rubidium concentrations (Figures 6.9 and

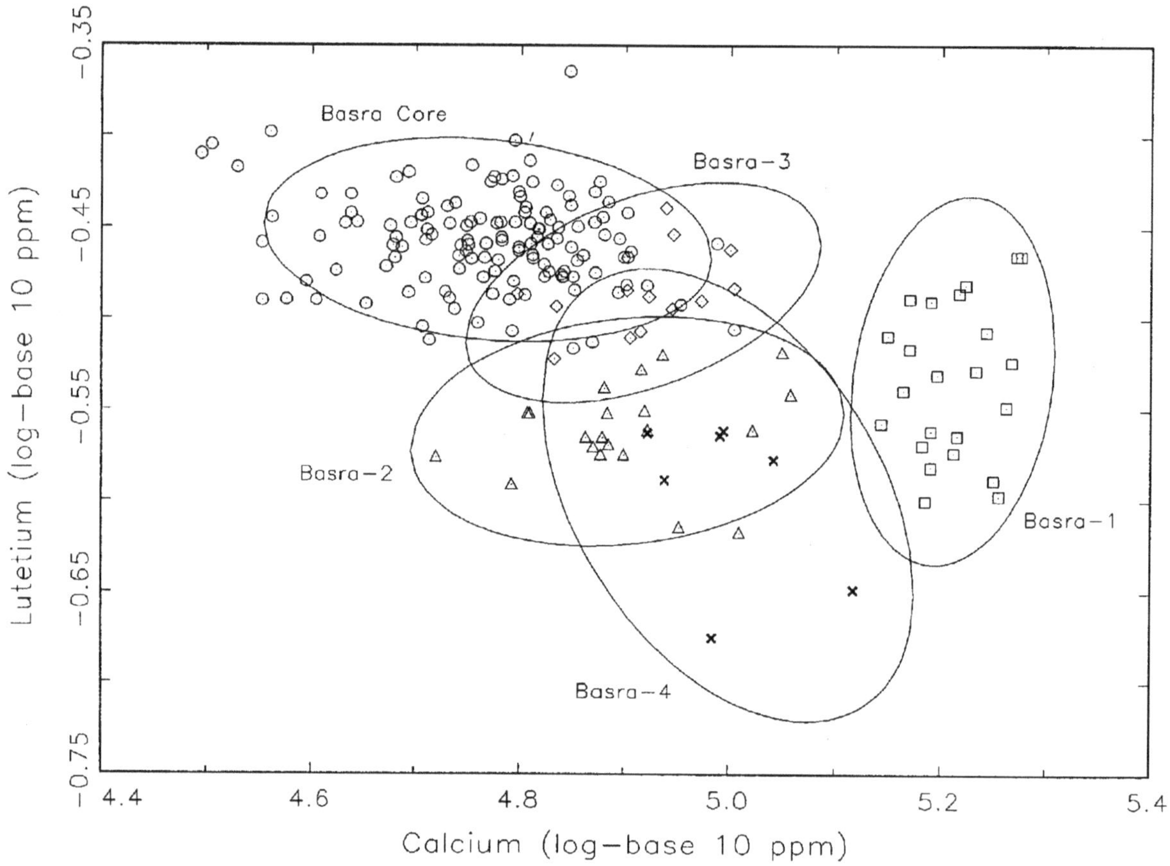

Figure 6.7 Bivariate Plot of Calcium and Lutetium Concentrations in the Basra Core Group and Four Smaller Groups Recognized in the NIST Sample From Al-Basra. Ellipses Represent 90% Confidence Level for Membership in the Groups.

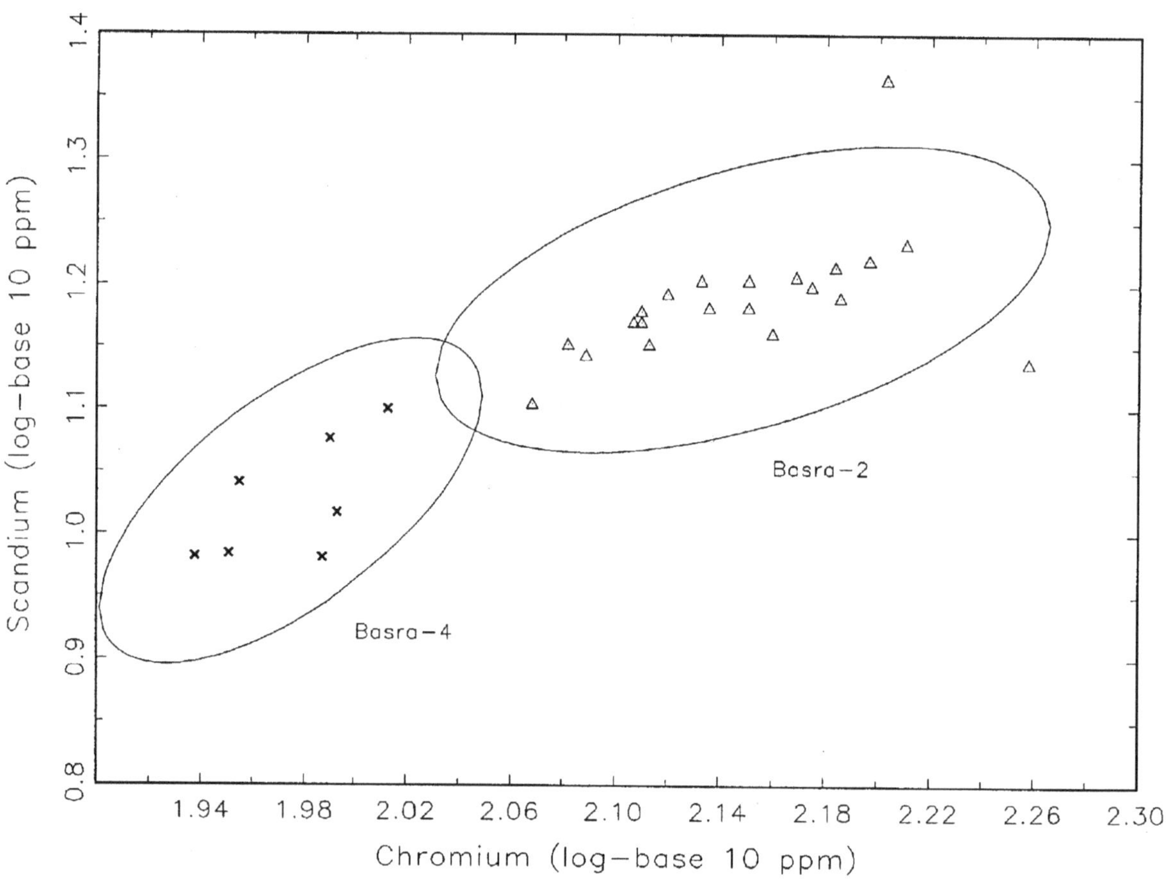

Figure 6.8 Bivariate Plot of Chromium and Scandium Concentrations in the Basra-2 and Basra-4 Groups. Ellipses Represent 90% Confidence Level for Membership in the Groups.

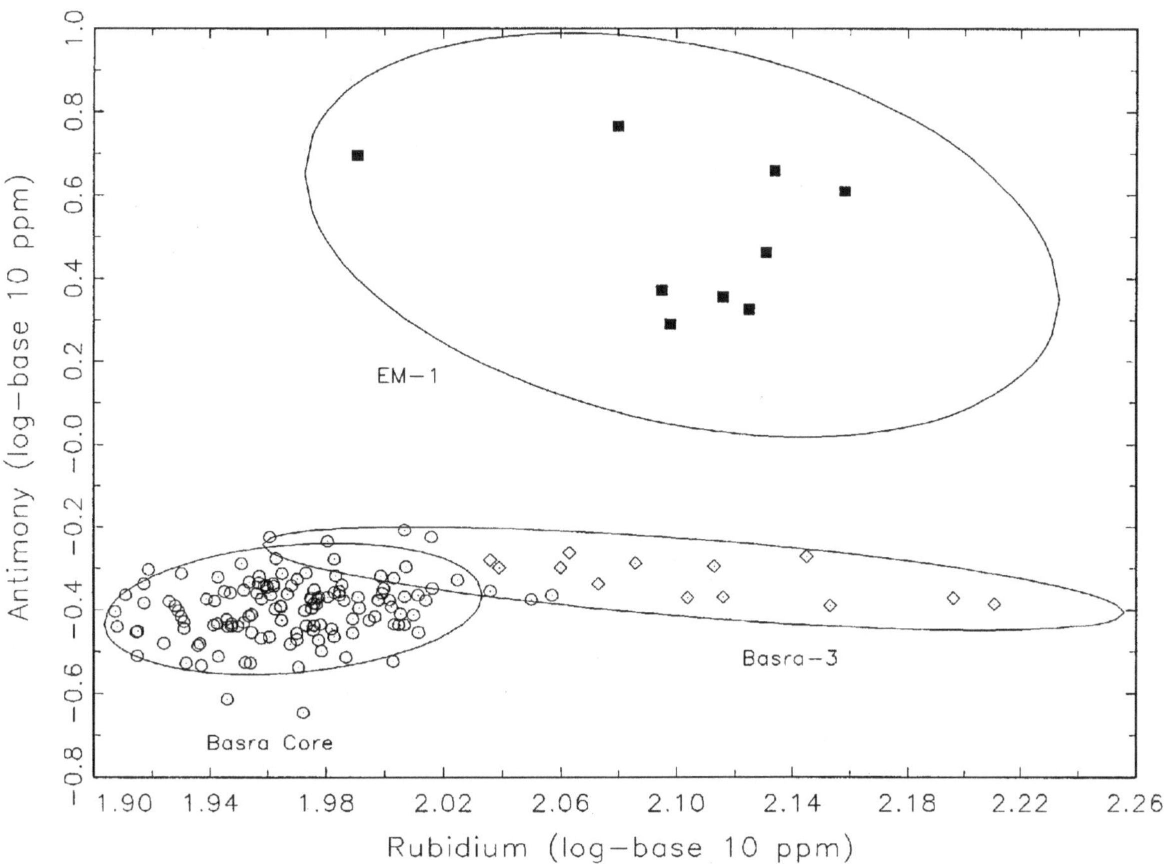

Figure 6.9 Bivariate Plot of Rubidium and Antimony Concentrations in the Basra Core, Basra-3, and EM-1 Groups. Ellipses Represent 90% Confidence Level for Membership in the Groups.

6.10), and calcium and potassium are very slightly enriched as well. As was observed in the Basra-2 and 4 groups, these compositional variations probably represent minor chemical variations in ceramic raw materials present in the region of al-Basra, in this case possibly associated with differences in feldspar content (e.g., more K-feldspars in the Basra-3 group). Although no clay samples fell into the Basra-3 group, many bivariate projections of the data show a general similarity of this group to the Basra core group. This can be interpreted as an indication of the Basra-3 group local origin.

The EM-1 Group

The group referred to as the EM-1 group contains eight glazed specimens and one gray ware specimen from al-Basra. It corresponds to the glazed ware compositional group defined by Benco and Blackman (1998) (Figure 6.3). Numerous bivariate projections of the data show this group as clearly discriminated from the Basra core group and the other Basra compositional subgroups. The EM-1 group is best defined as being higher in antimony concentrations than the other groups (Figure 6.9). This group can be tentatively associated with a non-local origin (i.e., outside al-Basra area source zone). This argument is supported by the fact that the EM-1 group has a unique chemical signature that clearly differentiates it from the other groups (presumed to be local). Furthermore, this group does not include any clay samples from al-Basra area.

The Hinterland-1 and Hinterland-2 Groups

The Hinterland-1 and Hinterland-2 groups designate two minor compositional variants identified in the pottery samples from hinterland sites. These two chemical groups are composed of 13 specimens or about 9% of the total number of samples analyzed at MURR (Table 6.2). The Hinterland-1 group has enriched lutetium and low rubidium (Figure 6.10), which might relate to higher relative amphibole proportions. Several specimens from this group appear to be coarsely textured, including a fragment of kiln brick and an unsieved raw clay sample from al-Basra. These observations suggest that the Hinterland-1 group may have been produced from raw materials present in the al-Basra vicinity.

The Hinterland-2 group is characterized by generally lower calcium concentrations than the Basra core group. A calcium-strontium plot neatly discriminates the two groups (Figure 6.11). However, most other bivariate projections of the data show near or complete overlap of both groups (i.e., both groups have very similar chemical signatures). Several specimens included in the Hinterland-2 group show non-negligible probability of membership in the Basra core group based on cross-validated Mahalanobis distances. One sample (BSR014; see Appendix F) falls just outside the 1% probability cutoff threshold. As in the case of the Hinterland-1 group, the pottery from the Hinterland-2 group was also likely produced locally using raw materials present in the al-

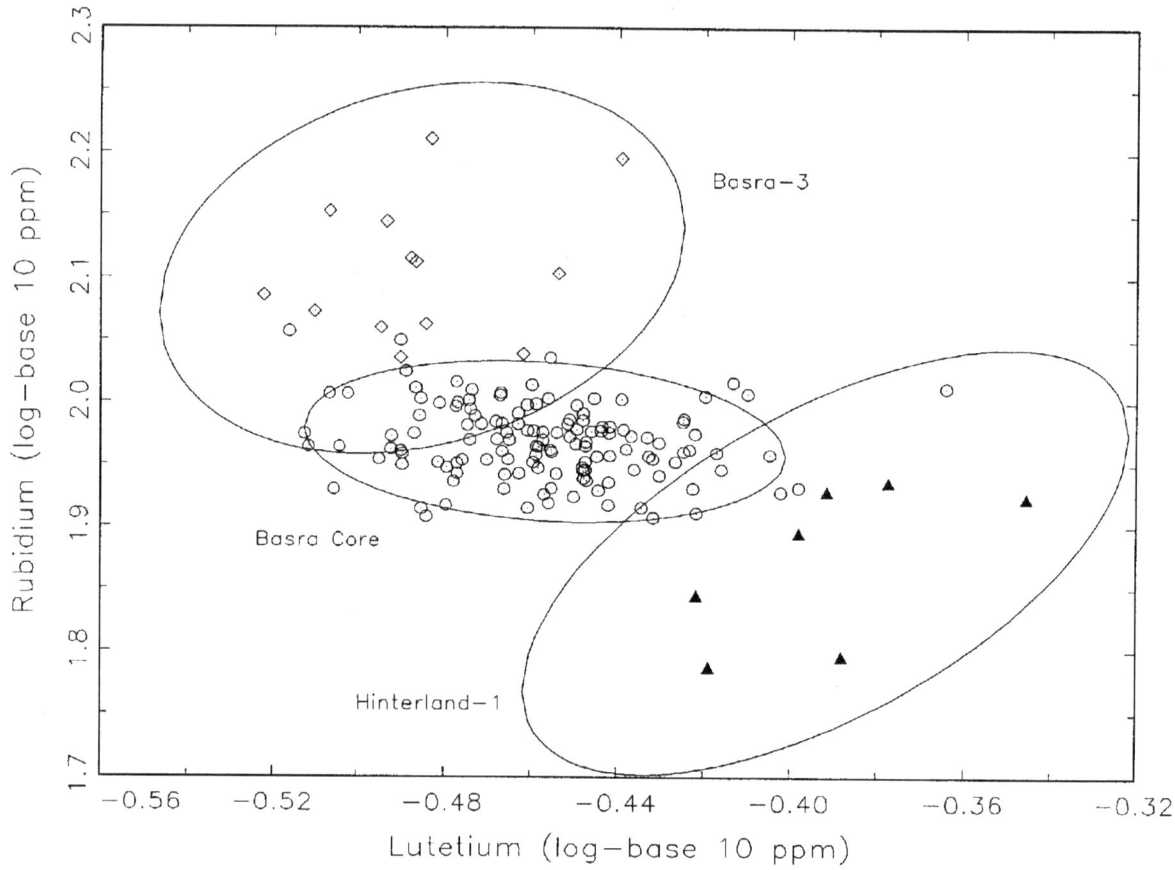

Figure 6.10 Bivariate Plot of Lutetium and Rubidium Concentrations in the Basra Core, Basra-3, and Hinterland-1 Groups. Ellipses Represent 90% Confidence Level for Membership in the Groups.

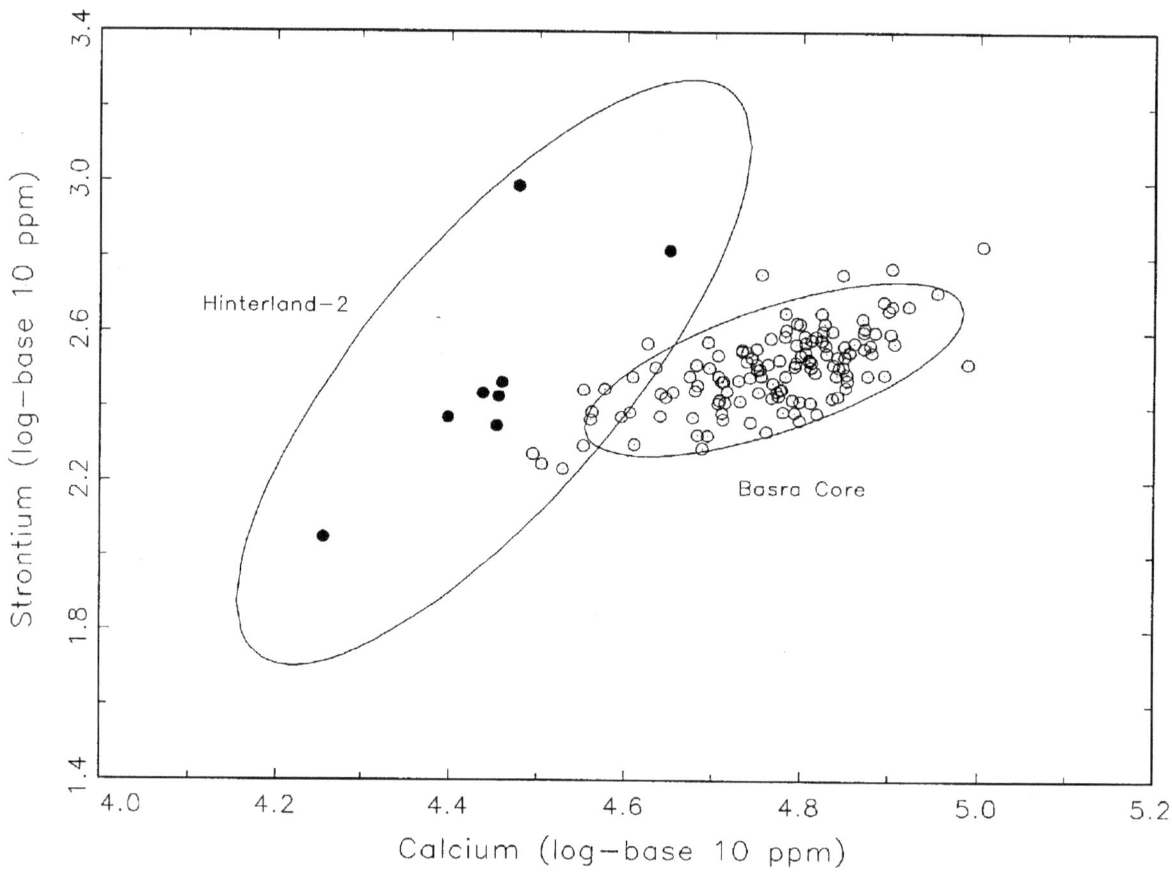

Figure 6.11 Bivariate Plot of Calcium and Strontium Concentrations in the Basra Core and Hinterland-2 Groups. Ellipses Represent 90% Confidence Level for Membership in the Groups.

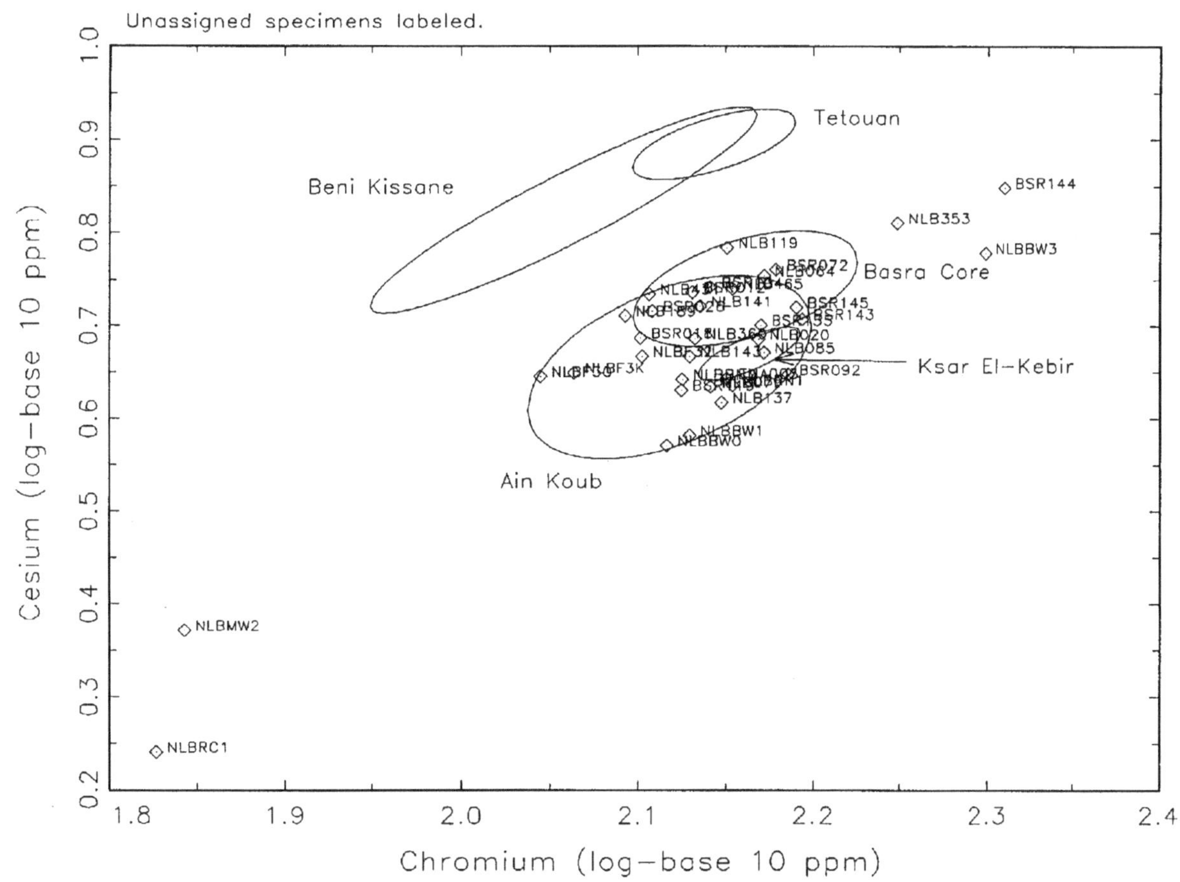

Figure 6.12 Bivariate Plot of Chromium and Cesium Concentrations of the Unassigned NIST and MURR Specimens. Individual Unassigned Specimens are Labeled by Analytical ID. Ellipses Represent 90% Confidence Level for Membership in the Basra Core, Basra-1, Basra-2, Basra-3, and Basra-4 Groups, but Individual Group Members are not Plotted.

Basra area. However, six of the eight samples included in this group, all come from a single site in the al-Basra hinterland (ARB13; see Figure 3.2), which may indicate the presence of a minor non-Basra production around this site.

Unassigned Specimens

A total of 38 pottery samples from al-Basra and the hinterland sites could not be confidently assigned to any of the chemical groups.[6] Unassigned specimens constitute close to 10% of the hinterland sample (14 specimens, see Table 6.2). Unassigned specimens also include many clay samples from al-Basra. Inclusion of clay samples in the category of unassigned specimens may point to a selective pattern in raw materials exploitation. In other words, al-Basra potters were selective in their choice of raw materials. It should be stressed, however, that the difference in chemical composition between clays and fired pottery may as well be due to the processing of clay materials prior to the actual phase of vessel forming (e.g., adding tempering materials and/or removing inclusions and impurities; see Rice 1987:118-119).

Unassigned specimens do not seem to originate from distant pottery production centers. On a chromium-cesium plot (Figure 6.12), the majority of them fall within a cluster that includes the Basra core group and the two southern ethnographic groups of Ksar el-Kebir and Ain Koub (this latter is located at 45 km northeast of al-Basra). Not a single sample shows a chemical signature what would align it with the northern ethnographic groups of Beni Kissane or Tetouan. The bivariate projection of the data on a calcium-lutetium plot (Figure 6.13) shows that most of the unassigned specimens cluster in the general vicinity of the Basra core group. Based on these observations, the unassigned specimens would seem to represent low-frequency procurement patterns of al-Basra potters (i.e., clay deposits that were only sporadically exploited by al-Basra potters) or to be statistical outliers from the Basra core group.

Discussion of INAA Results

The most important finding of this study is that most of the archaeological specimens from hinterland sites fall within a single core group, namely, the Basra core group (Tables 6.1 and 6.2). This supports the premise that al-Basra was not only an important ceramic production center but also an important distribution center in the region. Al-Basra served as a major supplier of utilitarian ware to hinterland communities. Except for glazed ware (the EM-1 group), almost all the archaeological samples submitted for analysis were produced at al-Basra or at its immediate vicinity.

6 A specimen is considered as "unassigned" if it is either likely to belong to more than one group or is statistically unrelated to any group (Duff 1999:6.32).

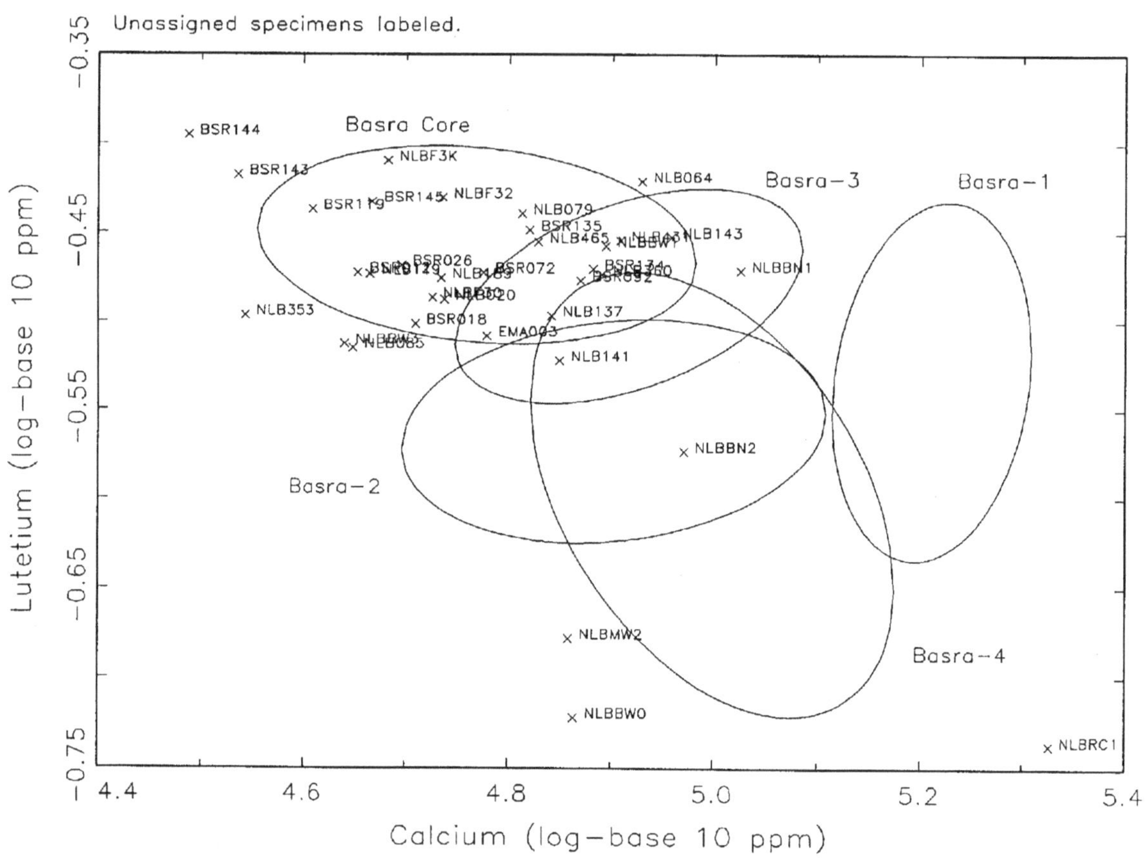

Figure 6.13 Bivariate Plot of Calcium and Lutetium Concentrations of the Unassigned NIST and MURR Specimens. Individual Unassigned Specimens are Labeled by Analytical ID. Ellipses Represent 90% Confidence Level for Membership in the Basra Core, Basra-1, Basra-2, Basra-3, and Basra-4 Groups, but Individual Group Members are not Plotted.

The INAA results discussed in this chapter do not support Redman's argument regarding al-Basra's relations with its hinterland. Redman (1983, 1983-84, 1986a) investigated the degree of integration between al-Basra (among a number of other medieval sites in northern Morocco) and its hinterland by looking for ceramic evidence from hinterland communities at the site, and not the other way around - as it was accomplished in this study. Based on the assumption that handmade pottery was made in rural areas, Redman argued that "high amounts of hand built ceramics [indicate] strong interaction with the rural elements and/or maintenance of small-scale productive units within the city" (Redman 1986a:17; see also 1983:374). Based on this argument, the low proportions of handmade pottery at al-Basra were considered as evidence for al-Basra's "urbaness", but most importantly, as evidence for its weak ties with its hinterland communities (Boone and Benco 1999:54; Redman 1983:374, 1983-84:347, 1986a:17).

This study shows that al-Basra and its hinterland communities were tightly linked through a network of political/administrative, socio-cultural, and economic relations. In fact, the very survival of al-Basra - as a city with an essentially agrarian-based economy - depended on the surplus of its hinterland. Most importantly, these results show the limitation of using the ratios of handmade vs. wheelmade pottery to address complex aspects of past human behavior.

Although, historical data point to the economic and political role of al-Basra as a major Idrisid provincial capital (Abû al-Fidâ 1848:184-185; Ibn Abî Zar' 1860:130), no archaeological evidence had existed to support this idea. The results of this study represent the first purely archaeological evidence in this respect. As shown in Table 6.1, 80 to 100% of specimens from most hinterland sites fall within the Basra core group. Only four sites show a relatively low degree (40 to 60%) of affiliation to the Basra core group (ARB7, ARB13, MBK1, and MBS2).

MBK1 and MBS2 are located 21 km southeast and 37.5 km west of al-Basra, respectively (Figure 3.2). It is possible that these two sites were involved in other local exchange systems, possibly centered around Mulây Bû Salhâm (medieval Bu<u>h</u>ayrat Ariâ<u>gh</u>) or medieval Kurt. The ceramic data from Mulây Bû Salhâm and Kurt are not yet adequately analyzed to allow for further comparison.

Six specimens out of eight from ARB13 fall within the Hinterland-2 group (Appendix F), which may indicate the presence of a minor non-Basra production around this site. However, none of the specimens from ARB8 and ARB18 (both located at less than 5 km from ARB13) was assigned to the Hinterland-2 group, and four specimens from ARB13 itself were assigned to the Basra core group (Table 6.1).

The low proportion of the Basra core group samples from ARB7, which is only about 3 km from al-Basra, is intriguing. As I pointed out above, one ARB7 sample (BSR014; see Appendix F) falls just outside the 1% probability cutoff threshold of membership in the Basra core group based on cross-validated Mahalanobis distances.

Among the specimens included in the Basra core group are four samples (out of a total of five) that were collected at the site of Frigidae (LLM4) (Figure 3.2; Table 6.1), a Roman military camp that was occupied some time before the fourth century A.D. (Limane and Rebuffat 1995:305; Rebuffat 1987:36; Tissot 1876:256, 258, 1878:276). The site contains little surface material. Siraj (1995b:597-599) argues that Frigidae may be the site of medieval al-Aklâm based on textually derived data. I reexamined his sources, and found it unlikely that Frigidae corresponds to medieval al-Aklâm. Textual evidence indicates that the city of al-Aklâm: (1) was located at less than one *marhala* (less than 40 km) from al-Basra, (2) was founded by an Idrisid prince (Yahya Ibn Idrîs, A.D. 905-919), (3) was fortified, (4) was surrounded by abundant water resources, dense woodlands, and "high" mountains, and (5) had a congregational mosque (*Djâmi'*) (see Appendix B).

While some of the textual details about al-Aklâm are applicable to Frigidae, others are clearly not so. Frigidae is located at about 30 km northwest of al-Basra (Figure 3.2); it has abundant water resources (e.g., Soueir River) and a forest in the immediate vicinity of the site. But, unlike al-Aklâm, there are no mountains nearby; in fact, the site is only 85 m above sea level. Most important of all, the site of Frigidae is simply too small to have been occupied by a fortified city with a sizable population (as indicated by the presence a congregational mosque). The site is less than one hectare (0.71 ha) in size (Rebuffat 1987:59). Tissot (1878:276), who visited Frigidae in 1874, wrote: "la station de Frigidae, à en juger par le caractère particulier et le peu d'importance des vestiges qu'elle a laissés, n'a jamais dû être autre chose qu'un poste militaire."

The discovery of al-Basra produced pottery at Frigidae, however, suggests an Idrisid occupation at the site. How many people were living at Frigidae during the Idrisid period? Who were they? What was the nature of their interaction with al-Basra? These are questions that need to be answered in future work.

The spatial distribution of al-Basra hinterland sites show a number of patterns. Al-Basra's local exchange system included relatively distant communities. As shown in Figure 3.2, LLM14 and MBS2, are located at 32.5 km and 37.5 km west of al-Basra, respectively. More importantly, both sites are located at the immediate vicinity of Mulây Bû Salhâm (medieval Buhayrat Ariâgh). Although textual sources indicate that Buhayrat Ariâgh (MBS1) was the port of al-Basra (Eustache 1955; Picard 1996:47-49), the archaeological evidence found at the site date to later periods (Appendix E). The ceramic material collected at LLM14 is strikingly similar to al-Basra's assemblage, both in form and category of ware. Compositional analysis shows that 12 out of 15 specimens from LLM14, and more than half of the specimens from MBS2, could be assigned to the Basra core group (Table 6.1; Appendix F). It appears that al-Basra ceramics were moving west towards Buhayrat Ariâgh. It is possible that al-Basra pottery vessels and/or their contents (e.g., oil, honey, salted butter, olives, etc) were being transported, along a succession of "staging posts" (e.g., LLM14 and MBS2), to Buhayrat Ariâgh for shipment to more distant markets.

In addition to this western axis, al-Basra pottery appears to have moved south towards the Idrisid city of Kurt. Three specimens out of five from MBK1 fall within the Basra core group (Table 6.1). MBK1 is located at about 21 km southeast of al-Basra, and 10 km southwest of HDK1 (possible site of medieval Kurt) (Figure 3.1; Appendix E). Although, several lines of evidence (e.g, toponymy and textual sources) point to HDK1 as the possible site of medieval Kurt, the ceramic material found at the site bears no resemblance, be it stylistic or typological, to al-Basra pottery.

Al-Basra pottery also moved along a northern axis towards al-Kasr al-Kabîr via ARB8. ARB8 consists of the modern-day village of Jajouka (possible site of medieval Zahdjûka). Nine out of 10 specimens from ARB8 were assigned to the Basra core group (Table 6.1). The site must have imported its pottery from al-Basra or at least its immediate vicinity. ARB8 is located about 6 km southeast of al-Kasr al-Kabîr (Figure 3.2). Textual sources indicate that Zahdjûka (ARB8?) was an Idrisid city (al-Bakrî 1965:224). During the early Idrisid period, al-Kasr al-Kabîr (known at the time as Sûk al-Kutâmî or Sûk Kutâma) was a small settlement (Yver 1978) (Appendix B). Al-Kasr al-Kabîr did not become an important city until after the collapse of al-Basra (Abû al-Fidâ 1848:184-185).

One plausible interpretation of these results is that ARB8 (Zahdjûka?), and possibly al-Kasr al-Kabîr, were getting their ceramics from al-Basra, the biggest production center (of ceramics among other things) in the region. After the Idrisid period and the collapse of al-Basra, al-Kasr al-Kabîr may have taken over and become the new capital, but no evidence of medieval pottery production at al-Kasr al-Kabîr has been identified. It is worth noting, however, that al-Kasr al-Kabîr is now a major pottery production center of both traditional and contemporary forms (Vossen and Ebert 1986:22-23). It would be worth while to trace the origin of this production, and determine whether it dates to medieval times when al-Kasr al-Kabîr was a regional capital.

It is possible that the northern axis, once it reached al-Kasr al-Kabîr, turned west towards the port of Tushummush (LAR1, ancient Lixus) via the Lukkûs River. Documentary sources attest that Tushummush was the residence of an Idrisid prince (al-Bakrî 1965:223; Appendix B) and that al-Basra's merchants shipped their products along the Lukkûs River. According to Ibn Hawkal (1842:192): "les habitants de Basra s'embarquent avec des marchandises sur la branche [of the Lukkus River] qui passe chez eux; ils deçendent alors jusqu'à l'Océan, et se dirigent ensuite où ils veulent se rendre." The coastal entrepôt of Tushummush, located at the mouth of the Lukkûs River, must have played an important role in al-Basra's maritime trade (Anonymous 1958:140, 1985:189; Eustache 1955:232). Surprisingly, the Islamic ceramic material found at the site, which includes sherds with incised motifs on a painted background (*sgraffito*?), date to the twelfth to fourteenth centuries A.D. (Akerraz 1992:385; Ataallah 1967:633). Nevertheless, the hypothesis that al-Basra vessels and/or their contents were moving, via the Lukkûs River, towards Tushummush is a valid one.

To recapitulate, the results of the INAA study show that al-Basra pottery moved along three axes: a western axis leading towards Mulây Bû Salhâm (medieval coastal entrepôt of Buhayrat Ariâgh), a southern axis leading towards medieval Kurt, and a northern axis leading towards al-Kasr al-Kabîr and, possibly, along the Lukkus River to the port of Tushummush. Unfortunately, the ceramic materials found at these end points do not show any similarities to al-Basra pottery. They are either dated to later periods (the case of Mulây Bû Salhâm and Tushummush) or not yet adequately identified (the case of Kurt and, especially medieval al-Kasr al-Kabîr).

Overall, the INAA results indicate that the majority of the archaeological specimens from of al-Basra and its hinterland sites have the same chemical profile. This finding supports the hypothesis that al-Basra was a major supplier of pottery in the region. The subgroups identified in this study may represent variant choices of ceramic raw materials or paste preparation by potters in al-Basra or its immediate vicinity.

This study also demonstrates the potential of combining textual evidence with compositional data in investigating medieval Islamic societies. In the case of medieval al-Basra, textual sources provide useful information on the city's regional and macro-regional exchange systems involving neighboring towns as well as distant regions (e.g., Tushummush, Buhayrat Ariagh, Tâmasnâ of the Barghwâta, and Ifrîkiya). Historical evidence also provides fined-grained data on the type of products exchanged (e.g., cotton, flax, cereals, and dairy products). However, the utility of textual sources is limited when it comes to documenting micro-regional exchange systems (i.e., exchange systems involving cities and their immediate hinterland communities). Chemical characterization of ceramics by INAA represents a good solution to circumvent this limitation.

This study represents the first application of INAA to investigate local exchange and community interaction between a medieval Moroccan city and its hinterland. The results of this research, although very positive, could be strengthened further by including clay samples from the region around al-Basra and archaeological specimens from other medieval production centers (not necessarily contemporaneous to al-Basra) within the region. I hope that the MURR and NIST data sets generated by Benco and myself will constitute a useful resource for other scholars to build upon.

Modeling al-Basra's Pottery Distribution

The resolution of the archaeological data on al-Basra pottery distribution (both from survey and compositional analysis) is not yet sufficiently fine-grained to allow the application of a sophisticated model of pottery distribution. The sampling strategies I implemented in my survey and surface collection were relatively simple to allow the discussion of al-Basra pottery distribution in quantitative terms (see Plog 1977:129, 132-133). Moreover, there are fewer models on the distribution of locally produced commonware pottery - which constitutes the bulk of al-Basra pottery production - to draw upon, compared to model's on the distribution of glazed ware and elite items in general (for example, Plog 1977; see also Baugh and Ericson 1994; Earle and Ericson 1977; Ericson and Baugh 1993).

Regardless of the limitations of the data at hand, fall-off or decay models seem to be the most appropriate ones to explain the mechanisms of al-Basra pottery distribution. Fall-off models "graph a decline in interaction (distribution) as effective distance from the source of supply increases (the so-called friction effect of distance)." (Rice 1987:198). Based on this premise, it is expected that different exchange mechanisms would form different fall-off curves[7] (see Hodder and Orton 1976).

Typically, bulky, non-elite goods are expected to be found near their source of supply. This is especially the case for utilitarian ware, which, in addition to its low value and bulkiness, has a low transportability.[8] There is no reason not to expect that the same pattern applies to al-Basra pottery. In a fall-off graph, this mechanism shows as a steep gradient (i.e., high frequencies near the source, followed by a sudden drop in frequency at a short distance from it). A steep gradient is typical of what is known as a "supply-zone behavior" (Rice 1987:198-199).

Assuming that the spatial occurrence of al-Basra pottery at hinterland sites reveals a "supply-zone behavior", the question remains as how it was distributed. In other words, what mechanisms of exchange were in operation between producers and consumers? Of the five mechanisms of pottery distribution defined by Renfrew (1977:9-10), two of them (No. 3 and 4) seem to be applicable to medieval Morocco. In the context of the first mechanism, the producer and consumer meet at third location, usually a market, to conduct the transaction. The pottery is then sold to local consumers or merchants who carry it to farther locations through secondary distribution (Renfrew 1977:9; Rice 1987:193). The second mechanism involves the intervention of a middleman or wholesaler. The producer exchanges his pots with the middleman who carries them to, and exchanges them with, consumers in other (relatively farther) locations (Renfrew 1977:9).

There is supporting evidence, both historical and ethnoarchaeological, that these two mechanisms may have operated at al-Basra. Documentary evidence indicates that pottery (both glazed and utilitarian) was sold at urban markets.

7 See Riley (1984:59) for an example (from the region of Palenque, Mexico) on the difficulties of using fall-off curves to identify exchange system when the assemblage under investigation involves a wide variety functional classes.

8 See a critique by Riley (1984:58) who argued that the generally held assumption that coarse utilitarian pottery is made at or near the location where it is found is not always valid. He pointed to petrographic evidence showing that "coarse, undecorated utilitarian wares" were moving on a significant scale throughout the classical Mediterranean.

In his description of the various markets at the city of Fez, the sixteenth-century geographer Leo Africanus (1956:193) states that: " Puis viennent les marchands de vases: leurs poteries sont belles, avec de jolis coloris; les unes sont monochromes, d'autres de deux couleurs. Ces marchands ont une centaines de boutiques." The same source indicates that potters' shops were located in the vicinity of the potting community: "Près des murs de la ville [Fez] sont les briquetiers et les fours des potiers.[9] En-dessous de ceux-ci on trouve un grand marché où se vend de la poterie blanche, c'est-á-dire, non vernissée, telle que terrines écuelles, marmites" (Leo Africanus 1956:202). This passage shows that utilitarian ware was sold in a "special" market near its locus of production. It is possible that some consumers may have purchased their pots directly from the potters themselves.

The same processes of pottery distribution are still observable in modern-day Fez. Pottery is sold directly to local consumers in the new potters' quarter of Ain Nokhbi, in the various covered markets of Fez-al-Bali, and in the craftsmen's market in the new city (Vossen 1984:364-365; Vossen and Ebert 1986:149-155; see also Le Tourneau 1949). Some of the production of Fez pottery workshops (especially glazed ware intended for tourists) is sold to wholesalers (middlemen), who transport it to retailers scattered all over Morocco.

It is quite possible that al-Basra pottery production and distribution was organized in the same way as in medieval Fez (see Le Tourneau 1949, 1961). Similar to medieval Fez, the industrial zone at al-Basra, represented by pottery kilns F1 and F3, was located on the periphery of the city near the city walls (Figure 6.1). Al-Basra pottery was probably sold not far from its locus of production at the city's different markets. Some local consumers may have acquired their pots directly from pottery workshops.

Al-Basra pottery was distributed to hinterland communities either (1) directly via al-Basra market system, or (2) indirectly through a network of rural markets (*aswâk*, sing. *sûk*) operated by middlemen (secondary distribution). This second mechanism of pottery distribution still exists in several regions of modern-day Morocco. It is well documented ethnoarchaeologically. According to a model formulated by Vossen (1984:Figure 1), traditional pottery was distributed via a network composed of a "central market place center" and a set of subordinate markets of smaller size. Theoretically, this network is composed of seven markets, each one held on a different day of the week (Vossen 1984:367-368). This system of rotation must have been in existence for at least nine centuries; al-Bakrî (1965:212) mentioned a market that was "held every Friday" at the village of Naṣr Ibn Djarw. Along the same lines, Leo Africanus (1956:175-176) referred to a market that was held "outside the city [of Maknâs] every Monday."

In terms of the spatial distribution of pottery workshops and rural markets in modern-day Morocco, Vossen argues that ideally (1) a pottery workshop is required at every 20 km interval (Vossen 1984:369), and that (2) a central market, which is also considered in Vossen's model as a "supra-regional manufacturing center," should be found every 35 km (Vossen 1984:371-373). Some "supra-regional central markets" are visited by consumers living as far as 40-50 km away (Vossen 1084:369).

These patterns may have existed at al-Basra and its hinterland. All of the hinterland sites that acquired their pots from al-Basra were located between 20 to 40 km from the city (Figure 3.2). It is possible that a number of small workshops and small rural markets may have existed, at regular intervals, between the city of al-Basra and other major pottery production and distribution centers. It is also possible that some of al-Basra pottery was sold at nearby urban markets in Mûlây Bû Salhâm (?), al-Kaṣr al-Kabîr, Tushummush, and Kurt. It is doubtful, however, that al-Basra pottery, especially the unglazed utilitarian ware, moved over long distances to more distant markets.

At al-Basra, and possibly in medieval Morocco, there is no evidence of state involvement in pottery production and distribution. Benco's analyses of al-Basra's pottery production show no evidence of state control of the production process (Benco 1987, 1989a). Benco (1987:168) argued that "pottery production in the early medieval town of al-Basra was undertaken by independent artisans in relatively small workshops and was affected primarily by economic and cultural factors, similar to most pottery industries in the Islamic world."[10] Apparently, al-Basra's local exchange system was a purely entrepreneurial affair. With the exception of taxes and market duties collected by state officials, state involvement in the distribution process was minimal if not non-existent.

Although there is no evidence of state involvement in local exchange, the al-Basra market system must have been fairly complex because of the use of coinage (dirhams and, possibly, *fulûls*, sing. *fals*[11]) in market transactions. We know from numismatic evidence that al-Basra issued its own currency (Eustache 1970-71:118-122). Furthermore, textual evidence indicates that flax (linen textiles?) was used as currency. Al-Bakrî (1965:216) wrote that "elle [al-Basra] s'appelle aussi Basrat al-Kattân 'Basra du lin', parce que, à l'époque où elle commença à se peupler, on y employait du lin en guise de monnaie dans toutes les opérations commericales."

The INAA results presented in this chapter constitute an important step towards understanding al-Basra's local exchange system. In fact, conducting INAA was absolutely essential in this context, since one cannot adequately discuss exchange without first locating, with a reasonable amount of certainty, the locus of manufacture. At present, the bulk of our data on al-Basra's local exchange system - and the Idrisid political economy in general - is still mostly drawn from

[9] Pottery workshops were located at the periphery of the city possibly to reduce the population exposure to fumes and odors.

[10] For a historical view of craft production in pre-industrial societies with an emphasis on pottery production in the Islamic world, see Benco 1987:6-15.

[11] A *fals* is a low denomination bronze coinage that was used primarily for local exchange. The circulation area of the *fals* is limited to nearby its locus of emission (Udovitch 1965:769).

documentary and ethoarchaeological evidence. One future direction is to use these data (1) to refine existing anthropological models (or formulate new ones) so that they can be applied to medieval Morocco, and (2) to build upon our current knowledge of al-Basra local exchange system to conduct more archaeological investigations in al-Basra hinterland.

Chapter 7

SUMMARY AND CONCLUSIONS

Theoretical Contributions

This study has provided an anthropological discussion of the political economy of medieval Morocco. It used documentary and numismatic data to assess the applicability of recent anthropological concepts and ideas to medieval Moroccan complex societies. The results of this study support the Boone et al. (1990) argument that the economic structure of medieval Morocco witnessed a radical change in the eleventh century. State finance systems shifted from reliance on agricultural surplus to reliance on the sub-Saharan gold trade.

During the Idrisid period, agricultural surplus was the primary source of state finance. This type of finance system is known in the archaeological literature as *staple finance* (D'Altroy and Earle 1985; Earle 1994). Idrisid settlements were located in rich agricultural regions and were hierarchically distributed. The distribution of Idrisid settlements within a number of micro-regional settlement systems administered by a set of provincial capitals came as a response to (1) the fragmentary nature of the Idrisid political system, and (2) the need to maximize the amount of agricultural surplus levied from hinterland settlements.

Although documentary evidence confirms that the Idrisids levied taxes on farmland (*kharâdj*), there is no clear documentary or archaeological evidence, of how these taxes were collected, who collected them, and where they were stored - assuming they were paid in kind. Another component of the Idrisid political economy that is poorly understood is how surplus was distributed to finance state institutions (i.e., payment of state personnel, construction and maintenance of public works). There is ample documentary and numismatic evidence for the presence of a market system and for the use of currency (Idrisid silver dirhams). It is possible that currency - given as salaries to state personnel - was converted into consumable goods through market exchange.

During subsequent dynastic periods (Almoravids, Almohads, and Marinids), sub-Saharan gold became the primary source of state finance (*wealth finance*). The concern to control, protect, and facilitate long-distance gold trade gave rise to a "primate" settlement system with a few very large urban centers, located at major nodes along long-distance trade routes (e.g., Fez and Marrakech), and a number of urban centers of much smaller size.

Post-Idrisid dynastic states accumulated substantial wealth through their role as intermediary agents between gold-producing regions of sub-Saharan West African and the western Mediterranean Basin. Their territory expanded exponentially covering almost all of North Africa and southern Spain during the Almohad period. Considering the size of post-Idrisid dynastic empires, a wealth finance system was the most appropriate one to efficiently manage state resources. The proceeds from sub-Saharan gold trade were minted into currency (dinars) at a number of ports of trade (e.g., Sidjilmâsa). Part of the proceeds was disbursed locally to finance local governments, while the rest was sent to the state capitals of Marrakech and Fez. As opposed to agricultural surplus, sub-Saharan gold (*tibr*) was easier to transport over long-distances and to store over long periods of time.

Compared with the rudimentary nature of the Idrisid state apparatus, post-Idrisid dynastic empires established a true form of central government (*makhzan*). Documentary evidence shows that a minister of finance (*Sâhib al-Ashghâl*) was in charge of state fiscal affairs. State revenue was stored in special facilities. Most importantly, cash revenue and revenue in kind were stored in separate facilities under the supervision of two different state officials. This suggests a high level of specialization within the post-Idrisid wealth finance system. There is, however, no archaeological evidence of these facilities.

Another major component of the Boone et al. model that was examined in this study concerns the material impact of changing political economies. This study used documentary and numismatic evidence to record the change in the size, location, and distribution of medieval settlements between the Idrisid and subsequent dynastic periods. This research shows that there was a shift in settlement systems from a multitiered hierarchy of settlement size distribution to a "primate" one. The Idrisid settlement system was composed of the state capital (Fez), a number of provincial capitals (e.g., al-Basra), and several smaller towns and villages surrounding each provincial capital. The Idrisid settlement system was dominated by mid-sized settlements; the tenth century al-Mukaddasî (1950, 1994) listed 51 cities in northern Morocco alone.

The post-Idrisid settlement system was composed of a few very large urban centers followed by much smaller settlements. Documentary evidence shows that the cities of Fez and Marrakech had populations of more than 100,000 inhabitants each. More importantly, the number of mid-sized cities in northern Morocco was reduced by nearly 70%. Several of these cities were considered as a threat to the central authority and, therefore, were destroyed.

The analysis of the duration of occupation of medieval settlements in northern Morocco has shown that several coastal entrepôts were occupied for eight centuries or longer. The longevity of coastal entrepôts is explained by their involvement in a variety of mercantile activities related to long-distance gold trade.

The results of this research suggest that medieval Moroccan urban growth was not sustained during the post-Idrisid dynastic period. Except for state capitals, such as Fez, Marrakech, and Ribât al-Fath (Rabat), which continued to grow over time, most settlements either decreased in size or were abandoned. From the Idrisid to the Marinid periods, only about 30% of all the original settlements in northern Morocco remained occupied.

The examination of numismatic data provided supporting evidence for such a decrease in medieval Moroccan urban growth. The number of minting sites decreased steadily following the Idrisid period - assuming that a mint implies the presence of an urban center.

Building on previous research on al-Basra pottery, this study provides the first archaeological evidence for the role of al-Basra as a supplier of pottery vessels to its hinterland communities. Documentary evidence suggests that the Idrisid provincial capital of al-Basra was the center of a local exchange system. To examine local exchange and community interaction between al-Basra and its countryside, 145 samples from 15 hinterland sites were subjected to instrumental neutron activation analysis (INAA).

The results of compositional analysis ascertained that al-Basra pottery was moving across its hinterland. The bulk of the hinterland samples shows the same chemical composition as that of al-Basra samples. Some of al-Basra's pottery was found at sites 40 km away from its origin of manufacture.

Documentary and ethnoarchaeological evidence suggests that al-Basra pottery was distributed to hinterland communities either (1) directly via al-Basra market system, or (2) indirectly through a network of rural markets operated by middlemen (secondary distribution). To explain the mechanisms of al-Basra pottery distribution, this research proposes the use of fall-off, or decay, models. In a fall-off graph, al-Basra pottery distribution is expected to show as a steep gradient, typical of a "supply-zone behavior"; al-Basra pottery is composed mostly of utilitarian ware, which is not expected to travel far from its source of supply.

Methodological Contributions

By adopting an archaeological-historical approach, this study has brought together several lines of evidence in an investigation of Medieval Moroccan political economy and settlement systems. Although archaeological, documentary, and numismatic evidence has been used in previous studies in Morocco, this research introduced a new method to effectively combine multiple lines of evidence to answer specific anthropological questions (see Chapter 2).

Textual information drawn from more than twenty documentary sources was classified into five settlement categories: (1) duration of occupation, (2) phase of foundation, (3) state of occupation, (4) archaeological status, and (5) size. Because of the importance of site size for settlement studies, I formulated a number of criteria for inferring settlement size from medieval Arabic documentary sources (Table 2.1). These criteria are applicable not only to medieval Maghribian settlements but to all Islamic settlements as well.

Based on these criteria, it was possible to classify settlement information into six settlement size classes (Table 2.1). Once settlement size information was quantified (i.e., converted into numerical values), it was possible to establish a number of graphs to visually monitor urban growth in northern Morocco. In addition to using documentary evidence to monitor change in settlement systems, it was also utilized to record the change in medieval Moroccan political economy from a reliance on agriculture to a reliance on long-distance gold trade (Chapter 4).

In this study, numismatic evidence was tailored to address specific issues on political economy and settlement systems. Three categories of information were particularly important in this regard: (1) the number of mints founded by each dynastic state, (2) their total production - as opposed to individual specimens, and (3) their spatial distribution. These categories of information were analyzed in terms of the main theoretical premise of this research (i.e., the shift in political economy and its material impact on settlement systems).

From a broader methodological vantage point, the archaeological-historical approach implemented in this study shows that multiple lines of evidence can be effectively combined without the risk of circular argument. Each line of evidence shed light on a particular aspect of medieval Moroccan society (Figure 1.2).

Archaeological evidence, in the form of survey and chemical compositional data, contributed primarily to our understanding of local exchange and community interaction between al-Basra and its hinterland, an aspect that is poorly depicted in historical records. The interpretation of the spatial patterns identified through INAA was corroborated by ethnoarchaeological observations on exchange mechanisms in modern-day Morocco.

Finally, by adopting a regional and comparative framework, this study is expected to be of interest to a wider audience of scholars and students in anthropological archaeology, economy, and history. Moreover, by combining theories and methodologies from two different anthropological schools (American and French), this research will help bridge the gap between Islamic-period archaeologists on both sides of the Atlantic.

Substantive Contributions

This study generated important data for settlement studies in Morocco. These data consist of (1) an inventory of 61 archaeological sites in northern Morocco (Appendix E), (2) INAA elemental data for 145 ceramic samples from sites in al-Basra region (Appendices F and G), (3) settlement information on nearly 100 sites in northern Morocco based on documentary and numismatic evidence (Appendix B), and finally (4) a list of 43 historical texts of potential significance to studies of medieval Moroccan economy and settlement systems (see Textual Sources Cited).

The inventory of the archaeological sites found during this project will contribute to the Moroccan national inventory of archaeological sites (*La Carte Archéologique du Maroc*). Although only the surface collections from al-Basra's hinterland sites were analyzed and the results incorporated in this project, the ceramic material from other sites was counted, photographed, and briefly described. This material is now curated at the Institut National des Sciences de l'Archéologie et du Patrimoine (INSAP).

The INAA elemental data from al-Basra's hinterland sites will be available to other scholars investigating other medieval local exchange systems in northern Morocco. The compilation - in one place - of a large corpus of documentary and numismatic information on medieval settlements in northern Morocco will make this information readily available to scholars and students, especially outside Morocco. In case more in-depth information is needed, I included a list of several medieval Arabic documentary sources of relevance to Islamic-period archaeologists. To make this literature available to a broader audience of American and British scholars, it needs to be translated into English by specialists who master the Arabic, French, and English languages.

Directions for Future Research

To conclude, this study suggests two main directions for future research in Morocco. First, building on the methods and results achieved in previous research in northern Morocco, it is important to establish and/or complete good ceramic typologies for other Islamic sites (e.g., Kurt, Walîla, Tu<u>sh</u>ummu<u>sh</u>) based on well-controlled stratigraphic excavations. As the results of the archaeological survey around al-Basra have shown, it is only when there is a good ceramic typology that survey data can be effectively used to address specific anthropological questions. Without previous knowledge of al-Basra material, it would have been difficult to draw any meaningful information from the al-Basra hinterland sites.

Essentially, what is suggested here is (1) to establish a good ceramic typology for a particular Islamic site based on excavated material, then use this knowledge to direct archaeological survey in the hinterland of the site, and (2) to apply the same research strategy at other sites and their hinterland in northern Morocco. Combining archaeological data from several sites and their hinterlands will eventually result in a better understanding of regional settlement patterns in all northern Morocco.

The second direction for future research is to utilize documentary and numismatic evidence to investigate issues related to political economy and settlement systems in other areas of Morocco, such as the Atlantic plains south of Bû Ragrâg, the <u>H</u>awz, the Sûs, and the Tâfilâlt. It is possible that other settlement patterns will emerge, especially since each of these areas followed relatively different economic and urban trajectories.

The value of this research is not limited to Moroccan and/or North African state societies. The archaeological-historical approach used in this study can be applied to other complex societies - not necessarily Islamic - in other parts of the world.

REFERENCES CITED

Akerraz, A.

1992 Lixus, du Bas-Empire à L'Islam. *Lixus*, Collection de L'Ecole Française de Rome 166:379-385.

1998 Recherches sur les Niveaux Islamiques de Volubilis. In *Genèse de la Ville Islamique en al-Andalus et au Maghreb Occidental*, edited by P. Cressier and M. Garcia-Arenal, pp. 295-304. Casa de Velazquez, CSIC., Madrid.

Alberich, C., J.

1954 *Cultos Primitivos de Marruecos*. Instituto de Estudios Africanos, Madrid.

Ammerman, A.

1981 Surveys and Archaeological Research. *Annual Review of Anthropology* 10:63-88.

Ataallah, M.

1967 La Céramique Musulmane à Paroi Fine Incisée ou Peinte de Lixus. *Bulletin d'Archéologie Marocaine* VII:627-639.

Baugh, T. and E. J. Ericson (editors)

1994 *Prehistoric Exchange Systems in North America*. Plenum Press, New York.

Baxter, M. J.

1994 *Exploratory Multivariate Analysis in Archaeology*. Edinburgh University Press, Edinburgh.

Bazzana, A., L. Erbati, Y. Montmessin, and A. Touri

1983-84 Première Prospection d'Archéologie Médiévale et Islamique dans le Nord du Maroc (Chefchaouen, Oued Laou, Bou Ahmed). *Bulletin d'Archéologie Marocaine* XV:367-450.

Bazzana, A. and Y. Montmessin

1995 Quelques Aspects de la Céramique Médiévale du Maroc du Nord: Problèmes Typologiques et Chronologiques. In *Actes du 5ème Colloque International: La Céramique Médiévale en Méditerranée Occidentale*, edited by R. El Hraiki and E. Erbati, pp. 241-269. Institut National des Sciences de l'Archéologie et du Patrimoine, Rabat.

Ben Romdhane, K.

1978 *Les Monnaies Almohades: Aspects Ideologiques et Économiques*. Thèse du 3ème cycle, Université de Paris VII.

Benco, N.

1987 *The Early Medieval Pottery Industry at al-Basra, Morocco*. BAR International Series 341. British Archaeological Reports, Oxford.

1989a Diversity in Ceramic Production: A Case Study from Medieval North Africa. In *Medieval Archaeology*, edited by C. L. Redman, pp. 99-118. Medieval and Renaissance Text Studies Press. State University of New York, Binghamton.

1989b Material Correlates of Specialized Pottery Production: An Ethnoarchaeological Example from Morocco. Paper presented at the 88th Annual Meeting of the American Anthropological Association, Washington, D.C.

1989c Morphological Variability: An Approach to the Study of Craft Specialization. In *A Pot for All Reasons: Ceramic Ecology Revisited*, edited by C. C. Kolb and L. M. Lackey, pp. 57-72. Laboratory of Anthropology, Temple University Press, Philadelphia, PA.

1990 1990 Archaeological Investigations at al-Basra, Morocco. *Bulletin d'Archéologie Marocaine* In press.

1992 *Compositional Analysis of Ethnographic Clays and Pottery from Morocco*. Proposal submitted to the MURR Archaeometry Laboratory.

1994 *Preliminary Report on Archaeological Excavations at Al-Basra, Morocco.* Submitted to Institut National des Sciences de l'Archéologie et du Patrimoine (INSAP), Rabat.

1995a A Historical Model of Pottery Production from Medieval North Africa. Paper presented at the 60th Annual Meeting of the Society for American Archaeology, Minneapolis.

1995b *Preliminary Report on Archaeological Excavations at al-Basra, Morocco.* Submitted to Institut National des Sciences de l'Archéologie et du Patrimoine (INSAP), Rabat.

2000 The Moroccan Site of al-Basra in Historical and Archaeological Perspective. Paper presented at the 65th Annual Meeting of the Society for American Archaeology, Philadelphia, PA.

in press Five Seasons of Archaeological Research at al-Basra, Morocco: 1980, 1981, 1990, 1994, and 1995. Paper presented at the *Actes du Colloque sur Plus d'un Siècle de Recherches Archéologiques au Maroc*, Societé Marocaine d'Archéologie et du Patrimoine, Rabat 1-4 Juillet, 1998.

Benco, N. and J. Blackman

1998 Chemical Homogeneity and the Standardization Hypothesis. Paper presented at the 63rd Annual Meeting of the Society for American Archaeology, Seattle, Washington.

in prep Neutron Activation Analysis of Medieval Islamic Pottery from al-Basra, Morocco. Manuscript in preparation.

Benco, N., S. Ennahid, J. Blackman, and H. Neff

in prep Pottery Production and Exchange in Medieval Morocco: A Chemical and Mineralogical Study. Manuscript in preparation.

Benjelloun-Laroui, L.

1990 *Les Bibliothèques du Maroc*. Islam d'Hier et d'Aujourd'hui 34. Maisonneuve & Larose, Paris.

Bishop, R. L. and H. Neff

1989 Compositional Data Analysis in Archaeology. In *Archaeological Chemistry*, vol. IV, edited by R. O. Allen, pp. 57-86. American Chemical Society, Washington, D.C.

Blachère, R.

1957 *Extraits des Principaux Géographes Arabes du Moyen Age*, Paris.

Boone, J. and N. Benco

1999 Islamic Settlement in North Africa and the Iberian Peninsula. *Annual Review of Anthropology* 28:51-71.

Boone, J. L., E. Myers and C. L. Redman

1990 Archaeological and Historical Approaches to Complex Societies: The Islamic States of Medieval Morocco. *American Anthropologist* 92:630-646.

Boone, J. L. and C. L. Redman

1982 Alternate Pathways to Urbanism in the Medieval Maghreb. *Comparative Urban Research* IX(1):28-38.

Bosworth, C. E., E. Van Donzel, B. Lewis and C. Pellat
1986 Leo Africanus. In *Encyclopaedia of Islam*, vol. V, pp. 723-724. E. J. Brill, Leiden.

Bovill, E. W.
1968 *The Golden Trade of the Moors*. 2nd ed. Oxford University Press, New York.

Brethes, J. D.
1939 *Contribution à l'Histoire du Maroc par les Recherches Numismatiques*, Casablanca.

Brett, M. and E. Fentress
1996 *The Berbers*. The Peoples of Africa. Blackwell Publishers, Oxford.

Brignon, J., A. Amine, B. Boutaleb, G. Martinet, and B. Rosenberger
1967 *Histoire du Maroc*. Hatier, Casablanca.

Brumfiel, E. M. and T. K. Earle
1987 Specialization, Exchange, and Complex Societies: An Introduction. In *Specialization, Exchange, and Complex Societies*, edited by E. Brumfiel and T. Earle, pp. 1-9. Cambridge University Press, Cambridge.

Cahen, C.
1981 L'Or du Soudan, Mythe ou Réalité Avant les Almoravides. In *Mélanges en Hommage à Raymond Mauny*, pp. 539-545, Paris.

Calasso, G.
1992 Les Remparts et la Loi, les Talismans et les Saints. La Protection de la Ville dans les Sources Musulmanes Médiévales. *Bulletin d'Etudes Orientales* XLIV(Numéro special: Sciences Occultes et Islam):83-104.

Chabbi, J. and N. Rabbat
1995 Ribâṭ. In *Encyclopaedia of Islam*, vol. VIII, pp. 493-506. E.J. Brill, Leiden.

Cherif, M.
1991 L'Importance de Ceuta dans le Réseau du Commerce Méditerranéen (XIIe-XIIIe Siècles). *Revue de la Faculté des Lettres de Tétouan* 5.

Colin, G. S.
1936 Les Mines Marocaines et les Marocains. *Bulletin Economique du Maroc* 13:194-200.

Conrad, D. C. and H. Fisher
1982 The Conquest that Never Was: Ghana and the Almoravids, 1076. Part 1: The External Arabic Sources. *History in Africa* 9:21-59.
1983 The Conquest that Never Was: Ghana and the Almoravids, 1076. Part 2: The Local Oral Sources. *History in Africa* 10:53-78.

Cressier, P.
1981 *Prospection Archéologique dans le Rif (Zone de l'Ancien Royaume de Nakur). Premiers Résultats*. Thèse du 3ème cycle, Université de la Sorbonne, Paris IV.
1983 Fortifications du Rif. *Castrum I, Habitats Fortifiés et Organization de l'Espace en Méditerranée Médiévale*, vol. IV:45-55. Travaux de la Maison de l'Orient (Lyon).
1984 Mastasa, Un Site Rural Médiéval Complexe sur la Côte du Rif (Maroc). *Photo Interpretation* 2-3:46-62.
1992 Le Développement Urbain Des Côtes Septentrionales du Maroc au Moyen Age: Frontière Intérieure et Frontière Extérieure. In *5ème Colloque International du C.T.H.S: Afrique du Nord Antique et Médiévale. Spectacles, Vie Portuaire, Religions*, pp. 173-187, Paris.
1995 La Fortification Islamique au Maroc: Eléments de Bibliographie. *Archéologie Islamique* 5:163-196.

Cressier, P., A. El Boudjay, H. El Figuigui, and J. Vignet-Zunz
1998 Hagar al-Nasr "Capital" Idrisside du Maroc Septentrional: Archéologie et Histoire (IVe H./Xe ap. J.C.). In *Genèse de la Ville Islamique en al-Andalus et au Maghreb Occidental*, edited by P. Cressier and M. Garcia-Arenal, pp. 305-334. Casa de Velazquez, CSIC, Madrid.

Cressier, P. and M. Garcia-Arenal (editors)
1998 *Genèse de la Ville Islamique en al-Andalus et au Maghreb Occidental*. Casa de Velazquez, CSIC, Madrid.

Cressier, P., M. Naimi and A.-A. Touri
1992 Maroc Saharien et Maroc Méditerranéen au Moyen Age: Le Cas des Ports de Nul Lamta et de Badis. In *5ème Colloque International du C.T.H.S: Afrique du Nord Antique et Médiévale. Spectacles, Vie Portuaire, Religions*, pp. 393-407, Paris.

Cressier, P. and M. Picon
1995 Céramique Médiévale d'Importation à Azelik-Takadda (République du Niger). In *Actes du 5ème Colloque International: La Céramique Médiévale en Méditerranée Occidentale*, edited by R. El Hraiki and E. Erbati, pp. 390-399. Institut National des Sciences de l'Archéologie et du Patrimoine, Rabat.

Cuoq, J.
1975 *Recueils des Sources Arabes Conçernant l'Afrique Occidentale du VIIIe au XVIe Siècle*, Paris.

D'Altroy, T., N. and T. K. Earle
1985 Staple Finance, Wealth Finance, and Storage in the Inka Political Economy. *Current Anthropology* 26(2):187-206.

De Cardinal-Breton, M.
1985-1986 Ramassage de Surface à Ayn Karuash: Méthodes, Résultats et Perspectives. *Bulletin d'Archéologie Marocaine*: 339-343.

Delpy, A.
1955 Note sur Quelques Vestiges de Céramique Recueillis à Salé. *Hésperis* 42:129-152.

Dermenghem, E.
1954 *Le Culte des Saints dans l'Islam Maghrebin*, Paris.

Deverdun, G. and M. Rouche
1949 Notes sur de Nouveaux Documents de la Céramique Marocaine Découverts à Marrakech. *Hésperis* 36:451-55.

Devisse, J.
1972a Routes de Commerce et Echanges en Afrique Occidentale en Relation avec la Méditerranée: Un essai sur le Commerce Africain Médiéval du XIe au XVIe Siècle, 1re Partie. *Revue d'Histoire Economique et Sociale* 50(1):42-73.
1972b Routes de Commerce et Echanges en Afrique Occidentale en Relation avec la Méditerranée: Un essai sur le Commerce Africain Médiéval du XIe au XVIe Siècle, 2e Partie. *Revue d'Histoire Economique et Sociale* 50(3):357-397.
1985 Sijilmassa: Les Sources Ecrites, l'Archéologie et le Controle des Espaces. In *Colloque Euro-Africain d'Erfoud*, p. 19.
1988 Trade and Trade Routes in West Africa. In *General History of Africa: Africa from the Seventh to the Eleventh Century*, edited by M. E. Fassi, vol. III, pp. 367-435. UNESCO, General History of Africa. University of California Press, Berkeley.
1996 Or d'Afrique. *Arabica* 43(1):234-243.

Devisse, J. and I. Hrbek
1988 The Almoravids. In *General History of Africa: Africa from the Seventh to the Eleventh Century*, edited by M. El Fassi, vol. III, pp. 336-366. UNESCO, General History of Africa. University of California Press, Berkeley.

Devisse, J. and M. Picon

1995 Questions de Pots: A Propos des Céramiques de Tegdaoust (Maurétanie). In *Actes du 5ème Colloque International: La Céramique Médiévale en Méditerranée Occidentale*, edited by R. El Hraiki and E. Erbati, pp. 235-240. Institut National des Sciences de l'Archéologie et du Patrimoine, Rabat.

Doutté, E.

1984 *Magie et Religion dans l'Afrique du Nord.* P. Gauthier. Maisonneuve, Paris.

Duff, A.

1999 Regional Interaction and the Transformation of Western Pueblo Identities, A.D. 1275-1400. Unpublished Ph.D. Dissertation, Department of Anthropology, Arizona State University. Tempe.

Dufourq, C. E.

1966 *L'Espagne Catalane et le Maghreb aux XIIIe-XIVe Siècles*, Paris.

Earle, T.

1994 Wealth Finance in the Inka Empire: Evidence from the Calchaqui Valley, Argentina. *American Antiquity* 59(3):443-460.

Earle, T. K. and J. E. Ericson (editors)

1977 *Exchange Systems In Prehistory*. Academic Press, New York.

Echalier, J.-C.

1976 Mise en Evidence d'un Courant d'Echange dans le Sahara Médiéval par l'Etude Minéralogique de Poteries Communes. *Archéologie Médiévale* VI:329-333.

Eickelman, D.

1976 *Moroccan Islam: Tradition and Society in a Pilgrimage Center*. University of Texas Press, Austin.

El-Hraiki, R.

1989 *Recherche Ethno-archeologique sur la Céramique du Maroc.* Thèse de Doctorat, Université Lyon 2.

El-Hraiki, R., D. Robert, and M. Picon

1986 Ateliers Producteurs et Commerce Transsaharien à l'Epoque Médiévale. In *La Ceramica Médiévale nel Mediterreneo Occidentale*, pp. 51-54, Florence.

El-Hraiki, R., A. Schmitt, and M. Picon

1995 Trans-Saharan Commerce in the Medieval and Post-Medieval Eras: Results from the Laboratory Study of Ceramics. In *Trade and Discovery: The Scientific Study of Artefacts from Post-Medieval Europe and Beyond*, edited by D. R. Hook and D. R. M. Gaimster, pp. 117-122. Occasional Paper 109. British Museum Press, London.

Elisseeff, N.

1988 Manzil. In *Encyclopaedia of Islam*, vol. VI, pp. 454-456. E. J. Brill, Leiden

Ennahid, S.

1992 *Contribution à l'Etude de la Céramique Médiévale d'al-Basra, Morocco.* Unpublished B.A. thesis, Institut National des Sciences de l'Archéologie et du Patrimoine, Rabat.

1995 *Archaeological Survey and Documentary Research: Reconstructing Early Islamic Settlement Patterns Around al-Basra, Northern Morocco.* Unpublished Master's thesis, Department of Anthropology, Arizona State University, Tempe, AZ.

Ericson, J. E. and T. G. Baugh (editors)

1993 *The American Southwest and Mesoamerica: Systems of Prehistoric Exchange.* Plenum Press, New York.

Eustache, D.

1955 El-Basra, Capitale Idrissite et Son Port. *Hésperis* 42:218-38.

1970a Idrisids. In *Encyclopaedia of Islam*, vol. III, pp. 1035-1037. E. J. Brill, Leiden.

1970b Les Ateliers Monétaires du Maroc. *Hespéris-Tamuda* 11:95-102.

1970-71 *Corpus des Dirhams Idrissites et Contemporains: Etudes sur la Numismatique et l'Histoire Monétaire du Maroc I.* Banque du Maroc, Rabat.

Euzennat, M.

1962 *Les Voies Romaines du Maroc dans l'Itinéraire Antonin.* Hommages Albert Grenier 2, Bruxelles.

Fish, S. and S. Kowalewski (editors)

1990 *The Archaeology of Regions: A Case for Full-Coverage Survey.* Smithsonian Institution Press, Washington, D.C.

Fogg, W.

1939 The Importance of Tribal Markets in the Commercial Life of the Countryside of North-West Morocco. *Africa* 12(4):445.

1941 Changes in the Lay-out, Characteristics, and Function of a Moroccan Tribal Market, Consequent on European Control. *Man* 41:72.

Garcia-Arenal, M. and E. Manzano Moreno

1995 Idrissisme et Villes Idrissides. *Studia Islamica* 82(2):5-33.

1998 Légitimité et Villes Idrissides. In *Genèse de la Ville Islamique en al-Andalus et au Maghreb Occidental*, edited by P. Cressier and M. Garcia-Arenal, pp. 257-284. Casa de Velazquez, CSIC, Madrid.

Geertz, C.

1968 *Islam Observed.* Yale University Press, New Haven.

Glascock, M.

1992 Characterization of Archaeological Ceramics at MURR by Neutron Activation Analysis and Multivariate Statistics. In *Chemical Characterization of Ceramic Pastes in Archaeology*, edited by H. Neff, pp. 11-26. Monographs in World Archaeology, vol. 7. Prehistory Press, Madison, Wisconsin.

Godinho, V. M.

1947 *Historia Economics e Social da Expansao Portuguesa.* Marroco I. Terra Editora, Lisbon.

1956 *O mediterraneo Saariano e os Caravanas de Oro, Geografia Economica e Social do Saara Occidental e Central do XI as XVI Secolo*, St.-Paul, Brazil.

1969 *L'Economie de l'Empire Portugais aux XVe et XVIe Siècles*, Paris.

Grenier De Cardenal, M.

1980 Recherches sur la Céramique Médiévale Marocaine. In *La Céramique Médiévale en Méditerranée Occidentale: Xe-XVe siècles,* edited by G. Démains D'Archimbaud and M. Picon, pp. 227-249. Colloques Internationaux CNRS: Paris.

Gsell, S.

1928 Vieilles Exploitations Minières dans l'Afrique du Nord. *Hespéris* 7:1-21.

Harbottle, G.

1976 Activation Analysis in Archaeology. In *Radiochemistry*, vol. 3, edited by G. W. A. Newton, pp. 33-72. The Chemical Society, London.

Hazard, H. W.

1952 *The Numismatic History of Late Medieval North Africa.* Numismatic Studies 8. The American Numismatic Society, New York.

Hinz, W.

1965 Farsakh. In *Encyclopaedia of Islam*, vol. II, pp. 812-813. E. J. Brill, Leiden.

Hirth, K. G.

1996 Political Economy and Archaeology: Perspectives on Exchange and Production. *Journal of Archaeological Research* 4(3):203-239.

Hodder, I. and C. Orton

1976 *Spatial Analysis in Archaeology*. Cambridge University Press, Cambridge.

Hopkins, J. F. P.

1958 *Medieval Muslim Government in Barbary*, London.

Idris, R.

1968 L'Invasion Hilalienne et ses Conséquences. *Cahiers de Civilization Médiévale* XI.

Ismail, A. A.

1972 Origin, Ideology and Physical Patterns of Arab Urbanization. *Ekistics* 33(195):113-123.

Issawi, C. P.

1987 *An Arab Philosophy of History*. The Darwin Press, New Jersey.

Jacques-Meunié, Dj.

1951 *Grenier-Citadelles au Maroc*. Larose, Paris.

Jacques-Meunié, D.

1982 *Le Maroc Saharien dès Origines à 1670*. Librairie Klinsieck, Paris.

Johnson, G.

1975 Locational Analysis and the Investigation of Uruk local Exchange Systems. In *Ancient Civilization and Trade*, edited by J. A. Sabloff and C. C. Lamberg-Karlovsky, pp. 285-339. University of New Mexico Press, Albuquerque.

Kamal, Y.

1926-1951 *Monumenta Cartographia Africae et Aegypti*, Cairo.

Laallaoui, M.

1993 Agmat, Atelier Monétaire Idrisside. In *Actes du XIe Congrès International de Numismatique*, vol. III, pp. 287-290. Louvain-la-Neuve.

Lacoste, Y.

1966 *Ibn Khaldun*. Maspero, Paris.

1974 The General Characteristics and Fundamental Structures of Medieval North African Society. *Economy and Society* 3:1-17.

1984 *Ibn Khaldun: The Birth of History and the Past of the Third World*. Verso, London.

Laroui, A.

1995 *L'Histoire du Maghreb: Un Essai de Synthèse*. Centre Culturel Arabe, Casablanca.

Le Tourneau, R.

1949 *Fès avant le Protectorat: Etude Economique et Sociale d'une Ville de l'Occident Musulman*. Publications de l'Institut des Hautes Etudes Marocaines XLV, Casablanca.

1961 *Fez in the Age of the Marinides*. Translated by Besse Alberta Clement. University of Oklahoma Press, Norman.

Lessard, J.-M.

1970 Sijilmassa, la Ville et ses Relations Commerciales au XI Siècle d'après El Bekri. *Hespéris-Tamuda* 11:5-56.

Lévi-Provençal, E.

1941 Un Recueil de Lettres Officielles Almohades. *Hespéris*.

1953 Marabout. In *Shorter Encyclopaedia of Islam*, edited by H. A. R. Gibb and J. H. Kramers, pp. 325-326. E. J. Brill, Leiden.

1960 Abu 'Ubayd al-Bakrî. In *Encyclopaedia of Islam*, vol. I, pp. 155-157. E.J. Brill, Leiden.

Levtzion, N.

1978 The Sahara and Sudan from the Arab Conquest of the Maghrib to the Rise of the Almoravids. In *The Cambridge History of Africa*, vol. 2, edited by J. Fage, pp. 637-680. Camridge University Press, Cambridge.

Levtzion, N. and J. F. P. Hopkins (editors)

1981 *Corpus of Early Arabic Sources for West African History*. Cambridge University Press, Cambridge.

Lewarch, D. E. and M. J. O'Brien

1981 The Expanding Role of Surface Assemblages in Archaeological Research. In *Advances in Archaeological Method and Theory*, vol. 4, edited by M. B. Schiffer, pp. 297-342. Academic Press, New York.

Lightfoot, D. R. and J. A. Miller

1996 Sijilmassa: The Rise and Fall of a Walled Oasis in Medieval Morocco. *Annals of the Association of American Geographers* 86(1):78-101.

Limane, H. and R. Rebuffat

1995 Voie Romaine et Système de Surveillaince Militaire sur la Carte d'Arbaoua. In *Actes du VI Colloque International: Productions et Exportations Africaines, Actualités Archéologiques*, pp. 299-342. L'Afrique du Nord Antique et Médiévale, CTHS, Paris.

Louhichi, A. and M. Picon

1983 Importation de Matériel Ifriqiyen en Mauritanie. *Revue d'Archéometrie* 7:45-58.

Loyet, M.

2000 Food and Fuel: The Faunal Remains from al-Basra. Paper presented at the 65th Annual Meeting of the Society for American Archaeology, Philadelphia, PA.

Mahoney, N.

1994 *Economy and Environment at al-Basra: An Archaeobotanical Analysis of a Medieval Islamic Urban Center*. Unpublished Master's thesis, Department of Anthropology, George Washington University, Washington, DC.

Maqbul, A., S.

1965 Djughrâfiya. In *Encyclopaedia of Islam*, vol. II, pp. 575-587. E. J. Brill, Leiden.

1995 *A History of Arab-Islamic Geography: 9th-16th Century A.D.* Al al-Bayt University, Mafraq, Amman.

Marçais, G.

1913 *Les Arabes en Bérberie du XIe au XIVe Siècle*, Constantine-Paris.

1939 Poteries Estampées du Moyen Age. In *Actes du IVe congrès de la Féderation des Societés Savantes de l'Afrique du Nord*, Algiers.

Massignon, L.

1906 *Le Maroc dans les Premiéres Années du XVI Siècle ap. J.C.: Tableau Géographique d'Après Léon l'Africain*. Mémoires de la Société Historique Algérienne I, Algiers.

Mauny, R.

1961 Tableau Géographique de l'Ouest Africain au Moyen Age d'après les Sources Ecrites, la Tradition et l'Archéologie. *Bulletin de l'Institut Fondemental de l'Afrique Noire/Bulletin de l'Institut Français de l'Afrique Noire* 61.

Messier, R.

1974 The Almoravids: West Africa and the Gold Currency of the Mediterranean Basin. *Journal of Economic and Social History of the Orient* 17(1):31-47.

1980 Quantitative Analysis of Almoravid Dinars. *Journal of Economic and Social History of the Orient* 23(1-2):102-118.

1995 Sijilmassa: Intermédiaire entre la Méditerranée et l'Ouest de l'Afrique. In *L'Occident Musulman et l'Occident Chrétien au Moyen Age*, edited by M. Hammam, pp. 181-196, Rabat.

1997 Sijilmassa: Five Seasons of Archaeological Inquiry by a Joint Moroccan-American Mission. *Archéologie Islamique* 7:61-92.

Miles, G. C.

1965a Dînâr. In *Encyclopaedia of Islam*, vol. II, pp. 297-299. E. J. Brill, Leiden.

1965b Dirham. In *Encyclopaedia of Islam*, vol. II, pp. 319-320. E. J. Brill, Leiden

Miller, R.

1997 Gold as a Commodity in West Africa. *The Numismatist* 110(9):1023.

Miquel, A.

1967 *Géographie Humaine du Monde Musulman Jusqu'au Milieu du XIe Siècle: Géographie et Géographie Humaine dans la Littérature Arabe dès origines à 1050*. Civilisations et Societés: 7, vol. 1, Ecole Pratique Des Hautes Etudes, Mouton & Co., Paris-La Haye.

1971 Ibn Hawkal. In *Encyclopaedia of Islam*, vol. III, pp. 786-788. E. J. Brill, Leiden

1987 Quelques Aspects de la Ville dans la Géographie Arabe du Xs. *Mondes et Cultures* XLVII(2):153-168.

1993 al-Mukaddasî. In *Encyclopaedia of Islam*, vol. VII, pp. 492-493. E. J. Brill, Leiden.

Monaes Farias, F. P.

1967 The Almoravids. *Bulletin de l'Institut Français de l'Afrique Noire/Bulletin de l'Institut Fondamental de l'Afrique Noire* XXIX(Serie B):863-865.

Montagne, R.

1929 Un Magazin Collectif de l'Anti-Atlas: L'Agadir des Ikounka. *Hésperis* 9:145-266.

Monteil, V.

1968 Routier de l'Afrique Blanche et Noire du Nord-Ouest. *Bulletin de l'Institut Fondemental de l'Afrique Noire/Bulletin de l'Institut Français de l'Afrique Noire* XXX(Serie B):39-116.

Myers, E.

1984 The Political Economy of Pottery Production: An Archaeological Study of the Islamic Commonware Ceramics of Medieval Qsar es-Seghir. Unpublished Ph.D. dissertation, Department of Anthropology, State University of New York, Binghamton, NY.

Nance, J. D.

1983 Regional Sampling in Archaeological Survey: The Statistical Perspective. In *Advances in Archaeological Method and Theory*, vol. 6, edited by M. B. Schiffer, pp. 289-356. Academic Press, New York.

Neff, H.

1992 Introduction. In *Chemical Characterization of Ceramic Pastes in Archaeology*, vol. 7, pp. 1-10. Monographs in World Archaeology. Prehistory Press, Madison, Wisconsin.

Neff, H. and M. Glascock

1993 *Compositional Analysis of Ethnographic Clays and Pottery form Morocco*. Research Report on file, Missouri University Research Reactor, University of Missouri, Columbia.

2000 *Instrumental Neutron Activation Analysis of Ceramics from Northern Morocco*. Research Report on file, Missouri University Research Reactor, University of Missouri, Columbia.

Norris, F.

1971 New Evidence on the Life of Abdullah Ibn Yasin and the Origins of the Almoravid Movement. *Journal of African History* 12:2.

Oman, G.

1971 al-Idrîsî. In *Encyclopaedia of Islam*, vol. III, pp. 1032-1035. E. J. Brill, Leiden.

Pellat, C.

1991 al-Masâlik wa 'l-mamâlik. In *Encyclopaedia of Islam*, vol. VI, pp. 639-640. E. J. Brill, Leiden.

Picard, C.

1995 Le Commerce des Produits Agricoles entre le Maghreb Occidental et l'Andalus au XII Siècle. In *Actes du VI Colloque International: Productions et Exportations Africaines, Actualités Archéologiques*, pp. 177-187. L'Afrique du Nord Antique et Médiévale, CTHS, Paris.

1996 Fortifications et Fonctions Portuaires sur le Littoral Atlantique Musulman. *Archéologie Islamique* 6:45-66.

Plog, F.

1977 Modeling Economic Exchange. In *Exchange Systems In Prehistory*, edited by T. Earle and J. Ericson, pp. 127-140. Academic Press, New York.

Plog, F. T., S. Plog, and W. Wait

1978 Decision Making in Modern Surveys. In *Advances in Archaeological Method and Theory*, vol. 1, edited by M. B. Schiffer, pp. 383-421. Academic Press, New York.

Poncet, J.

1967 Le Mythe de la "Catastrophe" Hilalienne. *Annales: Economie, Sociétés, Civilizations*:1099-1120.

Rebuffat, R.

1987 L'Implantation Militaire Romaine en Maurétanie Tingitane. *L'Africa Romana*, pp. 31-78.

Redman, C.

1973 Multistage Fieldwork and Analytical Techniques. *American Antiquity* 38(1):61-79.

1983 Comparative Urbanism in the Islamic Far West. *World Archaeology* 14:355-77.

1983-84Survey and Test Excavation of Six Medieval Islamic Sites in Northern Morocco. *Bulletin d'Archéologie Marocaine* XV:311-349.

1986a Methods Used to Compare Islamic Ceramic Assemblages from Northern Morocco. In *Ceramica Medieval del Mediterraneo Occidental*, pp. 11-19, Madrid.

1986b *Qsar es-Seghir: An Archaeological View of Medieval Life*. Academic Press, New York.

Redman, C. L. and P. J. Watson

1970 Systematic Intensive Surface Collection. *American Antiquity* 35:279-291.

Renfrew, C.

1977 Introduction: Production and Exchange in Early State Societies, the Evidence of Pottery. In *Pottery and Early Commerce: Characterization and Trade in Roman and Later Ceramics*, edited by D. P. S. Peacock, pp. 1-20. Academic Press, London.

Ricard, P.
1925 *Le Maroc*. Les Guides Bleus. Hachette, Paris.

Ricard, P. and A. Delpy
1931 Notes sur la Découverte de Spécimens de la Céramique du Moyen Age. *Hespéris* 13:227-237.

Ricard, R.
1936 Le Commerce de Berberie et l'Organization Economique de l'Empire Portugais au XV et XVI Siècles. *Annales de l'Institut des Etudes Orientales d'Alger* II.
1938 Les Places Portugaises du Maroc et le Commerce d'Andalousie. *Annales de l'Institut d'Etudes Orientale d'Alger* IV.
1955 *Etudes sur l'Histoire des Portugais au Maroc*, Coimbra.

Rice, P.
1987 *Pottery Analysis: A source book*. The University of Chicago Press, Chicago.

Riley, J.
1984 Pottery Analysis and the Reconstruction of Ancient Exchange Systems. In *The Many Dimensions of Pottery: Ceramics in Archaeology and Anthropology*, edited by S. E. Van der Leeuw and A. Pritchard, pp. 57-78, CINGULA 7. Institute for Pre- and Proto-history, University of Amsterdam, Amsterdam.

Rosenberger, B.
1964 Autour d'une Grande Mine d'Argent du Moyen Age Marocain: Le Jbel Aouam. *Hespéris-Tamuda* 5.
1967 Note sur Kouz, un Ancien Port à l'Embouchure de l'Oued Tensift. *Hespéris-Tamuda* 8:23-66.
1970a Les Vieilles Exploitations Minières et les Centres Métallurgiques du Maroc: Essai de Carte Historique. *Revue de Géographie du Maroc* 17:71-108.
1970b Les Vieilles Exploitations Minières et les Centres Métallurgiques du Maroc: Essai de Carte Historique. *Revue de Géographie du Maroc* 18:59-102.
1970c Tamdult, Cité Minière et Caravanière Pre-Saharienne: IXe-XIVe Siècles. *Hespéris-Tamuda* 11:103-139.
1998 Les Premières Villes Islamiques du Maroc: Géographie et Fonctions. In *Genèse de la Ville Islamique en al-Andalus et au Maghreb Occidental*, edited by P. Cressier and M. Garcia-Arenal, pp. 229-255. Casa de Velazquez, CSIC., Madrid.

Sayre, E. V.
1975 *Brookhaven Procedures for Statistical Analyses of Multivariate Archaeometric Data*. Manuscript on file, Brookhaven National Laboratory, BNL-23128.

Schiffer, M. B., M. A. Sullivan, and T. Klinger
1978 The Design of Archaeological Surveys. *World Archaeology* 10(1):1-28.

Sinopoli, C. M.
1994 The Archaeology of Empires. *Annual Review of Anthropology* 23:159-180.

Siraj, A.
1995a De l'Antiquité au Haut Moyen Age: Produits et Voies de Commerce dans la Maurétanie Occidentale (Le Maghrib al-Aksa). In *Actes du VI Colloque International: Productions et Exportations Africaines, Actualités Archéologiques*, pp. 189-207. L'Afrique du Nord Antique et Médiévale, CTHS, Paris.
1995b *L'Image de la Tingitane: L'Historiographie Arabe Médiévale et l'Antiquité Nord-Africaine*. Collection de l'Ecole Française de Rome: 209, Paris.
1998 Vie et Mort d'une Cité Islamique: A Propos du Phénomen Urbain dans le Maroc Idrissid Septentrional. In *Genèse de la Ville Islamique en al-Andalus et au Maghreb Occidental*, edited by P. Cressier and M. Garcia-Arenal, pp. 285-294. Casa de Velazquez, CSIC., Madrid.

Smith, A. B.
1993 Sijilmasa, Morocco, and the Saharan Gold Trade. *Digging Stick* 10(2):5-8.

Stambouli, F. and A. Zghal
1976 Urban Life in Pre-Colonial North Africa. *British Journal of Sociology* 27:1-20.

Taouchikht, L.
1995 La Céramique Médiévale de Sijilmassa: Approche Générale. In *Actes du 5ème Colloque International: La Céramique Médiévale en Méditerranée Occidentale*, edited by R. El Hraiki and E. Erbati, pp. 224-234. Institut National des Sciences de l'Archéologie et du Patrimoine, Rabat.

Terrasse, H.
1936 Note sur les Ruines de Sijilmassa. *Revue Africaine* 79(368-369):581-589.
1937 La Céramique Hispano-Maghrébine du XIIe Siècle d'Après les Fouilles du Chateau de l'ain Ghaboula, Dchira. *Hésperis* 37.
1947a L'Ancien Maroc Pays d'Economie Egarée I. *Revue de la Méditerranée* IV(17):37-53.
1947b L'Ancien Maroc Pays d'Economie Egarée II. *Revue de la Méditerranée* IV(18):147-160.
1950 *Histoire du Maroc dès Origines à l'Etablissement du Protectorat Français*. 2 vols, Casablanca.
1953 La Forteresse Almoravide d'Amargou. *Al-Andalus* XVIII:389-400.

Terrasse, H. and J. Meunié
1957 *Nouvelles Recherches Archéologiques à Marrakech*. Publications de l'Institut des Hautes Etude Marocaines LXII, Paris.

Tissot, C.
1876 Itinéraire de Tanger à Rbat. *Bulletin de la Société de Géographie*:225-294.
1878 *Recherches sur la Géographie Comparée de la Maurétanie Tingitane*. Mémoires de l'Académie des Inscriptions et Belles Lettres, Paris.

Touri, A.
1988 Prospections Archéologiques dans les Jbala-Ghomara (Maroc). Méthodes et Résultats. In *Castrum 2. Structures de l'Habitat et Occupation du Sol dans les Pays Méditerranéens. Les méthodes et l'Apport de l'archéologie Extensive*, pp. 29-41. Collection de l'Ecole Française de Rome 105, Collection de la Casa de Velazquez 21, Rome-Madrid.
1997 *Patrimoine Culturel et Territoire: Etude Préliminaire pour la Mise en Valeur de la Région du Gharb*. Submitted to Direction du Patrimoine Culturel, Secretariat d'Etat Chargé de la Culture, Ministère de l'Enseignement Superieur de la Formation des Cadres et de la Culture, UNESCO, Rabat.

Troin, J.-F.
1975 *Les Souks Marocains: Marchés Ruraux et Organisation de l'Espace dans la Moitié Nord du Maroc*. Edisud, Aix-en-Provence.

Udovitch, A. L.
1965 Fals. In *Encyclopaedia of Islam*, vol. II, pp. 768-769. E. J. Brill, Leiden

Vanacker, C.

1973 Géographie Economique de l'Afrique du Nord selon les Auteurs Arabes, du IX au milieu du XII siècles. *Annales: Economie, Sociétés, Civilizations* 28(3):659-680.

Vossen, R.

1984 Towards Building Models of Traditional Trade in Ceramics: Case Studies from Spain and Morocco. In *The Many Dimensions of Pottery: Ceramics in Archaeology and Anthropology*, edited by S. E. Van der Leeuw and A. Pritchard, pp. pp. 341-406, CINGULA 7. Institute for Pre- and Proto-history, University of Amsterdam, Amsterdam.

Vossen, R. and W. Ebert

1986 *Marokkanische Topferei: Topferorte und-zentren Eine Landesaufnahme (1980)*. Dr. Rudolf Habelt GmbH, Bonn.

Webb, J. and D. Frankel

1994 Making an Impression: Storage and Surplus Finance in Late Bronze Age Cyprus. *Journal of Mediterranean Archaeology* 7(1):5.

Weigand, P. C., G. Harbottle, and E. V. Sayre

1977 Turquoise Sources and Source Analysis: Mesoamerica and the Southwestern U.S.A. In *Exchange Systems in Prehistory*, edited by T. K. Earle and J. E. Ericson, pp. 15-34. Academic Press, New York.

Westermarck, E.

1926 *Ritual and Belief in Morocco*. Macmillan, London.

1935 *Survivances Paiennes dans la Civilisation Mohametaine*. Payot, Paris.

Wheatley, P.

1976 Levels of Space Awareness in the Traditional Islamic City. *Ekistics* 42(253):354-366.

Yver, G.

1960 al-Basra. In *Encyclopaedia of Islam*, vol. I, pp. 1087-1088. E. J. Brill, Leiden.

1978 al-Kasr al-Kabîr. In *Encyclopaedia of Islam*, vol. IV, pp. 729. E. J. Brill Leiden.

TEXTUAL SOURCES CITED

Abû al-Fidâ

1848 *Géographie d'Aboulfeda*. Translated by A. Reinaud and St. Guyard. 2 vols. Imprimerie Royale, Paris.

Anonymous

1958 *Kitâb al-istibsâr fî 'adjâ'ib al-amsâr*. 1st ed. Alexandria University, Alexandria.

1981 *Akhbâr madjmû'a fî fathi-l-andalus wa dhikri 'umarâ'ihâ*. al-Maktaba al-Andalusiyya, Beirut.

1985 *Kitâb al-istibsâr fî 'adjâ'ib al-amsâr*. 2nd ed. Dar al-Nashr al-Maghribiyya, Casablanca.

al-Bakrî

1965 *Description de l'Afrique Septentrionale*. 3rd ed. Translated by M. De Slane. Adrien-Maisonneuve, Paris.

Fagnan, E.

1924 *Extraits Inédits Relatifs au Maghreb (Géographie et Histoire)*. Translated by E. Fagnan. J. Carbonel, Algiers.

al-Himyarî, Ibn 'Abd al-Mun'im

1975 *al-Rawd al-mi'târ fî khabar al-aktâr*. Maktabat Lubnan, Beirut.

Ibn Abî Zar' al-Fâsî

1843 *Annales Regum Mauritaniae (al-Anis al-mutrib rawdh al-kirtas)*. Translated by Carolus Johannes Tornberg. 2 vols. Litteris Academicis, Upsaliae.

1860 *Roudh el-Kartas, Histoire des Souverains du Maghreb et Annales de la Ville de Fès*. Translated by A. Beaumier, Paris.

1964 *Rawd al-qirtas*. Translated by A. Huici Miranda. 2 vols, Valence.

Ibn Battûta

1859 *Al-Rihla*. Translated by C. Defremery and B.R. Sanguinetti. Collection d'Ouvrages Orientaux. 4 vols. Société Asiatique, Paris.

Ibn al-Fakîh al-Hamadânî

1949 *al-Buldân*. Translated by M. Hadj Sadok. J. Carbonel, Algiers.

1973 *Abregé du Livre des Pays*. Translated by Henri Massé. Institut Français de Damas, Damascus.

Ibn Hawkal

1842 Description de l'Afrique. *Journal Asiatique* XIII (Février):153-196; 209-258.

1873 *al-Masâlik wa-l-mamâlik*. Bibliotheca Geographorum Arabicorum II, Leiden.

1938-39*Sûrat al-ard*. Bibliotheca Geographorum Arabicorum II, edited by J. K. Kramers. 2nd ed. 2 vols, Leiden.

1965 *Configuration de la Terre*. Translated by G. Wiet. Maisonneuve et Larose, Paris.

1967 *Kitâb sûrat al-ard (Opus Geographicum)*. Bibliotheca Geographorum Arabicorum II, edited by J. H. Kramers. E. J. Brill, Leiden.

Ibn 'Idhârî

1948 *al-Bayân al-mughrib fî akhbâr al-Maghrib*. 4 vols. E. J. Brill, Leiden.

Ibn Khaldûn

1847 *Kitâb al-'ibar (Histoire des Berbères et des Dynasties Musulmanes de l'Afrique Septentrionale)*. Translated by M. De Slane. 2 vols, Algiers.

1967 *al-Muqaddimah*. Translated by F. Rosenthal. 3 vols. Princeton University Press, Princeton.

Ibn Khurdâdhbah

1889 *al-Masâlik wa-l-mamâlik*, Leiden.

1949 *al-Masâlik wa-l-mamâlik (Description du Maghreb et de l'Europe au IIIe Siècle/IX Siécle)*. Translated by M. Hadj Sadok. J. Carbonel, Algiers.

Ibn Rustah

1967 *Kitâb al-a'lâk al-nafîsa*. Bibliotheca Geographorum Arabicorum VII, edited by M. J. De Goeje. 2nd ed. E. J. Brill, Leiden.

Ibn Sa'îd al-Maghribî

1958 *Bast al-ard fî tûliha wa-l-'ard*. Instituto Muley Hasan, Tetuan.

al-Idrîsî

1864-1866*Description de l'Afrique et de l'Espagne*. 2 vols. E. J. Brill, Leiden.

1957 *Description de l'Afrique Septentrionale et Saharienne (Texte arabe extrait du Kitâb nuzhat al-mushtâk fî ikhtirâk al-âfâk)*. La Maison des Livres, Algiers.

1983 *Le Maghrib 6 siècle de l'hégire (12 siècle après J.C.)*. Publishid, Paris.

al-Istakhrî

1948 al-Masâlik wa-l-mamâlik. *Bulletin des Etudes Arabes* 37(March-April):91-96.

Leo Africanus (al-Hasan al-Wazzân)

1956 *Description de l'Afrique (Della Descrittione dell'Africa e delle cose notabili che quivi sono)*. Translated by A. Epaulard, Th. Monod, H. Lhote, and R. Mauny. 2 vols. Maisonneuve, Paris.

Lévi-Provençal, E.

1928 *Documents Indédits d'Histoire Almohade*. P. Geuthner, Paris.

al-Mukaddasî

1950 *Description de l'Occident Musulman au IVe=Xe Siècle*. Translated by Charles Pellat. Bibliothèque Arabe-Française (IX), Algiers.

1963 *Ahsan al-takâsîm fî ma'rifat al-akâlîm (la meilleure répartition pour la connaissance des provinces)*. Translated by André Miquel. Institut Français de Damas, Damascus.

1994 *The Best Divisions for Knowledge of the Regions: A Translation of Ahsan al-Taqasim fi Marifat al-Aqalim*. 1st ed. Translated by Basil Anthony Collins and reviewed by Muhammad Hamid al-Tai. Centre for Muslim Contribution to Civilisation. Garnet Publishing, Reading.

Miquel, A.

1973 La Description du Maghreb dans la Géographie d'al-Içt'akhri. *Revue de l'Occident Musulman* 2ème semestre:231-239.

al-Ya'kûbî

1892 *Kitâb al-buldân*. Translated by G. Wiet. Bibliotheca Geographorum Arabicorum VII. E. J. Brill, Leiden.

1937 *al-Buldân (Les Pays)*. Translated by G. Wiet. Oriental Authors, Institut Français d'Archéologie Orientale, Cairo.

Yâkût al-Hamawî

1852-1869 Marâsid al-ittilâ' 'alâ asmâ' al-amkina wa-l-bikâ'. In *Lexicon Geographicum*, edited by Juynboll. 5 vols, Leiden.

1866-1873 *Mu'djam al-buldân*. 6 vols, Leipzig.

1906-1907 *Mu'djam al-buldân*, vol. 10, Cairo.

al-'Umarî

1927 *Masâlik al-absâr fi mamâlik al-amsâr (L'Afrique moins l'Egypte)*. Translated by M. Gaudefroy-Demombynes. Bibliothèque des Géographes Arabes, Paris.

al-Watwât

1924 Mabâhidj al-fikr wa manâhidj al-'Ibar. In *Extraits Inédits Relatifs au Maghreb*, pp. 41-61. Translated by E. Fagnan, Algiers.

al-Zuhrî

1968 Kitâb al-djughrâfiya. *Bulletin d'Etudes Orientales* 21:9-312.

APPENDIX A

CHRONOLOGICAL LISTING OF THE MEDIEVAL GEOGRAPHERS AND CHRONICLERS CITED IN THIS STUDY

1. Ibn Khurdâdhbah (272 A.H./A.D. 885)[1]
2. al-Ya'kûbî (276 A.H./A.D. 889-890)
3. Ibn al-Fakîh al-Hamadânî (after 290 A.H./A.D. 903)
4. al-Istakhrî (340 A.H./A.D. 951)
5. al-Warrâk (292-363 A.H./A.D. 904-973)*
6. Ibn Hawkal (378 A.H/A.D. 988)
7. al-Mukaddasî (375-380 A.H./A.D.985-990)
8. al-Bakrî (460 A.H./A.D. 1068)
9. al-Zuhrî (532 A.H./A.D. 1137)
10. al-Idrîsî (548A.H./A.D. 1154)
11. al-Baydak (565 A.H./A.D. 1170)*
12. *Kitâb al-Istibsâr* (587 A.H./A.D. 1191)
13. Yâkût al-Hamawî (621 A.H./A.D. 1224)
14. Ibn Sa'îd al-Maghribî (685 A.H./A.D. 1286)
15. Ibn 'Idhârî (712 A.H./A.D. 1312)
16. al-Watwât (al-Kurtubî) (632-718 A.H./A.D. 1235-1318)*
17. Ibn Abî Zar' al-Fâsî (between 710-720 A.H./A.D. 1310-1320)*
18. Abû al-Fidâ (721 A.H./A.D. 1321)
19. al-'Umarî (737-738 A.H./A.D. 1337-1338)
20. Ibn Battûta (756 A.H./A.D. 1355)
21. Ibn Khaldûn (808 A.H./A.D. 1406)*
22. al-Himyarî, Ibn 'Abd al-Mun'im (A.D. 1461?)
23. Leo Africanus (al-Hasan al-Wazzân) (906-956 A.H./A.D. 1496?-1548)

[1] Dates refer to the year (s) when the source was written. Dates followed by (*) indicate the author's year of death. A.H. (After Hidjra) indicates the year in Muslim calendar.

APPENDIX B

SYNOPTIC TABLE OF SETTLEMENT INFORMATION BASED ON TEXTUAL AND NUMISMATIC EVIDENCE (MEDIEVAL NORTHERN MOROCCO)

Name	Founding	Size/Economy	Textual/Numismatic Sources
Aftis	Idrisid	"Ville appartenant a Djannun b. Ibrahim, et habitee par des Kutama... riche et florissante."	(al-Bakri 1965:223)
Aghigha	"Elle devait sa fondation aux Rabedis espagnols [202 A.H./A.D. 818]."; Idrisid?	"Cette ville est maintenant deserte."	(al-Bakri 1965:295)
Agla	"Batie par les Africains" pre-Idrisid?	"Une ville antique... ruinee dans les guerre passees..." (Leo Africanus 1956:257). Destroyed in the 10th century A.D. (Massignon, 1906:241)	(Leo Africanus 1956:257, Massignon, 1906:241)
Aklam (al-)-1	"Fondee recemment par Yahya b. Idris [b. 'Umar; Yahya IV; A.D. 905-919]"; Idrisid	[City]; "Il y a une chaire (minbar) et une mosquee djami' (congregational mosque) construite par les Idrisides." (Ibn Hawkal 1967:80)	(Ibn Hawkal 1938-39:77, 1967:80)
Aklam (al-)-2 (Bab Aklam)	Built by 'Abd Allah b. Idris; Idrisid	[Prosperous city]	(al-Idrisi1957:109)
Amardjuwa-1	Almoravid	Fortress	(Anonymous 1985:190)
Amardjuwa-2 (Mergo)	"Elle fut batie par les Romains"; [Almoravid]	"Cette ville est aujourd'hui inhabitee... il ya sur la pente de la montagne une autre petite ville [Mulay Bu Shta village]..."	(Leo Africanus 1956:256)
Ara'ish (al-)-1 (Ribat Harat al-Ahshis?)	[pre-Almoravid?]	"Bourg [village] bien peuple qui touche a une vaste plaine."	(al-Bakri 1965:223-224)
Ara'ish (al-)-2	[pre-Almoravid?]	[City]; annual tax payment to the Marinid treasury: 10.000 mithkâl (dinâr).	(al-'Umari 1927:171)
Ara'ish (al-)-3 (Lharais)	"Ville fondee par les anciens Africains"; [pre-Almoravid?]	"Cette ville etait tres peuplee... [it was abondoned from A.D. 1471 to A.D. 1506]... A cette epoque un fils de l'actuel roi de Fez decida de la repeupler, la fortifia tres bien... le coton se recolte en effet en grande quantite."	(Leo Africanus 1956:251-252; Encyclopedia of Islam, 2 ed., vol. I:604-605)
Asada	"Ruines antiques" (al-Bakri 1965:114); "[Asada] renferme quelques restes d'anciens monuments." (al-Bakri 1965:224); [pre-Idrisid]	[City]	(al-Bakri 1965:114, 224)
Asila-1	[Idrisid]	"[Asila] est une grande ville... riche et pleine de ressources."	al-Istakhri in (Miquel, 1973:233).
Asila-2 (Azîlâ)	Idrisid	One of the 41 main cities of the district of Fas (Sus al-Adna).	(al-Mukaddasi 1950:7)
Asila-3	[Idrisid]	"[Asila] est une ville... [abundant] cereales, ble, orge...L'eau... est pure et agreable... marches..."	(Ibn Hawkal 1938-39:75-76)
Asila-4	"Ville de construction moderne"; Idrisid	"Ville... mosquee...cinq nefs... cimetiere... murraille percee de cinq portes... marche tres frequente...port... offre un bon abri aux navires."	(al-Bakri 1965:218-219)
Asila-5 (Azila)	[Idrisid]	"Une tres petite cite dont il ne subsiste (qu'une petite partie)... plusieurs marches se tiennent sur son territoire..."	(al-Idrisi1983:168)
Asila-6	[Idrisid]	"[Asila] etait une grande et ancienne ville... peuplee... florissante... bien fournie en produits de terre avec un port frequente..."	(Anonymous 1958:51-52)
Asila-7	"Une ville antique...a ete reconstruite ensuite... elle est de construction moderne..."; [Idrisid]	[City]	(Ibn `Idhari 1948:232)
Asila-8	"Ancienne"; [Idrisid]	"Pays (ou region)... C'est une grande ville... peuplee... florissante et abondante en richesses. Autrefois...avait un port frequente."	(al-Himyari 1975:42)
Asila-9 (Arzilla)	"Ville batie par les Romains... [taken by the Muslims in A.D. 713]"; [Idrisid]	"[Asila] a ete une grande ville batie par les Romains... les souverains et pontifes de Cordoue (...) la restaurerent et la mirent en meilleur etat et plus forte qu'auparavant [around A.D. 997]... La contree produit beaucoup de cereales et de fruits..."	(Leo Africanus 1956:260-261)
Asila-9a	Idrisid	[City]; minting activities: Idrisid currency (209 A.H. /A.D. 824-25).	(Eustache 1970-71:109, 1970:96)

Name	Founding	Size/Economy	Textual/Numismatic Sources
Awsadja	Idrisid?	[City]	Ibn Ghazi in (Massignon 1906:218)
Ayn al-Shams	[pre-Almoravid?]	"la source appelee 'Ayn al-shams est tres abondante... Village de Nasr b. Djarw endroit florissant et bien peuple qui possede un Djami'... On y tient un marche tous les vendredi."	(al-Bakri 1965:212)
Baht	Idrisid	[City]; minting activities: Idrisid currency; the only mention of the site is found in al-Bakri (1965:263); "ville Barghwata" (Massignon 1906:218).	(Eustache 1970:96)
Balash	Idrisid	One of the 41 main cities of the district of Fas (Sus al-Adna).	(al-Mukaddasi 1950:7)
Balyunash-1	[pre-Almoravid?]	[Port]	(al-Bakri 1965:208, Siraj 1995b:331)
Balyunash-2	pre-Almoravid	"makan [a location]... prosperous"; [a city?]	(al-Idrisi1957:107)
Bani 'Attush	Almoravid	A small city located between [Bani] Tawra and Bani Ziad, east of al-Kasr (Kasr Abi Musa). Abundance of fruits; [sold] for a cheap price.	(al-Idrisi1957:52)
Bani Basil	Built "par les Africains" (Leo Africanus 1956:179); built in the 12th century A.D. (Massignon 1906:217); Almoravid	"Une petite ville... la ville a ete ruinee... [around A.D. 1413 during the war between the Marinids Muhammad known as al-Sa'id and the Sultan of Fas Abu Sa'id 'Uthman]... partly reoccupied around A.D. 1515."	(Leo Africanus 1956:179, Massignon 1906:217)
Bani Radjik	[pre-Almoravid]	[City]	(Ibn Hawkal 1967:65)
Bani Sadal	[pre-Almoravid]	[City]	(Ibn Hawkal 1967:65)
Bani Tawda-1	Almoravid	"The first of al-Gharb cities (mudun al-Gharb) to be destroyed by the Almohads." (al-Idrisi1957:55); "[Bani Tawda] suffisait a elle-meme... profusion de ses cereales... ses recoltes... laitages... marches...." (al-Idrisi1983:101)	(al-Idrisi1957:55, 1983:101)
Bani Tawda-2	Almoravid	"[Bani Tawda] etait une grande ville... entouree de tribus... Elle est le chef-lieu d'un canton riche en cereales et en bestiaux."	(Anonymous 1958:141-142)
Bani Tawda-3 (Bani Teuda)	"Une ville tres ancienne batie par les Africains"; [Almoravid]	[City]; "Au temps jadis elle a fait 8.000 feux, mais elle fut totalement detruite, a l'exception des murs [possibly in A.D. 1144 by the Almohad 'Abd al-Mu`min]... ses terrains sont tres fertiles est extremement productifs."	(Leo Africanus 1956:256)
Bani Tawda-4	Almoravid	[City]	(Eustache 1970:96; Hazard 1952:330)
Bani Tawra	Almoravid	The city was very populated and prosperous (markets, workshops, etc.).	(al-Idrisi1957:52)
Bani Ziad	Almoravid	A big city [madina 'amira]; During the time of al-Mulththam [Almoravids], it was the second largest settlement (kutr) [in the area] after Tagrart [Maknas]. The two cities are located at about a quarter mile from each other.	(al-Idrisi1957:52)
Basra (al-)-1	[Idrisid]	"Une grande ville, vaste et riche... Al-Basra et Azila relevent de la region de Tanger..."	al-Istakhri in (Miquel, 1973:233).
Basra (al-)-2	[Idrisid]	"al-Basra etait une grande ville, florissante et importante mais elle est en ruines." (al-Mukaddasi , 1950:27); One of the 41 main cities of the district of Sus al-Adna.	(al-Mukaddasi 1950:7, 27)
Basra (al-)-3	[Idrisid]	"Ville..grandeur moyenne (madina muktasida)... ses produits les plus serieux consistent en coton, exporte vers l'Ifrikiya et autres lieux..." (Ibn Hawkal 1938-39:76); Trading with Barghwata (1967:83); shipping activities along the Lukkus River (1842:192).	(Ibn Hawkal 1842:192, 1938-39:76, 1967:80, 83).
Basra (al-)-4	"Une ville de construction moderne... la meme epoque qu'Asila."; [Idrisid]	"Ville qui occupe un grand espacement... dix portes... mosquee a sept nefs et deux bains... [two cemeteries]... surpasse toutes les localites voisines par l'etendue de ses paturages et le nombre de ses troupeaux..."	(al-Bakri 1965:216-217)
Basra (al-)-5	[Idrisid]	"[al-Basra] fut une ville moyenne [muktasida]... autour de laquelle existent des villages et des fermes... "cererales... coton... ble... banlieue florissante..."; shipping activities along the Lukkus River (al-Idrisi 1957:109).	(al-Idrisi1957:109, 1983: 168-69)

Name	Founding	Size/Economy	Textual/Numismatic Sources
Basra (al-)-6	[Idrisid]	"Grande ville... dix portes... riche en cereales et en troupeaux... lait... Basra al-Alban... Basra al-Kattan... lin en guise de monnaie..."	(Anonymous 1958:139)
Basra (al-)-7	[Idrisid]	"al-Basra est aussi un pays [balad]... Elle est ruinee."(Yakut al-Hamawi, 1866-1873, vol. 1:440?); shipping activities along the Wadi Shafdad [Lukkus River] (Yakut al-Hamawi, 1866-1873, vol.2:22?).	(Yakut al-Hamawi, 1866-1873, vol. 1:440?, vol. 2:22?)
Basra (al-)-8	"Auparavant une ville antique... fondee vers la meme epoque qu'Asila."; [Idrisid]	"Ville... dix portes... Basra al-Kattan... lin en guise de monnaie..."	(Ibn `Idhari 1948:103)
Basra (al-)-9	Idrisid	"Leur [Idrisids] domination s'etendit depuis le Sous el-Aksa jusqu'a la ville d'Oran, et ils eurent pour [dynastic] capitale Fes, et plus tard El-Basra." (Ibn Abi Zar' 1860:130)	(Ibn Abi Zar' 1860:130)
Basra (al-)-9a	[Idrisid]	"Le chef-lieu de la province etait autrefois Basra... Apres la destruction de la ville, le chateau de 'Abd al-Karim prit le rang de capitale."	(Abu al-Fida 1848:184-185)
Basra (al-)-9b	[Idrisid]	"[al-Basra] etait autrefois... une ville considerable... son territoire renferme des bourgades et des champs... principaux produits sont le ble et le coton..."	al-'Umari in (Fagnan 1924: 79-80)
Basra (al-)-9c	"Ville moderne... construite vers la meme epoque qu'Asila"; [Idrisid]	"[al-Basra city-wall has] dix portes..."; "ville moderne"; "De toute cette region, al-Basra est la localite la plus riche en paturage et en cereales... Basra al-Dhubban... Basra al-Kattan... lin en guise de monnaie..."	(al-Himyari 1975:108-109)
Basra (al-)-9d	"Batie... par Mahumet, fils d'Idris"; Idrisid	"Une ville de peu d'etendue qui a fait dans les 2.000 feux... Elle fut tres policee tant que regna la maison d'Idris... a ete tres habitee... Mais lors de la decheance des Idrisides... Il n'en reste plus debout que les murailles."	(Leo Africanus 1956:259)
Basra (al-)-9e	Idrisid	[City]; minting activities: Idrisid currency (Idrisid dirham dated to 182A.H./A.D. 798-99 and 197A.H. /A.D. 812-13).	(Eustache 1955:229)
Baydâ' (al-)	[Idrisid?]	One of the main cities of the territory of Tandja.	(al-Mukaddasi 1950:7-9)
Buhayrat Ariagh-1 (Righa)	Idrisid	"Buhayrat Aryagh communique avec l'ocean ou mouillent les vaisseaux espagnols qui viennent charger les produits agricoles de la region..."; [Ariagh Lake] is used by al-Basra merchants for their shipping activities.	(Ibn Hawkal 1938-39:81)
Buhayrat Ariagh-2	Idrisid	"Un mouillage pour les bateaux a une etape de l'oued Fas"; [anchorage site]	(Yakut al-Hamawi 1852-1869, vol. I:131; vol.IV:271-272; al-Himyari, 1975:141)
Dakhla	[pre-Almoravid]	[City]	(Ibn Hawkal 1967:65)
Damna (al-)	Conquered by Yusuf b. Tashfin in 1072 A.D.; pre-Almoravid	[City]	(Ibn Abi Zar' 1860)
Djâhid (al-)	Idrisid	One of the 41 main cities of the district of Fas (Sus al-Adna).	(al-Mukaddasi 1950:7)
Djami' al-Hammam (Gemih el Chemmem)	"Ville ancienne"; Marinid?	"Ville ancienne... detruite lors des guerres de Sahid [destroyed around A.D. 1413 during the war between the Marinids Muhammad known as al-Sa'id and the Sultan of Fas Abu Sa'id 'Uthman]"	(Leo Africanus 1956:178)
Djarmana	[Idrisid]	[City]	(Ibn Hawkal 1938-39, 1967:80)
Djazira (al-) (Gezira)	"Ville ancienne"; [pre-Idrisid?]	"Une petite ville... a ete abondonne au debut des guerre avec les Portugais."	(Leo Africanus 1956:258)
Djum'a (al-) (El-Giumha) ['Ayn Karwash?]	"Batie de notre temps par les Africains"; [Marinid]	"Une petite ville... Cette ville a ete tres habitee et policee [destroyed around A.D. 1413 during the war between the Marinids Muhammad known as al-Sa'id and the Sultan of Fas Abu Sa'id 'Uthman]"	(Leo Africanus 1956:251)
Fankur-1	Idrisid	[City]	(Ibn Khurdadhbah 1889:88-89)
Fankur-2	Idrisid	[a city]	(Ibn al-Fakih 1973:98)

Name	Founding	Size/Economy	Textual/Numismatic Sources
Fanzara	"Batie… par un des rois Almohades"; Almohad	"Une ville pas bien grande… [destroyed around A.D. 1413 during the war between the Marinids Muhammad known as al-Sa'id and the Sultan of Fas Abu Sa'id 'Uthman]"	(Leo Africanus 1956:171-172)
Fas-1	Idrisid	Seat of the Idrisid authority.	(Ibn Khurdadhbah 1889:88-89)
Fas-2	"C'est la que reside Yahya b. Yahya… la ville (quartier) nommee Ville des Andalous est occupee par Dawud b. Idris."; Idrisid	"[The city of Fas is] considerable et tres peuplee… il ya trois mille moulins qui travaillent…"	(al-Ya'kubi 1892:357-358)
Fas-3	Idrisid	Seat of the Idrisid authority.	(Ibn al-Fakih 1973:98)
Fas-4	"C'est la ville de Yahya le Fatimide."; Idrisid	"La ville principale [de la circonscription (kura) de Tanger], qui est aussi le chef-lieu (Kasaba), se nomme Fes."	al-Istakhri in (Miquel, 1973: 233)
Fas-5	Idrisid	Fâs (the city) is the administrative capital or Kasaba of the Sûs al-Adna district. Fâs is also the name of one of the districts (Kuwar, sing. Kura) of the province of the Maghreb (al-Mukaddasi 1950:7).	(al-Mukaddasi 1950:7, 27)
Fas-6	Built by Idris b. Idris (Ibn Hawkal 1967:90); Idrisid	"Ville importante [madina djalila] qu'un cours d'eau partage en deux parties que gouvernent deux emirs differents… le produit des taxes et impots surpassent en quantite ce qui se trouve [in other urban settlements]." (Ibn Hawkal 1873:57, 59)	(Ibn Hawkal 1873:57, 59; 1967:65, 90)
Fas-7	Idrisid	"Fez etait la capitale des Etats qui appartenaient aux descendants d'Idris [Idris I]." (al-Bakri 1965:231); "les deux villes renferment plus de trois cents moulins et environs une vingtaine de bains." (al-Bakri1965:226)	(al-Bakri 1965:226-231)
Fas-8	Idrisid	"Fas is the pole and the center around which revolves the cities of al-Maghrib al-Aksa [madinat Fas kutb wa madar li muduni al-Maghrib al-Aksa]."	(al-Idrisi1957:53)
Fas-9	Idrisid	"Elle etait la capitale de la mer [Hadirat al-Bahr] et la ville la plus importante avant la fondation de Farrakech."; [cours d'eau] "actionne environs six cents moulins… Fas possede trois mosquees-cathedrales."	(Yakut al-Hamawi 1906-1907 vol. VI:29-331)
Fas-9a	Idrisid	During the reign of al-Mansur and his son al-Nasir [Almohads]: 785 mosques, 122 public fountains, 93 hammams, 472 mills. Census under al-Nasir: 89,236 households [5 persons/household = 446.180 inhabitants]; 19.041 misriyya (Ibn Abi Zar' 1843:25-26).	(Ibn Abi Zar' 1843:15-27)
Fas-9b	Idrisid	[Major city]; 400 mills; annual tax payment to the Marinid treasury: 150.000 mithkâl (dinâr)	(al-'Umari 1927:171)
Fas-9c (Fez)	Idrisid	"Grande cite, capitale de toute la Mauretanie… on construisit au bord de la riviere a l'Est [A. al-Andalus] une petite ville qui compta environ 3.000 feux…. [Almoravid period] 30.000 personnes y [Fas] furent tuees… [16th c.] 700 temples et mosquees…"	(Leo Africanus 1956:179-241)
Fas-9d (al-'Aliya)	Idrisid	Major city; minting activities: Idrisid currency; "al-'Aliya Madinat Idris" inscribed on an Idrisid dirham.	(Eustache 1970:98, 1970-71:146)
Fas-9e	Idrisid	Major city; minting activities: Almoraivd currency (36 dinars); Almohad currency (14 dinars), Marinid currency (61 dinars) (Hazard 1952:335-336); Miknasan Zanata currency (Eustache 1970:98).	(Eustache 1970:98; Hazard 1952:335-336)
Ghimd (al-) (La Vergogna)	"Tres ancien"; [Almohad?]	"Chateau [fortress]"	(Leo Africanus 1956:247)
Ghuzza-1	Idrisid	[City]	(Ibn Khurdadhbah 1889:88-89)
Ghuzza-2	Idrisid	[City]	(Ibn al-Fakih 1973:98)
Ghuzza-3	[Idrisid?]	One of the main cities of the territory of Tandja.	(al-Mukaddasi 1950:7-9)
Habash (al)	[pre-Almoravid]	[City]	(Ibn Hawkal 1967:65)
Hadjar al-Nasr-1 (Kal'at an-Nusûr)	Idrisid	One of the 41 main cities of the district of Fas (Sus al-Adna).	(al-Mukaddasi 1950:7)

Name	Founding	Size/Economy	Textual/Numismatic Sources
Hadjar al-Nasr-2 (al-Hadjar)	"(de construction moderne)... appartient aux Idrisides..."; [Idrisid]	"Une grande ville... une de leurs [Idrisids] villes les plus precieuses et les plus importantes..."	(Ibn Hawkal 1938-39:81)
Hadjar al-Nasr-3 (Sakhrat al-Nasr)	"Fortresse batie en l'an 317 A.H/(A.D. 929) par Ibrahim fils de Muhammad, fils al'Kasim, fils d'Idris, fils d'Idris." (al-Bakri 1965:247-248); Idrisid	"[The city is the] residence des Bani Muhammad [famille Idriside]."	(al-Bakri 1965:223)
Hadjar al-Nasr-4 (al-Hadjar)	Idrisid	[City]; "Riche et prospere, elle possede l'eau a l'interieur, ainsi que des jardins et vergers."	(al-Idrisi1983:69-70)
Hadjir (al-)-1	Idrisid	[City]	(Ibn Khurdadhbah 1889:88-89)
Hadjir (al-)-2	Idrisid	[City]	(Ibn al-Fakih 1973:98)
Hâdjir (al-)-3	[Idrisid?]	One of the main cities of the territory of Tandja.	(al-Mukaddasi 1950:7-9)
Hadjna	[pre-Almoravid?]	[City]	(Ibn Hawkal 1967:65)
Humar (Homar)	"Batie par un certain Hali fils de Mahomet ['Ali b. Muhammad b. Idris b. Idris, A.D. 836-848]" (Leo Africanus 1956:260); Idrisid	"Une ville... Ce ne fut pas une grande ville... La ville est demeuree deserte depuis qu'Arzila a ete prise par les Portugais [A.D. 1471]." (Leo Africanus 1956:260); Destroyed in the 10th century A.D. (Massignon 1906:241).	(Leo Africanus 1956:260)
Idjadjin-1	"Elle appartient a Djannun b. Muhammad [al-Kasim b. Muhammad b. Idris b. Idris]."; Idrisid	"Ville... referme un Djami',... un bain... fait partie du pays de Djinyara... Elle est habitee par les Bani Masara [Masmuda]."	(al-Bakri 1965:224)
Idjadjin-2 (Zadjdjan)	[Idrisid]	"De Sabta a Fas par la route de Zadjdjan, (on compte huit jours)."; [a city]	(al-Idrisi1983:186)
Idjadjin-3	"Appartient aux Masmuda"; [Idrisid]	"C'est une ville prestigieuse et riche... un Djami'... un bain"	(al-Himyari 1975:617)
Idjadjin-4 (Ezaggen)	"Batie par les anciens Africains" [Idrisid]	"Une ville... Elle fait dans les 500 feux... ville bien policee... Le canton peut donner un revenu de dix mille ducats..."	(Leo Africanus 1956:255)
Idjarhan	Idrisid	[City]; minting activities: Mu'tazilite Berbers currency; Idrisid currency.	(Eustache 1970:100)
Kakammariyya	[pre-Almoravid?]	"Village qui appartient a des Sanhadjiens... possede des carrieres ou l'on taille des meules de moulin."	(al-Bakri 1965:222)
Kal'a (al-)	[pre-Almoravid?]	Fortress?	(al-Bakri 1965:222)
Kal'at Ibn Djundub (Kal'at Ibn Kharrub?)	[pre-Almoravid?]	It was a big city (madina kabira).	(Anonymous 1985:190)
Kal'at Ibn Kharrub	[Idrisid?]	"Une grande ville... elle possede des bois, des vergers, beacoup de betail et de champs cultives."	(al-Bakri 1965:215)
Kal'at Sadina-1	Domain of Muh. b. 'Umar b. Idris; Idrisid.	"Pays [territory] important"	(al-Ya'kubi 1937:223)
Kal'at Sadina-2	[Idrisid]	"Une bourgade [of a Masmuda tribe]."; a big village.	(al-Bakri 1965:210)
Kal'at Shamît	"C'est la [district of Fas?] que se trouvent la citadelle de Chamit construite par Ibn Buri (...)"; Idrisid	One of the 41 main cities of the district of Fas (Sus al-Adna).	(al-Mukaddasi 1950:9, 25 note 55)
Kanisa (al-)	[pre-Idrisid]	"[al-Kanisa] est un village florissant situee sur une colline appartenant [a la tribu des] Kutama."	(al-Bakri 1965:222-223)
Karzawa (of Bani Husayn)	[pre-Almoravid?]	The biggest village in the Wargha River vicinity.	(al-Bakri 1965:224)
Kasr (al-) (Kasr Abi Musa)	Built by an Almoravid prince; Almoravid	A small city located between [Bani] Tawra and Bani Ziad; only a few markets; limited trading activities."	(al-Idrisi1957:52)
Kasr (al-) al-Kabir-1 (Sûk al-Kutâmî)	pre-Idrisid	One of the 41 main cities of the district of Fas (Sus al-Adna).	(al-Mukaddasi 1950:7)
Kasr (al-) al-Kabir-2 (Kasr Danhadja)	"Il renferme des monuments antiques"; [pre-Idrisid]	"Chateau qui s'eleve sur une colline et qui domine une grande riviere... c'est la que les rois du Maghreb s'etaient etablis dans les temps anciens."; Fortress	(al-Bakri 1965:216)

Name	Founding	Size/Economy	Textual/Numismatic Sources
Kasr (al-) al-Kabir-3 (Suk Kutama)	pre-Idrisid	"[Suk Kutama] etait la capitale des Etats gouvernes par Idris, fils d'al-Kasim b. Ibrahim. Cette grande et magnifique ville est situee sur la riviere Lukkus. Elle possede un Djami'... lieu de marche... possede un marche bien achalande"	(al-Bakri 1965:215)
Kasr (al-) al-Kabir-4 (Kasr 'Abd al-Karim)	[Fortress built by the Danhadja tribe in the 8th century A.D.; pre-Idrisid]	"Petite ville habitee par un ramassis de Berberes appeles Danhadja... un marche bien achalande et diverses activites artisanales." (al-Idrisi1983:90)	(al-Idrisi1983:90,168)
Kasr (al-) al-Kabir-5 (Kasr Sanhadja)	"Monuments anciens" [pre-Idrisid]	"[City nearby] Lukkus qui est navigable... le souverain actuel [the AlmohadYa'kub al-Mansur] y a fait construire deux caravanserails remarquables. Ce lieu constitua ainsi un centre et se fit connaitre, les marchands le frequenterent et s'y etablirent."	(Anonymous 1958:140)
Kasr (al-) al-Kabir-6 (Kasr 'Abd al-Karim)	[pre-Idrisid]	"Une ville... le chef-lieu de la province etait autrefois Basra... Apres la destruction de la ville, le chateau de 'Abd al-Karim prit le rang de capitale."	(Abu al-Fida 1848:184-185)
Kasr (al-) al-Kabir-7 (Kasr 'Abd al-Karim)	[pre-Idrisid]	"Une petite ville"; annual tax payment to the Marinid treasury: 20.000 mithkâl (al-Umari 1927:171).	al-'Umari in (Fagnan 1924: 80; al-'Umari 1927:171)
Kasr (al-) al-Kabir-8 (Kasr 'Abd al-Karim)	[pre-Idrisid]	"Petite ville... habitee par une population Berbere... possede des terres de cultures fertiles, des resouces en gibier et en poisson, un marche achalande et diverses activites artisanales"	(al-Himyari 1975:376)
Kasr (al-) al-Kabir-9 (Casar el Cabir)	"Batie au temps de Mansor, roi et pontife de Marrakech et sur son ordre"[The Almohad Ya'kub al-Mansur, A.D. 1184-1199]; pre-Idrisid	"Une grande ville ...devint en peu de temps, a cause de la fertilite du pays, une cite de 400 feux... le roi avait coutume de passer l'ete dans les environs et ce fut aussi une raison de la prosperite de la ville."	(Leo Africanus 1956:252-254)
Kasr (al-) al-Saghir-1 (Marsa Bab al-Yam)	[Idrisid]	"Marsa bab al-Yam, rade sans abri... quelques habitations, un ribat..."; [anchorage]	(al-Bakri 1965:206)
Kasr (al-) al-Saghir-2 (Kasr Masmuda)	[Idrisid]	"Kasr Masmuda... une grande forteresse... ou l'on construit des navires et des barques (utilisees pour le passage en Andalousie)."	(al-Idrisi1983:166)
Kasr (al-) al-Saghir-3 (Kasr Masmuda)	[Idrisid]	"A Marsa bab al-Yam se trouve un village nomme Kasr Masmuda..."	(Anonymous 1958:138)
Kasr (al-) al-Saghir-4 (Kasr Masmuda)	[Idrisid]	"C'est un grand chateau..."; fortress	(al-Himyari 1975:476)
Kasr (al-) al-Saghir-5 (Casar ez Zaghir)	"Batie par Mansor, roi et pontife de Marrakech [the Almohad Ya'kub al-Mansur]"; Idrisid	"Petite ville... Casar fut une ville tres policee... Ses habitants etaient presque tous des marins qui assuraient le passage entre la Berberie et l'Europe."	(Leo Africanus 1956:264, 272)
Khadra (al-)-1	Idrisid	[City]	(Ibn Khurdadhbah 1889:88-89)
Khadra (al-)-2	Idrisid	[City]	(Ibn al-Fakih 1973:98)
Khadrâ (al-)-3	[Idrisid?]	One of the main cities of the territory of Tandja	(al-Mukaddasi 1950:7-9)
Khamis Matghara (Camis Metgara)	"Batie par les Africains" (Leo Africanus 1956:178); "Ville Idrisid" (Massignon 1906:217); [Idrisid?]	"Petite ville... ruinee pendant la guerre de Sahid [destroyed around A.D. 1413 during the war between the Marinids Muhammad known as al-Sa'id and the Sultan of Fas Abu Sa'id 'Uthman]... [reoccupied by immigrants from Granada in A.D. 1496]"	(Leo Africanus 1956:178; Massignon 1906:217)
Khawlan (Chaulan)	"Un ancien chateau..."; [Marinid]	Fortress?; "[Abu-l-Hasan 'Ali (A.D. 1331-1348) fit construire un tres bel edifice sur cette source thermale [located nearby Khawlan]." (Leo Africanus 1956:242-3)	(Leo Africanus 1956:242-3)
Kurt-1	Idrisid	"Tous les lieux de cette region, ainsi que Tanger, appartiennent auxEdrisites, qui en recuiellent les taxes et les impots [djibaya, Kharadj]." (Ibn Hawkal 1842:193). "les habitants [de la ville] sont adonnes au commerce." (Ibn Hawkal 1967:81)	(Ibn Hawkal 1967:65, 80-81)
Kurt-2	Idrisid	"Le Rdat... fleuve qui baigne le pied d'une montage dont le sommet (est domine par une ville nommee Kurt, et qui est ruinee de nos jours...)."	(al-Bakri 1965:217)
Kurt-3	Idrisid	"Ville... Eux tous [Berbers and Arabs] ainsi que la population du district dont il est question ici c'est a dire celui de Tanger, sont soumis aux Idrisides... les habitants sont adonnes au commerce."	(al-Idrisi1983:80-81)

Name	Founding	Size/Economy	Textual/Numismatic Sources
Kurt-4	[Idrisid]	"[Kurt] etait autrefois une grande et forte ville… et qu'habitaient des Berberes nommes (Biyatha). Ce n'est plus aujourd'hui qu'une bourgade (florissante)… bien pourvue en vivres, de laquelle depenadait un grand canton…"	(Anonymous 1958:189)
Ma'mura-1	Built by the Banu Yafran in the 10th century A.D (Eustache 1955:226-227); [pre-Almoravid?]	[City?]	(al-Idrisi1957:53; Eustache 1955:226-227)
Ma'mura-2 (Mahmora)	"Batie par un des rois Almohades"; [pre-Almoravid?]	"Une petite ville… la ville a ete detruite [around A.D. 1413 during the war between the Marinids Muhammad known as al-Sa'id and the Sultan of Fas Abu Sa'id 'Uthman]"	(Leo Africanus 1956:172-173)
Madînat Djabal Zâlâgh	"Elle a ete construite par Khaluf ibn Ahmad al-Mu'tali [Maghili?]" (al-Mukaddasi 1950:25); Idrisid	One of the 41 main cities of the district of Fas (Sus al-Adna) (al-Mukaddasi 1950:9); "Le siege [mustakar] des Emirs de Fas nommes par le Fatimide est a Jabal Zalagh." (al-Mukaddasi 1950:27).	(al-Mukaddasi 1950:9, 25, 27)
Madraka-1	Idrisid	[City]	(Ibn Khurdadhbah 1889:88-89)
Madraka-2	[Idrisid?]	One of the main cities of the territory of Tandja.	(al-Mukaddasi 1950:7-9)
Maghila-1	pre-Idrisid?	"[Maghila] fut auparavant une ville peuplee [mutahaddira]… (habitations) ininterrompues… Aujourd'hui, on y voit des vestiges et des ruines…"	(al-Idrisi1983:87-88)
Maghila-2 (Maghila al-kat)	pre-Idrisid?	A big fortress; Djami' (mosque); a big market.	(Anonymous 1985:193)
Maghila-3	"Ville antique batie… par les Romains"; pre-Idrisid?	"Une petite ville… un beau territoire dans la montage entierement plante d'oliviers et aussi un beau territoire dans la plaines ou l'on trouve de nombreuses et grosses sources… [it produces] beacoup de chanvre et de lin."	(Leo Africanus 1956:247)
Makarmada (al-) (Macarmeda)	"Batie par les souverains de Zenata"; [pre-Almoravid?]	"Une ville… Jadis elle fut le chef-lieu d'un grand canton et elle fut tres policee… [destroyed around A.D. 1413 during the war between the Marinids Muhammad known as al-Sa'id and the Sultan of Fas Abu Sa'id 'Uthman]…"	(Leo Africanus 1956:241)
Maknas-1 (Miknâsa)	[pre-Almoravid]	One of the 41 main cities of the district of Fas (Sus al-Adna).	(al-Mukaddasi 1950:7)
Maknas-2 (Miknasa)	[pre-Almoravid]	"les Miknasa, qui habitent des cabanes construites de broussailles."(al-Bakri 1965:177-178); [a village?]; In A.D. 1063, Maknas was already a city governed by an Amir (Terrasse 1950:224).	(al-Bakri 1965:177-178; Terrasse 1950:224).
Maknas-3 (Maknasa)	[pre-Almoravid]	Maknasa constitutes several cities [mada'in 'idda]; Madinat Maknasa is named Tagrart, [the city as it stands now] was not affected by any major changes.	(al-Idrisi1864-1866:87-88)
Maknas-4	[pre-Almoravid]	[Major city]; annual tax payment to the Marinid treasury: 60.000 mithkâl (dinâr)	(al-'Umari 1927:171)
Maknas-5 (Mecnase)	"Batie par [the Maknasa tribe]" (Leo Africanus 1956:175-176); [Idrisid Warzigha?] (Massignon 1906:214); [pre-Almoravid]	"Une grande ville… Elle fait pres de 6.000 feux et sa population est tres dense… [the city's and its district revenue is estimated to] le tiers de tout ce que rapporte le royaume de Fez."	(Leo Africanus 1956:175-176; Massignon 1906:214)
Maknas-6 (Miknas)	[pre-Almoravid]	[City]; minting activities: Almoravid currency (2 dirhams); Almohad currency (2 dinars) (Hazard 1952:337)	(Eustache 1970:99; Hazard 1952:337)
Malhas	Domain of 'Ali b. 'Umar b. Idris; Idrisid	"Un caravanserail" (al-Ya'kubi 1937:223); caravansary; The site of future Ezaggen (Massignon 1906:238).	(al-Ya'kubi 1937:223; Massignon 1906:238)
Masina-1 (Masita)	pre-Idrisid	"Une des villes qui est de leur [Idrisids] ressort et qui entre sous leur autorite… La plaine est peuplee de Berberes… Il y a beacoup de cours d'eau et un systeme d'irrigation qui assure aux riverains un riche revenu."	(Ibn Hawkal 1938-39:77, 1967:81)
Masina-2	According to al-Bakri, Idris I conquered the city in 173 A.H/A.D. 789-790). The city must have existed before the Idrisid period (before the 8th century A.D.) (al-Bakri 1965: 231); pre-Idrisid	"[Masina] etait la capitale des Etats d''Isa, fils de Hasan le Hasanide, surnomme al-Hadjdjam" (al-Bakri 1965:218); "Masita [Masina] grand canton ou la culture du coton reussit parfaitement." (al-Bakri 1965:295).	(al-Bakri 1965:218, 295)

Name	Founding	Size/Economy	Textual/Numismatic Sources
Masina-3	pre-Idrisid	"Grand village qui ressemle plutot a une petite ville... C'etait jadis une ville avec un rempart et marches; aujourd'hui, elle est en ruines."	(al-Idrisi1983:169)
Matruka-1	Idrisid	[City]	(Ibn Khurdadhbah 1889:88-89)
Matruka-2	Idrisid	[City]	(Ibn al-Fakih 1973:98)
Matrûka-3	[Idrisid?]	One of the main cities of the territory of Tandja.	(al-Mukaddasi 1950:7-9)
Mudrika	Idrisid	[City]	(Ibn al-Fakih 1973:98)
Mulay Idris (Gualili)	"Ville fondee... par les Romains... [Idris I] se mit aussitot a rebatir la ville et y habita"; pre-Idrisid	"Ruinee par les Africains dans l'antiquite... [Idris II] l'abandonna... Aujourd'hui il n'existe plus dans la ville que deux ou trois maisons qui servent de logement a ceux qui assurent l'entretien de la tombe [Idris I] et le culte dont elle est l'objet."	(Leo Africanus 1956:245)
Nabrash	[pre-Almoravid?]	"Bourg [kariya]... appartient a des Luwata... florissant, bein peuple, riche en fruits et en sources."; a village.	(al-Bakri 1965:221)
Narandja (Narangia)	"Chateau batie par les Africains"; [Marinid?]	"Un chateau... sacage par les Portugais. Il est demeure jusqu'a present inhabite et desert depuis l'an 895 de l'hegire [A.D. 1490]"; a fortress.	(Leo Africanus 1956:258)
Ribat-1 (Barbat?)	[pre-Almoravid]	[a city?]	(Ibn Hawkal 1967:65)
Ribat-2 (al-Fath)	"Il [the Almohad, 'Abd al-Mu`min in 548 A.H/A.D. 1153-1154] ordonna aussi de creuser les fondations du Ribat al-Fath..."; [pre-Almoravid]	"Il [the Almohad, 'Abd al-Mu`min] y fit batir un chateau. Il resta la cinq mois a surveiller les travaux de la conduite [aqueduct to bring water to Sala], des fondations et de la construction du chateau."	al-Baydak in (Levi-Provencal 1928:185)
Ribat-3 (Rabat)	"Batie aux temps modernes par Mansor [Abu Yusuf Ya'kub al-Mansur in A.D. 1197]..."; [pre-Almoravid]	[Tamasna province]; "Une grande ville... ressemble a Marrakech... mais elle est tres petite en comparison de Marrakech... Aujourd'hui Rabat est dans un pire etat que jamais.. On y trouverait a grand peine quatre cent maisons habitees pres de la citadelle..."	(Leo Africanus 1956:164-166)
Ribat-4 (al-Fath)	pre-Almoravid	[City]; minting activities: 1 Almohad dinar (Hazard 1952:332).	(Eustache 1970:97; Hazard 1952:332)
Sabta-1	pre-Idrisid	"Le roi de cette ville s'appelle Iiman [le comte Julien]"	(Ibn Khurdadhbah 1889:88)
Sabta-2	pre-Idrisid	One of the 41 main cities of the district of Fas (Sus al-Adna); "c'est un des ports d'embarquement celebres."	(al-Mukaddasi 1950:7, 25)
Sabta-3	"La ville ressortit aujourd'hui aux Ummayyades."; [pre-Idrisid]	"Ville... avec des vergers et des jardins qui suffisent aux besoins des habitants... Elle a un port (d'acces facile)... "Dans la banlieue sont installes des Berberes dont les contributions, les impositions et l'impot foncier etaient percus par le gouverneur..."	(Ibn Hawkal 1938-39:75, 1967:78)
Sabta-4	"Ville d'une haute antiquite"; pre-Idrisid	"Une grande ville... renferme un bain tres ancien... [un] Dajmi' (cinq nefs) [trois cimetieres], l'hotel du gouverneur (Dar al-'Imara)."	(al-Bakri 1965:202-204)
Sabta-5	[pre-Idrisid]	[City]; "Nulle part on ne fait des peches aussi fructueuse... En ville existe un (marche) pour la taille et le polissage du corail [mardjan]..."; "Sabta est un bon port ou les navires jettent l'ancre a l'abri de tous les vents."	(al-Idrisi1983:164-165)
Sabta-6	"Une ville ancienne"; pre-Idrisid	[City]	(Anonymous 1958:46)
Sabta-7	[pre-Idrisid]	[City]	(Abu al-Fida 1848:186)
Sabta-8	[pre-Idrisid]	[City]; annual tax payment to the Marinid treasury: 50.000 mithkâl (dinâr).	(al-'Umari 1927:171)
Sabta-9 (Sebta)	"Elle a ete fondee... par Romains"; The city was partly destroyed by the Almohad 'Abd al-Mu`min in A.D. 1148; pre-Idrisid	"Une tres grande ville... Ce fut le chef-lieu de toute la Mauretanie parce que le gouvernement romain y resida... Sebta, depuis cette epoque [Islamic occupation in A.D. 708] jusqu'a ces dernieres annees, est toujours allee en s'accroissant..."	(Leo Africanus 1956:265-267)
Sabta-9a	[pre-Idrisid]	[City]; minting activities: Hammudid currency, Almoravid currency, Almohad currency, Marinid currency; 2 Almoravid dinars; 11 Almohad dinars; 11 Marinid dinars (Hazard 1952:332).	(Eustache 1970:97; Hazard 1952:332)

Name	Founding	Size/Economy	Textual/Numismatic Sources
Sadak	[pre-Almoravid]	"Ville situee dans le territoire des Maghila et la residence de Khaluf b. Ahmad al-Maghili"	(al-Bakri 1965:218)
Sakuma	pre-Idrisid	"Chateau [fortress] situe dans le voisinage de Fez." [Musa b. Nusayr writing to al-Walid b. 'Abd al-Malik states that:] "dans le partage des prisonniers faits a Sakuma, on vous a reserve cent mille individus."	(al-Bakri 1965:230)
Salâ-1	pre-Idrisid	One of the 41 main cities of the district of Fas (Sus al-Adna).	(al-Mukaddasi 1950:7)
Sala-2 (Ribat Sala)	"La vielle ville de Sala [Sala al-Kadima], qui remonte a la plus haute antiquite."; pre-Idrisid	"Elle est en ruine, les habitants se groupent dans des couvents qui entourent la ville... Leurs couvents sont destines a la lutte contre les Barghwata."	(Ibn Hawkal 1842:195-196, 1938-39:78, 1967:65, 81)
Sala-3	"Une ville de la plus haute antiquite... qui se nomme Shalla.."; pre-Idrisid	[City]	(al-Bakri 1965:175-176)
Sala-4	"(La ville moderne [haditha] de Sala) est au bord de la mer, alors qu'autrefois la ville de Shalla etait a deux milles de la mer."; pre-Idrisid	[City]; "Les navires d'Ishbiliyya (Seville) et de toutes les villes maritimes d'Andalousie y jettent l'ancre et en repartent avec toutes sortes de marchandise..."	(al-Idrisi1983:81-82)
Sala-5	[pre-Idrisid]	"Sala est le chef-lieu d'une vaste province qui s'etend au midi, et qu'on nomme Tamasna... il s'y [Tamasna] trouve un grand nombre de villes, entre autres le port d'Anfa..."; "C'est une ville ou regne une grande aisance et ou les vivres sont a bas prix..."	(Abu al-Fida 1848:183)
Sala-6	pre-Idrisid	[Major city]; annual tax payment to the Marinid treasury: 40.000 mithkâl (dinâr).	(al-'Umari 1927:171)
Sala-7 (Sela)	"Ville tres ancienne batie par les Romains."; pre-Idrisid	[City]; "ayant un bon port, il a ete frequente par les commercants chretiens de diverses nationalites... parce qu'il sert de port a tout le royaume de Fez... [Sala] demeura depuis [the Spanish attack in A.D. 1260] et bien moins peuple et moins bien soigne..."	(Leo Africanus 1956:169-170)
Sala-8	[pre-Idrisid]	[City]; minting activities: Almoravid currency (1 dinar), Almohad currency (2 dinars), Marinid currency (1 dinar) (Hazard 1952:335).	(Eustache 1970:98; Hazard 1952:335; Encyclopedia of Islam, 1 ed., vol. IV: 87)
Shalla (Sella)	"Batie par les Romains."; pre-Idrisid	[Tamasna province]; "Une petite ville... cette ville a ete ruinee lors de la guerre des heretiques [Barghwata]."	(Leo Africanus 1956:166)
Subu-1 (Sabû)	Idrisid	One of the 41 main cities of the district of Fas (Sus al-Adna).	(al-Mukaddasi 1950:7)
Subu-2	Idrisid	[City]; minting activities: Idrisid currency; "Hamza b. Dawud b. Idris governed the Sebou region" (al-Ya'kubi 1937:223 note 7).	(Eustache 1970:97, al-Ya'kubi 1937:223 note 7)
Tadjradjra-1	Idrisid	[City]	(Ibn Khurdadhbah 1889:88-89, Eustache, 1970-71:129).
Tadjradjra-2 (Madjradjra)	Idrisid	[City]	(Ibn al-Fakih 1973:98)
Tadjradjra-3 (Tâdjarâdjarâ)	Idrisid	One of the main cities of the territory of Tandja.	(al-Mukaddasi 1950:9)
Tadjradjra-4 (Tagragra)	Idrisid	[City]; minting activities: Idrisid currency	(Eustache 1970:96)
Tafalfalt (Tefelfelt)	[Marinid?]	"Une petite ville... [destroyed around A.D. 1413 during the war between the Marinids Muhammad known as al-Sa'id and the Sultan of Fas Abu Sa'id 'Uthman]"	(Leo Africanus 1956:175)
Tahaddart	[pre-Almoravid?]	"Grand village florissant."	(al-Bakri 1965:221)
Tahlit-1	This Idrisid city was still known at the end of the 12th century A.D. since it was mentioned in the "Memoires" of al-Baydak; Idrisid	"[the city of] Tahlit, au-dessous d'al-Kasr d'Ibn 'Abd al-Karim."	al-Baydak in (Levi-Provencal 1928:149)
Tahlit-2	Idrisid	[City]; minting activities: Idrisid currency	(Eustache 1970:97)
Tandja-1	pre-Idrisid	"Une immense circonscription [kura] englobant des villes, des villages et force steppes appartenant aux Berberes..."	al-Istakhri in (Miquel, 1973:233).

Name	Founding	Size/Economy	Textual/Numismatic Sources
Tandja-2	pre-Idrisid	Tandja cette ville si eloignee." (al-Mukaddasi 1950:3); "Le district de Fas comprend deux regions: Tanger et le Zab." (al-Mukaddasi 1950:5) "Tandja est une region importante... riche et belle, avec des villes prosperes (al-Mukaddasi 1950:27).	(al-Mukaddasi 1950:3, 5, 27)
Tandja-3	"Ville d'une antiquite reculee... plus tard les habitants ont edifie une nouvelle cite, a la distance d'un mille sur le flanc d'une montagne."; pre-Idrisid	"La raison de cette fondation [the city] etait la peur de la famille d'Idris, qui avait occupe Ceuta pendant sa domination dans le pays." (Ibn Hawkal 1938-39:75; Tandja paid tribute to the Idrisids (Ibn Hawkal 1842 1842:193).	(Ibn Hawkal 1938-39:75; 1842:190, 193; 1967:79)
Tandja-4	"on y trouve beaucoup des monuments antiques... La ville actuelle est batie sur une hauteur plus elevee que l'emplacement de l'acienne Tanger..."; pre-Idrisid	"(On a raconte) que la juridiction de cette ville s'etendait sur un territoire dont la langueur et la largeur etaient egalement d'un mois de marche... Elle renferme un beau Djami'... (...un marche) tres frequente."	(al-Bakri 1965:213-215)
Tandja-5	"Ville ancienne [kadima `azaliyya]"; pre-Idrisid	"[City]; Son territoire porte son nom... Le territoire sur lequel elle est batie se prolonge, vers l'interieur du pays ou existent des exploitations agricoles productives... Son port est le point de depart et d'arrivee des bateaux..."	(al-Idrisi1983:166)
Tandja-6	pre-Idrisid	"Tandja est la Kasabah et le chef-lieu du pays des Berberes."	(Anonymous 1958:15)
Tandja-7	"Ville ancienne"; pre-Idrisid	"[The city]a dans sa dependance une province longue et large d'un mois de marche et ou on trouve comme villes du littoral al-'Ara'ish, Tushummus, Azila ou Asila et Sala..."	al-Watwat (Fagnan 1924:46)
Tandja-8	pre-Idrisid	"Edriss et son serviteur marcherent jusqu'a ce qu'ils eussent atteint la ville de Tanger. Tanger etait alors la capitale du Maghreb, la mere de ses villes, la plus belle alors et la plus vieille."	(Ibn Abi Zar' 1860:14)
Tandja-9	"Une antique capitale."; pre-Idrisid	"Elle fut la capitale de ce pays avant l'Islam et a l'epoque de la conquete de l'Espagne."; annual tax payment to the Marinid treasury: 30.000 mithkâl (dinâr) (al-Umari 1927:171)	(al-'Umari 1927:171, 199)
Tandja-9a (Tangia)	"[Tandja] a ete fondee dans l'antiquite"; pre-Idrisid	"Grande ville... Tangia a toujours ete une ville policee, noble et bien habitee... Le territoire qui l'environne n'est pas tres propice a la culture des cereales..."	(Leo Africanus 1956:264)
Tandja-9b	pre-Idrisid	[Major city]; minting activities: Idrisid currency (198 A.H./A.D. 813-14 and 206 A.H./A.D.821-22) (Eustache 1970-71: 145); Umayyad gold currency (Eustache 1970:98); Almoravid currency (Hazard 1952:335)	(Eustache 1970:98, 1970-71:145; Hazard 1952:335; Encyclopedia of Islam, 1 ed., vol. IV: 683)
Tansor	[Marinid?]	"Une ville... contient trois cents maisons... "	(Leo Africanus 1956:257)
Tawarat	[Idrisid]	[City]	(Ibn Hawkal 1967:65)
Tazgha	Idrisid?	[City]	Ibn Ghazi in (Massignon 1906:218)
Tittawan-1	[pre-Almoravid?]	"[Tittawan] forme le chef-lieu du territoire appartenant aux Bani Sikkin."; "domine la partie inferieure de Wadi Ras... qui dans cette localite, est assez large pour permettre aux petits navires de remonter depuis la mer jusqu'a Titawan."	(al-Bakri 1965:210)
Tittawan-2 (Tetteguin)	"Batie par les anciens Africains... [In A.D. 1492, it was restored by Abu-l-Hasan al-Mandari] La ville est restee a l'un de ses petits-fils."; pre-Almoravid	"Une petite ville"	(Leo Africanus 1956:267-269)
Tittawan-3	pre-Almoravid	[City]; minting activities: Marinid currency (775-796 A.H.).	(Hazard 1952:330)
Tûnaktâyân (Pietra Rossa?)	"Batie par les Romains."; [Almoravid]	"Une ville... petite... aujourd'hui une sorte de hameau ou de village"; "Le terrain cultive abonde en oliviers et en cereales..."	(Leo Africanus 1956:246)
Tushummush-1	"[Tushummush] remonte a la plus haute antiquite." "kadima azaliyya awaliyya djahiliyya" (Ibn Hawkal 1967:79); [pre-Idrisid]	[City]; "les habitants de Basra s'embarquent avec des marchandises sur la branche [of Lukkus River] qui passe chez eux; ils decendent alors jusqu'a l'Ocean, et se dirigent ensuite ou ils veulent se rendre." (Ibn Hawkal 1842:192)	(Ibn Hawkal 1842:192, 1938-39:76, 1967:79)
Tushummush-2	"Grande ville antique."; pre-Idrisid	[City]; "la residence de Maymun b. al-Kasim [Idrisid prince]."; "habitee par une nombreuse population et qui abonde en eau et en fruits."	(al-Bakri 1965:223)

Name	Founding	Size/Economy	Textual/Numismatic Sources
Tushummush-3	pre-Idrisid	"[Tushummush] etait une grande ville... possede des villages peuples par divers clans des Berberes."	(al-Idrisi1983:166)
Tushummush-4	"Ancienne ville"; "grand fort antique nomme Tushummus... L'alide Idris b. al-Kasim b. Ibrahim le releva et le fit (renaitre); il est encore habite de nos jours..."; pre-Idrisid	"[Tushummush] a dans sa dependence un vaste canton... Entre le lac et la mer il y a une mosquee (frequentee)."; "abonde en produits de la terre, en cereales et bestiaux... Des bateaux y chargent des cereales."	(Anonymous 1958:52, 140, 1985:140, 189)
Tushummush-5	"Ville ancienne"; pre-Idrisid	[City]; "Les gens d'al-Basra y [Wadi Shafdad] transportent leurs biens de commerce a l'aide des barques; une fois qu'ils aient atteint la mer oceanique, il se dirigerent vers la mer occidentale pour aller ou il souhaitent."	(Yakut al-Hamawi 1866-1873, vol. 2:22)
Ubbad (al-) (Hubbed)	[Marinid?]	"Un chateau... inhabite"; fortress?	(Leo Africanus 1956:242)
Ukasha-1	[Idrisid?]	A village [karya] located at about the distance of one day from Bani Tawda.	(al-Idrisi1957:55)
Ukasha-2 (Suk Ukasha)	Idrisid	A fortress controlled by the Idrisid Muhammad b. Hasan	(Ibn 'Idhari 1948)
Waldja (al-)	Almoravid	[City]; minting activities: Almoravid currency.	(Eustache 1970:100)
Walila-1	pre-Idrisid	"Dand le pays de Tanger, a-t-on-dit, la ville principale est Volubilis; la plupart des habitants sont Mu'tazilites; leur chef est aujourd'hui Ishak b. Muh. 'Abd al-Hamid, compagnon d'Idris b. Idris..."	(al-Istakhri 1927:84)
Walîla-2	pre-Idrisid	One of the main cities of the territory of Tandja.	(al-Mukaddasi 1950:7-9)
Walila-3	pre-Idrisid	"Oulili, ville situee dans le territoire de Fez et a une journee de cette capitale, du cote de l'occident." (al-Bakri 1965:226); "cette grande et ancienne ville, qu'il ne faut pas confondre avec Tanger, est situee a l'occident de Fez."	(al-Bakri 1965:226, 231)
Walila-4 (Tisra)	Roman; pre-Idrisid	"[The city] s'appelle aujourd'hui [end 12th A.D.] Taysara (or Tisra)"; "[the territory of the Awraba tribe] renfermait de nombreuses villes, notamment celle de Sakuma, qui etait voisine de Fez."	(Anonymous 1958:150, 1985:194)
Walila-5	pre-Idrisid	"Ancienne capitale du Maghreb... elle est maintenant deserte et en ruine."	Ibn Sa'id al-Maghribi in (Fagnan 1924:13)
Walila-6	pre-Idrisid	"chef-lieu des montagnes de Zraoun [Zarhun]. Walila etait une ville entouree de superbes murs de construction antique..."	(Ibn Abi Zar' 1860:14)
Walila-7 (Kasr Fir'awn)	"Ville antique fondee par les Romains a un peu moins de 8 milles (3 milles) de Gualili [Mulay Idris]"; pre-Idrisid	"Une petite ville"; "les collines d'alentour sont plantes d'oliviers"	(Leo Africanus 1956:246)
Walila-8	pre-Idrisid	[City]; minting activities: 'Abbasid currency, Idrisid currency.	(Eustache 1970:100, 1970-71:162)
Wargha-1	Idrisid	One of the 41 main cities of the district of Fas (Sus al-Adna).	(al-Mukaddasi 1950:7)
Wargha-2	Idrisid	[City]; minting activities: Idrisid currency.	(Eustache 1970:100)
Warzigha-1	According to al-Bakri, the "village" of Warzigha was destroyed by the Fatimid general Maysur in A.D. 935-6." (al-Bakri 1965:295); The future site of Maknas (Massignon 1906:214); Idrisid	"Village large... tres peuple."; "bien arrose; les fruits et les vivres s'y trouvent en abondance."	(al-Bakri 1965:294-295; Massignon 1906:214)
Warzigha-2	Idrisid	[City]; minting activities: Idrisid currency.	(Eustache 1970:100)
Watit	Idrisid	[City]; minting and mining activities (silver): Idrisid currency.	(Eustache 1970:100)
Winakam	Idrisid	"Autrefois chef-lieu du pays [entre Sabta et Titawan] qui appartient a Hammud b. Ibrahim [un arriere petit fils d'Idris II]."; "[located] sur le flanc d'une montagne, et possede des eaux courante et des vergers en quantite."	(al-Bakri 1965:211)
Zahdjuka (Djadjuka)	Idrisid	"Ville d'Ibrahim b. Muhammad [Idrisid prince]... Zahdjuka appartient maintenant aux Zarhuna"	(al-Bakri 1965:224)
Zallul-1 (Zalûl)	Idrisid	One of the 41 main cities of the district of Fas (Sus al-Adna).	(al-Mukaddasi 1950:7)

Name	Founding	Size/Economy	Textual/Numismatic Sources
Zallul-2	Idrisid	"Ville charmente a l'est d'Azila… Elle etait administree dans le temps par un delegue (mu'awwal) de Hasan Ibn Djannun al-Hasani al-Fatimi qui la reconstruite."; "possedant des marches qui se touchent (kariba)…"	(Ibn Hawkal 1938-39:75, 1967:79)
Zawiyya (al-) (Zauia)	"Batie par [Abu Ya'kub Yusuf al-Nasir], second roi merinide"; Marinid	"Une petite ville… tomba en ruines"	(Leo Africanus 1956:242)

APPENDIX C

SETTLEMENT TERMINOLOGY USED IN ARABIC SOURCES

A. Terms (nouns) used to refer to settlement types:

'amal (pl. a'mâl) [settlement's jurisdiction]
ard (pl. arâdî) [territory; country]
bâdiya [rural area; hinterland]
balad [country; territory]
balda [city]
dâr al-mulk [seat of government]
dâr mamlaka [capital of kingdom]
hâdira (pl. hawâdir) [metropolis]
hadjar [fortress; refuge]
hawz [suburb]
hisn [fortress]
iklîm [province; clime]
kâ'ida [residence; chief-seat; capital]
kâ'idat al-mulk [seat of authority]
kal'a [fortress]
karya[1] [village]
kasaba [citadel; chief-seat; provincial capital]
khâna [caravansary]
kûra (pl. kuwar) [district]
kursî al-mamlaka [capital of the kingdom]
kursî-l-mulk [seat of government]
kutb [pole; capital]
kutr [district]
madâr [central-place]
madîna [city]
makân [locality]
mamlaka [kingdom]
manzil [residence; travel-station; caravansary]
marsa [port; anchorage]
maskan [residence]
mawdi' [locality]
misr [city; metropolis]
munya [country house]
mustakar [seat of authority]
nâhiyya [territory; region]
nazar (pl. anzâr): [settlement's jurisdiction]
rabad (pl. arbâd) [suburb]
ribât [convent; hospice; caravansary]
rustâk [agricultural territory]
sakhra [fortress; refuge]

[1] Masîna "grand village qui ressemle plutôt à une petite ville [karya kabîra kal madîna al-saghira] (al-Idrîsî 1957:109).

suk' (pl. askâ') [region; district]
um al-kura[2] [capital]
um al-mudun[3] [capital]

B. Terms (adjectives) used to refer to settlement size:

madîna 'âmira [populous; prosperous]
madîna 'azîma [immense]
madîna 'uzma [immense]
madîna âhila [populous]
madîna djalîla [prestigious]
madîna kabîra [big]
madîna ma'mûra [urbanized]
madîna mashhûra [renowned]
madîna muktasida [medium-sized]
madîna mutahadira [urbanized; civilized]
madîna mutawassita [medium-sized]
madîna saghîra [small]
madîna wâsi'a [spacious]

C. Terms (adjectives) used to refer to settlement chronology:

madîna awwaliyya [ancient]
madîna azaliyya [ancient]
madîna dhâhiliyya [pre-Islamic]
madîna hadîtha [modern]
madîna kadîma [old]
madîna muhdatha [modern; recently founded]

D. Other expressions used to refer to settlement chronology:

madîna ahyâ rasmahâ... [a city renovated by...]
madîna djaddadahâ[4] (from *tadjdîd* or renovation)... [a city renovated by...]
madîna ikhtattahâ... [a city created by...]
madîna istahdathahâ[5] (from *istihdâth* or creation)... [a city created by...]
madîna rasama hudûdahâ [a city designed by...]

[2] The literal meaning of Um al-kura is "mother of all cities" referring to Makka (Mecca). It is used in textual evidence to refer to a regional capital (e.g., "Tandja is the kasaba [chief-seat] and the 'Um al-kura' [the capital] of the country of the Berbers..." (Anonymous 1981:15).

[3] The literal meaning of Um al-mudun is "mother of all cities". This term is used in textual evidence in the same way as Um al-kura.

[4] See an example in the description of Malîla in (al-Bakrî 1965:178-179; al-Himyarî 1975:545-6).

[5] See an example in the description of Tangier in (Ibn Hawkal 1842:193).

APPENDIX D

DISTRIBUTION OF SETTLEMENTS BY PHASE OF OCCUPATION AND SETTLEMENT SIZE CLASS

Site Name	Founding Period	Phase I	Phase II	Phase III	Phase IV
Aftîs	Idrisid	V	0	0	0
Aghîgha	Idrisid?	V	0	0	0
Agla	pre-Idrisid?	V	0	0	0
al-Aklâm	Idrisid	V	V	0	0
Amardjuwa	Almoravid	0	VI	0	0
al-'Arâ'ish	pre-Almoravid?	0	VI	V	V
Asâda	pre-Idrisid	V	0	0	0
Asîla	Idrisid	V	V	VI	V
'Awsadja	Idrisid?	V	0	0	0
'Ayn al-Shams	pre-Almoravid?	0	VI	VI	0
Baht	Idrisid	V	0	0	0
Balash	Idrisid	V	0	0	0
Balyunash	pre-Almoravid?	0	VI	VI	0
Banî 'Attush	Almoravid	0	VI	0	0
Banî Bâsil	Almoravid	0	VI	VI	0
Banî Radjîk	pre-Almoravid	V	0	0	0
Banî Sadâl	pre-Almoravid	V	0	0	0
Banî Tâwda	Almoravid	0	III	0	0
Banî Tâwra	Almoravid	0	V	0	0
Banî Ziyâd	Almoravid	0	V	0	0
al-Basra	Idrisid	IV	V	0	0
al-Baydâ'	Idrisid?	V	0	0	0
Buhayrat Ariâgh (Rîgha)	Idrisid	VI	VI	VI	0
Dakhla	pre-Almoravid	V	0	0	0
al-Damna	pre-Almoravid	V	V	0	0
al-Djâhid	Idrisid	V	0	0	0
Djâmi' al-Hammâm (Gemih el Chemmem)	Marinid?	0	0	0	V
Djarmâna	Idrisid	V	0	0	0
al-Djazîra (Gezira)	pre-Idrisid?	VI	VI	VI	VI
al-Djum'a (El-Giumha) ['Ayn Karwâsh?]	Marinid	0	0	0	VI
Fankur	Idrisid	V	0	0	0
Fanzâra	Almohad	0	0	V	V
Fâs (al-'Âliya)	Idrisid	III	II	I	I
al-Ghimd (La Vergogna)	Almohad?	0	0	VI	VI
Ghuzza	Idrisid	V	0	0	0
al-Habash	pre-Almoravid	V	0	0	0
Hadjar al-Nasr (Kal'at al-Nusur)	Idrisid	V	VI	0	0
al-Hadjîr	Idrisid	V	0	0	0
Hadjna	pre-Almoravid?	V	0	0	0
Humâr (Homar)	Idrisid	V	VI	VI	VI
Idjâdjîn	Idrisid	V	V	V	V
Idjarhân	pre-Idrisid	V	0	0	0
Kakammariyya	pre-Almoravid?	VI	0	0	0
al-Kal'a	pre-Almoravid?	VI	0	0	0
Kal'at Ibn Djundub (Kal'at Ibn Kharrub?)	pre-Almoravid?	V	VI	0	0
Kal'at Ibn Kharrub	Idrisid?	V	0	0	0
Kal'at Sadîna	Idrisid.	VI	0	0	0
Kal'at Shamît	Idrisid	V	0	0	0
al-Kanîsa	pre-Idrisid	VI	0	0	0

Site Name	Founding Period	Phase I	Phase II	Phase III	Phase IV
Karzâwa (of Banî Husayn)	pre-Almoravid?	VI	0	0	0
al-Kasr (Kasr Abî Musa)	Almoravid	0	VI	0	0
al-Kasr al-Kabîr	pre-Idrisid	V	V	V	V
al-Kasr al-Saghîr	Idrisid	VI	VI	VI	V
al-Khadra	Idrisid	V	0	0	0
Khamîs Matghâra (Camis Metgara)	Idrisid?	VI	VI	VI	VI
Khawlân (Chaulan)	Marinid	0	0	0	VI
Kurt	Idrisid	V	VI	VI	0
Madînat Djabal Zâlâgh	Idrisid	V	0	0	0
Madrâka	Idrisid	V	0	0	0
Maghîla	pre-Idrisid?	V	0	VI	VI
al-Makarmâda (Macarmeda)	pre-Almoravid?	V	VI	VI	VI
Maknâs (Miknâsa)	pre-Almoravid	V	IV	IV	III
Malhas	Idrisid	VI	0	0	0
Ma'mura	pre-Almoravid?	VI	VI	V	V
Masîna (Masîta)	pre-Idrisid	V	VI	0	0
Matruka	Idrisid	V	0	0	0
Mudrîka	Idrisid	V	0	0	0
Mulây Idrîs (Gualili)	pre-Idrisid	VI	0	0	0
Nabrash	pre-Almoravid?	VI	0	0	0
Narandja (Narangia)	Marinid?	0	0	0	VI
Ribât (Barbât?)	pre-Almoravid	VI	V	II	V
Sabta	pre-Idrisid	V	V	IV	III
Sadâk	pre-Almoravid	V	0	0	0
Sakuma	pre-Idrisid	VI	0	0	0
Salâ	pre-Idrisid	V	V	V	IV
Shalla (Sella)	pre-Idrisid	VI	VI	0	0
Subu (Sabu)	Idrisid	V	0	0	0
Tadjrâdjra	Idrisid	V	0	0	0
Tâfalfalt (Tefelfelt)	Marinid?	0	0	0	VI
Tahâddârt	pre-Almoravid?	VI	0	0	0
Tahlît	Idrisid	V	V	V	0
Tandja	pre-Idrisid	IV	IV	IV	IV
Tansor	Marinid?	0	0	0	VI
Tâwarat	Idrisid	V	0	0	0
Tâzgha	Idrisid?	V	0	0	0
Tittâwân	pre-Almoravid?	VI	V	V	V
Tunaktâyân (Pietra Rossa?)	Almoravid	0	V	VI	0
Tushummush	pre-Idrisid	V	V	V	VI
al-'Ubbâd (Hubbed)	Marinid?	0	0	0	VI
'Ukâsha (Suk 'Ukâsha)	Idrisid	VI	0	0	0
al-Waldja	Almoravid	0	V	0	0
Walîla	pre-Idrisid	IV	V	VI	0
Wargha	Idrisid	V	0	0	0
Warzîgha	Idrisid	V	0	0	0
Watît	Idrisid	V	0	0	0
Winâkam	Idrisid	V	0	0	0
Zahdjuka (Djadjuka)	Idrisid	V	0	0	0
Zallul (Zalul)	Idrisid	V	0	0	0
al-Zâwiyya (Zauia)	Marinid	0	0	0	VI

APPENDIX E

INVENTORY OF SURVEYED SITES

This appendix includes an inventory of the archaeological sites surveyed during this project. With a few exceptions, most of the sites described in this inventory were discovered during the 1998 and 1999 field-seasons. This appendix is organized into two sections: (1) archaeological sites included in INAA study (see Chapter 6), (2) archaeological sites not included in INAA study.

In both sections, sites are presented in ascending order according to their numbers. Sites numbers were assigned using a notational system composed of the first three letters of the 1/50,000 topographic map in which the site was located, followed by a sequential number. The x, y, and z coordinates are based on "Lambert kilometric grid" (*quadrillage kilométrique Lambert*). The map projection is that of Lambert Conformal Conic (Ellipsoid: Clarke 1880).

The information provided for each site includes site number, site name, site coordinates, site description, and a bibliography[1] when applicable. Only the ceramic material found in archaeological sites included in INAA study is discussed in terms of pottery types.[2] The system used to describe surface collections includes the pottery type and the number of samples collected. For example, **Form 40:10** indicates that Form 40 is represented by 10 samples. The description of pottery types is based on Benco's typology (Benco 1987). A list of the pottery types collected and their descriptions is included at the end of this appendix.

Archaeological Sites Included in INAA Study

Map: Arbaoua (ARB)

ARB1, Douar J'aouna al-Basra (medieval al-Basra), x 456.8, y 467.5, z 222
Site of medieval al-Basra (see Chapter 6).

ARB2, al-Ghzalat, x 457.1, y 465, z 335
Located at 2.3 km southeast of al-Basra (Figure 3.2). The site is now occupied by the modern village of al-Ghzalat. The village area is about 0.16 km². The surface scatter area is 300 m in diameter. While plowing their fields, local farmers found beads, ceramic vessels, and round grinding stones (*R<u>h</u>a*). The surface material includes wheelmade and glazed wares (honey and brown), fragments of roof-tile (red and yellow), and a round grinding stone fragment of 35 cm in diameter. The site was used for quarrying; large blocks of stone were located at the periphery of the site, which may have been part of an enclosing wall. The closest water source to the site is Ain el-Bir located at 500 m northwest of the site.

Pottery types collected: Form 12:1, Form 19:2, Form 40:11, Form 41:1, Form 42:1, Form 43:5, Form 44:2, Form 80:11, Form 81:1, Form 83:1 (glazed), Form 93:2, Form 99:1, Form 120:4, and Form 121:1.

ARB7, Bhalla, x 459, y 469, z 172
Located at 3 km northeast of al-Basra and occupied by modern village of Bhalla (Figure 3.2). The surface scatter area is 100 in diameter. The ceramic material includes handmade, wheelmade, and glazed wares (green and honey). The surface material also includes fragments of roof-tile and slag. According to local farmers, the slag was possibly left behind by itinerant blacksmiths who used to visit the village during the colonial period.

Pottery types collected: Form 19:5, Form 40:9, Form 44:1, Form 80:8, Form 82:1, and Form 121:3

ARB8, Jajouka (Mslâla), x 457.1, y 483.1, z 82
Located at about 8 km southeast of Ksar Kebir and overlooks the Loukous River (Figure 3.2). The site is known to the locals as Mslâla nearby the local cemetery of <u>K</u>lî'a, both toponyms not shown on the topographic map. There is another location with the same toponym (Jajouka) at 15 km northeast of the site.

The site is now occupied by the modern village of Jajouka. The western section of the site is delimited by outcroppings. The surface scatter area is 500 m in diameter. The ceramic material includes handmade, wheelmade, and glaze wares (green and honey). The surface material also includes fragments of roof-tile and round grinding stone. Although there is abundant stone material on the ground, no wall alignments were identified. This is possibly the site of Zah<u>dj</u>ûka mentioned by al-Bakrî (1965:224) (Appendix B).

Pottery types collected: Form 12:1, Form 13:1, Form 40:6, Form 41:3, Form 44:1, Form 48:4, Form 80:3, Form 84?:2, Form 99:2, Form 120:10, and Form 121:1.

ARB13, Sidi Bou Douma, x 456.2, y 482.2, z 250
Located at 15 km north of al-Basra on top of Jbel Rheni Mountain (Figure 3.2). It overlooks the nearby village of Jbel Rheni. The site is badly eroded. The surface scatter area is about 250 m in diameter. The surface material includes handmade, wheelmade and glazed wares (green and dark brown), in addition to fragments of roof-tile.

Pottery types collected: Form 40:6, Form 42:1, Form 43:1, Form 44:2, Form 80:2, Form 121:1, and Form 120:1.

ARB15, Sidi Bou Dmama (Kudyat Srafah), x 456.3, y 466.1, z 257
Located at 1.5 km south of al-Basra (Figure 3.2). The surface scatter area is 250 m in diameter. The ceramic material consists almost exclusively of wheelmade pottery. The surface material

[1] For references cited in site description but not included in site bibliography, see the main reference section (in References Cited).

[2] With the exception of Moulay Bouselham's site description which includes a detailed list of the ceramic material excavated by Redman in 1981 (Redman 1983-84).

also includes fragments of roof-tile and round grinding stone. Most of the site surface is covered with building stones. Several wall alignments are still visible on the ground, including a section of a building (s) that is about 22.30 m long; a 10 m section of it is clearly visible on the surface (oriented SW-NE).

Pottery types collected: Form 40:19, Form 41:2, Form 42:11, Form 43:3, Form 44:6, and Form 99:2.

ARB18, Ketama (Merksa), x 460.3, y 480.3, z 320
Located at 13.5 km north of al-Basra (Figure 3.2). The site is now occupied by the modern village of Ketama. It overlooks the dam of Oued al-Makhazin on Loukkous River. A large portion of the site is now used to grow olive trees. The surface of the site is covered with rock-piles. The southern section of the site is delimited by outcroppings. The local farmers use the stones to enclose their houses and fields. The larger blocks are cut into disks of 50 to 70 cm in diameter and used to make oil presses.

The ceramic material was found at several locations of the site - within a perimeter of about 500 m in diameter. It includes handmade, wheelmade, and glazed wares (honey). The surface material also includes fragments of roof-tile and round grinding stones.

Pottery types collected: Form 19:1, Form 40:4, Form 41:3, Form 80:6, Form 81:2, Form 99:1 (glazed), and Form 120:2.

Map: Lalla Mimouna (LLM)

LLM1, Shkayfa, x 443.3, y 478.8, z 170
Located at 18 km northwest of al-Basra near the modern village of Chograne and the local marabout of Sidi Mohammed Chrif (Cheikh?) (Figure 3.2). Interestingly, the site toponym (Shkayfa) is a diminutive for "sherd".

This site is characterized by high densities of surface scatter. The largest area of surface scatter is about 700 m in diameter. The ceramic material is made almost exclusively of wheelmade pottery. The ceramic material is also visible below surface in some areas of the site that were exposed by rainwater.

There are abundant water sources around the site including two springs and three wells. No archaeological features were identified at the site. It is possible that building stones were cleared from the surface of the site to allow farming. Although not shown on the topographic map, large areas around the site are now planted with eucalyptus trees.

Pottery types collected: Form 40:16, Form 41:4, Form 42:9, Form 43:8, Form 44:11, Form 48:1, Form 49:1, Form 54?:1, Form 78?:1, Form 80:2, Form 81:1, Form 99:5, and Form 120:5.

LLM4, Frigidae, x 431.4, y 485.5, z 85
A Roman military camp located at 32 km northwest of al-Basra (Figure 3.2). The site was occupied some time before the fourth century A.D. (Limane and Rebuffat 1995:305; Rebuffat 1987:36; Tissot 1876:256, 258, 1878:276).

The area of Frigidae is less than one hectare (0.71 ha) (Rebuffat 1987:59). Tissot (1878:276), who visited Frigidae in 1874 described it in the following terms: "La station de Frigidae, à en juger par le caractère particulier et le peu d'importance des vestiges qu'elle a laissés, n'a jamais dû être autre chose qu'un poste militaire." INAA data show that the site was reoccupied during the Idrisid period (see Chapter 6).

Pottery types collected: Form 40:1 and Form 43:1.

LLM5, Sidi Ahmed al-Niyya, x 441.4, y 467.3, z 24
Located at 15 km west of al-Basra (Figure 3.2). The site is now occupied by the cemetery of Mrija village. A small stream (Oued Bouhrira) flows at the immediate vicinity of the site. The site is cut by a dirt road leading to a nearby village. An exposed cross-section of the site shows evidence of intensely burned clay (a kiln?). A large section of the site is inaccessible due to the presence of a fence. The surface scatter area is 50 m in diameter. The surface material is composed mainly of wheelmade pottery (including what may be a waster) and roof-tiles. No architectural features were visible on the ground.

Pottery types collected: Form 40:10, Form 41:3, Form 42:2, Form 43:4, Form 44:1, Form 48:1, Form 81:1, Form 120:3, and Form 121:2.

LLM8, Sidi Ahmed Bourziguine, x 427.1, y 488, z 50
Located at 37 km northwest of al-Basra at the immediate vicinity of Soueir River (Figure 3.2). The surface scatter area is 150 m in diameter. The ceramic material includes wheelmade and glazed wares (green and honey).

Pottery types collected: Form 40:5, Form 41:3, Form 42:2, Form 43:1, Form 44:2, Form 80:1, and Form 84:1.

LLM9, Jbel ad-Dal (el-Arab), x 440.9, y 462.9, z 155
Located at about 17 km southwest of al-Basra near the modern village of el-Arab (Figure 3.2). The site occupies a hilltop where a relay radio station ("*relais hertzien*") has been recently built. The surface scatter area is about 250 m in diameter. With the exception of a few handmade and green-colored glazed sherds, most of the ceramic material found at the site is composed of wheelmade pottery. The surface material also includes several fragments of roof-tile and one fragment of a round grinding stone. Sites LLM9 and LLM10 are possibly part of the same settlement divided by a small stream.

Pottery types collected: Form 40:12, Form 41:6, Form 42:4, Form 43:2, Form 81:3, Form 93:2, Form 120:5, and Form 121:1.

LLM10, Kudyat Sma, x 440.2, y 463.1, z 90
Located at about 17 km southwest of al-Basra near the tomb of Sidi Abdellah (the cemetery of el-Arab village) (Figure 3.2). The surface scatter area is about 200 m in diameter. The ceramic material includes handmade, wheelmade, and glazed wares (green). The surface material also includes fragments of roof-tile. LLM9 and LLM10 are possibly part of the same settlement. LLM10 has a higher surface density than LLM9.

Pottery types collected: Form 12:9, Form 13:1, Form 40:40, Form 41:17, Form 42:7, Form 43:8, Form 48:8, Form 80:4, Form 99:2, Form 120:2, and Form 121:6.

LLM14, Sidi Yssef, x 424.1, y 473.7, z 11
Located at 32.5 km northwest of al-Basra near the modern village of Ksaksa (Oulad Ziane on the topographic map) (Figure 3.2). Drader River is less than 1 km south of the site. The surface scatter area is about 200 in diameter. Higher densities of ceramic material are found near the domed structure which constitutes the marabout of Sidi Yssef. With the exception of a few handmade sherds, most of the ceramic material is composed of wheelmade pottery.

The area around the site - or what remains thereof - has been seriously damaged due to the building of a new highway and a toll station (not shown on the topographic map, which needs to be updated).

Pottery types collected: Form 40:20, Form 41:4, Form 42:9, Form 43:2, Form 80:7, Form 81:2, Form 84:3, and Form 120:6.

Map: Machraa Bel-Ksiri (MBK)

MBK1, al-Ayyach (al-'Asimi), x 466.2, y 448.5, z 40
Located at 21 km southeast of al-Basra near the cemetery of al-Ayyach village. This village is now abandoned. The site overlooks the et-Tnine River (Oued et-Tnine). There is a stone quarry in the vicinity of the site. The only standing structure at al-Ayyach is the domed marabout of Sidi Ahmed el-Haj. The surface scatter area is about 100 m in diameter. The ceramic material at the site includes handmade, wheelmade, and glazed wares (brown, honey, and green). The surface material also includes fragments of roof-tile, round grinding stones, and fired bricks.

Pottery types collected: Form 12:1, Form 19:3, Form 40:16, Form 41:6, Form 42:2, Form 44:4, Form 82:4, Form 84?:3, Form 120:6, and Form 121:4.

Map: Moulay Bouselham (MBS)

MBS2, Sidi Mostefa (Douar Riah), x 420.1, y 475.8, z 29
Located at 37.5 km west of al-Basra near the cemetery of the modern village of Riah (Figure 3.2). The installation of new sewage lines badly disturbed the site. Only a few ceramic sherds were found on the surface. The surface scatter area is about 50 m in diameter. The ceramic material includes handmade and wheelmade pottery.

Pottery types collected: Form 42:1, Form 43:1, Form 81:3, Form 120:1, and Form 121:1.

Archaeological Sites Not Included in INAA Study

Map: Arb'a Ayacha (ACH)

ACH1, Souiyyar, x 462.2, y 536.4, z 45
Located at 1 km west of el-Kebir River (Oued el-Kebir) and 2.5 km east of the *Route Principale* No. 37. A Roman site with visible stone and brick architecture, and abundant surface material. No Islamic period material was found at the site.

Bibliography:
Lenoir, M. 1993 Ad Mercuri Templum: Voies et Occupation Antiques du Nord du Maroc. *Sonderdruck aus Mitteilungen des Deutchen Archaeologischen Instituts Roemische Abteilung* Band 100.

ACH2, al-Kharroub, x 465, y 540.3, z 250
A modern village located at about 1 km east of et-Tlata Jbel Habib at the foot of the Jbel Habib Mountain. The village area is about 0.6 km². At the immediate vicinity of the village, there is evidence of smelting activities as attested by the presence of slag. There are also traces of wall alignments and rock-piles from wall collapse. There were few ceramic sherds on the ground (handmade, wheelmade, and green-colored glazed wares). This is possibly a late medieval or colonial-period site.

The village representative (*mukaddam*) informed the author that there are other "ancient" ruins, known as al-Mardj or Gharz Shurfa, at the vicinity of Sîdî al-Makhfî (Douar al-'mârât). The toponym of Kal'at Ibn Kharrûb was mentioned by al-Bakrî (1965:215) (Appendix B). Furthermore, according to Leo Africanus (1956:270) "Il y a dans cette montagne [Chebib (Djabal Habîb)] environ six ou sept châteaux."

Map: Arbaoua (ARB)

ARB3, Ouald Amer Moussa, x 460.2, y 466.7, z 260
Located at 3.5 km east of al-Basra on a hilltop offering an excellent view of all the Mda River Valley (Figure 2.6). The site is now occupied by the modern village of Ouald Amer Moussa. The village area is about 0.18 km². The surface scatter area is 250 m in diameter centered around the tomb of Sidi Ahmed in the village cemetery. The surface material includes wheelmade and green-colored glazed wares. The site was used for quarrying. The closest water source is the Ain Doufane spring located at about 500 m northwest of the site. Period of occupation is unknown.

ARB4, Sidi Salem, x 461.5, y 466.1, z 277
Located at 5 km east of al-Basra, and occupied by the marabout of Sidi Salem (Figure 2.6). The surface scatter area is 175 m in diameter. The western section of the site is delimited by outcroppings. The surface material includes handmade, wheelmade, and glazed wares (green, honey, and brown). Most of the site surface is covered with building stones. Some of the stone material was used by local farmers to delimit their fields.

The major archaeological feature at this site is a stone wall running north-south. This wall is 8 m long and 0.7 m wide. Only the first course of this wall is still in place. As attested by the wall collapse nearby, this wall must have been part of a large stone structure. The spring nearby the site (Ain Sidi Salem) is the main source of drinking water for the surrounding villages of Oulad Ziane and Sefiane. Period of occupation is unknown.

ARB5, Loubat, x 458.4, y 470.9, z 120
Located at 3.5 km northeast of al-Basra and 1.5 km southwest of the modern village of Loubat (Figure 2.6). The site is cut through by a dirt road leading to the village. Traces of wall alignments are visible on the ground. The surface scatter area is about 200 m in diameter. The site is covered with shrub and dwarf palm. The ceramic material found at the site includes wheelmade (especially coarse ware) and glazed wares (green and honey). Period of occupation is unknown.

ARB6, Sidi Ahmed Cheikh, x 456.6, y 474.4, z 231
Locate at 7.5 km north of al-Basra (Figure 2.6). The surface scatter area is 200 m in diameter. The ceramic material includes wheelmade and glazed wares (green). Period of occupation is unknown.

ARB9, no toponym, x 458.1, y 482.1, z 16
Section of a wall protruding from a steep embankment leading down to the Loukous River. The visible section of the wall is 1 m wide. The surface material consists of large fragments of coarse ware with thick walls possibly used for canalization. Period of occupation is unknown.

ARB10, Kudyat al-Mriyyas, x 456.5, y 476.6, z 190
Located at 9 km north of al-Basra (Figure 2.6). The site toponym on the topographic map is K^{at} el-Meriach. The visible section of the site is 200 m in diameter. The presence of unharvested fields made it difficult to assess the actual area of the surface scatter. Although, there is relatively abundant stone material on the surface, no wall alignments were identified. The surface material consists of handmade, wheelmade, and glazed wares (green and honey). The surface material also includes fragments of round grinding stones. There are no water sources nearby the site. Period of occupation is unknown.

ARB11, Ain Gharra, x 461.5, y 470.6, z 212
Located at 5.5 km northeast of al-Basra (Figure 2.6). The site toponym on the topographic map is Ain Hadra. The site is made of two hills (Ain Gharra and Bsibisa). The surface scatter area is 500 m in diameter. The surface material includes handmade, wheelmade, and glazed wares (honey). There was a spring at the site that is now dried up. Period of occupation is unknown.

ARB12, Lalla Bbarka, x 459.1, y 470.3, z 172
Located at 4 km northeast of al-Basra (Figure 2.6). The site consists of a small ceramic scatter nearby a saint tomb. The ceramic material includes handmade and wheelmade wares. Period of occupation is unknown.

ARB14, Lalla Menni, x 453.8, y 462.3, z 197
Located at 6 km southwest of al-Basra (Figure 2.6). The visible section of the site is about 100 m in diameter. The presence of unharvested fields made it difficult to assess the actual area of the surface scatter. The surface material is composed of wheelmade pottery. This is possibly a late medieval or a colonial-period site.

ARB16, Swayyar (Lalla Meriem), x 455.4, y 485.3, z 40
Located at 3.5 km southeast of Ksar Kebir (Figure 2.6). The site is now occupied by a farmer's house. As its toponym indicates (*swayyar*, Arabic diminutive for wall), the only archaeological feature at the site is a section of a wall made of stone and *pisé*; stone was used in lower courses to support pisé blocks - using a system of wood casing. This feature is oriented north-south and measures 30 m long and at least 2 m high. Other sections of it are still visible on the ground. The surface material consists of wheelmade pottery (possibly modern).

According to the locals, this structure was built by the Spaniards. Farmers also found human remains (a cemetery?) in the vicinity of the site. This is possibly a late medieval site (Alawite?).

ARB17, El Hamri, x 446.6, y 485.9, z 130
Located at 7.5 km southwest of Ksar Kebir in the vicinity of the modern village of Rzigat (Figure 2.6). The site is located on a hilltop overlooking the Krem River Valley. The surface scatter area is about 150 m in diameter. The ceramic material includes handmade, wheelmade, and glazed wares (green, brown, and honey). The surface material also includes fragments of roof-tiles and round grinding stone. The geological deposits in the area are made of a reddish soil mixed with gravel. Period of occupation is unknown.

Map: Asilah (ASL)

ASL1, al-Houmar, x 444.5, y 533.4, z 131
Located at 7.5 km southeast of Asilah and 1 km east of the Homar River. The site is now occupied by the modern village of el-Houmar. A few ceramic sherds were found nearby the village's mosque. The ceramic material includes handmade, wheelmade, and glazed wares (green). The surface material also includes a piece of bloated glass (evidence for manufacture or accidental exposure to fire?). The village spring is called Ain Soumata.

It is possible that the village of el-Houmar was built on top of medieval Homar mentioned by Leo Africanus (1956:260) (see Appendix B).

Map: Beni-Ammar (BNA)

BNA1, Qasbat Nasrani (Kasabat al-Nasrânî), x 501.2, y 378.6, z 987
An important Almoravid fortress west of Fez (Figure 3.1). Several scholars argued that this fortress corresponds to the site of Tûnaktâyân mentioned by the twelfth century al-Baydak (Lévi-Provençal 1928:221) and to that of Pietra Rossa (al-Hadjar al-Ahmar) mentioned by Leo Africanus (1956:246) (see Appendix B).

Very few ceramic sherds were found on the surface (due to the non-residential nature of the site) including glazed ware (green, white, and honey). For a complete site description see bibliography below.

Bibliography:
Berthier, P. 1938 *Essai sur l'Histoire du Massif de Moulay Idris: De la conquête à l'établissement du Protectorat Français*, Rabat.

BNA2, Mghila, x 511.5, y 380.2, z 360
Located north of the route linking Fez to Meknès at about 4 km north of the small town of Mhaya. The site is now occupied by the modern village of Mghila. The village area is about 0.25 km². The ceramic material is found at several areas around the village in scatters of moderate densities. It includes handmade, wheelmade, and glazed wares.

It is possible that important archaeological remains lie beneath the modern village of Mghila. While plowing their fields, local farmers occasionally find complete ceramic vessels (some of them glazed) and round grinding stones. According to informants, an underground conduit made of pottery tubes was discovered while repairing the dirt road that cuts through the village. The archaeological importance of this site has yet to be recognized. Sites BNA2 and BNA3 were possibly parts of the same medieval settlement (Maghîla, see Appendix B).

BNA3, Ain Jouaou, x 512, y 380, z 340
Located at about 0.5 km southeast of the modern village of Mghila (BNA2). The site is divided into two sections by a small stream (Oued Jouaou). The surface material includes pottery, fragments of bricks and roof-tile. Limane (1997:9), who first identified the site, has found fragments of type RIIB Spanish amphorae (*amphores espagnoles*).

To the west of Oued Jouaou, in an area of 150 m in diameter, a high density of ceramic material was found. This material includes handmade, wheelmade, and glazed wares (green). The most important feature at the site is a *pisé* structure known locally as al-Sum'a (the minaret). This structure (5.5 m high) was possibly part of a tower reinforcing one of the angles of a fortification wall. In fact, the southern side of this structure shows a section of a wall that is 1.5 m wide.

Limane (1997:9) recorded several other important features on the eastern side of Oued Jouaou including a section of a wall (city-wall?) 5 m long, 1.5 m high, and 1 m wide, and a stone block that was used for oil processing. In addition to these features, the site also contains a number of *pisé* structures along Oued Jouaou that are most likely late medieval (Alawîte?). The archaeological importance of this site has yet to be recognized. Sites BNA2 and BNA3 were possibly parts of the same medieval settlement (Maghîla, see Appendix B).

Bibliography:
Limane, H. 1997 Un Site Romain dans la Région de Mhaya. *Nouvelles Archéologiques et Patrimoniales* I:9.

BNA4, Ahl Zaouia, x 508.9, y 401.5, z 370
Located at 7 km southeast of Souk Sebt of Oudayas. The site is now occupied by the modern village of Ahl Zaouia. Due to the absence of building stones in the area, most of the houses in the village were built using mud-brick. While building their houses, local farmers found ceramic material and traces of earlier structures. The main water source at the village is a tributary of the Mkes River.

A few ceramic sherds were found including handmade, wheelmade, and glazed wares (green). Local informants attribute the site to the Wattasid period (A.D. 1420-1550). The toponym of al-Zawiyya is mentioned by Leo Africanus (1956:242) (see Appendix B).

Map: Had Kourt[3] (HDK)

HDK1, Kourt, x 475.8, y 449.7, z 443
Located on a small plateau on the top of the Kourt Mountain (Jbel Kourt) (Figure 3.1). The site is mostly known to the locals for the presence of a cave believed to be the hermitage (*khalwa*) of Mûlây 'Abd al-Kâdir al-Djîlânî - a well-known twelfth-century saint (see Mounès 1957:14-15). Every year an annual fair (*mawsim* or moussem) is held in his honor in the vicinity of the cave.

The site area is about 0.14 km². The most important archaeological feature at the site is its fortifications. The perimeter of the site is enclosed by a combination of outcrops and a thick enclosing wall. This latter was essentially built to fill in gaps between outcrops. The southwestern section of the enclosing wall is 77 m long and 1.8 m wide. This wall was built using lime mortar and roughly shaped building stones.

The central area of the plateau is covered with shrubs and wall collapse. Fifty years ago, when Mounès (1957:16) visited the site, some of the walls were still standing. Mounès also found several fragments of well-made bricks, roof-tile, and ceramics. At the southeastern corner of the site, a few meters from the cave, there is historic stone structure that was possibly used by pilgrims visiting the cave.

The ceramic material found at the site consists of handmade, wheelmade, and glazed wares (green and honey). Preliminary analysis of ware and form categories shows that this material is different from that found in al-Basra. Other surface material includes fragments of roof-tile and slag.

The archaeological importance of the site has yet to be recognized. Most importantly, the site has to be dated. There are several hypotheses in this regard. Some scholars argued that, in order to control the route linking Tangier to Volubilis, the Romans must have recognized the excellent strategic location that the site offers, and used it to build a fortified post (the Roman site of Viposcianae?) (Mounès 1957:16-17; Tissot 1878:296).

Is this the site of medieval Kurt? Archaeological evidence does not seem to support this hypothesis. First, the site is simply too small to be the medieval city mentioned in textual records (see Appendix B). Moreover, there are no springs at the site to sustain an urban population. The closest spring is Ain el-Hafa, located at the foot of the mountain (i.e., *extra muros*). As it is the case in other medieval Moroccan fortresses, rain water - captured and stored in cisterns - must have been the main source of water for the population of the site.

Second, according to al-Bakrî (1965:217) the city of Kurt overlooks the Rdat River, which is in fact 7.5 km to the south

[3] Feuille NI-30-XIII-3b; Aerial photos: 1/20.000-62:1810, 1811, 1812 (Available from La direction de la cartographie, Rabat).

of the site. Furthermore, the archaeological evidence discussed above clearly contradicts the information provided by al-Idrîsî (1983:169) who states that the city (1) had no fortifications, (2) was located at the foot of a mountain, and (3) had abundant water resources. The site must have been more of a fortress-refuge than an actual urban center. This site needs immediate archaeological attention. In order to understand its function and its period of occupation, it needs to be mapped and test excavated.

Bibilography:

Mounès, J. 1957 Notes sur Quelques Villes Disparues du Maroc Septentrional. *Bulletin de l'Enseignement Public au Maroc* 44(239):5-28.

Map: Lalla Mimouna (LLM)

LLM2, Lalla Rahma, x 434.7, y 486.4, z 108
Located at about 30 km northwest of al-Basra near the modern village of Ouled Bou Azza (Figure 2.6). The surface scatter is 300 m in diameter. According to informants, the spring at the site (Ain Stal) was associated with a stone structure now inextant. The ceramic material includes handmade, wheelmade, and glazed wares (green and brown). Period of occupation is unknown.

LLM3, Sidi el-Houari, x 435.6, y 487.9, z 132
Located at 30 km northwest of al-Basra at the immediate vicinity of the marabout of Sidi el-Houari (Figure 2.6). The surface scatter is about 300 m in diameter. The ceramic material includes handmade, wheelmade, and glazed wares (green). Period of occupation is unknown.

LLM6, Sidi Hlal, x 440.8, y 470.2, z 53
Located at 17 km west of al-Basra (Figure 2.6). A few ceramic sherds (handmade and wheelmade) were found around the marabout of Sidi Hlal and near the modern village of Ouled Nafkha (Nafrha). Period of occupation is unknown.

LLM7, Kudyat Kniz, x 428.6, y 487.2, z 75
Located at 35 km northwest of al-Basra near the modern village of Ouled Mosbah (Figure 2.6). This is a Roman site as attested by the finding of several *terra sigillata* (*Sigillée*) sherds, fragments of amphorae, roof-tile, and three large building blocks. The site area is about 250 m in diameter. This site needs immediate archaeological attention since it is being transformed into a farm using modern irrigation systems.

LLM11, Sidi Bouzakri, x 441, y 462.3, z 110
Located at about 17 km southwest of al-Basra (Figure 2.6). The surface scatter area is about 200 m in diameter. The ceramic material includes handmade, wheelmade, and glazed wares (green, brown, and honey). The glazed wares include a green-colored fragment of a lamp pedestal. The surface material also includes fragments of roof-tile and fired bricks. Period of occupation is unknown.

LLM12, Sidi Ahmed el-Jahid, x 441.5, y 465.4, z 64
Located at 15 km west of al-Basra near the modern village of Sder Mghitane (Mrhitane Sder on the topographic map) (Figure 2.6). The surface scatter area is about 100 in diameter. The ceramic material includes handmade, wheelmade, and glazed wares (green). Period of occupation is unknown.

LLM13, Ain Gsab, x 432.2, y 464, z 80
Located at 25 km west of al-Basra near the cemetery of Mouaouka village. The site is named after a nearby spring (Ain Tsob on the topographic map) (Figure 2.6). The surface scatter area is about 100 m in diameter. The ceramic material is composed mostly of wheelmade pottery. Period of occupation is unknown

Although, there is no major body of water in the area, large deposits of solidified shell are found near the site. On a hilltop 0.5 km north of the site, there are remains of a *pisé* structure, which according to the locals was a residence of a local chief (Caid or K̲â'id).

LLM15, Lalla Zahra, x 426.7, y 466.1, z 82
Located at 30 km west of al-Basra and shown on the topographic map as "*Minaret en Ruines*" (Figure 2.6). The surface scatter area is about 150 m in diameter. Most of the ceramic material is composed of wheelmade pottery. A few glazed sherds were found including a fragment of green-colored pedestal lamp. The surface material also includes fragments of roof-tile, fired bricks, and round grinding stones. Interestingly, a fragment of a round grinding stone was reused in the building of the minaret (described below).

The most important archaeological feature at the site is a stone-built minaret. This is a square structure 10 m high and 3 m on each side. The upper part is missing - or never completed as was the case for the Almohad Hassan Tower in Rabat.

A brief description of the monument by Ahmed Ettahiri, a member of the field crew and a specialist in Islamic monuments: "Un minaret construit en grès dunaire, tuile, brique, avec un mortier en chaux et en sable très solide. Le chainage du minaret est fait de pierre de taille. Les faces extérieures sont décorées de deux niches aveugles en arc brisé outrepassé, clavaux en brique cuite sur des pilastes. L'intérieur du minaret s'ouvre sur le côté sud - comme le tombeau en dome de Lalla Zahra. L'entrée est en berceau, avec un petit réduit à l'intérieur, aussi en berceau. Le haut du minaret est accessible à l'aide de marches en gradins."

The period when this structure was in use is still unknown. More in-depth architectural analysis will certainly shed more light in this regard. Considering the size of the site, this latter was possibly a medieval *zâwiya* (convent). Furthermore, the site must have predated the cemetery nearby since a stone base of a door-post was reused in the construction of one of the tombs.

Map: Larache (LAR)

LAR1, Lixus, x 435.4, y 511.4, z 85
Lixus (medieval Tus̲h̲ummus̲h̲) is one of the most important Roman-period sites in Morocco (Figure 3.1). The site has been the object of several archaeological projects. Archaeological evidence suggests that Lixus was abandoned in the beginning of the fifth century A.D. (Akerraz 1992:383-

384). The following description focuses on the Islamic phase of occupation at the site.

The site was reoccupied during the Islamic period. It was mentioned - as Tushummush - in several medieval Arabic texts (Appendix B). Archaeological evidence for the Islamic period at the site is represented by a mosque, a house with a central courtyard, and a number of water management facilities.[4]

The mosque is located within the boundaries of the reduced city (*"la ville réduite"*) in what is known as "the quarter of the temples". The original function of this structure was a subject of debate among classical period archaeologists. Ponsich (1981:113-114) argued that this structure was originally a Christian basilica before it was converted into a mosque. Akerraz (1992:382-383) and Euzennat (1974:175-181) attributed this structure to the Islamic period.

In addition to the *mihrâb* (apse), the base of the minaret, and traces of a staircase leading to this latter, the mosque at Lixus is composed of three sections (Akerraz 1992:Figure 6; Ponsich 1981:114-117; Figure 32): (1) a covered prayer-hall (15.20 m by 11.10 m) with three naves of equal width, (2) a paved open courtyard (the *sahn* of the mosque) (11.40 m wide, and (3) a rectangular back room (3.50 m by 11 m).

The Islamic house at Lixus is built against the later city-wall within the reduced city (Ponsich 1981:126-127, Figure 36). It has a central courtyard with portico and a basin in the middle. A series of rooms with plastered walls open into the courtyard. This house is equipped with is a private bath (*hammâm*) with its own small cistern.

El-Khatib-Boujibar's work (1992) on the water management system at the city identified several water facilities dating to the Islamic period. This includes a well (Well B) and two cisterns (El-Khatib-Boujibar 1992:306, 310). Cistern 19, the only square cistern at the site, was built during the Islamic period to store water for the *hammâm* of the Islamic house (El-Khatib-Boujibar 1992:306; see also Ponsich 1981:127). Cistern 15, located underneath the mosque's open courtyard, is dated to the Roman period but is believed to have been modified during the medieval period (El-Khatib-Boujibar 1992:307).

The ceramic material found at Lixus consists of handmade, wheelmade, and glazed wares (green and honey). With the exception of Ataallah's study (1967) of a special decorated ware (dated between the twelfth and fourteenth centuries A.D.), Islamic period ceramics found at the site are not yet adequately studied.

The presence of a mosque with three naves[5] (300 m^2) suggests that there was a relatively sizeable population at the site. Since all the archaeological evidence for the Islamic occupation was found within the boundaries of the reduced city, it is most likely that medieval Tushummush occupied the reduced Roman city.

Bibliography:

Akerraz, A. 1992 Lixus, du Bas-Empire à L'Islam. *Lixus*, Collection de L'Ecole Française de Rome 166:379-385.

Ataallah, M. 1967 La Céramique Musulmane à Paroi Fine Incisée ou Peinte de Lixus. *Bulletin d'Archéologie Marocaine* VII:627-639.

El-Khatib-Boujibar, N. 1992 Le Problème de l'Alimentation en Eau à Lixus. *Lixus*, Collection de L'Ecole Française de Rome 166:305-323.

Euzennat, M. 1974 Les Edifices du Culte Chrétien en Maurétanie Tingitane. *Antiquités Africaines* 8:175-190.

Ponsich, M. 1966 Contribution à l'Atlas Archéologique du Maroc: Region de Lixus. *Bulletin d'Archéologie Marocaine* VI:377-423.

1981 Lixus: Le Quartier des Temples. *Etudes et Travaux d'Archéologie Marocaine* IX.

Rebuffat, R. 1985 A Propos du Quartier des Temples de Lixus. *R. A. (Revue Archéologique)*:123-128.

Map: Manzla (MNZ)

MNZ1, Kouass, x 445.5, y 548.2, z 45
Located at 8 km north of Asilah at the mouth of the Gharifa River. This is an important Roman site with a possible Islamic component (possibly the port of Nabrash mentioned by al-Bakrî [1965:221]). The Islamic period ceramics at the site have not yet been studied. Surface collection at Dchar includes handmade, wheelmade, and glazed wares (green and honey).

Bibliography:

Ponsich, M. 1966 Kouas Port Atlantique et Carrefour des Voies de la Tingitane. *Bulletin d'Archéologie Marocaine* VI:369-405.

MNZ2, Sidi Kacem, x 450.4, y 568.9, z 25
The remains of a Roman watchtower located on the Atlantic coast at 1.5 km northwest of the modern village of Hajreièn. No surface material was found at the site.

Bibliography:

Ponsich, M. 1964 Contribution à l'Atlas Archéologique du Maroc: Région de Tanger. *Bulletin d'Archéologie Marocaine* V:253-290.

1970 *Recherches Archéologiques à Tanger et dans sa Région*, Paris.

MNZ3, Chrif, x 453.3, y 571.9, z 60
A Roman site located at 0.5 km northeast of the modern village of Jbila on what is now the cemetery of the village. The surface scatter area is about 150 m in diameter. In addition to Roman period ceramics, the surface material also includes Islamic and/or colonial period pottery (handmade, wheelmade, and glazed wares [green and honey]) and fragments of round grinding stones.

[4] For a general map of the site, see *Lixus*, Collection de L'Ecole Française de Rome, 1992(166):417.

[5] The mosque at al-Basra has seven naves (al-Bakrî 1965:216-217).

Bibliography:
Ponsich, M. 1964 Contribution à l'Atlas Archéologique du Maroc: Région de Tanger. *Bulletin d'Archéologie Marocaine* V:253-290.
1970 *Recherches Archéologiques à Tanger et dans sa Région*, Paris.

MNZ4, Jbila, x 452.5, y 471.5, z 134
A Roman site near the modern village of Jbila. The surface scatter area is about 200 m in diameter. In addition to Roman period ceramics, the surface material also includes Islamic and/or colonial period pottery (handmade, wheelmade, and glazed wares [green and honey]) and fragments of roof-tile and fired bricks.

Bibliography:
Ponsich, M. 1964 Contribution à l'Atlas Archéologique du Maroc: Région de Tanger. *Bulletin d'Archéologie Marocaine* V:253-290.
1970 *Recherches Archéologiques à Tanger et dans sa Région*, Paris.

MNZ5, Zilil, x 453.1, y 546.9, z 87
Recent archaeological evidence found at the Roman site of Dchar Jdid confirmed that this latter was in fact the Roman site of *Colonia Iulia Constantia Zilil*, founded by Augustus between 33 and 27 B.C. (Lenoir 1993:507). Of the six pedestals discovered at the site in 1986, the toponym of the site was inscribed on five of them (Lenoir 1993:509). No Islamic period ceramics were found at the site.

Bibliography:
Lenoir, M. 1993 Ad Mercuri Templum: Voies et Occupation Antiques du Nord du Maroc. *Sonderdruck aus Mitteilungen des Deutchen Archaeologischen Instituts Roemische Abteilung* Band 100.

MNZ6, Souiyar Tahadart, x 447, y 553.4, z 6
A Roman industrial compound for fish processing located at about 300 m east of the Mohammed V bridge on the Tahadart River. Siraj (1995b:346) signals the presence of another Roman site with an Islamic component northeast of Souiyar Tahadart (AM22).

Bibliography:
Ponsich, M. 1964 Contribution à l'Atlas Archéologique du Maroc: Région de Tanger. *Bulletin d'Archéologie Marocaine* V:253-290.
Ponsich, M. and M. Tarradell 1965 *Garum et Industries Antiques de Salaison dans la Méditerranée Occidentale*, Paris.

Map: Meknès (MKS)

MKS1, Ouarzigha, x 486.5, y 371, z 375
The toponym of Warzîgha is known through both documentary and numismatic evidence (Appendix B). The name of Warzîgha is found on six Idrisid dirhams dated between A.D. 838-9 and A.D. 861-2 (Eustache 1970-71:155). There is a modern village north of Meknès with the same toponym (Warzîgha). Local farmers found several mud-brick wall alignments and an Idrisid dirham bearing the name of the site (the author was not able to verify this information). Inside one of the village houses[6], traces of what may be a mud-brick wall were identified. The survey around the village did not reveal any archaeological material.

MKS2, Ain Kebira, x 489, y 371.5, z 450
A *pisé* structure (6.5 m by 6.5 m) located at about 2.5 km east of the Ouarzigha village (MKS1). The presence of a spring (Ain Kebira, Ain Hallouf on the topographic map) suggests that this structure was a cistern used by the population of Ouarzigha. No archaeological material was found at the site. This is a possibly a late medieval or a colonial period site.

Map: Moulay Bouselham (MBS)

MBS1, Moulay Bouselham (medieval Buhayrat Ariagh), x 419.4, y 474.8, z 7
Located at 38 km west of al-Basra and overlooking the lake of Merja Zerga (Figure 2.6). The site is now totally silted up. Only a few sherds were found on the ground. The site has been the object of several archaeological investigations (Eustache 1955; Redman 1983-84). Documentary evidence points to the role of Buhayrat Ariagh as the port of al-Basra (Appendix B). The following discussion focuses on the 1981 archaeological excavation conducted at the site by Redman[7].

The site forms an irregular trapezoid 100 m by 60 m (Eustache 1955:219-222, Figure 2). The site area is about 4,000 m². The northern section of this structure is occupied by a gate 3 m wide with two imposing square towers (5 m by 5 m) on each side. The interior of this structure contains traces of what is possibly a staircase leading to the parapet and traces of a rectangular structure (11.60 m by 3.60 m).

In 1981 remnant outcroppings of the defensive wall could still be seen in some areas. Being constructed from a locally-quarried sandstone, these remnants were badly eroded. Seven 2x2 meter test squares were conducted at the site, five within the fortification wall and two at its immediate periphery. In one of the peripheral squares substantial concentration of shell and a net-weight were found suggesting that (1) the area may have been used for shell-fish processing (for consumption) or (2) a locus for waste discard. Interestingly, one of the test squares produced a fragment of a millstone that would have been used for processing grain (Redman 1983-84:345). With the exception of several sections of the fortification wall, very few architectural features were found at the site.

The site is characterized by low overall ceramic densities. Preliminary analysis of the ceramic material excavated at the site shows a wide range of variation in ceramic forms and wares:

6 Owner's name is Farès Ben Isa.

7 The material discussed in this section was synthesized from the report and field notes of the 1981 excavation at the site. This material was made available by Charles Redman, Department of Anthropology, Arizona State University.

- 18 tentative ware categories, established based on either surface preparation (e.g., glazing or incision) or temper.
- 26 potentially diagnostic form categories, established based on very few examples or on small fragments. Few largely complete vessels were recovered.

Ware Categories found at MBS1 (medieval Bu<u>h</u>ayrat Aria<u>gh</u>):

1- Handbuilt (sand-tempered)
2- Limestone Tempered
3- Coarse Limestone Tempered
4- Mica Tempered
5- Red Plainware
6- Red Clinky clear Glaze 1 (characterized by a transparent glaze)
7- Red Clinky Clear Glaze 2 (characterized by more opaque glaze)
8- Green Glaze
9- Slipped Ware
10- Cream Ware (coarse paste with surface pitting probably caused by the combustion of carbonaceous inclusions)
11- Coarse Ware
12- Brown Glaze on Buff
13- Painted Buff (characterized by painted decorative strokes)
14- Lusterware (characterized by traces of a patina)
15- Brown Glaze
16- Ribbed
17- combed/Incised
18- Incised Pattern

Form Categories found at MBS1 (medieval Bu<u>h</u>ayrat Aria<u>gh</u>):

Bowls

1- Simple Rimmed Bowl
2- Double Rimmed Bowl
3- Squat Handbuilt Bowl
4- Thin-walled Wide Bowl
5- Handbuilt Bowl with Flange Below Rim
6- Handbuilt Bowl with Indented Flange Below Rim

Jars

1- Simple Rimmed Jar
2- Jar with Handle on Simple Rim
3- Flanged Ring-based Jar
4- Miniature Flat-based Jar with String-cut Base
5- Squat Widemouthed Jar
6- Flat-rimmed Squat Jar
7- Double-rimmed Beanpot Jar

Rims

1- Simple Everted Rim
2- Triangular-lipped Rim

Bases

1- Flat Base
2- Non-flanged Ring Base
3- Inset Base
4- String-cut Base

Miscellaneous Forms

1- Beaker (Flat-rimmed with band on external wall)
2- Basin (Thick rounded rim with impressed decoration on rim exterior)
3- Strainer
4- Game Piece/Disc (net weight?)
5- Rectangular Handbuilt "Palette"-lamp?
6- Short-necked Flask
7- Spout

The ceramic material found at the site suggests that this entrepôt was occupied during the Almohad[8] or Marinid period. There is still no definitive archaeological evidence that MBS1 is the site of medieval Bu<u>h</u>ayrat Aria<u>gh</u> mentioned in the textual records.

Map: Ouezzane (OZN)

OZN1, Djnan al-Makhzen (medieval I<u>dj</u>â<u>d</u>jîn?), x 479.7, y 472, z 230

Located in the modern town of Asjen at about 7 km northwest of Ouezzane (Figure 3.1). The toponym of I<u>dj</u>â<u>d</u>jîn was first mentioned by al-Bakrî (1965:224) (see Appendix B).

A preliminary study of the site was conducted by Safsafi (1990:72-79). The site forms a slightly irregular rectangle enclosed by walls 1 m wide and 5 m high. The building material consists of *pisé* and stone. Clockwise from the north, the walls are 199 m, 112 m, 135 m, and 95.5 m. Only the south wall is still in fairly good condition. Its upper part shows traces of crenelations. Four square towers were placed at each corner of this structure. Several collapsed buildings occupy the central area (Safsafi 1990:Plan 8).

There is still no conclusive archaeological evidence that the Djnan al-Makhzen is the medieval I<u>dj</u>â<u>dj</u>în. According to Mounès (1957:6-7) the toponym of I<u>dj</u>â<u>dj</u>în mentioned by al-Bakrî is not to be confused with Asjen. He argued that the site of I<u>dj</u>â<u>dj</u>în is to be found southeast of Ain Defali. The author's investigations in the area proposed by Mounès (i.e., around the village of Oulad Ktir and in the vicinity of Jbel Aouf) did not uncover any archaeological sites. Furthermore, the toponym of I<u>dj</u>â<u>dj</u>în is unknown to the local population.

Archaeological evidence shows that Djnan al-Makhzen was an important fortress. The text of Leo Africanus (1956) corroborates this information. Ezaggen (I<u>dj</u>â<u>dj</u>în?) was about 500 hearths (2,500 inhabitants) and paid 10,000 ducats to the central treasury (Leo Africanus 1956: 255). But more importantly, Leo Africanus (1956: 255, 269) states that the governor of Ezaggen was in charge of defending the region against Portuguese raids. A portion of the region's tax revenue was used to support a contingent made of 400 cavalrymen.

Archaeological survey around the site uncovered a few ceramic sherds including green-colored glazed ware. The surface material also includes fragments of bricks and roof-tile. In order to determine the site function and chronology a number of test excavations has to be conducted both within the enclosing walls and outside.

[8] An Almohad <u>k</u>irâ<u>t</u> (a square silver coin) was found at the site (Eustache 1955:222).

Bibliography:
Mounès, J. 1957 Notes sur Quelques Villes Disparues du Maroc Septentrional. *Bulletin de l'Enseignement Public au Maroc* 44(239):5-28.
Safsafi, N. 1990 *Sites et Monuments Historiques d'Ouazzane et de sa Périphérie.* Mémoire de Fin d'Etudes du II Cycle des Sciences de l'Archéologie et du Patrimoine INSAP, Rabat.

OZN2, Djamaa Tabiya, x 479.3, y 472.7, z 260
Located at about 0.7 km north of Djnan al-Makhzen (ONZ1). The major archaeological feature at the site is the remains of a *pisé* structure known as Djamaa Tabiya (literally, Pisé-built mosque). A preliminary study of this structure was conducted by Safsafi (1990:72-79). Local tradition attributes the construction of this mosque to the Marinid period (A.D. 1258-1420) (Mounès 1957:11).

In contrast to Djnan al-Makhzen, there is abundant surface material in the area around the collapsed mosque. The ceramic material consists of handmade, wheelmade, and glazed wares (green, honey, and blue). The surface material also includes fragments of roof-tile, round grinding stones, and bricks. It is possible that the ceramic material found at the site was produced locally as attested by the finding of a spur (a piece of kiln furniture) by Safsafi (1990:79).

Bibliography:
Mounès, J. 1957 Notes sur Quelques Villes Disparues du Maroc Septentrional. *Bulletin de l'Enseignement Public au Maroc* 44(239):5-28.
Safsafi, N. 1990 *Sites et Monuments Historiques d'Ouazzane et de sa Périphérie.* Mémoire de Fin d'Etudes du II Cycle des Sciences de l'Archéologie et du Patrimoine, INSAP, Rabat.

Map: Sidi Kacem (SKM)

SKM1, Volubilis (medieval Walîla), x 485.3, y 386.1, z 370
Located at 27 km north of Meknès (Figure 3.1). Volubilis is the most important Roman period site in Morocco. Both archaeological and documentary evidence show that the site was continuously occupied until the Islamic period (see Appendix B). Akerraz (1985a:185-191) identified two main phases of post-Roman occupation. The first phase extends from A.D. 285 (date of Roman withdrawal), to the sixth century A.D. The second phase began with the building of the late city-wall ("*enceinte tardive*") enclosing the western section of the city and ends with the arrival of Idris I. The Idrisid occupation of the site is attested by the finding of several Idrisid dirhams the earliest of which is dated to A.D. 789-790 (Akerraz 1998:299; Eustache 1970-71:162-169).

As in Lixus (medieval Tus͟hummus͟h), most of the Islamic occupation at Volubilis was centered within the reduced city ("*la ville réduite*") enclosed by the late city-wall (Akerraz 1998:Plan 1). However, recent archaeological excavations north of *la Maison au Compas* and *extra-muros* have shown that the Islamic occupation extends beyond the boundaries of the reduced city (Akerraz 1998; El Khayari 1990-91, 1994).

There exists an abundant literature about the site of Volubilis. The bibliography below focuses on the archaeological and numismatic evidence that pertains to the Islamic component of the site (Walîla).

Bibliography:
Akerraz, A. 1985a *La Maurétanie Tingitane du Sud de Diocletien aux Idrissides.* Thèse de 3eme Cycle, Université de Paris IV.
1985b Note sur l'Enceinte Tardive de Volubilis. *Bulletin Archéologique du C.T.M.S.* 19:429-438.
1998 Recherches sur les Niveaux Islamiques de Volubilis. In *Genèse de la Ville Islamique en al-Andalus et au Maghreb Occidental*, edited by P. Cressier and M. Garcia-Arenal, pp. 295-304. Casa de Velazquez, CSIC., Mardrid.
El Khayari, A. 1990-91 *Les Thermes Extra-muros à Volubilis.* Mémoire de Fin d'Etudes du II Cycle des Sciences de l'Archéologie et du Patrimoine, INSAP, Rabat.
1994 Les Thermes Extra-muros à Volubilis. *L'Africa Romana* 10:301-312.
Eustache, D. 1956 Monnaies Musulmanes Trouvées à Volubilis. *Hespéris*:133-195.
1966 Monnaies Musulmanes Trouvées dans la Maison au Compas (Volubilis). *Bulletin d'Archéologie Marocaine* VI:349-364.
1970 Les Ateliers Monétaires du Maroc. *Hespéris-Tamuda* XI:95-102.
1970-71 *Corpus des Dirhams Idrissites et Contemporains: Etudes sur la Numismatique et l'Histoire Monétaire du Maroc I.* Banque du Maroc, Rabat.
Karim-el-Ghoumari, M. 1990-91 *La Céramique des Niveaux Islamiques de Volubilis.* Mémoire de Fin d'Etudes du II Cycle des Sciences de l'Archéologie et du Patrimoine, INSAP, Rabat.
Lenoir, E. 1983-84 Volubilis des Baquates aux Rabedis: Une Histoire Sans Paroles? *Bulletin d'Archéologie Marocaine* XV:299-309.
1985 Volubilis du Bas-Empire à l'Epoque Islamique. In *Actes du II Colloque International sur l'Hisoire et l'Archéologie de l'Afrique du Nord*, vol. 19, pp. 425-428, BCTH, Grenoble.

Map: Souk al-Kolla (SKL)

SKL1, Doura el-Hajar (medieval H̱adj̱ar al-Nasr), x 471, y 507.7, z 614
H̱adj̱ar al-Nasr (the Rock of the Eagle) is an Idrisid fortress located at about 30 km southeast of Jbel Sidi Habib (Figure 3.1). The site is now occupied by the modern village of Douar el-Hajar. The site was mentioned in several medieval Arabic texts (Appendix B). H̱adj̱ar al-Nasr was recently discovered by a team of Moroccan, French and Spanish archaeologists (Cressier et al. 1998).

The site is located on a *mesa* of about 5 hectares. Several archaeological features were found at H̱adj̱ar al-Nasr including an enclosing wall and a large central complex (7.5 m by 19.5 m) arranged in the shape of the letter L. Although textual evidence points to the presence of water within Hadjar al-Nasr, no storage facilities for food (silos) or water (cisterns) were found at the site (Cressier et al. 1998:323-326, 331).

The little ceramic material found at the site consists mainly of plain wheelmade pottery in addition to honey-colored glazed ware similar to pottery production of the Caliphal and late Caliphal periods in Muslim Spain. Overall, the ceramic material found at Hadjar al-Nasr date to the tenth century A.D. (Cressier et al. 1998:329, 332).

Bibliography:
Cressier, P., A. El Boudjay, H. El Figuigui and J. Vignet-Zunz 1998 Hagar al-Nasr "Capital" Idrisside du Maroc Septentrional: Archéologie et Histoire (IVe H./Xe ap. J.C.). In *Genèse de la Ville Islamique en al-Andalus et au Maghreb Occidental*, edited by P. Cressier and M. Garcia-Arenal, pp. 305-334. Casa de Velazquez, CSIC, Madrid.

Map: Tafrant-Wargha (TWR)

TWR1, Beni Taouda (Banî Tâwdâ), x 523.5, y 441, z 190
Banî Tâwdâ (also known as Fès el-Bali) is an Almoravid city located at about 50 km north of Fez (Figure 3.1) (Cressier 1995:Figure 4). The site is located on a plateau that overlooks the rich Ouergha River Valley (now the location of the al-Wahda Dam). The site area is about 65 hectares. Banî Tâwdâ was mentioned in several medieval Arabic texts (Appendix B). Several archaeological features were still visible in the early 1900s including the city-wall, a central *Kasaba* (a citadel), and a *hammâm* (bath) (Saladin 1916).

The city-wall is made of stones extracted from the nearby mountain of Amergou. It is characterized by the absence of towers. The remaining portion of it ranges between 2 to 5 m in height and 1.5 m in width. The *hammâm* is a stone-built structure that is still in relatively good condition. It forms a rectangle 11.50 m by 10.70 m and has three rectangular rooms of equal area. The walls are 0.75 m wide. Test units conducted within this structure revealed a floor made of marble slabs (0.55 m by 0.48 m) (Touri 1997:105).

The building materials and construction techniques used at both Banî Tâwdâ and the nearby fortress of Amerjou (*Amardjuwa*) (TWR2) clearly indicate that both sites were built during the same period (Lévi-Provençal 1918:196).

The surface material includes wheelmade pottery, glazed wares (green and honey), roof-tiles and bricks. The site has a high interpretive potential and needs immediate archaeological attention (systematic surface collections, test excavations, and restoration of existing monuments).

Bibliography:
Cressier, P. 1995 La fortification Islamique au Maroc: Eléments de Bibliographie. *Archéologie Islamique* 5:163-196.

Lévi-Provençal, E. 1918 Ruines Almoravides du Pays de l'Ouergha. *Bulletin Archéologique du Comité des Travaux Historiques et Scientifiques*:194-200.

Saladin, H. 1916 Note Sur un Essai d'Identification des Ruines de Bani Teude, Mergo, Tansor et Agla, situées dans la Région de l'Ouergha (subdivision de Fez) et Relevées par le Capitaine Odinot. *Bulletin Archéologique du Comité des Travaux Historiques et Scientifiques*:118-131.

Terrasse, H. 1953 La Forteresse Almoravide d'Amargou. *Al-Andalus* XVIII:389-400.

Touri, A. 1997 *Patrimoine Culturel et Territoire: Etude Préliminaire pour la Mise en Valeur de la Région du Gharb*. Submitted to Direction du Patrimoine Culturel, Secretariat d'Etat Chargé de la Culture, Ministère de l'Enseignement Superieur de la Formation des Cadres et de la Culture, UNESCO, Rabat.

Vicaire, M. and R. Thouvenot 1938 Vestiges Archéologiques dans la Région de Fès el-Bali. *Hespéris* XXV:367-376.

TWR2, Amerjou (Amardjuwa), x 525, y 433.5, z 680
An Almoravid fortress located at 8 km south of Banî Tâwdâ (Fés el-Bali) on the top of Amergou Mountain (Figure 3.1). This stone-built fortress overlooks the whole area of the Ouergha River Valley. The fortification wall is 5 m high, 1.35 m wide, and 370 m in circumference forming an elongated polygon oriented northwest/southwest. The site area is about 1.4 hectares. The fortification wall is reinforced with 12 towers (Lévi-Provençal 1918:194-195). The main features inside the fortress are a *Kasaba* (a citadel) and a cistern (3.40 m by 9.50 m) near a water spring.

Bibliography:
Cressier, P. 1995 La fortification Islamique au Maroc: Eléments de Bibliographie. *Archéologie Islamique* 5:163-196.

Lévi-Provençal, E. 1918 Ruines Almoravides du Pays de l'Ouergha. *Bulletin Archéologique du Comité des Travaux Historiques et Scientifiques*:194-200.

Saladin, H. 1916 Note Sur un Essai d'Identification des Ruines de Bani Teude, Mergo, Tansor et Agla, situées dans la Région de l'Ouergha (subdivision de Fez) et Relevées par le Capitaine Odinot. *Bulletin Archéologique du Comité des Travaux Historiques et Scientifiques*:118-131.

Terrasse, H. 1953 La Forteresse Almoravide d'Amargou. *Al-Andalus* XVIII:389-400.

Map: Tanger (TNG)

TNG1, al-Kal'a, x 457.2, y 577.4, z 90
Located at less than 5 km west of Tangier on a promontory overlooking the sea (Agla on the topographic map). The main archaeological feature at the site is a small square structure (40.50 m by 40.50 m) built by alternating courses of stones and bricks. Four square towers (4 m by 4 m) are located in each corner. The author was denied access to this building which now "converted" into a farmer's house. At about 100 m southwest of this building the remains of several stone structures are visible on the ground. The surface material consists of handmade and wheelmade pottery. The surface scatter area is about 200 m in diameter.

The main building at the site was possibly a citadel (*Kal'a*) as the toponym of the site indicates. Interestingly, al-Bakrî

(1965:222) mentioned this toponym along the route between Ishbârtâl (Spartel Cape) and Tangier. However, there is still no conclusive archaeological evidence to support the hypothesis that this site is in fact the one mentioned by al-Bakrî (see Siraj 1995b:341-342).

Map: Teroual (TRW)

TRW1, Ain Karouach ('Ayn Karwâsh), x 494.9, y 434.8, z 86
Located at about 50 km south of Ouezzane near the modern village of Ma'arif (Figure 3.1). The material discussed below was synthesized from De Cardenal-Breton (1985-1986), Hassar-Benslimane (1979-80) and Touri (1997).

Excavations at the site by Hassar-Benslimane uncovered an important architectural complex which consists of a rectangular structure (4.90 m by 5.35 m) with an intricate multi-colored mosaic tile pavement and a circular water fountain in the middle. These excavations also uncovered a complex underground canalization system.

After conducting a magnetometer survey at the site three pottery kilns were identified. De Cardenal-Breton (1985-1986) conducted a systematic surface collection at the site and identified four areas of potential functional variability. The ceramic material at the site consists of handmade (8%), wheelmade (88%), glazed wares (4%) (green, yellow, and ochre), and several pottery wasters. The ceramic types found at the site includes conical plates, cooking pots, water jars, and lamps (De Cardenal-Breton 1985-1986:342-343). It is possible that the site of 'Ayn Karwâsh is in fact the medieval al-Djum'a or Gemaa el Caruax mentioned by Leo Africanus and Marmol respectively (Leo Africanus 1956:251, note 383).

Bibliography:

De Cardenal-Breton, M. 1985-86 Ramassage de Surface à Ain Karuash: Méthodes, Résultats et Perspectives. *Bulletin d'Archéologie Marocaine*:339-343.

Hassar-Benslimane, J. 1979-80 Ain Karuash: Un Nouveau Site Islamique dans le Gharb. *Bulletin d'Archéologie Marocaine* XII:364-376.

Touri, A. 1997 *Patrimoine Culturel et Territoire: Etude Préliminaire pour la Mise en Valeur de la Région du Gharb.* Submitted to Direction du Patrimoine Culturel, Secretariat d'Etat Chargé de la Culture, Ministère de l'Enseignement Superieur de la Formation des Cadres et de la Culture, UNESCO, Rabat.

A List of the Pottery Types Collected

(This typology was established by Benco)[9]

Bowls and Basins

Form 12 Bowl with simple rounded lip - relatively shallow and broad; smoothly curving sides (Benco 1987:Figure 5.10).

Form 13 Bowl with beveled lip - relatively shallow and broad; lip beveled toward interior; smoothly curving sides; flat base (Benco 1987:Figure 5.10).

Form 19 Basin - heavy form with thick everted lip, often with deep cord impression in the outside of the lip; may have combed design just inside rim; very large in diameter; well-finished surfaces but no noticeable burnishing marks.

Jars and Pitchers

Form 40 Jar with everted lip and sloping body - everted lip which may be grooved on interior; body slopes outward to a sharp, often ridged or grooved carination; below carination body slopes back inward toward base; occasionally upper body has comb incised decoration (Benco 1987:Figure 5.9).

Form 41 Jar with folded triangular lip and low neck - rim is often folded over to exterior to form triangular shaped cross-section; rather short curved neck; body resembles an inverted pear shape; flat base; shoulder frequently has combed incised decoration or occasionally grooving; lower body of vessel may be ribbed. Rim diameter is larger than 10 cm (Benco 1987:Figure 5.4).

Form 42 Jar with band rim and short curved neck - body is pear shaped; lower body of vessel may be ribbed. (Body is similar in shape to type 41 and 43) (Benco 1987:Figure 5.4).

Form 43 Jar with grooved band rim and short curved neck - band rim with groove in exterior; frequently there is a groove in interior of rim possibly to hold stopper or lip; short curved neck; inverted pear-shaped body; may have comb incisions or grooved decoration on shoulder; lower body is often ribbed (Benco 1987:Figure 5.5).

Form 44 Jar with folded triangular lip and tall ridged (or unridged) neck - rim is folded over to exterior to form triangular shaped cross-section or snub nosed profile; tall neck slopes outward slightly toward shoulder and may have a ridge on the exterior at approximately its midpoint; neck curves into shoulder without a sharp break; large handle extends from neck (ridge) possibly to shoulder; sloping shoulder which may have comb incised decoration; probably large rounded, elongated body. Rim is less than 10 cm in diameter (water storage jar) (Benco 1987:Figure 5.7).

Form 48 Pitcher with simple lip and tall straight neck - simple rounded or beveled lip; relatively tall, straight and nearly vertical neck; clear demarcation between neck and shoulder; may have handle from rim to shoulder (Benco 1987:Figure 5.8)

Form 49 Jar with flaring rim - rounded lip which may be thickened on the inside; rim flares outward; short curved neck; rounded shoulder.

Form 54 Jar with flattened, everted lip and low neck; very low neck; broadly sloping shoulder. Usually chinky red ware.

Form 78 Jar with triangular rim and short vertical neck; body is rounded and may be corrugated; cream-ware (Benco 1987:Figure 5.14).

[9] See bibliography at the end of this section.

Bases

Form 80 Flat base - simple flattened base; nearly all are clearly jar bases.

Form 81 Convex base.

Form 82 Ring base - most are probably bowl bases.

Form 83 Inset base.

Form 84 Flanged base.

Lamps and Miscellaneous Forms

Form 93 Nosed lamp - flattened, round bowls with short, flask-like neck and flaring rim; handle from neck to bulge of bowl; long "nose", frequently with charred tip; some variation in shape of nose (Benco 1987:Figure 5.11).

Form 99 Disk - small, round or nearly round piece, deliberately worked around edge. Approximately 3 cm in diameter. May have smooth or ribbed surface.

Handles

Form 120 Strap - somewhat flattened in cross-section, often with finger groove down center.

Form 121 Round - round in cross-section; crook-shaped; usually associated with cup forms.

Bibliography:

Benco, N. 1987 *The Early Medieval Pottery Industry at al-Basra, Morocco*. BAR International Series 341. British Archaeological Reports, Oxford.

1998 Al-Basra Pottery: Form Classification. Manuscript on file, Department of Anthropology, George Washington University, Washington, DC.

APPENDIX F

DESCRIPTIVE INFORMATION AND GROUP ASSIGNMENTS FOR ARCHAEOLOGICAL POTTERY FROM AL-BASRA'S HINTERLAND SITES

Chemical Group	Analytical I.D. (N=145)	Site name	Site No.	Ware category	Description	Chronology: Period/Phase	Basra Core probability
Basra Core	BSR001	al-Ghzalat	ARB2	sandy buff	Form 40; carinated jar	Idrisid?	97,325
Basra Core	BSR002	al-Ghzalat	ARB2	orange, with sandy texture	Form 40; carinated jar	Idrisid?	62,546
Basra Core	BSR003	al-Ghzalat	ARB2	fine buff	Form 40; carinated jar	Idrisid?	97,213
Basra Core	BSR004	al-Ghzalat	ARB2	cream-colored--brown/orange	Form 40; carinated jar	Idrisid?	23,304
Basra Core	BSR005	al-Ghzalat	ARB2	fine gray	Form 40; carinated jar	Idrisid?	69,872
Basra Core	BSR006	al-Ghzalat	ARB2	fine buff	Form 40; carinated jar?	Idrisid?	99,618
Basra Core	BSR007	al-Ghzalat	ARB2	cream-colored	Form 42; jar with band rim	Idrisid?	69,519
Basra Core	BSR009	al-Ghzalat	ARB2	cream-colored	Form 43; jar with groov ed-band rim	Idrisid?	53,722
Basra Core	BSR010	al-Ghzalat	ARB2	cream-colored--brown hue	Form 43; jar with groov ed-band rim	Idrisid?	85,738
Basra Core	BSR011	Bhalla	ARB7	orange, with fine texture	Form 40; carinated jar	Idrisid?	45,951
Basra Core	BSR013	Bhalla	ARB7	sandy buff	Form 40; carinated jar	Idrisid?	85,263
Basra Core	BSR015	Bhalla	ARB7	fine buff	Form 40; carinated jar	Idrisid?	18,814
Basra Core	BSR016	Bhalla	ARB7	fine buff	Form 40; carinated jar	Idrisid?	58,373
Basra Core	BSR020	Bhalla	ARB7	sandy gray	Form 80; flat base	Idrisid?	53,209
Basra Core	BSR021	Jahjouka	ARB8	fine buff	Form 40; carinated jar	Idrisid?	82,575
Basra Core	BSR022	Jahjouka	ARB8	orange with very fine texture	Form 40; carinated jar	Idrisid?	12,173
Basra Core	BSR023	Jahjouka	ARB8	very fine buff	Form 40; carinated jar	Idrisid?	8,877
Basra Core	BSR024	Jahjouka	ARB8	cream-colored--olive green hue	Form 40; carinated jar	Idrisid?	63,167
Basra Core	BSR025	Jahjouka	ARB8	cream-colored--brown/orange	Form 40; carinated jar	Idrisid?	67,377
Basra Core	BSR027	Jahjouka	ARB8	very fine buff	Form ?	Idrisid?	50,688
Basra Core	BSR028	Jahjouka	ARB8	cream-colored--olive green hue	Form 44; tall-necked water storage jar	Idrisid?	75,204
Basra Core	BSR029	Jahjouka	ARB8	very fine buff	Form 41; jar with triangular rim	Idrisid?	63,808
Basra Core	BSR030	Jahjouka	ARB8	sandy buff	Form 41; jar with triangular rim	Idrisid?	83,261
Basra Core	BSR034	Sidi Bou Douma	ARB13	cream-colored	Form 40; carinated jar?	Idrisid?	47,451
Basra Core	BSR038	Sidi Bou Douma	ARB13	cream-colored	Form ?	Idrisid?	48,558
Basra Core	BSR039	Sidi Bou Douma	ARB13	very fine buff	Form ?	Idrisid?	6,764
Basra Core	BSR040	Sidi Bou Douma	ARB13	sandy buff	Form ?	Idrisid?	8,095
Basra Core	BSR041	Kudyat Srafah	ARB15	sandy gray	Form 40; carinated jar	Idrisid?	81,285
Basra Core	BSR042	Kudyat Srafah	ARB15	orange, with fine texture	Form 40; carinated jar	Idrisid?	41,653
Basra Core	BSR043	Kudyat Srafah	ARB15	sandy gray	Form 40; carinated jar	Idrisid?	69,997
Basra Core	BSR044	Kudyat Srafah	ARB15	orange colored	Form 40; carinated jar	Idrisid?	82,854
Basra Core	BSR046	Kudyat Srafah	ARB15	sandy gray	Form 43; jar with groov ed-band rim	Idrisid?	19,547
Basra Core	BSR047	Kudyat Srafah	ARB15	fine buff	Form 43; jar with groov ed-band rim	Idrisid?	97,717
Basra Core	BSR048	Kudyat Srafah	ARB15	sandy gray	Form 43; jar with groov ed-band rim	Idrisid?	43,131
Basra Core	BSR049	Kudyat Srafah	ARB15	fine buff	Form 43; jar with groov ed-band rim	Idrisid?	63,006
Basra Core	BSR050	Kudyat Srafah	ARB15	orange colored	Form 43; jar with groov ed-band rim	Idrisid?	22,577
Basra Core	BSR051	Ketama	ARB18	fine gray	Form 40; carinated jar	Idrisid?	42,433
Basra Core	BSR052	Ketama	ARB18	very fine buff	Form 40; carinated jar	Idrisid?	61,278
Basra Core	BSR053	Ketama	ARB18	fine buff	Form 40; carinated jar	Idrisid?	94,113
Basra Core	BSR054	Ketama	ARB18	sandy buff	Form 40; carinated jar	Idrisid?	96,251
Basra Core	BSR055	Ketama	ARB18	orange colored	Form 41; jar with triangular rim	Idrisid?	8,340
Basra Core	BSR056	Ketama	ARB18	sandy buff	Form 41; jar with triangular rim	Idrisid?	99,682
Basra Core	BSR057	Ketama	ARB18	sandy buff	Form ?	Idrisid?	90,949
Basra Core	BSR058	Ketama	ARB18	orange with very fine texture	Form ?	Idrisid?	9,246
Basra Core	BSR059	Ketama	ARB18	fine buff	Form ?	Idrisid?	47,053
Basra Core	BSR060	Ketama	ARB18	very fine buff	Form ?	Idrisid?	18,212
Basra Core	BSR061	Shkayfa	LLM1	sandy buff	Form 40; carinated jar	Idrisid?	69,353
Basra Core	BSR062	Shkayfa	LLM1	fine buff	Form 40; carinated jar	Idrisid?	58,873

Chemical Group	Analytical I.D. (N=145)	Site name	Site No.	Ware category	Description	Chronology: Period/Phase	Basra Core probability
Basra Core	BSR063	Shkayfa	LLM1	fine gray	Form 40; carinated jar	Idrisid?	90,176
Basra Core	BSR064	Shkayfa	LLM1	sandy gray	Form 40; carinated jar	Idrisid?	8,392
Basra Core	BSR065	Shkayfa	LLM1	sandy gray	Form 40; carinated jar	Idrisid?	76,351
Basra Core	BSR066	Shkayfa	LLM1	sandy gray	Form 42; jar with band rim	Idrisid?	53,322
Basra Core	BSR067	Shkayfa	LLM1	orange with very fine texture	Form 43; jar with grooved-band rim	Idrisid?	91,031
Basra Core	BSR068	Shkayfa	LLM1	cream colored	Form 43; jar with grooved-band rim	Idrisid?	88,169
Basra Core	BSR069	Shkayfa	LLM1	sandy buff	Form 43; jar with grooved-band rim	Idrisid?	48,822
Basra Core	BSR070	Shkayfa	LLM1	cream-colored--brown/orange	Form 43; jar with grooved-band rim	Idrisid?	17,590
Basra Core	BSR071	Frigidae	LLM4	sandy buff	Form 40; carinated jar	Idrisid?	41,220
Basra Core	BSR073	Frigidae	LLM4	sandy buff	Form ?	Idrisid?	52,064
Basra Core	BSR074	Frigidae	LLM4	sandy buff	Form ?	Idrisid?	1,932
Basra Core	BSR075	Frigidae	LLM4	sandy buff	Form ?	Idrisid?	43,457
Basra Core	BSR076	Sidi an-Niyya	LLM5	sandy buff	Form 40; carinated jar	Idrisid?	59,422
Basra Core	BSR077	Sidi an-Niyya	LLM5	orange colored	Form 40; carinated jar	Idrisid?	29,445
Basra Core	BSR078	Sidi an-Niyya	LLM5	orange colored	Form 40; carinated jar	Idrisid?	5,763
Basra Core	BSR079	Sidi an-Niyya	LLM5	sandy buff	Form 40; carinated jar	Idrisid?	26,508
Basra Core	BSR080	Sidi an-Niyya	LLM5	sandy buff	Form 40; carinated jar	Idrisid?	68,036
Basra Core	BSR081	Sidi an-Niyya	LLM5	sandy buff	Form 43; jar with grooved-band rim	Idrisid?	97,415
Basra Core	BSR083	Sidi an-Niyya	LLM5	sandy buff	Form 41; jar with triangular rim	Idrisid?	86,639
Basra Core	BSR084	Sidi an-Niyya	LLM5	orange colored	Form 40; carinated jar?	Idrisid?	97,014
Basra Core	BSR085	Sidi an-Niyya	LLM5	fine buff	Form ?	Idrisid?	8,759
Basra Core	BSR086	Sidi Ahmed Bourziguine	LLM8	cream-colored--brown/orange	Form 40; carinated jar	Idrisid?	16,872
Basra Core	BSR087	Sidi Ahmed Bourziguine	LLM8	fine buff	Form 43; jar with grooved-band rim	Idrisid?	40,750
Basra Core	BSR088	Sidi Ahmed Bourziguine	LLM8	sandy gray	Form 41; jar with triangular rim	Idrisid?	15,644
Basra Core	BSR089	Sidi Ahmed Bourziguine	LLM8	sandy gray	Form 41; jar with triangular rim	Idrisid?	91,328
Basra Core	BSR090	Sidi Ahmed Bourziguine	LLM8	cream colored	Form 41; jar with triangular rim	Idrisid?	95,383
Basra Core	BSR093	Sidi Ahmed Bourziguine	LLM8	sandy gray	Form ?	Idrisid?	18,496
Basra Core	BSR094	Sidi Ahmed Bourziguine	LLM8	sandy gray	Form ?	Idrisid?	14,991
Basra Core	BSR095	Sidi Ahmed Bourziguine	LLM8	orange colored	Form ?	Idrisid?	76,190
Basra Core	BSR096	el-Arab	LLM9	sandy buff	Form 40; carinated jar	Idrisid?	62,786
Basra Core	BSR097	el-Arab	LLM9	sandy buff	Form 40; carinated jar	Idrisid?	86,169
Basra Core	BSR098	el-Arab	LLM9	fine buff	Form 40; carinated jar	Idrisid?	94,502
Basra Core	BSR099	el-Arab	LLM9	cream colored	Form 40; carinated jar	Idrisid?	28,060
Basra Core	BSR100	el-Arab	LLM9	sandy buff	Form 40; carinated jar	Idrisid?	93,734
Basra Core	BSR101	el-Arab	LLM9	sandy gray	Form 43; jar with grooved-band rim	Idrisid?	19,967
Basra Core	BSR102	el-Arab	LLM9	sandy buff	Form 43; jar with grooved-band rim	Idrisid?	75,873
Basra Core	BSR103	el-Arab	LLM9	orange with very fine texture	Form 41; jar with triangular rim	Idrisid?	11,620
Basra Core	BSR104	el-Arab	LLM9	orange colored	Form 44; tall-necked water storage jar	Idrisid?	3,140
Basra Core	BSR105	el-Arab	LLM9	sandy buff	Form 42; jar with band rim	Idrisid?	54,060
Basra Core	BSR106	Kudyat Sma	LLM10	sandy gray	Form 40; carinated jar	Idrisid?	98,717
Basra Core	BSR107	Kudyat Sma	LLM10	orange colored	Form 40; carinated jar	Idrisid?	83,732
Basra Core	BSR108	Kudyat Sma	LLM10	fine gray	Form 40; carinated jar	Idrisid?	2,291
Basra Core	BSR109	Kudyat Sma	LLM10	fine buff	Form 40; carinated jar	Idrisid?	78,574
Basra Core	BSR110	Kudyat Sma	LLM10	sandy buff	Form 40; carinated jar	Idrisid?	93,792
Basra Core	BSR111	Kudyat Sma	LLM10	sandy gray	Form 43; jar with grooved-band rim	Idrisid?	39,805
Basra Core	BSR112	Kudyat Sma	LLM10	sandy gray	Form 43; jar with grooved-band rim	Idrisid?	27,021
Basra Core	BSR113	Kudyat Sma	LLM10	sandy gray	Form 43; jar with grooved-band rim	Idrisid?	1,113
Basra Core	BSR114	Kudyat Sma	LLM10	sandy buff	Form 43; jar with grooved-band rim	Idrisid?	41,042
Basra Core	BSR115	Kudyat Sma	LLM10	fine buff	Form 43; jar with grooved-band rim	Idrisid?	27,095

Chemical Group	Analytical I.D. (N=145)	Site name	Site No.	Ware category	Description	Chronology: Period/Phase	Basra Core probability
Basra Core	BSR116	Sidi Yssef	LLM14	sandy buff	Form 40; carinated jar	Idrisid?	17,059
Basra Core	BSR117	Sidi Yssef	LLM14	orange colored	Form 40; carinated jar	Idrisid?	7,069
Basra Core	BSR118	Sidi Yssef	LLM14	sandy buff	Form 40; carinated jar	Idrisid?	71,874
Basra Core	BSR120	Sidi Yssef	LLM14	sandy gray	Form 40; carinated jar	Idrisid?	13,039
Basra Core	BSR121	Sidi Yssef	LLM14	sandy buff	Form 40; carinated jar	Idrisid?	56,633
Basra Core	BSR122	Sidi Yssef	LLM14	very fine buff	Form 41; jar with triangular rim	Idrisid?	78,346
Basra Core	BSR123	Sidi Yssef	LLM14	fine buff	Form 41; jar with triangular rim	Idrisid?	75,028
Basra Core	BSR124	Sidi Yssef	LLM14	sandy buff	Form 42; jar with band rim	Idrisid?	90,865
Basra Core	BSR126	Sidi Yssef	LLM14	fine buff	Form 43; jar with grooved-band rim	Idrisid?	11,571
Basra Core	BSR127	Sidi Yssef	LLM14	sandy gray	Form 44; tall-necked water storage jar	Idrisid?	38,542
Basra Core	BSR128	Sidi Yssef	LLM14	sandy buff	Form ?	Idrisid?	42,119
Basra Core	BSR130	Sidi Yssef	LLM14	sandy gray	Form ?	Idrisid?	1,348
Basra Core	BSR131	al-'Asimi	MBK1	fine buff	Form 40; carinated jar	Idrisid?	34,045
Basra Core	BSR132	al-'Asimi	MBK1	orange colored	Form 40; carinated jar	Idrisid?	64,159
Basra Core	BSR133	al-'Asimi	MBK1	sandy gray	Form 40; carinated jar	Idrisid?	22,315
Basra Core	BSR136	Douar Riah	MBS2	sandy buff	Form 68; flask with outset band rim	Idrisid?	82,967
Basra Core	BSR137	Douar Riah	MBS2	orange colored	Form 43; jar with grooved-band rim	Idrisid?	89,621
Basra Core	BSR138	Douar Riah	MBS2	sandy buff	Form 70? flask with rolled rim	Idrisid?	37,167
Basra Core	BSR139	Douar Riah	MBS2	very fine buff	Form ?	Idrisid?	52,042
Basra Core	BSR141	Douar Riah	MBS2	sandy buff	Form ?	Idrisid?	34,905
Basra Core	BSR142	Douar Riah	MBS2	orange with very fine texture	Form ?	Idrisid?	83,167
Hinterland-1	BSR082	Sidi an-Niyya	LLM5	sandy buff	Form 41; jar with triangular rim	Idrisid?	0,000
Hinterland-1	BSR091	Sidi Ahmed Bourziguine	LLM8	cream colored	Form 40; carinated jar	Idrisid?	0,000
Hinterland-1	BSR125	Sidi Yssef	LLM14	fine buff	Form 43; jar with grooved-band rim	Idrisid?	0,000
Hinterland-1	BSR129	Sidi Yssef	LLM14	orange colored	Form ?	Idrisid?	0,000
Hinterland-1	BSR140	Douar Riah	MBS2	sandy buff	Form ?	Idrisid?	0,000
Hinterland-2	BSR014	Bhalla	ARB7	sandy buff	Form 40; carinated jar	Idrisid?	0,409
Hinterland-2	BSR019	Bhalla	ARB7	fine buff	Form 80; flat base	Idrisid?	0,001
Hinterland-2	BSR031	Sidi Bou Douma	ARB13	fine buff	Form 40; carinated jar	Idrisid?	0,003
Hinterland-2	BSR032	Sidi Bou Douma	ARB13	fine buff	Form 40; carinated jar	Idrisid?	0,000
Hinterland-2	BSR033	Sidi Bou Douma	ARB13	fine buff	Form 40; carinated jar	Idrisid?	0,098
Hinterland-2	BSR035	Sidi Bou Douma	ARB13	fine gray	Form 43; jar with grooved-band rim	Idrisid?	0,000
Hinterland-2	BSR036	Sidi Bou Douma	ARB13	very fine buff	Form ?	Idrisid?	0,055
Hinterland-2	BSR037	Sidi Bou Douma	ARB13	orange with very fine texture	Form ?	Idrisid?	0,000
Unassigned	BSR008	al-Ghzalat	ARB2	cream-colored--brown hue	Form 42; jar with band rim	Idrisid?	0,000
Unassigned	BSR012	Bhalla	ARB7	orange, with fine texture	Form 40; carinated jar	Idrisid?	0,028
Unassigned	BSR017	Bhalla	ARB7	sandy buff	Form 42; jar with band rim	Idrisid?	0,017
Unassigned	BSR018	Bhalla	ARB7	very fine buff	Form ?	Idrisid?	0,455
Unassigned	BSR026	Jahjouka	ARB8	sandy buff	Form 40; carinated jar	Idrisid?	0,000
Unassigned	BSR045	Kudyat Srafah	ARB15	cream-colored--brown/orange	Form 40; carinated jar	Idrisid?	0,000
Unassigned	BSR072	Frigidae	LLM4	sandy buff	Form 43; jar with grooved-band rim	Idrisid?	0,253
Unassigned	BSR092	Sidi Ahmed Bourziguine	LLM8	very fine gray	Form ?	Idrisid?	0,001
Unassigned	BSR119	Sidi Yssef	LLM14	sandy buff	Form 40; carinated jar	Idrisid?	0,282
Unassigned	BSR134	al-'Asimi	MBK1	orange colored	Form 43; jar with grooved-band rim	Idrisid?	0,001
Unassigned	BSR135	al-'Asimi	MBK1	sandy gray	Form 43; jar with grooved-band rim	Idrisid?	0,000
Unassigned	BSR143	Douar Riah	MBS2	orange colored	Form ?	Idrisid?	0,000
Unassigned	BSR144	Douar Riah	MBS2	fine gray	Form ?	Idrisid?	0,000
Unassigned	BSR145	Douar Riah	MBS2	fine gray	Form ?	Idrisid?	0,000

APPENDIX G

ELEMENTAL CONCENTRATIONS FOR ARCHAEOLOGICAL POTTERY FROM AL-BASRA'S HINTERLAND SITES

Analytical ID. (N=145)	Site No.	As	La	Lu	Nd	Sm	U	Yb	Ce	Co	Cr	Cs
BSR001	ARB2	7,2864	36,9156	0,3404	32,5496	6,3951	2,76	2,4012	73,3124	14,14	144,2681	6,103
BSR002	ARB2	7,3581	34,4934	0,3237	28,676	6,0391	2,24	2,4482	71,0646	15,0579	136,8697	5,2835
BSR003	ARB2	12,2114	38,3675	0,3356	31,5974	6,5166	3,02	2,4515	77,1219	14,8432	153,8808	5,9952
BSR004	ARB2	3,0906	35,7196	0,3239	32,44	6,0114	2,95	2,3771	71,9213	12,5578	140,2753	5,2505
BSR005	ARB2	3,6918	38,5158	0,3499	31,2056	6,6662	2,91	2,5373	78,5105	14,1166	150,1588	6,2642
BSR006	ARB2	8,131	37,0764	0,3302	31,2806	6,3651	2,33	2,3545	74,5393	14,5679	148,6272	5,8884
BSR007	ARB2	6,1286	34,5571	0,3314	28,5222	6,0775	2,41	2,3628	69,0109	14,0569	133,2046	5,0881
BSR008	ARB2	12,0966	42,5765	0,404	34,4823	7,7627	2,94	2,9957	86,5592	20,5864	121,3644	11,463
BSR009	ARB2	4,3652	33,6944	0,3239	27,896	5,8685	2,19	2,2749	68,5209	12,5895	136,1409	5,3836
BSR010	ARB2	5,6674	36,1481	0,3489	34,7705	6,666	1,97	2,3523	71,8184	13,4602	141,6695	5,2899
BSR011	ARB7	4,361	36,3076	0,3221	33,3215	6,6353	2,51	2,3694	72,347	12,2166	141,4435	5,7494
BSR012	ARB7	4,7258	33,7982	0,3367	29,6047	6,8479	2,33	2,4532	69,3553	15,5688	135,278	5,4506
BSR013	ARB7	4,3784	34,5998	0,3332	31,3282	6,4154	2,13	2,2158	68,6499	13,9821	138,7058	5,5487
BSR014	ARB7	2,1879	35,8337	0,3472	30,4231	6,2032	2,34	2,3446	76,4289	15,2751	143,5219	5,1778
BSR015	ARB7	4,4292	33,8928	0,3471	29,3597	6,4649	2,39	2,485	65,148	13,8876	132,4191	5,1326
BSR016	ARB7	3,3365	33,4428	0,3515	27,9192	6,1155	2,59	2,3463	65,9811	13,1854	129,6029	5,066
BSR017	ARB7	6,4739	30,5288	0,3311	28,3104	5,7166	1,6	2,3459	62,7463	12,6757	125,9297	3,9921
BSR018	ARB7	4,3472	31,1347	0,3152	28,0343	5,2065	2,1	2,2174	60,8468	10,2882	126,3216	4,8632
BSR019	ARB7	6,0173	35,909	0,3395	29,4287	6,2691	2,32	2,3343	72,6361	11,4461	138,8012	4,9103
BSR020	ARB7	1,9672	33,2216	0,3344	28,7708	6,0285	2,1	2,4152	64,9968	12,6612	132,6189	5,3588
BSR021	ARB8	4,82	36,4218	0,3469	33,2505	6,5506	3,1	2,5409	74,2058	13,1464	148,5576	5,9566
BSR022	ARB8	7,4237	37,7696	0,3472	32,5499	7,2035	2,45	2,5279	75,6133	13,6916	145,0534	5,7876
BSR023	ARB8	10,8068	39,1455	0,3415	35,0815	7,1859	2,49	2,6128	81,1632	18,2247	157,3875	5,5617
BSR024	ARB8	5,5508	37,9045	0,3412	34,7885	6,5613	2,62	2,4697	77,6483	14,2691	150,6591	6,034
BSR025	ARB8	12,2178	33,7353	0,3476	29,5612	6,1502	1,8	2,4176	69,0035	13,4305	133,2124	5,5367
BSR026	ARB8	7,0117	31,75	0,3399	26,1781	5,6139	2,42	2,3904	62,4515	20,6051	128,329	5,2013
BSR027	ARB8	9,9701	39,8462	0,3599	37,2654	6,9361	3	2,5773	80,3908	15,0313	156,8864	5,5435
BSR028	ARB8	5,0271	37,3695	0,3359	33,3329	6,6517	2,21	2,4474	77,5756	13,3451	150,1444	5,8355
BSR029	ARB8	11,0817	38,5002	0,3783	32,459	6,8767	2,39	2,6182	74,6369	14,6223	148,7061	5,7495
BSR030	ARB8	6,1049	36,8421	0,3335	33,1104	6,6063	3,05	2,3124	74,3107	13,7391	152,2398	5,9902
BSR031	ARB13	1,5342	38,0569	0,3455	32,6157	6,6882	2,47	2,4408	74,8468	16,6343	151,575	4,7666
BSR032	ARB13	1,9867	39,9414	0,367	32,6083	7,4836	2,23	2,7009	78,0576	17,3781	161,2656	5,3033
BSR033	ARB13	7,8992	39,9526	0,3538	32,052	7,3102	3,01	2,3394	78,0996	16,4414	143,808	4,8276
BSR034	ARB13	4,1438	35,2448	0,3601	29,6871	6,4632	2,51	2,6267	70,3388	14,0844	138,1133	5,2891
BSR035	ARB13	4,1699	38,7668	0,3735	35,4105	6,8978	2,22	2,5878	73,8109	22,3667	152,6314	4,5289
BSR036	ARB13	5,2059	40,7133	0,3523	34,7792	7,618	2,74	2,6281	81,9696	16,0564	161,7541	5,8336
BSR037	ARB13	6,2635	40,046	0,3811	35,2273	8,0268	3,19	2,8196	85,0177	16,6453	145,3726	4,8646
BSR038	ARB13	8,3869	35,6289	0,3567	29,6217	6,5227	2,13	2,4674	71,0871	13,4615	140,8473	5,0889
BSR039	ARB13	4,0496	40,1292	0,3891	34,1563	7,4516	3,14	2,6867	79,2458	16,4202	159,5227	5,5014
BSR040	ARB13	7,5852	35,6382	0,3299	32,3388	6,1439	2,25	2,6374	69,7228	12,3982	140,3583	5,3543
BSR041	ARB15	3,7908	34,6636	0,3613	32,339	6,3512	1,86	2,5617	68,5455	14,4489	136,8005	5,2249
BSR042	ARB15	4,3284	35,8358	0,3267	33,1052	6,3714	2,48	2,4532	72,8159	12,2943	139,0547	5,7904
BSR043	ARB15	6,2538	34,7692	0,32	30,6542	6,0119	2,59	2,3457	70,8519	12,9797	134,3803	5,2815
BSR044	ARB15	6,1953	33,4931	0,3328	30,9182	6,2364	2,59	2,4922	67,282	13,298	132,3907	5,1466
BSR045	ARB15	4,3235	32,1312	0,3384	28,4114	5,9221	2,26	2,2674	69,1742	60,0083	126,3297	4,7067

Analytical ID. (N=145)	Site No.	Eu	Fe	Hf	Ni	Rb	Sb	Sc	Sr	Ta	Tb	Th
BSR001	ARB2	1,37	47346,3	5,1657	0	96,5709	0,4406	16,1775	355,13	1,2155	0,9117	9,7433
BSR002	ARB2	1,3524	49265	6,5195	0	91,4488	0,4322	15,383	242,6	1,1287	0,7937	9,5178
BSR003	ARB2	1,4415	49173,5	5,0276	75,17	100,4359	0,4202	16,6831	369,61	1,3195	0,8434	10,3017
BSR004	ARB2	1,2984	45498,1	5,2684	80,06	90,9765	0,4541	15,5506	280,75	1,181	0,7976	9,5925
BSR005	ARB2	1,4481	49162,5	4,5667	0	100,7651	0,3672	16,8304	265,86	1,2543	0,7492	10,1743
BSR006	ARB2	1,3862	49960,5	5,3397	18,69	99,8288	0,4368	16,3572	395,95	1,2486	0,7709	10,059
BSR007	ARB2	1,3528	48155,1	6,5201	60,91	82,6689	0,4138	15,0192	236,02	1,1276	0,8623	9,1696
BSR008	ARB2	1,5143	51264,5	4,4951	65,67	141,5217	2,1872	18,5348	263,88	1,2588	1,3315	13,082
BSR009	ARB2	1,3154	44702,5	5,3152	47,13	89,0763	0,3638	15,1101	263,39	1,2394	0,6322	9,2017
BSR010	ARB2	1,3527	47283,3	4,9256	0	93,3547	0,3496	15,7103	316,84	1,1825	0,5983	9,7022
BSR011	ARB7	1,3167	42463,1	4,6562	0	94,0527	0,4879	15,4721	275,7	1,2169	0,5477	9,4996
BSR012	ARB7	1,4682	44648	4,8481	51,87	92,1765	0,414	14,8594	236,41	1,0759	1,1385	9,0979
BSR013	ARB7	1,3136	46790,7	5,2189	0	99,2675	0,3837	15,1522	384,96	1,1628	0,6085	9,2404
BSR014	ARB7	1,5069	47008	6,0635	0	89,0934	0,303	16,0663	292,03	1,1782	1,0597	9,7531
BSR015	ARB7	1,2451	46549,1	5,2301	0	89,5062	0,371	14,4537	277,97	1,0819	0,5735	8,8096
BSR016	ARB7	1,2599	44653,8	5,9149	0	87,6348	0,3685	14,9085	277,61	1,1281	0,9366	8,9249
BSR017	ARB7	1,2423	50542,9	6,1316	0	71,4705	0,4205	13,9069	244,72	1,0933	0,6134	8,5431
BSR018	ARB7	1,2069	40180,8	5,0417	0	81,5837	0,343	13,4877	280,98	1,0347	0,5785	8,1513
BSR019	ARB7	1,3111	43570,9	5,7699	0	78,8937	0,3699	13,8705	268,16	1,2723	0,574	9,4482
BSR020	ARB7	1,2355	43407,4	5,7797	53,87	89,8682	0,3841	14,4259	306,56	1,08	0,5613	8,8446
BSR021	ARB8	1,3935	47694,9	5,1084	48,1	103,2769	0,4196	16,1154	341,82	1,2028	0,5934	9,905
BSR022	ARB8	1,4411	45342,2	5,4074	0	94,9527	0,3366	15,5398	276,08	1,2705	0,65	9,7713
BSR023	ARB8	1,4997	49948,3	4,9679	45,66	91,3757	0,5972	16,3287	326,45	1,402	0,6825	10,6556
BSR024	ARB8	1,4368	48145,4	5,2494	97,69	101,2939	0,3893	16,4795	305,35	1,2676	1,1683	10,2393
BSR025	ARB8	1,2979	44495,1	5,633	44,66	90,728	0,3401	15,1055	421,38	1,1894	0,6305	9,3573
BSR026	ARB8	1,2125	43822,2	7,4666	0	84,9037	0,3335	14,2772	262,24	1,0043	0,5933	8,6447
BSR027	ARB8	1,4647	48825,9	5,0684	33,6	94,9153	0,4233	16,1638	257,2	1,4419	0,6405	10,6063
BSR028	ARB8	1,3972	47906,1	4,9828	0	98,8102	0,3762	16,3511	321,22	1,2637	0,5916	10,2086
BSR029	ARB8	1,4293	47864,6	4,8909	0	94,4279	0,4215	15,5427	337,12	1,3131	0,6148	10,0808
BSR030	ARB8	1,3654	48578,8	5,0946	0	99,9636	0,4476	16,1361	381,2	1,2542	0,5852	9,9998
BSR031	ARB13	1,3761	48752,6	4,834	72,74	85,6906	0,4041	16,4582	235,09	1,3461	0,6009	10,1052
BSR032	ARB13	1,5501	52413	5,1753	49,53	93,0871	0,4506	17,9793	973,65	1,3686	1,06	10,5514
BSR033	ARB13	1,4626	49442,7	4,5893	0	81,5241	0,4025	15,4271	223,02	1,3021	0,6579	10,0303
BSR034	ARB13	1,3921	49133,1	5,9167	0	95,6527	0,427	15,748	346,87	1,1705	0,7061	9,9071
BSR035	ARB13	1,4367	50624,1	4,6727	41,3	84,5631	0,3078	16,9278	112,14	1,3076	0,577	9,984
BSR036	ARB13	1,537	50994,1	5,0637	43,79	100,3484	0,3716	17,3815	657,77	1,4581	0,6331	10,9101
BSR037	ARB13	1,7786	44938,7	5,2721	0	82,6421	0,4526	15,6318	273,09	1,3225	0,8334	10,3359
BSR038	ARB13	1,3872	48580,8	5,8787	36,65	86,8627	0,4227	15,8017	320,7	1,2693	0,5724	9,8947
BSR039	ARB13	1,5115	50701,9	4,8399	85,05	101,6081	0,3666	17,3865	187,64	1,332	0,6871	10,557
BSR040	ARB13	1,3267	41585,4	4,9771	0	89,4996	0,3712	15,2765	469,91	1,136	0,5628	9,4679
BSR041	ARB15	1,3524	45316,2	6,2647	81,42	86,2479	0,3265	14,9151	295,25	1,1435	0,6521	9,305
BSR042	ARB15	1,3694	45395,4	5,4497	63,29	97,5958	0,35	15,6816	376,26	1,1394	0,5624	9,4751
BSR043	ARB15	1,2417	44993,1	5,5913	0	90,0517	0,3509	14,9574	334,19	1,1518	0,5657	9,2368
BSR044	ARB15	1,3762	46138,3	6,1237	51,76	86,3952	0,3303	14,6626	295,01	1,1205	0,6109	9,0439
BSR045	ARB15	1,2701	45101,4	6,0432	88,46	79,0753	0,3534	14,0555	233	1,0786	0,6221	8,6583

Analytical ID. (N=145)	Site No.	Zn	Zr	Al	Ba	Ca	Dy	K	Mn	Na	Ti	V
BSR001	ARB2	109,663	138,2556	84721,7	247,8	71546,5	4,5668	18518	470,09	4792,72	4543,571	160,7339
BSR002	ARB2	113,147	140,6773	75632,8	276,62	40263,6	4,5394	18786,73	546,36	3970,62	4339,096	147,238
BSR003	ARB2	111,2379	144,3753	87598,5	192,71	67165,6	4,6579	17893,05	490,49	5407,42	4454,515	199,818
BSR004	ARB2	106,0519	129,6103	82882,4	583,75	37691,8	3,8584	20573,06	458,59	4705,99	5219,358	163,668
BSR005	ARB2	109,1975	125,8405	88907,5	172,3	68424,7	3,9818	19086,83	402,8	6485,22	4473,051	175,8178
BSR006	ARB2	115,5705	136,0137	84274,9	351,99	79667,1	4,2717	18600,67	570,93	5605,5	4957,84	184,6216
BSR007	ARB2	107,6543	179,5199	75176,3	378,57	39339,2	4,4421	18247,23	486,95	4599,65	4345,361	146,5955
BSR008	ARB2	117,0867	126,0824	98499,1	675,68	65616,3	4,8406	24355,28	1045,44	5956,19	4783,904	157,74
BSR009	ARB2	103,2468	152,5857	78826,1	280,83	61589,3	4,5064	17401,99	385,37	5284,45	4626,477	156,5962
BSR010	ARB2	115,9333	133,435	88269,9	611,83	56230,9	4,4305	19209,8	462,22	4400,19	4685,649	163,0854
BSR011	ARB7	96,5706	122,4186	82063,8	1143,69	45097,9	4,4379	19371,66	392,48	4657,98	4835,609	176,1853
BSR012	ARB7	107,1776	148,5561	79750,4	634,55	45150,9	5,1162	16558,16	433,89	4419,36	4782,476	145,803
BSR013	ARB7	107,7568	161,7671	83555,5	483,15	58199,8	4,4719	18068,58	417,87	4850,25	4951,226	157,7676
BSR014	ARB7	111,797	182,219	80251,3	1558,93	28819,3	4,1137	16486,99	466,36	3356,08	4526,313	158,2457
BSR015	ARB7	112,0163	119,6627	77236,2	581,24	47789,5	4,086	15941,26	449,76	4250,43	4483,563	151,2886
BSR016	ARB7	103,2855	169,7304	78524,5	497,76	51931,1	3,9695	17234,79	486,73	3985,87	4791,406	147,3507
BSR017	ARB7	106,4977	175,8295	68294	972,57	36100,1	3,9077	12448,55	383,71	3493,85	4173,269	138,4274
BSR018	ARB7	90,8605	145,8839	80031,2	591,89	51210,6	4,6321	15666,74	356,99	4677,8	4186,5	169,1637
BSR019	ARB7	94,6336	148,8641	78310,9	518,26	28570,7	4,1247	14940,03	339,03	3697,52	4218,925	159,5676
BSR020	ARB7	99,7128	168,9101	78230,1	297,84	69124,1	3,9702	15820,96	439,53	4791,79	4398,319	172,2013
BSR021	ARB8	111,6477	145,2761	85951	293,08	55447,6	4,1209	18644,25	392,39	6933,32	5231,211	155,4371
BSR022	ARB8	103,687	152,1641	86437,2	251,17	56392,1	4,9573	16507,24	381,94	4826,78	4693,202	175,8126
BSR023	ARB8	117,043	153,8103	91328,6	230,55	47959,8	4,5403	17678,65	433,62	4713,94	4621,11	198,8877
BSR024	ARB8	111,8715	151,3093	88466,9	346	56757,5	4,2914	19263,96	461,92	5706,73	4079,762	169,1384
BSR025	ARB8	108,2974	161,4008	76603,6	369,17	67043,2	3,8148	18226,56	461,24	4628,37	4183,742	161,1491
BSR026	ARB8	107,9523	214,3371	72539,3	317,36	49626,2	3,7776	16288,55	630,39	4421,31	4003,369	150,6708
BSR027	ARB8	113,4573	149,6158	89197,7	338,8	50736,8	4,7743	18140,48	482,24	4111,33	5031,273	195,7872
BSR028	ARB8	110,3548	146,3518	85313,6	188,78	69573,6	3,9824	19299,44	421,94	5828,15	4983,294	164,6198
BSR029	ARB8	116,1926	149,7773	87827,4	205,99	59520,7	4,4199	16451,73	437,24	4810,37	4734,955	184,6626
BSR030	ARB8	109,2665	138,139	86259,9	188,46	66522,1	4,2227	18761,79	376,73	7364,27	4347,856	166,3978
BSR031	ARB13	125,3849	135,7691	91685,6	408,56	24978,9	4,3407	19071,33	606,4	4998,48	5200,96	171,5233
BSR032	ARB13	127,9951	137,5645	92929,4	505,02	30032,4	4,3905	19027,95	536,97	4758,58	5486,514	172,0349
BSR033	ARB13	113,4655	117,4013	85117,7	318,11	28425,3	4,6183	18263,12	663,49	4578,53	4486,946	162,0164
BSR034	ARB13	113,2594	158,2925	79299,9	416,54	50720,3	4,478	18090,37	456,5	6172,21	4306,643	158,9609
BSR035	ARB13	128,1872	146,3846	97491,4	442,27	17937,7	4,968	17177,76	516,52	4166,71	5674,81	165,0899
BSR036	ARB13	120,991	120,5214	91141,2	313,06	44648,8	4,7094	17524,34	480,91	4568,28	5430,945	187,591
BSR037	ARB13	115,8285	159,3321	79853	433,64	27435,8	6,0909	18473,65	401,49	3393,21	4536,709	143,1321
BSR038	ARB13	109,304	176,6986	79817,7	433,01	49596,4	4,2682	17097,21	423,22	6297,74	4795,249	162,0136
BSR039	ARB13	121,2392	137,3927	94302,5	464,16	31236,2	4,362	17917,13	470,38	4194,71	4941,137	191,6284
BSR040	ARB13	105,9095	140,8494	79302,6	1126,65	83368,2	4,0528	14031,37	309,64	6128,98	4652,503	170,9904
BSR041	ARB15	115,7622	154,0647	79358,7	616,16	51445,9	4,2515	17936,48	430,62	4551,24	4333,013	155,1375
BSR042	ARB15	106,0001	152,4951	82457	284,48	49385,6	4,1797	17513,81	297,55	3587,29	4843,491	153,5273
BSR043	ARB15	100,6411	181,4004	83344,7	438,84	54679,6	3,9468	17694,67	371,11	5173,68	4939,651	160,544
BSR044	ARB15	107,7087	157,671	76382,4	433,28	51191,9	4,1527	15961,11	361,87	3469,34	4879,563	151,2605
BSR045	ARB15	123,3327	145,0628	76019,5	649,82	37687,7	4,165	16482,74	1093,23	3809,07	4610,353	149,0013

Analytical ID. (N=145)	Site No.	As	La	Lu	Nd	Sm	U	Yb	Ce	Co	Cr	Cs
BSR046	ARB15	2,6317	33,7014	0,3406	30,438	6,1291	2	2,4408	66,3609	13,5646	137,4672	5,2503
BSR047	ARB15	4,5494	36,8953	0,3444	35,8699	6,4721	2,58	2,3767	73,6456	12,4602	142,6097	5,8898
BSR048	ARB15	7,3814	33,2954	0,3492	29,0844	5,9506	2,55	2,31	66,8933	13,2055	129,4893	5,0332
BSR049	ARB15	6,0111	35,4439	0,3077	33,978	6,4695	2,52	2,3267	70,1522	13,3378	131,1902	5,5841
BSR050	ARB15	7,1598	35,7402	0,3537	32,129	6,1904	2,83	2,5311	70,1874	12,8143	139,1297	6,154
BSR051	ARB18	6,7069	41,6023	0,3591	34,3392	7,5768	2,73	2,5595	82,8266	15,2886	161,7136	5,5328
BSR052	ARB18	5,9705	41,1671	0,3566	34,4868	7,2226	2,78	2,2999	82,7055	15,0984	161,1785	5,6353
BSR053	ARB18	10,2536	35,2912	0,3426	31,9113	6,3068	2,76	2,2635	69,7386	12,9032	139,3601	5,4977
BSR054	ARB18	4,8237	36,6867	0,3415	32,4767	6,5583	2,81	2,5641	70,6718	13,2644	145,2893	5,8112
BSR055	ARB18	4,4145	36,3278	0,3477	29,8531	6,589	1,53	2,6252	70,9279	13,2772	145,2901	5,4461
BSR056	ARB18	4,2635	36,9088	0,3367	31,6598	6,4744	2,75	2,4739	72,8536	13,119	141,2779	5,8819
BSR057	ARB18	5,4546	36,7527	0,3261	33,4618	6,2972	2,77	2,3997	74,2039	14,1895	143,7686	6,0376
BSR058	ARB18	4,5299	41,5567	0,3804	36,6886	6,9803	2,56	2,5071	84,0236	18,1876	170,1647	5,9004
BSR059	ARB18	2,7642	37,0498	0,3565	27,9262	6,2408	2,92	2,4818	76,0379	12,696	152,951	5,9272
BSR060	ARB18	5,8664	41,4933	0,3937	34,0834	7,1519	2,81	2,7445	85,3953	16,2955	168,9874	5,4128
BSR061	LLM1	5,1236	35,4858	0,3759	32,3317	6,2497	2,49	2,2785	72,9287	14,7054	147,1292	5,8332
BSR062	LLM1	4,2514	37,0944	0,3477	27,3122	6,4071	2,54	2,3243	75,3881	15,2202	151,3164	6,11
BSR063	LLM1	6,9848	36,6065	0,3615	33,7584	6,2131	2,43	2,3861	75,0727	14,3345	148,5357	5,6722
BSR064	LLM1	3,9779	34,4123	0,3505	28,078	6,2221	2,05	2,3576	71,4874	13,0089	131,7509	5,1991
BSR065	LLM1	5,7629	37,1414	0,3647	30,2542	6,4619	2,53	2,5429	76,8313	14,2462	152,8528	5,5685
BSR066	LLM1	9,3666	33,4766	0,3334	29,4194	5,9321	2,77	2,3526	67,3981	14,0939	140,0944	5,588
BSR067	LLM1	6,0166	38,0515	0,3586	33,6525	6,4639	2,19	2,5154	77,0577	13,924	155,7896	6,2174
BSR068	LLM1	5,5249	35,209	0,3554	33,4364	6,2823	2,85	2,5762	72,3362	15,2803	143,1826	5,5364
BSR069	LLM1	5,7743	36,0361	0,357	29,6287	6,0924	2,44	2,2229	74,5544	17,0165	145,1517	5,6055
BSR070	LLM1	11,8367	39,18	0,3861	33,0377	6,7024	2,76	2,4139	80,302	14,8322	160,4822	6,1404
BSR071	LLM4	3,0846	37,5767	0,354	31,8079	6,2544	3,25	2,4904	76,269	14,6683	152,2722	6,0507
BSR072	LLM4	3,8831	36,596	0,3368	30,2834	6,6492	2,29	2,6529	73,9451	13,2896	150,8271	5,7626
BSR073	LLM4	7,1084	37,9468	0,3506	32,7825	6,4602	2,25	2,7503	75,4918	13,637	151,5444	5,1236
BSR074	LLM4	6,4462	35,1371	0,3998	28,2297	6,1689	1,99	2,8066	69,4245	14,5973	141,2293	4,7959
BSR075	LLM4	5,5169	36,4681	0,3259	31,8621	6,2882	2,71	2,1729	73,0485	11,885	148,9782	5,9254
BSR076	LLM5	7,583	33,7829	0,3446	31,1419	5,9436	2,96	2,2051	67,0839	13,5225	131,3421	5,3478
BSR077	LLM5	8,53	35,5323	0,3638	29,4651	6,4476	2,58	2,3244	71,5777	14,4565	139,4233	5,7173
BSR078	LLM5	9,7403	32,822	0,3271	28,827	5,8029	2,67	2,0845	65,5754	11,354	123,7082	4,8967
BSR079	LLM5	18,1442	37,5066	0,3615	31,6664	6,3173	2,43	2,1356	74,9845	13,8635	155,6682	5,8683
BSR080	LLM5	11,3438	34,9352	0,3388	29,301	6,1287	2,43	2,4089	69,4724	14,375	135,5231	5,0996
BSR081	LLM5	7,3818	36,3203	0,3581	28,4528	6,4983	2,35	2,4191	72,6689	13,7091	148,2522	5,8393
BSR082	LLM5	6,9877	33,7303	0,4512	29,5414	7,1881	2,52	3,0153	69,0934	16,3173	130,3869	4,9002
BSR083	LLM5	12,3137	34,7648	0,3419	29,4464	6,0275	2,38	2,3254	68,597	13,6835	137,7136	5,1491
BSR084	LLM5	6,9819	35,0988	0,3357	32,2326	6,2196	2,41	2,186	70,4158	13,4639	141,8321	5,3859
BSR085	LLM5	9,0731	35,0459	0,35	33,0393	6,2218	3,55	2,3324	67,5341	12,2583	135,0798	5,1612
BSR086	LLM8	11,2417	37,2576	0,37	33,4408	6,688	2,42	2,4759	76,3623	14,7079	151,9389	4,5678
BSR087	LLM8	6,5475	37,6588	0,3428	33,2766	6,3988	3,16	2,4431	73,1661	14,2257	149,0598	5,5158
BSR088	LLM8	5,2609	36,0422	0,3504	29,7286	6,1963	2,73	2,0558	71,9965	14,032	148,2359	5,6416
BSR089	LLM8	6,1665	38,8759	0,3541	34,0741	6,3977	2,5	2,4968	77,5662	15,3513	156,4239	5,5428
BSR090	LLM8	8,9828	38,4794	0,346	31,9677	6,5438	2,58	2,4519	76,3829	15,1173	154,2591	5,9867
BSR091	LLM8	5,0346	40,0943	0,3999	34,768	6,8924	2,03	2,5727	76,9438	17,042	149,9934	4,3223
BSR092	LLM8	5,0061	39,4253	0,3335	32,7572	6,5303	2,52	2,4057	77,5423	14,2792	153,3938	4,4397

Analytical ID. (N=145)	Site No.	Eu	Fe	Hf	Ni	Rb	Sb	Sc	Sr	Ta	Tb	Th
BSR046	ARB15	1,3066	46017,5	5,8182	0	93,4682	0,2901	14,6173	243,86	1,1477	0,6261	8,8994
BSR047	ARB15	1,3311	46499	4,9591	0	98,065	0,4021	15,7023	361,35	1,2001	0,5558	9,5
BSR048	ARB15	1,2862	44004,3	5,4578	0	84,3102	0,4174	14,4911	242,15	1,0748	0,6084	8,7631
BSR049	ARB15	1,3618	44747,4	6,0704	47,61	92,1937	0,3757	15,1196	258,43	1,0744	0,5997	9,2189
BSR050	ARB15	1,3191	47096,1	6,1795	64,58	96,158	0,4385	15,6801	233,12	1,2032	0,6092	9,4451
BSR051	ARB18	1,5118	50092,6	4,8786	72,93	90,4758	0,4369	16,609	243,5	1,3709	0,6683	10,7726
BSR052	ARB18	1,4992	50208,8	4,97	0	97,9884	0,4268	16,6424	321,34	1,4664	0,6433	10,8872
BSR053	ARB18	1,3307	47475,6	5,4777	42,69	89,9816	0,2964	15,3584	374,49	1,1812	0,6086	9,477
BSR054	ARB18	1,3567	46095,4	4,7935	0	96,2713	0,4806	15,601	266,53	1,1723	0,6081	9,5934
BSR055	ARB18	1,3954	46502,9	4,6954	64,91	92,2415	0,3758	15,6907	258,99	1,1303	0,6925	9,7017
BSR056	ARB18	1,3399	44536,8	5,1377	0	97,5835	0,3792	15,7171	228,84	1,172	0,6218	9,5931
BSR057	ARB18	1,3573	41997,8	4,8956	0	102,6852	0,4315	15,7679	269,61	1,1722	0,6448	9,785
BSR058	ARB18	1,5752	53753,3	5,1969	0	101,1554	0,3663	18,843	210,77	1,3409	0,9458	11,1587
BSR059	ARB18	1,3852	45831	5,2655	0	96,7641	0,457	16,4407	335,84	1,224	0,8528	10,1071
BSR060	ARB18	1,5698	51397,6	5,0779	0	90,7718	0,4227	17,7502	176,53	1,4533	0,9911	11,3471
BSR061	LLM1	1,3814	45799,7	5,0699	0	96,5657	0,4318	16,0234	322,68	1,2258	0,7962	9,7877
BSR062	LLM1	1,4263	49036,8	4,901	50,38	99,7377	0,48	16,5431	292,05	1,2082	0,8913	10,0059
BSR063	LLM1	1,3692	49746,5	5,0517	34,78	90,6147	0,4794	16,658	402,53	1,2134	0,7713	9,9077
BSR064	LLM1	1,3473	47787,2	6,5939	60,63	85,3055	0,3591	15,5852	312,64	1,171	0,809	9,6222
BSR065	LLM1	1,3976	47958,9	5,147	45,19	91,7715	0,4003	16,7146	367,38	1,1724	0,8924	10,2695
BSR066	LLM1	1,2824	47450,2	5,4098	0	89,3493	0,5135	15,2845	268,75	1,1335	0,7433	9,1271
BSR067	LLM1	1,4217	49235,9	5,0571	0	100,7694	0,4741	16,8689	328,93	1,3025	0,7796	10,1977
BSR068	LLM1	1,3819	49818,2	6,0637	0	95,1773	0,3171	15,7367	328,26	1,1769	0,7947	9,8415
BSR069	LLM1	1,3533	49102,6	5,7772	58,37	88,2932	0,3777	16,2253	318,85	1,188	0,8286	9,7388
BSR070	LLM1	1,4702	52605,1	4,8965	59,72	103,7596	0,5965	16,8843	338,26	1,3522	0,8457	10,7598
BSR071	LLM4	1,339	45256	5,221	0	96,9211	0,4194	16,5909	241,72	1,2548	0,7885	9,9792
BSR072	LLM4	1,5352	48479,7	5,3716	0	95,7614	0,4733	16,3938	356,02	1,2388	0,7832	9,7644
BSR073	LLM4	1,3864	49511,9	5,1046	0	91,2161	0,4507	16,4882	302,7	1,2371	0,8018	10,0665
BSR074	LLM4	1,3504	46827,1	5,2242	28,48	85,4373	0,2967	15,2075	232,15	1,1246	0,8509	9,4027
BSR075	LLM4	1,3415	47191,9	4,3043	0	94,4603	0,401	15,9795	374,75	1,1914	0,7941	9,7164
BSR076	LLM5	1,2531	44515,6	5,413	0	87,673	0,4763	14,8817	420,87	1,1112	0,699	9,0258
BSR077	LLM5	1,4365	46826,4	5,3231	53,56	100,5718	0,4045	15,5703	353,66	1,1123	0,7498	9,4491
BSR078	LLM5	1,2515	43114	5,1488	34,17	82,1542	0,352	14,5433	296,66	1,0789	0,716	8,5663
BSR079	LLM5	1,3714	44881,2	4,535	62,46	95,6691	0,5826	16,3126	592,91	1,2336	0,7803	10,0167
BSR080	LLM5	1,2877	46259,7	5,9156	0	89,8807	0,4641	15,1517	449,04	1,1378	0,7429	9,4752
BSR081	LLM5	1,4265	48330,7	5,2441	34,55	94,8319	0,411	16,0469	351,88	1,1798	0,8375	9,8389
BSR082	LLM5	1,7162	46110,8	6,399	47,44	83,6713	0,4435	14,9512	366,62	1,0858	1,1359	9,1434
BSR083	LLM5	1,3033	42941,4	5,4316	0	85,1319	0,4863	15,1573	469,07	1,1105	0,7705	9,2177
BSR084	LLM5	1,3631	47624,5	5,2578	45,18	93,3619	0,338	15,588	280,53	1,1381	0,8197	9,3669
BSR085	LLM5	1,2742	46640,8	6,1991	0	82,9655	0,4975	14,6996	308,18	1,1527	0,7677	9,3463
BSR086	LLM8	1,4265	52919,7	6,1508	0	80,7756	0,3943	16,3817	237,57	1,2891	0,9325	10,3639
BSR087	LLM8	1,3456	46395,4	5,5333	0	93,3902	0,4719	16,3138	333,02	1,1589	0,9194	9,8758
BSR088	LLM8	1,3716	46097,8	5,8717	50,65	91,6413	0,4601	15,9064	305,22	1,1796	0,7412	9,5312
BSR089	LLM8	1,3955	49198,4	4,6404	0	93,9555	0,3959	16,7474	389,98	1,2365	0,8024	10,299
BSR090	LLM8	1,398	48559,3	5,1086	0	99,56	0,4198	16,7796	231,53	1,2634	0,8767	10,2634
BSR091	LLM8	1,4845	53716,9	5,0571	73,6	78,4304	0,58	18,7867	332,82	1,2032	0,9082	10,4943
BSR092	LLM8	1,4277	49023,5	4,5134	0	84,1293	0,432	16,9144	373,26	1,3009	0,8271	10,1657

Analytical ID. (N=145)	Site No.	Zn	Zr	Al	Ba	Ca	Dy	K	Mn	Na	Ti	V
BSR046	ARB15	108,0397	168,0985	78873,4	222,04	60070,8	4,6908	16806,65	332,97	4503,65	4448,476	160,6311
BSR047	ARB15	99,513	148,346	82678,7	471,48	56097,1	3,8852	19117,26	351,99	5376,78	4461,497	163,2232
BSR048	ARB15	110,9821	153,7232	76537,8	468,71	51243	4,3158	19553,53	325,37	4894,51	4518,663	156,0978
BSR049	ARB15	103,7791	188,8511	77692	458,04	51657,8	4,135	17107,59	389,33	4434,67	4556,562	154,8036
BSR050	ARB15	102,666	189,2384	81714,3	315,6	51369,7	4,2931	17755,37	367,32	5132,47	4817,735	149,0386
BSR051	ARB18	115,7587	153,753	93265,8	370,45	36504,5	4,8292	19342,39	419,44	4702,06	5172,534	201,6616
BSR052	ARB18	116,3211	149,4632	90993,4	238,65	43059,9	4,6735	17608,49	394,02	4684,84	5348,989	186,0714
BSR053	ARB18	107,6339	158,6124	78603,2	214,68	72459,5	4,1781	17216,86	389,44	5563,8	4309,731	162,2561
BSR054	ARB18	112,6854	123,6371	82692,2	191,41	58380,3	4,4385	17776,63	340,58	4810,04	4528,452	161,7593
BSR055	ARB18	105,1075	141,5026	87853,6	244,44	64573,9	4,5052	15479,27	356,26	4960,08	5271	175,2959
BSR056	ARB18	108,7447	138,0265	84342,4	248,31	55256,4	3,9022	17020,06	340,78	5084,96	5077,964	144,088
BSR057	ARB18	108,3778	127,9907	85225,9	236,02	59385,2	4,1726	17737,12	341,65	5068,7	4812,808	162,518
BSR058	ARB18	135,9417	115,5189	97713,7	343,6	49373,7	4,6043	17812,17	473,78	4224,43	5401,995	183,3143
BSR059	ARB18	116,646	132,2225	85909,3	189,58	64436,3	4,3237	17832,45	326,13	4767,97	4818,625	176,4868
BSR060	ARB18	134,6943	160,4238	93716,8	370,77	31956,6	4,5884	16403,7	489,92	4437,98	5176,926	175,6758
BSR061	LLM1	117,2957	120,2751	84802,8	139,03	64708,8	4,4301	15331,52	397,06	5421,6	4863,165	154,7107
BSR062	LLM1	135,724	100,4048	89788,4	250,57	58534,3	4,5091	18303,65	419,14	5136,33	5282,93	161,4178
BSR063	LLM1	117,8859	136,5926	83814	211,46	66767,9	4,4294	16868,47	433,16	4791,69	5396,422	170,5962
BSR064	LLM1	102,4426	153,0503	80692,9	289,01	65404,9	4,2963	15692,92	373,13	4344,38	4783,155	157,4534
BSR065	LLM1	110,316	136,3611	85929,4	154,38	70568,4	4,8759	17169,57	441,86	5242,69	5076,654	170,6377
BSR066	LLM1	108,0638	150,1939	76606,6	204,18	69402,9	4,4302	16741,66	361,45	4382,31	4733,559	165,4542
BSR067	LLM1	101,9897	132,7826	91763,3	285,03	57744,9	4,4531	18791,1	370,57	4971,72	4792,864	176,4453
BSR068	LLM1	110,5996	160,0202	79489	223,42	56120,6	4,5222	16991,3	577,3	4571,75	4431,496	148,0107
BSR069	LLM1	110,0475	143,9406	80797	230,71	56631,8	4,0933	16328,8	372,12	4821,38	4732,967	149,9272
BSR070	LLM1	114,8113	107,9734	89348	150,9	64362,2	4,5012	16969,12	430,26	6036,01	5066,498	168,8019
BSR071	LLM4	122,5259	129,1395	92237,9	265,53	65746,2	4,4565	19400,99	357,73	5439,16	4964,989	185,8576
BSR072	LLM4	130,4499	121,6586	80297,4	335,56	59681,1	4,8403	17177,79	347,6	6134,73	4856,148	174,4679
BSR073	LLM4	123,7085	102,8351	86200,4	336,22	40553,8	4,6898	18696,21	413,27	4614,94	4941,256	167,7083
BSR074	LLM4	119,4053	119,9391	81463	329,52	36369,9	4,5205	17915,62	410,16	3992,87	4545,469	146,7015
BSR075	LLM4	111,6218	89,7887	86357,1	363,17	63735,6	4,1736	18754,14	345,91	5589,35	4822,376	168,3027
BSR076	LLM5	118,1514	132,3179	75004,1	801,41	62860,9	4,2076	17990,18	539,47	6874,88	5128,6	148,3651
BSR077	LLM5	118,0465	172,0296	84758,8	286,07	63766,1	4,2831	16882,54	342,36	5103,97	4900,69	155,3726
BSR078	LLM5	96,2197	137,7904	73545	760,58	53551	3,6702	15711,81	355,45	3555,08	4207,953	133,1908
BSR079	LLM5	112,5432	117,7241	86783,2	474,76	79808,3	4,1058	17963,73	417,07	6837,49	4829,413	195,4522
BSR080	LLM5	123,8982	131,8664	73248,3	815,5	66491,7	4,1326	19787,88	530,73	6224,69	4803,142	176,5542
BSR081	LLM5	107,5877	115,4946	80228,3	315,56	67362,5	4,4528	17869,49	369,38	4955,16	4101,342	183,2871
BSR082	LLM5	123,6962	191,7809	78223,9	390,41	58264,7	6,0009	13641,62	499,22	3879,88	4196,86	147,0119
BSR083	LLM5	111,7734	118,678	79327,6	387,8	79877,1	4,1758	17011,8	424,8	5390,27	4482,827	147,7587
BSR084	LLM5	106,1621	130,6227	80779,4	460,23	59696,7	4,0371	18566,21	427,62	4645,97	4643,633	162,6605
BSR085	LLM5	109,0281	164,0355	71034,4	224,23	78402,5	4,1085	15474,44	431,74	4716,17	4259,448	168,0383
BSR086	LLM8	123,8453	155,1821	83396	199,13	43616,5	4,7761	14615,69	431,48	3395,18	4949,042	152,3296
BSR087	LLM8	102,0564	133,8451	82439	200,44	64790,8	4,4351	18341,27	365,04	6484,12	5005,197	158,8386
BSR088	LLM8	107,399	138,1281	81275,6	113,43	60498,4	4,14	15359,34	389,71	6287,6	4328,924	173,8265
BSR089	LLM8	109,5344	108,9815	85760	190,74	65534,7	4,5252	16742,3	399,92	6676,35	4892,97	167,8001
BSR090	LLM8	117,3401	133,2779	87963,3	179,15	62788,7	4,5802	18088,58	384,5	6647,13	4934,794	139,2422
BSR091	LLM8	107,7086	157,9772	96128,9	382,37	61323,2	5,1956	15136,2	710,62	5246,01	4776,759	113,1564
BSR092	LLM8	123,4251	126,7097	91270,9	623,84	74105,8	4,3057	16565,54	429,49	6590,96	5083,813	177,994

Analytical ID. (N=145)	Site No.	As	La	Lu	Nd	Sm	U	Yb	Ce	Co	Cr	Cs
BSR093	LLM8	0	38,1573	0,3663	34,3381	6,6558	3,4	2,4106	75,7377	14,5039	154,5768	5,0489
BSR094	LLM8	0	38,8154	0,3688	35,4484	6,5037	2,84	2,4067	75,9234	14,0138	148,6344	5,3031
BSR095	LLM8	14,3688	36,962	0,3566	34,2803	6,4921	2,75	2,3693	73,8434	13,9946	147,9502	5,0805
BSR096	LLM9	5,954	38,5212	0,3333	31,2474	6,3998	2,35	2,2415	75,8932	12,9231	154,783	6,0048
BSR097	LLM9	14,7537	36,1644	0,3489	31,3249	6,3507	2,33	2,3502	73,0272	14,6031	143,3731	5,4832
BSR098	LLM9	5,9873	40,4506	0,3461	33,3581	6,7523	2,79	2,6166	78,717	14,0499	159,8345	5,6938
BSR099	LLM9	8,4683	36,8922	0,3772	33,499	6,4946	1,76	2,5884	74,0436	14,9495	144,8164	5,6171
BSR100	LLM9	6,9181	35,6367	0,3677	32,1259	6,4644	2,48	2,3747	71,0132	13,0382	138,7197	4,8255
BSR101	LLM9	0	35,2212	0,3614	30,2943	6,2648	2,69	2,3678	70,2325	13,7799	142,4199	5,6843
BSR102	LLM9	5,135	35,7934	0,3657	29,8759	6,3782	2,7	2,4525	72,5311	16,1369	143,0627	5,2351
BSR103	LLM9	2,9441	39,7052	0,3761	32,8857	6,6605	1,89	2,4076	79,0089	13,5864	160,7368	5,6857
BSR104	LLM9	7,9822	38,2523	0,4323	31,6198	6,5151	3,39	2,5084	74,5732	13,7864	152,9826	5,9596
BSR105	LLM9	7,8865	37,5576	0,3744	31,1787	6,5517	2,28	2,341	73,836	12,7337	150,61	5,559
BSR106	LLM10	11,7599	36,8289	0,3516	33,2983	6,364	2,72	2,1926	72,0691	14,1863	145,9292	5,5927
BSR107	LLM10	11,096	35,5536	0,3353	30,6096	5,9518	2,49	2,272	69,0919	11,9716	139,3984	5,7227
BSR108	LLM10	6,8857	34,5657	0,342	30,8332	6,2784	3,29	2,5478	67,9725	10,3202	133,3634	5,2185
BSR109	LLM10	10,9345	34,3007	0,357	28,8738	6,2583	3,26	2,5368	69,019	13,1135	136,2934	5,349
BSR110	LLM10	10,6173	34,3528	0,3315	28,2486	6,1359	2,42	2,4311	69,0286	14,1912	134,7868	5,3465
BSR111	LLM10	4,2704	33,2438	0,3552	27,7885	6,0581	1,96	2,4436	67,3817	14,1533	135,9535	5,2241
BSR112	LLM10	11,2113	36,3073	0,357	31,5786	5,9136	2,59	2,5125	75,486	14,4046	153,6571	5,6759
BSR113	LLM10	3,4004	33,8164	0,3572	28,4963	6,2714	2,96	2,4749	69,9267	15,2469	134,9977	5,1575
BSR114	LLM10	8,2795	34,5306	0,3712	29,9458	6,2413	2,68	2,4942	66,1145	13,9897	129,8838	5,2457
BSR115	LLM10	14,4716	32,5436	0,3279	27,2812	5,8831	2,61	2,4031	65,8068	12,9749	129,9815	4,8034
BSR116	LLM14	4,9616	34,3188	0,3779	27,3468	6,0766	2,82	2,5828	69,1528	14,0254	137,6357	5,1016
BSR117	LLM14	4,925	36,6057	0,348	30,434	6,5083	2,06	2,5466	74,4368	12,6372	148,1163	5,2124
BSR118	LLM14	2,463	34,3581	0,3444	30,3218	6,2172	2,71	2,3065	69,2624	13,8164	138,4853	5,6712
BSR119	LLM14	4,0944	34,8483	0,3654	32,1431	5,9635	2,81	2,6584	69,0693	13,7182	133,3447	4,2718
BSR120	LLM14	7,1909	34,9529	0,3691	28,1069	6,345	3,32	2,6515	71,0014	12,7007	143,1937	5,2728
BSR121	LLM14	4,9342	34,6646	0,3462	29,0574	5,9208	2,91	2,4865	70,3894	13,4493	141,5533	5,0881
BSR122	LLM14	8,7234	38,3865	0,3699	33,0067	6,7438	1,94	2,6826	75,4344	14,1578	150,5314	5,2229
BSR123	LLM14	5,4159	36,8143	0,3827	34,3029	6,921	2,92	2,782	74,1889	15,0431	148,2902	5,1155
BSR124	LLM14	3,8999	36,2363	0,3642	33,766	6,682	3	2,6638	72,2072	14,1915	141,4819	5,6785
BSR125	LLM14	15,2276	33,1963	0,3786	31,8252	6,6494	2,35	2,6063	68,4896	11,5799	125,6775	4,1553
BSR126	LLM14	5,1472	35,9919	0,3837	30,9696	6,2506	2,89	2,6186	71,1395	12,0672	145,733	5,0776
BSR127	LLM14	3,7478	35,3232	0,3548	30,7272	6,4053	3,44	2,5764	70,98	12,4335	142,2795	5,0638
BSR128	LLM14	7,0903	37,4722	0,376	31,7236	6,6267	2,46	2,6741	73,7907	14,7715	145,068	5,2618
BSR129	LLM14	5,8037	32,1347	0,4058	29,6323	6,2136	2,39	2,6682	61,8628	12,3147	104,0264	3,9838
BSR130	LLM14	9,1432	36,2741	0,3571	29,4665	6,0253	2,77	2,4948	72,872	12,7671	145,6919	5,2686
BSR131	MBK1	6,7551	32,3756	0,3334	26,8549	5,7582	2,3	2,3153	64,3814	11,4799	124,5238	5,1049
BSR132	MBK1	4,237	32,0006	0,313	27,5119	5,7992	2,37	2,2601	64,5581	14,8254	128,6862	5,3101
BSR133	MBK1	7,3468	33,1222	0,3481	29,0328	6,0891	2,45	2,516	66,7764	14,1663	128,1325	5,8586
BSR134	MBK1	5,8798	35,9471	0,3384	31,3357	6,38	2,84	2,4986	70,2189	16,2078	138,4415	5,518
BSR135	MBK1	3,065	36,1308	0,3558	32,8202	6,6079	2,95	2,4265	71,1986	17,9	147,8367	5,0239
BSR136	MBS2	4,6591	34,695	0,3564	29,6251	6,4616	2,57	2,6307	69,8456	14,2947	136,2129	5,144
BSR137	MBS2	8,842	38,0792	0,3424	33,5193	6,4273	2,6	2,4968	75,3067	13,7333	145,3198	5,8783
BSR138	MBS2	7,3603	39,5768	0,3413	34,9375	6,5495	2,5	2,5162	78,9402	14,8983	155,3652	6,1878
BSR139	MBS2	5,1493	38,4868	0,3711	31,5405	6,4634	3,58	2,5338	77,2832	14,302	154,4275	5,5214
BSR140	MBS2	39,8768	36,8394	0,4091	37,6172	6,8025	1,85	2,9208	73,1555	16,9449	142,4494	3,3999
BSR141	MBS2	8,7828	34,577	0,3612	31,9635	6,3252	2,7	2,5122	70,6716	14,4002	137,745	4,7709
BSR142	MBS2	6,1126	38,9159	0,3554	33,7003	6,8306	3,17	2,3589	77,008	13,2599	149,5945	5,8061
BSR143	MBS2	5,4099	38,3306	0,3822	31,1153	6,9714	2,71	2,8897	74,1727	18,4525	156,2601	5,0984
BSR144	MBS2	1,9872	47,5907	0,4025	41,3543	7,3987	3,37	2,8815	93,8445	20,5548	204,3384	7,0523
BSR145	MBS2	6,7477	38,8236	0,3691	35,2554	7,0188	2,58	2,8083	78,1401	15,0427	155,0353	5,2481

Analytical ID. (N=145)	Site No.	Eu	Fe	Hf	Ni	Rb	Sb	Sc	Sr	Ta	Tb	Th
BSR093	LLM8	1,4397	50582,9	5,7072	0	88,3335	0,2434	16,6663	399,17	1,2164	0,7867	10,2009
BSR094	LLM8	1,3366	45756,3	4,7457	71,69	93,8097	0,2258	16,1818	346,62	1,2263	0,8147	9,967
BSR095	LLM8	1,335	46794,6	5,3192	32,92	88,1393	0,4411	15,8476	281,11	1,2031	0,8018	9,8971
BSR096	LLM9	1,3281	47199,4	4,4797	39,88	103,8307	0,4485	16,5301	343,86	1,2816	0,8	10,1516
BSR097	LLM9	1,3745	48623,4	5,9119	36,9	94,6653	0,445	15,928	405,16	1,1377	0,8234	9,8999
BSR098	LLM9	1,4393	49831,9	4,66	0	95,005	0,4275	17,0034	344,32	1,3094	0,8005	10,4758
BSR099	LLM9	1,3915	47139,6	6,2269	55,96	91,6502	0,4536	16,2456	448,99	1,2647	0,7967	10,0274
BSR100	LLM9	1,3505	47509,6	6,6315	0	82,2481	0,354	15,3678	304,53	1,1823	0,7769	9,7411
BSR101	LLM9	1,3528	47919,8	5,6254	64,65	94,575	0,3549	15,4432	390,64	1,1639	0,9417	9,7005
BSR102	LLM9	1,3245	47688,6	6,1478	0	94,0525	0,3648	15,5675	354,5	1,1809	0,8156	9,9522
BSR103	LLM9	1,4102	49568	4,5622	0	97,062	0,3059	17,2291	306,25	1,3276	0,8251	10,4227
BSR104	LLM9	1,3622	50161,2	4,9771	29,9	102,7209	0,3509	16,6516	323,23	1,2218	0,8768	10,1811
BSR105	LLM9	1,3842	48640,3	5,6811	46,63	89,6099	0,2972	15,9534	402,21	1,1864	0,8028	10,0406
BSR106	LLM10	1,3472	45840,3	4,9358	45,33	94,6154	0,3646	15,9168	353,21	1,2038	0,8622	9,7737
BSR107	LLM10	1,2724	45970,2	4,579	0	95,9598	0,3586	15,4649	409,32	1,142	0,7529	9,4132
BSR108	LLM10	1,3101	42468,5	4,2702	56,04	87,4566	0,4186	14,8018	456,89	1,1412	0,573	9,2151
BSR109	LLM10	1,2831	44596,1	5,8742	0	89,5313	0,4442	14,9489	389,6	1,1619	0,5566	9,4208
BSR110	LLM10	1,3171	46296	5,438	31	88,6537	0,3637	15,1992	332,07	1,1248	0,5768	9,4051
BSR111	LLM10	1,2771	46012	5,9246	0	92,672	0,4351	14,9545	353,2	1,1205	0,509	9,2992
BSR112	LLM10	1,4022	50650,4	5,6221	0	92,2689	0,4869	16,3931	422,65	1,2532	0,5997	10,1554
BSR113	LLM10	1,3036	39147,1	6,0955	0	86,5084	0,2925	14,9654	400,47	1,1137	0,5884	9,4303
BSR114	LLM10	1,2666	44614,8	5,6202	88,14	87,3649	0,3659	14,5069	260,9	1,0527	0,5509	9,0873
BSR115	LLM10	1,2692	41479,8	5,4412	39,52	80,9124	0,363	14,4304	297,15	1,0267	0,5352	8,9521
BSR116	LLM14	1,4284	48063,9	7,2806	55,61	85,3035	0,373	15,6995	211,48	1,1348	0,5843	9,656
BSR117	LLM14	1,3655	49768,6	6,1326	62,04	88,5695	0,4371	16,6389	197,83	1,1905	0,5615	9,9474
BSR118	LLM14	1,3258	45138,2	5,5838	55,99	96,127	0,3433	15,3731	374,44	1,1278	0,5654	9,5361
BSR119	LLM14	1,3431	47547,6	6,9655	0	68,0967	0,342	15,037	296,71	1,0862	0,5766	9,5997
BSR120	LLM14	1,3995	46659,7	6,2868	0	90,5698	0,4615	15,6258	569,99	1,1654	0,5789	9,6159
BSR121	LLM14	1,3677	47245,7	6,0119	53,87	82,2119	0,3086	15,5012	194,97	1,1053	0,6466	9,4939
BSR122	LLM14	1,4452	49343,3	5,5191	0	90,0622	0,3881	16,3775	199,27	1,1798	0,6345	10,1115
BSR123	LLM14	1,5148	49249,7	6,3493	0	91,1398	0,4566	16,3715	171,65	1,2026	0,6731	10,0716
BSR124	LLM14	1,439	44680,8	5,3764	54,87	95,1213	0,3671	15,6475	261,15	1,1355	0,6474	9,6335
BSR125	LLM14	1,5403	41312,9	3,9461	44,9	69,872	0,5758	14,4823	390,2	0,9615	0,6493	8,5683
BSR126	LLM14	1,4265	50224,9	6,5564	0	88,3456	0,3625	15,6678	570,77	1,1596	0,6135	9,6989
BSR127	LLM14	1,362	48907,4	5,83	0	83,9433	0,3308	15,6426	327,5	1,1881	0,5672	9,4568
BSR128	LLM14	1,5289	50100,4	6,0274	42,65	91,3322	0,3429	16,5071	276,84	1,1114	0,6884	10,0051
BSR129	LLM14	1,5009	40647,1	6,8937	0	84,6889	0,5636	12,8973	237,79	1,0222	0,7001	8,4189
BSR130	LLM14	1,4999	48733,7	5,7781	0	92,9724	0,4549	16,0264	266,31	1,1354	0,6916	9,8161
BSR131	MBK1	1,1761	40879,1	5,3703	49,47	87,6935	0,3073	14,0871	284,7	1,0282	0,5284	8,5834
BSR132	MBK1	1,2739	44700,8	5,459	0	92,1541	0,4062	14,6229	262,46	1,0433	0,5785	8,6292
BSR133	MBK1	1,2847	43614,9	5,3822	41,9	92,1779	0,405	15,0659	330,36	1,1226	0,5881	9,1922
BSR134	MBK1	1,3338	47938,6	4,3636	0	93,1744	0,3966	16,8747	343,57	1,16	0,5979	9,4891
BSR135	MBK1	1,418	49163	5,2061	59,05	79,1731	0,422	16,8196	239,36	1,1821	0,535	9,7155
BSR136	MBS2	1,3956	47754,7	7,1727	0	88,6631	0,3685	15,164	359,25	1,0722	0,5984	9,5992
BSR137	MBS2	1,3779	47892,7	5,0917	0	94,6434	0,4127	16,0136	302,92	1,2003	0,5432	9,8166
BSR138	MBS2	1,422	50820,2	4,7618	0	101,7418	0,5051	16,9014	381,56	1,2547	0,6066	10,359
BSR139	MBS2	1,4018	45398	4,6362	38,24	92,8686	0,3295	16,685	362,7	1,3212	0,6077	10,3827
BSR140	MBS2	1,625	55929,5	6,8956	40,25	62,4165	0,462	15,7526	324,89	1,1241	0,6766	10,1216
BSR141	MBS2	1,4301	47625,1	6,6089	0	82,6525	0,4602	15,4684	273,24	1,0976	0,8836	9,7874
BSR142	MBS2	1,4283	48505,9	5,0565	0	99,4964	0,4206	16,6151	235,57	1,2668	0,595	10,126
BSR143	MBS2	1,4477	51384,3	5,3624	69,37	89,466	0,6261	17,5146	148,85	1,2056	0,6001	9,919
BSR144	MBS2	1,6858	47069,5	4,878	32,4	95,199	0,4753	18,9371	473,27	1,4509	0,6416	12,4591
BSR145	MBS2	1,7846	50772	5,654	45,71	84,4252	0,4605	15,9608	298,84	1,3161	0,7144	10,2763

Analytical ID. (N=145)	Site No.	Zn	Zr	Al	Ba	Ca	Dy	K	Mn	Na	Ti	V
BSR093	LLM8	108,8934	150,2854	86203,2	226,95	76455	4,6262	14560,71	440,56	5832,18	4493,167	197,0422
BSR094	LLM8	103,4931	112,0401	84816,6	157,11	63007,3	4,4989	16364,84	437,24	4571,98	4501,186	180,5213
BSR095	LLM8	109,1176	155,1568	84342,5	198,25	59861	4,4161	14767,52	445,74	4552,49	4787,696	178,8998
BSR096	LLM9	111,2103	176,1251	89273,9	146,02	69266,2	4,1403	18031,18	355,68	6720,16	4759,75	172,5161
BSR097	LLM9	107,4918	147,2754	80094,1	246,81	60552,8	4,3436	20035,14	493,6	6157,69	4331,312	148,3387
BSR098	LLM9	112,9399	131,8362	89723,4	203,81	70619,7	4,4748	16703,42	420,87	5542,13	5340,389	181,0749
BSR099	LLM9	113,8567	175,2045	80079	313,23	60491,3	4,7919	16381,34	446,6	5403,23	5003,424	160,8038
BSR100	LLM9	111,1072	172,8598	78803,1	229,87	50824,9	4,4746	16297,87	521,54	5542,11	4809,873	179,1713
BSR101	LLM9	107,1001	122,8816	78796,7	234,32	63653,4	4,1658	14868,81	476,81	6473,22	4873,515	172,2442
BSR102	LLM9	115,8937	183,3916	80692,8	272,78	54729,1	4,5085	16152,75	551,9	5669,02	4701,205	165,9653
BSR103	LLM9	115,4605	92,1916	88982,6	150,86	75038,2	4,3383	19906,26	407,64	6010,21	5378,779	181,7165
BSR104	LLM9	118,922	117,4814	87562,5	225,28	70369,6	3,886	19028,27	418,35	5185,73	4513,023	167,9939
BSR105	LLM9	110,4957	147,7915	84322,4	250,09	68409	4,5729	17551,14	425,11	5757,2	4545,021	184,4777
BSR106	LLM10	115,6888	114,6211	82899,1	294,67	75839,1	3,9752	17476,78	423,2	6057,03	4588,801	166,9164
BSR107	LLM10	109,858	121,8915	81342,6	302,86	74369,7	4,1157	20672,4	468,11	5647,94	4541,066	168,5174
BSR108	LLM10	89,483	97,9882	78939,2	258,97	79208,9	4,2157	18665,28	445,99	6255,55	4539,401	165,6122
BSR109	LLM10	104,3408	117,4448	80146,2	397,85	60381,2	4,4094	19386,32	462,74	5203,24	4599,727	180,9108
BSR110	LLM10	114,119	150,1492	79044,7	321,49	62126,3	4,3945	16547,46	529,18	6253,4	4859,446	153,994
BSR111	LLM10	119,0079	132,7757	76860,5	285,37	71610,8	4,4898	15211,92	449,11	4668,29	4068,922	148,535
BSR112	LLM10	110,1708	143,6254	80942,4	177,76	62317,9	4,1212	18915,78	484,74	6794,67	4564,39	190,8249
BSR113	LLM10	111,9683	125,3046	79271,4	210,84	74223,5	4,8547	17605,38	360,35	5055,78	4215,765	169,1738
BSR114	LLM10	118,2055	130,4048	78506	250,09	62856,8	3,8808	17782,41	542,26	5859,49	4241,897	152,8968
BSR115	LLM10	97,0655	109,2049	75990,8	288,7	71144,5	3,9703	16764,98	477,08	4900,78	4431,099	158,4377
BSR116	LLM14	126,2654	154,1603	76969	247,78	48100,8	4,9507	16535,11	518,23	5607,64	3474,09	148,3979
BSR117	LLM14	115,204	150,6494	82585,4	253,18	35723,4	3,7543	16861,46	441,48	3846,39	4327,419	165,72
BSR118	LLM14	99,8721	138,687	77511,9	363,35	80433,4	4,3067	16504,65	438,14	6401,34	4290,837	174,329
BSR119	LLM14	116,1922	155,3016	77116,5	321,05	40732,6	4,2888	17886,04	496,15	5738,84	4181,964	137,771
BSR120	LLM14	106,9847	115,7746	77045,5	242,93	70255,2	4,5457	19462,67	435,33	5892,39	4496,503	172,8292
BSR121	LLM14	107,4022	134,9671	75750,4	192,09	48711,3	4,4722	15311,98	403,86	4502,52	4356,868	157,9324
BSR122	LLM14	122,3815	121,8633	90259,7	305,87	40714,1	4,404	18803,4	628,18	4573,67	5231,928	180,5795
BSR123	LLM14	119,7481	144,1776	82940,2	290,69	33803,4	5,1136	16813,63	499,36	4423,87	4642,85	173,7678
BSR124	LLM14	101,3836	129,8741	80082,4	188,32	53762,4	4,5552	19398,67	380,17	5433,57	4709,983	159,8247
BSR125	LLM14	86,4256	96,4619	76223,6	356,84	63535,3	4,4488	14834,13	530,06	3598,72	4286,279	107,5781
BSR126	LLM14	107,5013	165,199	75779,5	374,78	56792,2	4,3827	16639,95	472,2	5579,42	4245,838	174,739
BSR127	LLM14	97,9117	152,0591	76290,7	216,87	68634,5	4,2982	14283,4	512,09	4593,35	4655,101	177,2912
BSR128	LLM14	110,1932	152,8566	83933,9	325,55	59109	4,9923	16885,73	580,59	6039,18	4427,141	140,8047
BSR129	LLM14	85,4258	174,2272	66878,3	343,27	47777,3	5,1088	18419,88	428,93	1819,69	3850,032	89,939
BSR130	LLM14	101,1821	136,5625	80221,1	271,34	44221,7	4,3913	18846,42	385,23	4043,87	4136,467	149,2126
BSR131	MBK1	95,5301	102,649	76020,7	457,43	70864,7	4,0456	16206,4	415,82	4461,58	3908,348	157,652
BSR132	MBK1	111,878	133,037	72531,8	358,84	50875,1	4,1552	17340,44	388,07	4296,47	4420,181	146,6888
BSR133	MBK1	103,3035	141,0815	75351,1	320,6	97205,1	4,328	18975,61	447,71	5138,57	4276,863	158,1522
BSR134	MBK1	111,8857	92,5104	84332,4	898,23	76197,8	4,3658	20599,51	648,93	4474,49	4640,022	169,7541
BSR135	MBK1	119,0054	147,5135	84241,1	414,89	66120,9	4,5239	15139,31	660,43	5166,99	4968,088	165,7631
BSR136	MBS2	102,6781	177,6117	75271,1	252,68	54078,9	4,7608	15460,04	513,77	6040,11	4304,673	144,9133
BSR137	MBS2	99,7744	143,1323	84989,5	262,74	55169,7	4,1571	17898,36	422,88	5778,76	5095,94	160,1892
BSR138	MBS2	115,3153	97,3217	89670,4	138,92	64840,5	4,0725	17362,58	404,72	6883,15	4554,683	166,5446
BSR139	MBS2	110,1654	109,7764	89638,6	180,13	74259,8	4,5684	16836,8	413,39	5076,25	5409,559	183,6235
BSR140	MBS2	101,9355	169,8402	79873,6	237,8	43279,4	5,034	12270,59	568,67	5033,58	4988,465	141,2994
BSR141	MBS2	108,4616	136,8028	78734,4	172,4	43623,7	4,1327	15530,56	550,35	6106,9	3952,03	140,0429
BSR142	MBS2	115,3318	110,8763	88277,1	207,93	47490,4	4,5114	18401,69	469,95	5307,17	4456,568	179,1175
BSR143	MBS2	118,3694	123,3644	88293,6	283,87	34317,6	4,7062	14231,77	651,28	5150,16	4243,014	156,4612
BSR144	MBS2	118,434	140,8175	108450,2	317,51	30708,6	4,8857	17252,93	624,46	5484,68	5059,29	209,577
BSR145	MBS2	108,2774	125,4697	85399,6	116,76	46511,2	5,2859	15638,53	399,99	6976,16	5446,82	183,4026

APPENDIX H

SURVEY FORMS

Global Positioning System (GPS):
Northing.................................... Time and date:...................................
Easting.................................... Map info:...
Altitude.................................... Recorder:...

Photos:
Roll.......-...... Frame .... From .... To ....
Roll ....-..... Frame .... From .... To ....
Roll ....-...... Frame ....From .... To ....

Provenience & References:
Province: ....Qiyada:..........Town/Village:......................Douar: ....
Site Name: ....
Site Number: ....
Site Type: ....
Bibliography: ....
Landowner: ....
Site Conditions:
Deposition/Type: *open-surface open-w/-depth open-?-depth buried stratified other*

Archaeologically: *collected undisturbed unknown*

Conditions: *destroyed disturbed intruded partial-destroyed undisturbed*

Source:	*construction*	*cultivation*	*erosion-slope*	*erosion-wave*	*excavation*
Degree:	L M H	L M H	L M H	L M H	L M H
	flooding	*grazing*	*mining*	*off-road*	*land-improvement*
	L M H	L M H	L M H	L M H	L M H
	stone extraction	*timbering*	*other*..........................		
	L M H	L M H	L M H		

Current Land Use: *agriculture grazing none other*................................

Discussion..
....
....
....
....
....
....
....
....
....
....
....
....
....
....
....
....
....cont. on back

(Adapted from K. Kintigh)

Site Number:………………………………….
Site Coordinates:…………………………….
Recorder:………………………………………

Environment Setting:
Elevation: ....m Exposure: .... [open N S E W etc.] Est. Slope......°
Soil Texture .... Soil Color ....
Association: ....…………… Geological Zone ....
Local Landform: *dune hill mesa ridge valley* Location: *base edge in/on slope top*

Adjacent Landforms, Outcrops, Water Sources	Distance	Direction
…………………………………………………	…………	…………
…………………………………………………	…………	…………
…………………………………………………	…………	…………
Nearest Arable Soil	Distance	Direction
…………………………………………………	…………	…………
…………………………………………………	…………	…………

Local Plant Community:
shrub (arbrisseau) dwarf palm (doum) xerophytic camel thorn (dru) fig (figuier)

pomegranate (grenadier) almond (amandier) olive (olivier) oak (chêne) pine (pin)

cactus scrub (broussailles) barren (stirile) other……………..

Adjacent Plant Communities	Distance	Direction
....	....	....
....	....	....

Schematic Land Profile in Direction of Max Slope Direction ← ....

Environment Discussion:
....
....
....
....
....
....
....
....
....
....
....
....
....cont. on back

(Adapted from K. Kintigh)

Site Number:………………………………….
Site Coordinates:……………………………..
Recorder:………………………………………

Archaeological Information:

Features: *bedrock-grinding brush-corral canal charcoal-stain depression fence field-house hearth road rock-pile scatter stone-feature*

terrace water-control well other ....

Room Block: # Blocks .... Shapes .... # Rooms .... Total Rooms ....
Dimensions: ....Max. Ht. .... Area:............m²

Construction Materials: *sandstone rocks fired bricks non-fired bricks tabya* (pisé) *other.........*

Degrees of shaping: *ground pecked shaped unshaped*

Common sizes: *debris construction-size oversize*

Density: *light dense covered mounded coursed*

Midden: # ...... Dims: .... Max. Ht. .... Area: .... m²

Scatters: # .... Dims: .... Area: .... m²

Loc Feature/Collection unit Description Samples: Dims Materials

0 .... N C D Q: .... Ceram Lith
1 .... N C D Q: .... Ceram Lith
2 .... N C D Q: .... Ceram Lith
3 .... N C D Q: .... Ceram Lith
4 .... N C D Q: .... Ceram Lith
5 .... N C D Q: .... Ceram Lith

Artifacts Present: *ceramic chipped-stone faunal firecracked-rock floral fossil ground-stone shell glass historic-ceramic metal other.....*

Diagnostic Types Observed: Hand-made: plain/decorated Wheel-made:plain/decorated
Glazed-ware: plain/decorated Other…………

Time: *Prehistoric Pre-Islamic Islamic Modern Unknown* Complex/Dates: ....

Culture: *Idrissid Almoravid Almohad Marinid Other*……………..

Interpretive Potential: *None Low Moderate High* (discuss Below)

Site Discussion: ....
....
....
....
....
....
....
....
....
....
....
....
....cont. on back

(adapted from K. Kintigh)

www.ingramcontent.com/pod-product-compliance
Lightning Source LLC
LaVergne TN
LVHW071219210926
848482LV00015B/852